FOLKTALES OF *Egypt*

FOLKTALES OF THE WORLD

GENERAL EDITOR : *Richard M. Dorson*

FOLKTALES OF
Egypt

COLLECTED, TRANSLATED, AND EDITED,
WITH MIDDLE EASTERN AND AFRICAN
PARALLELS, BY
Hasan M. El-Shamy

FOREWORD BY
Richard M. Dorson

THE UNIVERSITY OF CHICAGO PRESS
Chicago and London

HASAN M. EL-SHAMY, formerly director of the
Folklore Archives in the Ministry of Culture, Cairo, is
currently assistant professor of folklore and associate
chairman of the Folklore Department at Indiana
University. He has written several articles on folklore
for scholarly journals.

Library of Congress Cataloging in Publication Data

Shamy, Hasan M   1938–
   Folktales of Egypt.

   (Folktales of the world)
   Bibliography: p.
   Includes indexes.
    1. Tales, Egyptian.   2. Tales, Egyptian—
History and criticism.   3. Tales, Egyptian—Classi-
fication.   I. Title.
GR355.S48   398.2'0962   79-9316
ISBN   0-226-20624-6

The University of Chicago Press, Chicago 60637
The University of Chicago Press, Ltd., London
© 1980 by The University of Chicago
All rights reserved. Published 1980
Printed in the United States of America
84   83   82   81   80   5   4   3   2   1

Contents

VIII   HUMOROUS NARRATIVES AND JOKES

Foreword

No country in the history of Western civilization offers the student of modern folktales the sweeping opportunities to trace their links to antiquity as does Egypt. The ancient high civilization of the Pharaohs covers 3,000 years, from the middle of the fourth millennium B.C. to its conquest by the Persians in the sixth century B.C. There followed a long period of domination by a succession of invaders, during which the Arab conquest by Calif Omar in A.D. 639–42 erased the last remnants of independent Egyptian civilization and converted Egypt into an Islamic people and an Arab state. Not until Napoleon's army marched into Egypt in 1798 did western Europe develop an interest in Egypt's antiquities and treasures. In the nineteenth century Egyptology, the reconstruction of the pharaonic culture by archaeologists, art historians, philologists, and mythologists, developed into a discipline of its own. Napoleon transported a large staff of scholars to the land of the Nile, and in their wake Jean François Champollion deciphered the riddle of the hieroglyphics in his posthumously published *Egyptian Grammar* (1836–41). In our day we have seen the intense excitement aroused by the display of objects from Tutankhamen's tomb in various American cities.

Yet the folklorist who seeks to establish connections between ancient and modern Egypt will find the clues tenuous and treacherous. George Young has written that the national movements of Turkey, Greece, Ireland, and other nations—he could have included Finland—"begin with a renascence of the national language, legends and literature.... But Modern Egypt has no language, no literature, no legends of its own." He thereupon tells how Gaston Maspéro, compiler of *Popular Stories of Ancient Egypt,*[1] once heard a village tale that he recognized as containing a pharaonic theme. Maspéro traced its recital to a little girl who had read one of his own translations in a school primer.[2]

Long, adventurous tales known as romances, some of which are recognizable as international folktales, demonstrably did circulate in ancient Egypt. In 1852 Emmanuel de Rougé deciphered a romantic narrative, "The Story of the Two Brothers," from an Egyptian papyrus of the 19th Dynasty of the New Kingdom dated about 1250 B.C., resembling the fictions in *The Arabian Nights* and replete with familiar folktale motifs. For the rest of the century, new discoveries of papyri enlarged the known repertoire of tales from antiquity, the earliest, "The Shipwrecked Sailor," coming from the 12th Dynasty of the Middle Kingdom, 2000–1700 B.C. In the middle of the fifth century B.C., Herodotus, writing on the wars between the Greeks and the Persians, recounted a number of stories he heard while visiting Egypt, including the legend of "The Treasure House of Rhampsinitis," an international tale type.[3] "Such as think the tales told by the Egyptians credible are free to accept them for history," he commented circumspectly.[4]

Twentieth-century Egyptologists have repeatedly assembled, in new or reprinted translations, the papyrus tales from ancient Egypt, usually in conjunction with other literary forms. These scholars have experienced some difficulty in labeling and categorizing these tales of sailors and travelers, kings and gods and magicians. Gaston Maspéro used the term "contes populaires" in his French edition and "popular stories" in his English edition. W. M. F. Petrie called his selection simply *Egyptian Tales.* Ernest A. Wallis Budge subdivided the tales by

[1] English title of translation from the fourth French edition (New York, 1915).

[2] George Young, *Egypt* (London, 1927), p. x.

[3] Type 950. See Stith Thompson, *The Folktale* (New York, 1946), p. 276.

[4] *The Greek Historians,* 2 vols., trans. George Rawlinson (New York, 1942), 1:21.

content and theme: "Stories of Magicians Who Lived under the Ancient Empire," "Legends of the Gods," "Tales of Travel and Adventure," and "Fairy Tales," in his compilation *The Literature of the Ancient Egyptians;* but in another volume, *Egyptian Tales and Romances,* he grouped the contents, spanning ancient to modern times, as pagan, Christian (Coptic), and Muslim. Gustave Lefèbvre used the French equivalent of Budge's title in *Romans et contes égyptiens.* Aylward M. Blackman, in translating from the German of Adolf Erman, employed "Narratives." William Kelly Simpson had recourse to "Narratives and Tales of Middle Egyptian Literature," in part 1 of his edition and "Late Egyptian Stories" in part 2. In another recent anthology, Miriam Lichtheim utilized "Prose Tales" for the Middle Kingdom and simply "Tales" for the New Kingdom. No one adopted the term "folktales," although E. Brunner-Traut's title *Altägyptische Märchen* employed a German equivalent.[5] The old Egyptian language itself had no word for "narrative" or "story."

Some scholars have commented on folkloristic motifs and mythological themes in these tales. Stith Thompson considers these papyrus narratives in his study on *The Folktale* and, while recognizing that most of them are written by priests, states that they resemble traditional tales known today in Europe and western Asia. In particular he identifies a number of familiar motifs in "The Two Brothers," such as the obstacle flight (D672), life token (E76.1), and evil prophecy (M340).[6] On the side of localized tradition, Maspéro notes that the aggrieved peasant in "The Lamentations of the Fellah" suffered the same harassment from petty functionaries and uttered the same plaints in the

---

[5] See Gaston Maspéro, *Les contes populaires de l'Egypte ancienne* (Paris, 1882); W. M. F. Petrie, *Egyptian Tales,* 2 vols. (London, 1899); Ernest A. Wallis Budge, *The Literature of the Ancient Egyptians,* (London, 1914); Adolf Erman, *The Literature of the Ancient Egyptians,* trans. Aylward M. Blackman (London, 1927); Budge, *Egyptian Tales and Romances* (London, 1931); Gustave Lefèbvre, *Romans et contes égyptiens de l'époque pharaonique* (Paris, 1949); William Kelly Simpson, ed., *The Literature of Ancient Egypt* (New Haven, 1972); and Miriam Lichtheim, *Ancient Egyptian Literature: A Book of Readings,* 2 vols. (Berkeley, 1973).

[6] Thompson, pp. 273–76.

same rhetoric as does the modern fellah.[7] But Lichtheim asserts uncompromisingly that "it would be a mistake to think of these tales as being folklore, as being simply and artlessly told."[8] She sees the prose tales as written in a sophisticated art form, even though they contain elements of the miraculous and marvelous.

My own view is that this baker's dozen of pharaonic stories probably enjoyed some life in oral tradition but received literary revision from the scribes, as do folklore tales in every age. Lichtheim misapprehends the character of the folktale when she terms it simple and artless; folklorists take for granted today the oral artistry and personal style of storytellers, and they have also widened the concept of folk narrative to include personal histories, a category into which several of the old Egyptian tales fall. This recovered literature does succeed in establishing the antiquity of storytelling and the belief in magic and magicians 5,000 years ago. In one tale King Khufu (Kheops, Cheops) listens to his sons recite tales of wonders wrought by past magicians and then marvels at the feats of a living magician brought into his presence.[9]

We may contrast the glimpse Egyptologists have given us into the storytelling of ancient Egypt with a most remarkable close-up, from an unexpected source, of storytelling in modern Egypt.

For the student of the folktales of Egypt, or indeed the folktales of any country, a unique volume exists in Edward William Lane's *Account of the Manners and Customs of the Modern Egyptians,* first published in London in 1836. From its initial appearance, at the time of the rediscovery of Egypt and her treasured antiquities by western Europeans, the book attracted a wide readership; it subsequently passed through successive editions and remains in print today.[10] As a record by a meticulous

---

[7] Maspéro, p. 45. Simpson entitles this "The Tale of the Eloquent Peasant."

[8] Lichtheim, 1:211.

[9] Ibid., pp. 215–16.

[10] Edward William Lane, *An Account of the Manners and Customs of the Modern Egyptians,* 5th ed., ed. Edward Stanley Poole, with a new introduction by Jon Manchip White (New York, 1973).

observer of the daily behavior, social etiquette, religious observances, and street scenes in the capital city of an exotic culture,
The Modern Egyptians possessed an appealing formula. The
folklorist will find very special rewards over and beyond ethno-
graphic details, for Lane savored all aspects of traditional culture,
except the grossly indecent; he enjoyed a good tale, whether in
the form of an extended romance or a pithy anecdote; and he
spiced his account with abundant instances of both, set in the
midst of Cairene domestic and business life. In so doing he
achieved the great desideratum of the folklorist, so rarely
fulfilled, to set the tales in the beating heart of the society whose
people tell them. A book of folktales by itself, extrapolated from
its cultural matrix, tells us little or nothing about the reasons why
a given society cherishes particular kinds of traditional narratives. From the viewpoint of today's folklore scholarship, Lane's
account appears modern indeed, for he dealt with the folkloric
phenomena of a great metropolis, a city of a quarter million
people at the time of his writing. Urban folklore and personal
experience stories lie at the cutting edge of contemporary folk
studies, and the account is replete with both.

Edward Lane was born in Hereford in 1801, the son of a
clergyman and a great-nephew of the painter Thomas Gains-
borough. At the age of twenty-four, ill with consumption,
he sailed for the dry climate of Egypt and remained there until
1828, during which time he prepared a manuscript "Description
of Egypt" that he illustrated with over 100 sepia drawings. After
an interim in England, he returned to Egypt in 1833 for another
year and a half to complete revisions on the book, which immediately won him a reputation as a leading authority on Islamic
civilization. The rest of Lane's life proved anticlimactic. He
translated *The Thousand and One Nights* in an emasculated version and spent seven more years in Egypt and the remainder of
his life in England until his death in 1876, obsessively compiling
an exhaustive Arabic dictionary.

The Egypt—or practically speaking, the Cairo, for in that
period the two terms were nearly synonymous—of which Lane
wrote was governed in brutal fashion by a Turkish military adven-
turer, Muhammad Ali, who from 1805 until 1848 butchered
his enemies, fleeced the peasants, expanded his realm, and

systematically looted the lands under his dominion. Although Lane refers only obliquely to Muhammad Ali, the atmosphere of cruelty and licentiousness created by the self-styled "Lion of the Levant" pervades the pages of *The Modern Egyptians*.

Anecdotes about Tradesmen and Peasants

A number of anecdotes retold by Lane illustrate the severity of the officials regulating tradesmen and overseeing the peasants. He clearly believed them to be true incidents and not "folktales," and some he reports at first hand. A folklorist will note, first, that oft repeated, allegedly true stories may be apocryphal and, second, that a factual story which is retold frequently becomes traditional and assumes a formulaic structure.

In Cairo under Muhammad Ali an officer known as the *mohtesib* supervised the scale of goods at the markets and in the shops to ensure the accuracy of weights and measures and fairness of price. He might have been considered a hero to the consuming public, save that he served the interests of an oppressive government and wielded the power of life and death. The *mohtesib* rode about the city with executioners; stopped shopkeepers and servants; questioned them about their scales, goods, and prices; and if he discovered errors, punished them on the spot by floggings or ingenious tortures. Once he ordered a breadseller, accused of selling his product below weight, stripped naked save for a loincloth and tied to the window bars of a mosque with a bread cake hung from a string drawn through a hole bored in his nose. For three hours under the sun he thus faced the crowds.

A cycle of cruelty tales gathered around a *mohtesib* named Muṣṭafā Kāshif. Once when he discovered that a butcher had sold meat two ounces short of the proper weight, he ordered his minions to cut two ounces of flesh from the butcher's back. When a vendor of *kunāfah* (a baked vermicelli-like dish) overcharged his customers, Muṣṭafā caused him to be seated naked on the copper tray used to bake the *kunāfah* until his backside was scorched. Seeing a seller of earthen water bottles mislabel his product as made in Kine, when they actually came from Semennood, Muṣṭafā commanded his servants to break each bottle separately on the head of the vendor. On one occasion, a bath keeper balked at washing one of Kāshif's horses in the public marble bath and suggested he bathe the horse in his stable; Kāshif had him beaten to death. Lane also heard stories of another brutal officer who supervised the several trades and manufacturers of Pasha Muhammad Ali and inflicted ghastly punishments on transgressors. On locating owners of private looms not licensed by the government, or merchants selling linens from such looms, this officer, Ali Bey, sentenced them to be wrapped in a piece of the linen, which was soaked in oil and tar and hung from a tree limb and then ignited. Fittingly, Ali Bey himself was burned to death in the explosion of a powder magazine in 1824 (Lane, pp. 122–24).

In a few anecdotal accounts heard by Lane, the peasant manages to escape his punishment of mutilation or death. In the town of Ṭanṭā in the Delta, the Turkish governor, Suleyman Aghā, had acquired a reputation for barbarous cruelty. One night he found two peasants sleeping in the government granary, and on interrogating them he learned that one had brought 130 ardebs of corn from an outlying village and the other sixty ardebs from the lands of Ṭanṭā. On hearing this, the governor tongue-lashed the local peasant, who protested that he brought in corn daily, while the village peasant brought his share in but once a week. "Be silent," thundered the governor, and directed a servant of the granary to hang the peasant from a nearby tree.

Next day the governor returned to the granary and beheld a peasant bringing in a large measure of corn. The hangman explained, "This is the man, sir, whom I hanged by your orders last night; and he has brought 160 ardebs." "What!" cried out the governor, "has he risen from the dead?" The servant responded, "No, sir; I hanged him so that his toes touched the ground; and when you were gone, I untied the rope; you did not order me to *kill* him." The Turkish governor walked off muttering about the ambiguities of Arabic, a tongue in which hanging and killing required different words. This narrative turns on a motif well known in folktales, "Literal following of instructions."[11] usually employed by fools but here by a clever fellow.

[11] Ibid., p. 126. The general motif of "Literal obedience" is J2460.

In another colloquy, a peasant's effrontery saved his ear. An elderly vendor selling watermelons laden on the backs of asses met the dreaded inspection officer Muṣṭafā Kāshif, who cut off the earlobes of merchants at whim. Kāshif asked the price of one large watermelon, and the old fellow promptly pinched one of his earlobes and said, "Cut it, sir." To each repeated query about the price of the melon he replied in the same way. "Fellow, are you mad or deaf?" raged the *moḥtesib*, laughing in spite of himself. "No," answered the vendor. "I am neither mad nor deaf; but I know that if I were to say the price of the melon is ten *faddah*, you would say, 'Clip his ear'; and if I said five *faddah*, or one *faddah*, you would say, 'Clip his ear'; therefore clip it at once, and let me pass on." As in many comparable tales, a clever retort saved the underdog from the authority figure, who in amusement waved the peasant on.[12]

In one circumstantial narrative, the oppressed peasant gains revenge on his persecutor. This episode occurred in a village in the most southerly district of the Nile Delta, in between Lane's first two visits to Egypt. The governor of the district ordered a poor peasant, who owned only a cow as the means of support for his family, to pay a sixty-riyāl tax. Ordinarily when peasants defaulted on taxes, the officials settled for a severe pummeling, but this time the governor commanded other peasants to purchase the cow. When they pleaded inability to pay, he summoned a butcher to kill the cow, slice up sixty pieces, and offer each piece to a peasant for one riyāl; in this way he obtained the sixty riyāl, a sum amounting to only about half the cow's value. For his contribution the butcher received the cow's head. Reduced to beggary, the peasant now appealed over the governor to the bey, who brought all involved to court and took evidence. Thereupon he sentenced the butcher to slaughter the governor and cut him up into sixty pieces and sentenced the sixty peasants who had paid one riyāl for parts of the cow to pay two riyāls each for slices of the governor. The head of the cow went to the butcher and the 120 riyāl to the poor peasant who had owned the cow. Thus, according to the tale, did the bey mete justice, in a manner

---

[12] Lane, pp. 122–23. The general motif of "Clever practical retort" is J1500.

satisfying to one of the sixty-one peasants involved (Lane, pp. 126–28).

The high valuation placed on material goods, food, and money, both by government tax collectors and by the *fellahin* who paid the taxes, clearly emerges in all these anecdotes. Muhammad Ali bled his fiefdom for some 3 million pounds of revenue annually, exacted from taxes on hand-manufactured articles, palm trees, and produce; and his minions engaged in a continual battle of wits and blows to collect the taxes (ibid., p. 129). Peasants boasted of flagellations received for refusing to part with their money, a trait traceable back to the Roman occupation. Lane speaks of a peasant savagely whipped by his governor for withholding a small tax of about four shillings; struck on the mouth as a climax to his beatings, he coughed up a coin he had concealed even at the price of his pummeling (ibid., p. 294). Peasants mutilated their sons or paid old women who traveled from village to village to knock out teeth, blind eyes, or cut off fingers of their sons to render them ineligible for military service (ibid., p. 195).

An instance which Lane himself regards as "hardly credible" illustrates the Egyptian reverence for bread. On observing crumbs in the street, passersby would pick them up, bless them, and place them on the side of the road for a dog's repast. Once two servants were breaking their bread before their master's house when a bey rode by with several officers. Out of deference one servant arose, whereupon the bey accosted him. "Which is the more worthy of respect, the bread that is before you or myself?" And he signaled an attendant to behead the servant (ibid., p. 290).

This class of stories grows from the immediate exigencies of life in Islamic Egypt under the Turkish occupation. They deal with market controls and tax collection and property values, matters that lend themselves to storytelling fully as much as do romantic adventures.

Anecdotes about Supernatural Beings

The jinni who responded to Aladdin's wonderful lamp did not spring from a storyteller's or writer's imagination but from a belief system ingrained in the Egyptian culture and approved by the Koran. According to Lanes's informants, the jinn ("ginn" in his spelling, singular "ginnee") inhabited the solid earth and the skies up to the lowest heavens, where they eavesdropped on angels and reported forecasts to diviners and magicians in the world who sought their assistance. Jinn assumed the shapes of men, animals, or monsters or remained invisible; they procreated with each other or with mortals; and they died after centuries of life. Before Adam, the jinn were created of fire, in contrast to the angels, created of light. Good jinn follow Islam; evil jinn, who are known as afreets or ghouls, particularly relish ancient tombs and dark temples, feed on the dead, and kill and devour the living. Many Arabs believed that jinn erected the pyramids.

Lane reported widespread acknowledgment of the ubiquitous presence of jinn by the Egyptians, who uttered prayers and charms to pacify them before entering their territories, beheld them riding the whirlwinds of sand and dust sweeping the desert or hurling bricks from rooftops into the streets, and encountered them in the shapes of cats and dogs and dead persons. Lane heard a learned sheik, author of scientific works, relate an anecdote concerning a conversation he had overheard between his black cat and a jinni who appeared at the door. "Open the door," requested the jinni. "The lock has had the name of God pronounced upon it," replied the cat, to explain why the jinni could not enter. The jinni then asked for two cakes of bread and was told by the cat that the name had been pronounced on the bread basket too, and so also with the water jar. Nearly dead of hunger and thirst, the jinni beseeched the cat for help, and the cat told him to go next door. The following morning, after hearing this exchange, the sheik greatly increased the size of the breakfast he was wont to give his pet, saying, "O my cat, thou knowest that I am a poor man: bring me, then, a little gold." But the cat vanished and returned no more (ibid., pp. 224–25).

Apparently the sheik had in mind a belief current among the women of Cairo that jinn could reward mortals with gold. According to the belief, in the first ten days of the first month of the Muhammadan year, a period known as *Moḥarram,* the jinn appear in the guise of water carriers or mules. If one comes as a water carrier and knocks on the door of a sleeping inmate, saying, "I am the *sakka,* where shall he empty the skin?" the one within responds, "Empty into the water jar," and later finds gold in the jar. In the form of a mule, the jinni carries saddlebags full of gold, a dead man's head on his back, and around his neck a string of bells, which he jingles at the door of some lucky person. This favored one opens the door, removes the head, and bids the mule, "Go, O blessed!" During the *Moḥarram* women continually petition the Lord to send them the mule or the water carrier. Another way of obtaining the jinn's gold in the *Moḥarram* would be for citizens of Cairo to pass through a street in the southern part of the city called el-Ṣaleebeh, where formerly a sarcophagus fronted a mosque by an old palace. There the jinn congregated to hold a midnight market during the ten holy days, and whoever purchased dates, cakes, or bread from them found his foodstuffs turned to gold. Since the sarcophagus was removed to the British Museum, the jinn have discontinued their market (ibid., pp. 426–28).

Egyptian attitudes toward the jinn varied from dread of being devoured by them to hopes for quick riches from them to easy familiarity with them. Lane tells of a comical cook in his employ, addicted to hashish, whom he heard on the stairs saying to someone, "But why are you sitting here in the draft? Do me the favor to come up into the kitchen, and amuse me with your conversation a little." On approaching the stairs Lane could see no one, but the servant explained that his master, having a clear conscience, was unable to perceive the afreet of a Turkish soldier sitting on the stairs smoking his pipe; he had come up from the well below and refused to move. Later the cook learned that the house had long been haunted by the ghost of a Turkish soldier murdered there. The cook continued to see the afreet regularly (ibid., p. 227).

Tales about Magicians, Dervishes, and Saints

Egyptians accredited supernatural and magical powers not only to the jinn but also to men in their midst who practiced occult arts. At the public festivals, on the streets, in the mosques, shops, homes, and harems, Lane observed a procession of saints, charlatans, fools, jugglers, entertainers, conjurers, magicians, fortune-tellers, dervishes, acrobats, madmen, blind men, and beggars, who impressed the public with their skills, gifts, and esoteric knowledge. Learned individuals who practiced magic derived their capacities to do so from God, the angels, and the good jinn and at their highest achievement could revive the dead or transport themselves in an instant to any desired spot. Cycles of tales grew around some celebrated magicians, such as the sheik Isma'Aeel Abu-el-Roos of the town of Dasook. "Even the more learned and sober of the people of this country relate most incredible stories of his magical skill," noted Lane (p. 265). The populace believed he had obtained his beneficent arts from having married a jinni or in being able to command the services of jinn. Muhammad Ali, ruler of the country, was said to consult Abu-el-Roos frequently.

A Muslim friend recounted to Lane instances he had witnessed of the magician's abilities while visiting at his home. A sheik who was present asked Abu-el-Roos to serve coffee and sherbet in the cups and glasses belonging to the sheik's father in Cairo. The magician produced the utensils, and the sheik examined them and pronounced them indeed to be those of his father. Next the sheik wrote a letter to his father and asked the magician to have an answer delivered. Abu-el-Roos placed the letter behind a cushion on his divan, and a few minutes later lifted the cushion to show that the sheik's letter was gone and another was in its place, in the handwriting of the sheik's father. This new letter replied in detail to that of the sheik and set forth circumstances of family affairs, which the sheik confirmed on his return to Cairo a few days later.[13]

On first arriving in Egypt, Lane heard the English consul general tell how he had sent for a well-known magician to detect a thief, whom the consul suspected to be one of his servants. The magician promised to make the image of the thief appear to a boy not yet arrived at puberty. A young boy was brought to him, and in the boy's right palm the magician drew a diagram with a pen, poured a little ink on his hand, burned incense and papers with charms written on them, and called for different objects to

---

[13] Lane, pp. 265–66. Lane noted that he had given an account of an even more famous magician, Ahamd Saddōmeh, who lived in the last half of the eighteenth century, in his translation of *The Thousand and One Nights,* chap. 1, n. 15.

appear in the ink, all of which the lad beheld; and finally he saw
the image of the thief. The boy described his appearance and
dress and then ran down into the garden and accosted one of the
laborers who fit the image. The accused promptly confessed his
thefts to the master.[14]

His curiosity sharpened by these second-hand versions of
magical feats, Lane desired to see a magical happening for himself and made arrangements to meet and observe 'Aabd-el-
Qādir, the master magician known to the British consul. This
individual proved to be well proportioned, affable, somewhat
shabbily dressed, and wearing a green turban, a sign of his de-
scendance from the Prophet. He informed Lane that good spirits
made his marvels possible, but to others he stated that his magic
was satanic. In Lane's presence he wrote out a charm containing
the names of his two jinn, Tarshūn and Taryooshūn, on a piece
of paper which he then dropped into a chafing dish resting on
live coals and burning frankincense and coriander seed. The
charm enabled the prepubescent boy summoned by the magician to see into the invisible world. (A virgin, a black female
slave, or a pregnant woman could also be used.) Lane describes
in close detail the procedures in which the boy gazed into the
magic mirror of ink formed on his palm and beheld colored flags,
soldiers, pitched tents, a red bull, and a sultan and his court.

'Aabd-el-Qādir now turned to Lane and asked him if he
wished to suggest any person, living or dead, for the boy to see.
Lane named Lord Nelson. The magician told the boy to say to
the sultan, "My master salutes thee and desires thee to bring
Lord Nelson: bring him before my eyes, that I may see him,
speedily." Soon the boy reported seeing a man in European
clothes lacking his left arm. Looking intently into the ink, he
corrected himself, saying, "No, he has not lost his left arm; but it
is placed to his breast." This emendation increased the accuracy
of the boy's description, since Lord Nelson pinned his empty
sleeve to his coat front, but it was his right sleeve. Lane inquired
of the magician whether the objects seen in the ink appeared as

[14] Lane, p. 267. In my own field experience among Maine lobster-
men I have encountered a comparable technique of detecting thieves
and adulterers, by the invocation of a spirit medium. See my *American
Folklore* (Chicago, 1959), pp. 128–29.

in actuality or as in a mirror and was told the latter. Hence the boy, and the magician, scored perfectly. Lane pondered all possible deceptions or collusion and could not see how he might have been hoodwinked. He speculated as to whether leading questions put by the interpreter about the images provided clues to the boy, and he did admit to observing other cases where the magician's craft had failed (pp. 268–75).

The pervasive belief in magic and enchantment gave rise to first-hand tales, or memorates in the folklorist's terminology, such as the foregoing and to second- and third-hand tales, or fabulates, spreading from the original parties to become a common subject of excited discourse among the city population and even the highest officials. An example of the latter form in *The Modern Egyptians* involved the chief secretary in the court of the *qāḍi* (chief judge) of Cairo, who was suddenly dismissed from his office and then afflicted with a serious illness. The deposed secretary, Mustafa el-Digwi, thereupon wrote to the pasha of Egypt, Muhammad Ali, accusing his successor of having hired a magician to write a fatal spell against him. The new secretary admitted the action and named the magician, who was remanded to prison until it could be seen whether el-Digwi would live or die.

"Now for the marvellous part of the story," writes Lane. One of the prison guards, on hearing a strange noise, looked into the cell and saw the magician sitting on the floor, a candle lit before him, reciting some words. After some moments the candle went out, but another appeared in each of the four corners of the cell. The magician arose and knocked his forehead three times against a wall; each time the wall opened and a different man appeared, with whom the magician spoke. The three men separately withdrew, the four candles vanished, the one in the center of the cell lit up again, and the magician resumed his original position. Interpreters of these proceedings declared that the magician had dissolved his spell, and indeed next morning el-Digwi felt much improved, called for a basin and ewer to perform his ablution, and soon fully recovered. The pasha restored him to his post and banished the magician (pp. 266–67). Such were stories of magic told as true by Egyptians in the 1830s.

In a separate category but related to the magicians fall the dervishes ("darweeshes" in Lane's spelling), who belonged to Muslim religious orders, often subsisted on alms, and enjoyed a reputation for holiness and the ability to perform miracles. Their feats and antics also provoked oral anecdotes of wonder. In religious processions, parades, and festivals, the dervishes demonstrated their ability to thrust iron spikes into their eyes and arms, to swallow live coals and broken glass, to pass swords through their bodies and packing needles through their cheeks, to handle and partly devour live serpents and scorpions, all without any pain or wound. One dervish would carry a hollowed tree trunk aflame with oil-soaked rags under his arm while the fire and smoke curled over his bare chest (ibid., p. 241). In bridal processions of affluent families, individuals who could perform extraordinary feats of this sort would be encouraged and rewarded for their participation; one young man carried a silver tray on which he displayed a large part of his intestines, oozing from an incision he had made in his abdomen (p. 168).

A number of dervishes traveled throughout the Egyptian countryside offering their services to charm away serpents. By some power they professed to detect the presence of snakes in the recesses of a house. The charmer struck the walls with a palm tree stick, whistled, clucked, spit, and spoke these words: "I adjure you by the Most Great Name, if ye be obedient, come forth; and if ye be disobedient, die! die! die!" Usually a serpent dropped from the wall or ceiling. Lane heard of skeptics who searched the dervish beforehand to make sure he had concealed no snakes on his person, or questioned servants in the house to ascertain whether they had conspired with the charmer, but they found no evidence to support their suspicions (pp. 383–84).

Dervishes who handled and ate serpents first removed their fangs or bored holes in their upper and lower lips and tied them with silk string. Some dervishes of the Saadeeyeh order would gather in their sheik's home before a chosen audience and in a state of frenzy eat the head of a snake, which they grasped with their thumb on its back two inches below the head. Not always did they escape unscathed. A powerful and famous snake eater known as "The Elephant" kept a poisonous serpent in a basket without food for some days, then put his hand in the basket to extract its fangs; but the snake bit his thumb, and the women of the house were too frightened to assist him, so his arm swelled and turned black, and he died in a few hours (Lane, p. 455).

The dervishes known as *magharbah,* who were Arabs from west of Egypt, specialized in wild dances suggesting the antics of madmen, punctuated with screams, arm flapping, and gesticulating, to the accompaniment of tambourines and kettledrums: hence the expression known to European and American schoolboys, "whirling dervishes." In his fever a half-naked dervish would chew on a live charcoal, inhaling and exhaling deeply, breathing out sparks, and opening wide his mouth, which looked like a small furnace, and then after some minutes swallowing the coal, with no sign of discomfiture. One renowned fire and glass eater, Muhammad El-Selāwi, in his excitement would spring up to the rafters of the mosque where he was lamplighter, sixteen feet above, and run along them, striking his arm with a wet finger until the blood flowed (ibid., pp. 462–63).

In their most spectacular collective performance, 100 or more dervishes lay down tightly packed in the street, while other dervishes ran over them beating little drums and carrying black flags, praising Allah, and at length the sheik rode over them on his grey horse. Only the sheik of the Saadeeyeh order possessed the power to perform this miracle of the treading *(Doseh);* one was said to have ridden over glass bottles without breaking any. None of the dervishes trod upon by horse and rider appeared in any way injured, but each immediately jumped up and followed the animal. The day before the treading the dervishes repeated prayers and invocations to render themselves immune to the horse's hooves, and those who omitted this ceremony were said to have been injured or killed at the *Doseh* (ibid., pp. 451–53, 468, 469; illustration on p. 452).

A third group of figures regarded with awe by the multitude, who share some characteristics of the dervishes and magicians and similarly gave rise to tales about their deeds, was composed of devout saints, or *awliyā,* a term meaning "favorite of heaven." Many were fools, idiots, or lunatics whom the people treated with special consideration, since they believed their minds to reside in heaven. Some rogues paraded as madmen in order to receive the alms and attention awarded *awliyā.* Some assumed

saints walked naked in the streets, accosting women with im-
punity; others went about in patched cloaks of many colors
adorned with strings of beads and wearing ragged turbans, carrying staffs with colored strips of cloth fluttering from the top
and chewing on straw and glass. *Awliyā* were believed to have
power to perform miracles according to their degree of faith in
God (ibid., pp. 227–29). Lane heard reports of a *waliy* who had
lived in Cairo chained to a wall with an iron collar around his
neck for more than thirty years. Some declared that he had been
seen to cover himself with a blanket, but when the blanket was
removed, no one lay underneath. The Cairenes also talked of a
waliy beheaded for a crime he never committed, whose head
uttered words of protest after it was severed, as with Sage
Dooban in *The Thousand and One Nights,* and of a similar case, in
which the *waliy*'s blood spelled on the earth, "I am a *waliy* of
God; and have died a martyr" (p. 234).

One anecdote told to Lane concerned a pious tradesman who
wished to become a *waliy.* He obtained an interview with the
most holy *waliy,* known as the *quṭb,* who granted him the special
power and assigned him a certain district to superintend. As he
walked through his district, he saw a bean seller in a shop about
to serve boiled beans to his customers, but coiled within the jar
the *waliy* through his new gift perceived a poisonous serpent, so
he smashed the jar with a stone. The bean seller thereupon
thrashed the *waliy* with a palm stick and only discovered the
serpent after the uncomplaining saint had limped away. The next
day the *waliy* broke a large milk jar, at the bottom of which he
had espied a dead dog, and was again beaten for his pains. The
third day he tripped up a servant carrying a supper tray, scattering the meat, vegetables, and fruit all over the ground; the servant began pounding him, until a bystander noticed a dog eat
some of the spilled food and drop dead. Then all apologized to
the saint, but so disgusted was he with his successive beatings
that he requested the *quṭb* and God to divest him of his supernatural gift, and he returned to his role as ordinary tradesman.
Lane speculated that the short-term saint might have paid associates to secrete the serpent and dog in the jars and so gain
him a false reputation as a holy man. Some *awliyā* acquired their
reputations by such stratagems (pp. 232–34).

An unusual funeral custom reflected the veneration accorded *awliyā*. Instead of the mournful wailing by women following the bier of an ordinary person, the mourners uttered piercing cries of joy (*zaghareeṭ*) which propelled the bearers of the bier, for if the cries ceased for an instant, the bearers stood riveted in place, unable to proceed. Sometimes a *waliy* directed the pallbearers of his corpse to the spot where he wished to be buried (ibid., p. 517). A friend told Lane an anecdote concerning such a situation. The pallbearers could not pass through the gate of Bab el-Naṣr to the tomb prepared for the *waliy,* and on consulting with each other they decided to withdraw a few steps and then move quickly forward, hoping thereby to overcome the dead *waliy*'s resistance. This stratagem failed, whereupon they moved out of hearing of the bier, and one suggested this plan: "Let us take up the bier again, and turn it round quickly several times till the sheyk becomes giddy; he then will not know in what direction we are going, and we may take him easily through the gate." The pallbearers followed this suggestion, succeeded in baffling the departed saint, and entombed him in the spot he had sought to avoid (pp. 517–18).

While observing the festival of the *mi'Arāg* celebrating the Prophet's miraculous ascension to heaven, Lane found himself in conversation with a saint who had some days before begged alms from him to feed fakirs (performers of religious recitations, or *zikrs*). The saint regaled his benefactor with a tale explaining the origin of the festival, which also exalted the miracle-making powers of saints. A certain sultan mocked the story behind the *mi'Arāg,* that the Prophet left his bed at night, was carried from Mecca to Jerusalem by the beast *buraq,* ascended with the angel to the Seventh Heaven, returned to Jerusalem and Mecca, and found his bed still warm. The sultan who scoffed at this miracle was playing chess with his vizier when the saint El-Tashtooshi appeared and asked to play, on condition that if he won the sultan must do his bidding. It was agreed, they played, and the saint won and ordered the sultan to plunge into a tank of water. On emerging, the sultan found himself changed into a beautiful long-haired woman living in a splendid palace and married to a prince. She bore him three children successively. After delivering them the princess returned to the tank, regained the form of the sultan, and rejoined the vizier and the saint, to whom he recounted his experience. The saint reminded the sultan of his ridicule of the *mi'Arāg;* the sultan now professed his belief in the miracle and became an orthodox Muslim (pp. 468–69). Such tales of enchantment and miraculous events clearly did circulate as accurate accounts among the people of Cairo, according to Lane's evidence. The occasion of the *mi'Arāg* festival, held always in the vicinity of the mosque in which the saint El-Tashtooshi was buried, and at the time of his *moulid* (birthday celebration), honored both the Prophet and the saint and kept alive stories of their powers.

Tales of Paramours

"Innumerable stories of the artifices and intrigues of the women of Egypt have been related to me," Edward Lane observed, and he proceeded to set down some specimens (p. 297). The Victorian clearly found offensive the "libidinous" and "licentious" character of harem wives, dancing girls, and prostitutes. In part he blamed the sultry climate, in part excessive leisure, and in part the husbands who encouraged their wives to hear indecent tales and songs and to watch through their latticed windows voluptuous dances presented by street performers.

A circumstantial narrative disclosed an affair between the attractive wife of a slave dealer, who neglected her, and a dustman servicing her house. She bought the dustman a shop close to her home where he could pursue the more respectable occupation of feed seller and arranged for him to meet her in a tryst by entering the harem from a palm tree just outside her window. Before the night her lover was to call, the wife requested her servant to tip off her husband of the tryst! Seeking to catch her *in flagrante delicto,* the husband told his wife he was going out but lay in wait at home and at the appointed time rushed up to the harem, only to find the door shut. On hearing him the wife screamed, the lover leaped out the window to the palm tree and made his escape, and the neighbors ran to the harem. From inside the locked door she told them that a robber was trying to break in, as her husband had left the house. Shamefaced, the husband admitted his ruse but claimed that his wife was entertaining a lover. Thereupon he broke open the door, but he and the neighbors found no one inside with his wife.

Next day the wife took him to court with two of the neighbors as witnesses that her husband had slanderously accused her of a criminal intrigue, with no supporting evidence. The judge sentenced him to eighty stripes, according to the Koran's edict. His wife asked him to divorce her, but he refused. They returned home, and on the third night later the wife bound her husband hand and foot as he slept and tied him to the mattress, then admitted her lover to her room from the palm tree. The ex-dustman roused the husband, bade him be silent on pain of death, and spent several hours making love to the wife before his eyes. After the lover departed, the wife untied her husband, who began beating her violently, while both called out for the neighbors. When they rushed in, the wife charged that her husband had gone stark mad. Again all appeared in court, the neighbors supported the wife's contention, and the judge sentenced him to be borne to the public madhouse. Professing pity for his condition, the wife pleaded that she be given custody of him so that, while he was safely chained in her apartment, she could minister to his needs. The judge blessed her and assented.

For the next month the wife consorted with her lover in front of her husband, as he lay bound in chains and an iron collar. After each tryst she importuned her spouse to divorce her, but he steadfastly refused. When the neighbors came by to see how he was faring and heard his rantings against his wife, they soothed him, saying, "God restore thee. God restore thee." At length the wife released her cuckolded spouse to the madhouse, and the neighbors gathered to bid him Godspeed with such words as "There is no strength nor power but in God!" and "How sad! He was really a worthy man" and "*Bādingān* [the fruit of the black eggplant, said to induce madness] are very abundant now." For seven months the husband lay in the madhouse, refusing to grant a divorce to his unfaithful wife, who declared, "Then chained you may lie until you die; and my lover shall come to me constantly."

Finally the husband relented and granted the divorce. Because her lover was too low in the social scale to wed her, the conniver remained single but continued to receive him at will. "The maid revealed the true history of this affair; and it soon became a subject of common talk" (Lane, pp. 297–99).

This tale would seem to eclipse all others in its genre for the wife's sheer *chutzpah,* but Lane relates others that are comparable. One woman of Cairo married four separate husbands, three of whom usually worked out of the city, but unluckily for her they all came to town the same day and called at her mother's house, where her resident husband happened to be. She feigned illness and withdrew, whereupon each of the four prescribed a remedy for *his* wife, and they fell to quarreling as to whose wife she was. The truth came out, and the court sentenced her to drowning in the Nile. (Lane, pp. 300–301. This "true" story is actually related to an international tale, *The Man Hidden in the Roof,* type 1360.)

In another case, the pasha gave a slave from his harem to a rich slave merchant who neglected her. She formed an intimacy with another merchant. Upon her paramour being seen by a slave, she hid her lover in a closet, but the slave broke it open, and the lover cut him with a dagger and escaped. The slave reported the affair and showed his bleeding hand to his master. Thereupon the wife fled back to her original owner, the pasha, who felt so insulted by the husband's mistreatment of his former harem slave that, instead of sentencing her to death for criminal intercourse, he restored her to *his* harem and spat in her husband's face. Soon after the paramour was smothered to death by courtesans, though why the lover rather than the cuckold met this fate the tale does not state.[15]

Anecdotes about the Evil Eye

All the Mediterranean peoples as well as east Europeans and the Irish and Scots share a tenacious belief in the evil eye. Throughout *The Modern Egyptians* Lane refers to incidents, customs, and amulets involving the evil eye. On first arriving in Egypt he was struck by the incongruity of delicate ladies in glistening silk scented with musk accompanied by dirt-smeared children clad in

[15] Lane, pp. 301–2. Other stories in this genre are given on pp. 299–300, 179–80. The persistence of the Islamic attitude to adultery is seen in the July 1977 execution in Saudi Arabia of Princess bint Abdul Aziz and her lover for adultery, an affair widely reported in the British and American press. See *Time* (February 13, 1978), p. 46. "It was a story worthy of the thousand and one Arabian nights. . . ."

rags, until he learned that maternal affection, not indifference, explained the matter. Unkempt children in public would be less likely to draw admiring and covetous looks which could maim and kill. When a boy passed through the streets in his circumcision ceremony, he wore female ornaments to divert the evil eye from his person and concealed part of his face with an embroidered handkerchief for the same purpose. At meals with invited guests, the partakers uttered expressions to avert the evil eve, mindful of the saying that "in the food that is coveted [i.e., upon which an envious eye has fallen] there is no blessing." Friends complained to Lane of seeing freshly slaughtered sheep hung up in the butcher's stalls in full view of all envious beggars and opined that one might as well eat poison as such meat. Lane's cook actually walked to a distant part of the city to purchase meat from a butcher who hid his supply from public view. A whole panoply of physical and verbal charms protected children against the evil eye, and when the evil eye had found its mark in spite of these precautions, the parents or injured party burned alum over coals and watched the alum take the form of the guilty party. They then pounded the alum, put it into food, and gave it to a black dog to eat to counteract the spell. Lane once personally observed a man who suspected his wife of casting the evil eye on him burn the alum, which did assume the form of a woman in a posture the husband recognized as peculiarly hers. Another recourse was to burn a special preparation known as *mey'ah mubārakah,* sold during the first ten days of the new year, whenever some member of the family was thought to have fallen under the evil eye; the smoke would cure the afflicted one.

On the streets of Cairo wedding parties hung a chandelier in front of the bridegroom's house, and crowds assembled to admire the handsome object. Since an envious eye might cause the chandelier to fall, a member of the wedding group threw a large jar on the ground, where it smashed into pieces and so diverted the attention of the onlookers.

Failure to observe these precautions might lead to accidents or misfortunes. A friend related to Lane how he heard a woman remark, on seeing two very large jars of oil borne by a camel, "God preserve us! What large jars!" The camel driver failed to

tell her to bless the Prophet, and a few minutes later the camel
fell and broke both jars and one of its legs.[16]

Anecdotes about the Nile

As the central physiographic feature of the land of Egypt, the
Nile played a major symbolic and folkloric role in the imagina-
tive life of the Egyptians. Lane sets forth a series of customs,
traditional observances, and legends associated with the historic
river. On June 17, "The Night of the Drop," the people believed
that a miraculous drop falls into the Nile, which causes the river
to rise; astrologers predict the exact moment when the drop will
fall. People flock from the city, the suburbs, and the villages to
spend the night on the banks of the Nile. On this night many
place marked lumps of dough on the terrace of their houses, and
at daybreak the household examines the lumps; the ones with
cracks indicate that the markers of those lumps will not live long.
The lumps also forecast whether the Nile will rise high the
following season.

Criers of the Nile at this time proclaimed in the streets the
daily rise of the river, with formulaic utterances invoking the
blessings of God and the Prophet, so that a malicious wish or an
evil eye would not prevent the rising of the river. The opening
of the Canal of Cairo, breaching the dam that closed its mouth
when the river had risen a sufficient height, also involved
ritualistic announcements and ceremonies; one was the "forming
of the bride" (*'Aaroosah*) a conical pillar of earth raised in front of
the dam, with a flat top on which maize or millet was planted.
The rising tide washed away the bride before the river reached
its crest, a week or two before the dam was opened. Behind the
custom of forming the bride lay a tradition alluded to by Arab
historians. When the Arabs conquered Egypt, in A.D. 641, the
Arab general 'Aamr Ibn-al-'Aāṣ gave orders to the Egyptians to
cease their annual sacrifice of a young virgin to the Nile. As a
result the river did not rise for three months, and the people

---

[16] Lane, pp. 57–59, 145, 249–51. Evil eye tales that I collected in
Ireland in 1951 are given in my *Folklore and Fakelore* (Cambridge, Mass.,
1976), pp. 191–95.

became highly alarmed that a famine would ensue. The general wrote his superior, who returned to him the following note, with instructions to throw it into the Nile: "From 'Abd-Allah 'Omar, Prince of the Faithful, to the Nile of Egypt. If thou flow of thine own accord, flow not; but if it be God, the One, the Mighty, who causeth thee to flow, we implore God, the One, the Mighty, to make thee flow." General 'Aamr obeyed his prince, and the Nile rose sixteen cubits the next night.

Another survival of the sacrificial virgin rite took the form of a ride in a gaily bedecked pleasure boat, adorned with cannon, lamps, pennants, and a silk awning and available for hire on the day preceding the opening of the dam. In popular belief this boat represented a magnificent vessel used by the Egyptians before the Arab invasion, to convey the virgin along the Nile to her drowning place (Lane, pp. 489–95).

Anecdotes about Tricksters

Although rogues, deceivers, impostors, and charlatans intrude throughout *The Modern Egyptians,* Lane never grouped anecdotes about them under a single rubric. A folklorist will recognize the trickster character recurring in anecdotal tales dispersed through the volume. The sham wise man figure appears in a story told to Lane as true of a neighborhood schoolmaster who could neither read nor write. Since he could recite the Koran from memory, he was able to hear the boys recite their lessons, and he employed a monitor to do his writing for him, on the plea that his eyes were weak. Shortly after he assumed office, a poor illiterate woman brought him a letter from her son who had gone on pilgrimage, asking him to read it to her. He pretended to read it but said nothing. "Shall I shriek?" she asked, inferring from his silence that the letter contained bad news. "Yes," he answered. "Shall I tear my clothes?" "Yes." Distraught, she returned home and gathered her friends for the death lamentations.

A few days later her son returned, in good health. His mother repaired to the schoolmaster to inquire why he had led her to believe her son was dead. Unabashed, the schoolmaster replied, "God knows futurity. How could I know that your son would arrive in safety? It was better that you should think him dead

than be led to expect to see him and perhaps be disappointed."
Persons in the room commented on the wisdom of the new
schoolmaster, and his reputation increased.

After hearing this story, Lane encountered a close variant in
the Cairo edition of *The Thousand and One Nights* and appended
it to chapter 18 of his translation, but he still clung to the possibility of the truth of the incident.[17]

Another trickster anecdote deals with a class of persons
named "spongers" by the Egyptians, since they lived by their
wits sponging at entertainments and gaining hospitality at private
homes. Lane heard of two spongers who journeyed to the festival at Tantá and found themselves at the end of the first day in a
small town with no prospects for supper. One went to the local
judge and accused his companion of refusing to pay back fifty
purses which the complainant had lent him. The judge sent a
bailiff to fetch the accused and, expecting a good fee for his
judgment the next day, ordered a good supper to be brought for
the two, as was the custom in country towns. Next day the case
was tried, and the accused readily admitted possessing the fifty
purses, which he said he was quite willing to return, as they were
only paper purses used by coffee vendors. "We are spongers," he
explained, and the irate judge had no recourse but to dismiss the
case (pp. 289–90).

A close line divided trickery and thievery, and *The Modern
Egyptians* includes some anecdotes on the battle of wits between
thieves and police officers. Pardoned thieves prowled the streets
of Cairo at night as incognito policemen, alert to the practices
they themselves had once followed. "Very curious measures,"
writes Lane, "such as we read of in some of the tales of 'The
Thousand and One Nights,' were often adopted by the police
magistrates of Cairo, to discover an offender. . . ." (p. 120). He
proceeds to narrate an illustrative case of unquestioned authen-
ticity, which the folklorist places in the category of the trickster
tricked.

A poor man of Cairo informed the chief magistrate of police
that a strange woman borrowed 500 piasters from him and had

[17] Lane, p. 162. The sham wise man is hero of tale type 1641, "Doctor Know-All."

given as security a headdress ornament *(qurṣ)* supposedly of diamonds and gold. On examining the ornament after her departure, he found it to be yellow brass. The magistrate advised him to remove the contents of his shop, lock it securely, and go about the city beating himself with two clods and crying, "Alas for the property of others!" Should someone address him, he should respond, "The property of others is lost: a pledge that I had, belonging to a woman, is lost; if it were my own, I should not thus lament."

The woman who had cozened him heard this conversation and rode to his shop on an ass, to give herself importance. "Man, give me my property that is in thy possession," she demanded. He told her it was lost, whereupon she went up to the police magistrate to prefer charges against him for having lost her ornament of red Venetian gold. The magistrate then showed her the brass ornament she had given in pledge. She confessed her misdeed, returned the 500 piasters, and was beheaded at the public execution grounds (ibid., pp. 120–22).

Reciters of Romances

Not only supposedly veracious stories about miracles, dreams, prophecies, illicit love affairs, and cruel punishments filled the ears of Egyptians in the 1830s; they could also listen to interminable fictions of wondrous adventures recited and sung by professional narrators in coffee shops, particularly on festival evenings. Some fifty reciters in Cairo specialized in the romance of the life of Abu-Zeid, a hero of central Arabia and Yemen who lived in the third century after the Flight. While this and other romances were printed in works comprising as many as ten volumes, the reciters chanted the poetic parts and narrated the prose from memory with dramatic movements and to the accompaniment of one or two players on a viol. Another thirty storytellers concerned themselves with the life of el-Ẓāhir, a prince of Egypt who ascended the throne in the year of the Flight 658. A third group of only half a dozen narrators read from the romance of ʿAantar, a celebrated Arabian warrior-hero known to English readers through an 1820 four-volume translation by Terrick Hamilton and from other works as well, including *The Thousand and One Nights*. The scarcity of copies of the *Nights* raised its price beyond the means of most reciters.

Some idea of the contents of these recitations may be gained from a brief digest of the romance of Delhemeh as outlined by Lane. The beautiful wife of an Arab chief dreamed that fire issued from her and burned her clothing. An old sheik interpreted the dream to mean that she would bear a famous son, at peril to her life, and that this son would sire a son even more famous. The chief fell ill and died, and his widow fled back to her own tribe, accompanied by a black slave, who tried to seduce her. The fright brought on premature labor. As soon as she gave birth, the slave struck off her head.

By coincidence Emir Dārim, chief of the Arab settlement in that area, had just lost a son at childbirth, and while hunting to assuage his grief he discovered an infant suckling its dead mother in the shade provided by a flight of locusts called *gundub*. The Emir brought the foundling, called el-Gundubah after the locusts, back to his wife and reared him as his own son. El-Gundubah grew to manhood and became a peerless horseman, praised, in the Arabic way, as a viper, a calamity, and a bitter gourd.

One day on an expedition the Emir wandered into the territory of a dreaded female warrior, The Grizzle (*el-Shamṭa*), who killed most of his party and took him captive. His ten sons set out to rescue him and were also taken prisoner and their attendants put to death. Now el-Gundubah set out alone on his horse and met her in the desert. "She saw him approach, a solitary horseman; and perceived that his riding was that of a hero. In haste she descended, and mounted her horse, and went out to meet him. She shouted against him; and the desert resounded with her shout; but El-Gundubah was unmoved by it. They defied each other, and met; and for a whole hour the contest lasted: at length, El-Gundubah's lance pierced the bosom of El-Shamṭa; its glittering point protruded through her back, and she fell from her horse, slain, and weltering in her blood." El-Gundubah then freed his adoptive father and brothers and divided among them the treasures of the Grizzle.

In the next episode Emir Dārim discovered that el-Gundubah was the son of an old enemy and forced him to do battle. The

hero slew his adoptive father and two of his foster brothers and
departed for other lands. Arriving at a verdant valley, he beheld
an elegant warrior ride toward him and challenge him to combat.
At length el-Gundubah threw his opponent to the ground and
raised his sword to give the final blow, when a sweet voice
implored him to show mercy and revealed herself as a "virgin
damsel," known as The Slayer of Heroes. She had sworn never
to marry until she met one who could vanquish her; now she
asked for his hand. They married and proceeded to further adventures and battles from which they emerged triumphant
(Lane, pp. 416–25; the quotation is on p. 418).

Such was the story fare offered Egyptians by public reciters of
romances before the advent of cinema, radio, and television.

A number of the story themes and personalities reported in
Lane's account of Egyptian life in the 1830s resurface in the
present collection of folktales undertaken by Hasan El-Shamy in
the Egypt of the late 1960s and early 1970s, even though El-
Shamy includes fantasy tales while Lane restricted his annals to
supposedly true events, save for the romances presented by reciters. Saints, jinn, and magicians continue to perform their
miracles and magic in twentieth-century tales. A *maghrabi* magician performs his art in tale no. 6, "The Maghrabi's Apprentice,"
and a jinni assumes cat form in tale no. 40, "The Thigh of the
Duck." A murdered merchant acquires sainthood in tale no. 37,
and Lane's story of the saint's wayward bier is matched in tale no.
38, "The Grave That Wouldn't Dig." The mysterious creature
known as the *buraq,* who carried Muhammad to heaven in a
miracle repeated to Lane, appears here in tale no. 20, "The Beast
That Took a Wife," as the animal bridegroom familiar in European *Märchen.* Lane's tale of the saint who transformed a skepti-
cal sultan into a beautiful woman by immersing him in a tub of
water finds an analogue in one of the series of magical tricks
performed by the dervish in tale no. 5, "The Grateful Fish." That
Egyptians still believe in the malevolence of the evil eye is at-
tested to in the first-hand reports given in tales no. 45, "The
Stone in Bed," and no. 46, "The New Car." Possessors of the
evil eye split a stone that has been substituted for a baby and
cause an automobile to crash. Turks are denigrated by Egyptians

in tales no. 24 and 57. Tales no. 2 and 34 refer to the sacrifice of
a virgin to the Nile, or a crocodile from the Nile, to ensure its
annual rise. The paramour theme surfaces in tale no. 2, "The
Black Crow and the White Cheese," in which a black slave is
disguised as a woman and concealed in the king's harem by the
queen so that she may consort with him. The king orders the
executioner to decapitate the slave and all the guards and maids
in the confidence. 'Aantar, hero of one of the great romance
cycles, emerges in tale no. 31, a narrative that sets forth a con-
frontation between the pagan 'Aantar and the Islamic hero 'Aali.
The trickster theme that gives point to Lane's tales of the spongers, the sham wise schoolteacher, clever peasants, and other
figures becomes formularized in the characters of Goha and
Abu-Nawwas in tales no. 58–62 and Stingy and Naggy in tale no.
55 in El-Shamy's collection.

We can perceive these continuities linking anecdotes in *An
Account of the Manners and Customs of the Modern Egyptians* and
Folktales of Egypt.

A volume of folktales current in today's Egypt is a particularly
welcome addition to the Folktales of the World series, first because the Arab world and the Middle East are poorly represented by folklore scholarship and second because Egypt now
plays so pivotal a role in our destinies. Hasan El-Shamy is unusually, even uniquely qualified to present the folktales of Egypt to
an American audience. He was born in Cairo in 1938 and took a
bachelor's degree in Arabic and Islamic studies at Ain Shams
University in Cairo in 1959. Coming to the United States the
following year on a Fulbright scholarship, he entered the
folklore program at Indiana University and earned an M.A. in
folklore in 1964 and a Ph.D. in folklore in 1967. For his dissertation he engaged in fieldwork among immigrant Egyptian
families in Brooklyn and analyzed his data in terms of the
dynamics of folk-culture change in an urban environment. After
teaching a year in the department of anthropology and sociology
at Morehead State University in Kentucky, Dr. El-Shamy returned to Cairo and from 1968 to 1972 served as director of the
archives in the Folklore Center there. He also taught at the

American University in Cairo and undertook field trips to record folktales among the Egyptian fellahin and various ethnic
groups such as the Nubians, the Bedouins, and the Nomads.
From his collections he has selected and translated the seventy
tales in the present volume and annotated them extensively on
the basis of some 800 Arab, African, and ancient Egyptian
variants that he has identified. These annotations document a
hitherto unsuspected network of tale relationships between the
peoples of north and sub-Saharan Africa. The desert is seen to
be more a highway than a barrier between culture areas.

In his published work Dr. El-Shamy has stressed the need for
an understanding of Egyptian folk culture that permeates the
entire society if one is to know the mind and soul of Egypt.[18]
Anwar Sadat confirms this point in his autobiography, when he
writes of growing up in the village of Mit Abu el Kom, listening
to the bedtime stories of his mother and grandmother and ab-
sorbing the traditions of the land.[19] In one of his writings Dr.
El-Shamy documents the relationship of mental health to
folkloric behavior. He describes what he calls "stress-reducing
folk practices" in Egypt such as dances, games, joking, riddling,
storytelling, chanting, verbal duels, and mock rituals, which
drain off tensions, provide reassurance, and sustain the spirits of
the urban lower classes, the villagers, and the Bedouins.[20] Besides publishing pioneering studies of this sort in English, Dr.
El-Shamy has made the work of folklore scholarship in the Western world known in Egypt through his original Arabic articles
and his translations from English into Arabic.[21] Since 1972

[18] Hasan El-Shamy, *The Supernatural Belief-Practice System in the
Contemporary Arab Folk Culture of Egypt,* Folklore Forum Monograph
Series (Bloomington, Ind., in press).

[19] *Time* (January 2, 1978), p. 28.

[20] Hasan El-Shamy, "Mental Health in Traditional Culture: A Study
of Preventive and Therapeutic Folk Practices in Egypt," *Catalyst,* no. 6
(Fall 1972), pp. 13–28.

[21] E.g., "Systems of Classification of Folk Narratives: The Type
Index" (in Arabic), *al-Funūn al-Sha'Abiyyah* 2 (March. 1969): 29–40;
and Richard M. Dorson, "Concepts of Folklore and Folklife Studies,"
translated into Arabic with M. El-Gohary, with translators' preface,
comments, and critiques (Cairo, 1972).

he has been a member of the folklore faculty of Indiana University. His special role is to explain the folk-cultural traditions of Egypt to Americans intrigued by that ancient land. The present selection of tales representing the storytelling forms of modern Egyptians admirably fulfills that role.

RICHARD M. DORSON

Introduction

In 1966, Professor Richard M. Dorson and I discussed the possibility of editing a volume on Egypt for this series. Only a few accurate texts were available then in print and in archives. Therefore I decided to use only fresh field data from Egypt as the basis for this volume.

The opportunity to assemble the data for this book came in 1968, when I received an appointment to the Center for Folklore in the Ministry of Culture in Cairo (CFMC). This center, then a branch within the Mass Culture Division of the Ministry of Culture, has sponsored field trips to gather materials concerning folk literature, music, dance, customs, and material culture (e.g., costumes, jewelry, furniture). Starting a much needed central archive for these materials was my first task. In surveying the holdings of sound tapes, I learned that the overwhelming majority of the center's recordings consisted of songs, poetry, and epic-romances *(seeràh)*. Interest in the prose folk narrative was virtually nonexistent; fewer than twenty tale texts were to be found among the collections accumulated since the inauguration of the center in 1958.

This lack of interest in the oral prose tale can be traced back to pioneering works by leading Egyptian folklorists[1] and still further back to early Arabic scholars. Even when Ibn Khaldoun (1332–1406) defended the use of colloquial Arabic as a medium

[1] E.g., Ahmad Rushdi Saleh's *al-adab al-Sha'Abi* [Folk literature] (Cairo, 1955) contained no folk stories; *The Genres* contained only four abbreviated tales. Also, with the exception of a single review article on A. H. Sayce, the embryonic journal of the Folklore Center, *al-funūn al-sha'Abiyyah* [Folk arts; translated in the English section as "Folk-

for literary expression, he limited his examples of worthwhile colloquial literature to poetry.[2] Significantly, the classical Arabic language *(fuṣḥā)* is inseparable from the religion of Islam; it is the language of the holy Koran. Modern nationalistic ideologies have shunned local folk dialects and hold classical Arabic to be a major unifying force among the Arabic-speaking countries. It is not surprising that the novel and the short story emerged only in the late nineteenth century as a direct transplant from European literature.[3]

Recognizing the need for attention to the genres of prose narrative, several other researchers and I launched a concentrated campaign to collect folktales in Cairo and its environs. Some researchers donated copies from their private collections, while others collected tales from their friends, relatives, and pupils.

Our first major field trip took place in 1969 in the Nubian resettlement area in Aswan Province; three researchers ('Aumar Khidr, a native of Nubia; 'A. Hawwas; and Miss Widad Hamed, a cinematographer) and myself were involved. Although the trip lasted only five days, it yielded a total of thirty-eight hours of well-documented tape recordings in addition to several reels of movie films and a large number of color slides. The films and slides dealt with aspects of Nubian culture not directly related to storytelling.

The majority of our recordings of narrative were in Arabic, which was easy for us to understand and classify, but some tales and many ritualistic songs and poems were in Nubian, particularly in the Kenzi language. In order to ensure the accessibility

lore"], did not deal with the prose narrative. Currently, however, a number of studies which focus on the folktale have developed; among these we may mention the works by Nabila Ibrahim and Ahmad Morsi. See, e.g., Ibrahim's *Qaṣaṣunā al-sha'Abi, min al-roomānsiyyah ila al-wāqi-'Aiyyah* [Our folk narratives, from romanticism to realism] (Beirut, 1974), in which she applies morphological and other theories to abridged tale texts.

[2] *The Muqaddimah: An Introduction to History,* ed. Franz Rosenthal (New York, 1958), 3:412–80, esp. 479.

[3] See, 'Aabdul-Mushin Taha Badr, *Tatawwur al-riwāyàh al 'Aarabiyyah al-ḥadeethàh fi miṣr . . .* [The evolution of the modern Arabic novel in Egypt, 1870–1938] (Cairo, 1963).

and accurate handling of these materials, I devised the following archiving system: one channel of a stereo tape recorder held the Kenzi Nubian texts and interviews, while the other contained Khidr's simultaneous translation. Thus it was possible to listen to the original text, the Arabic translation, or both at the same time. The listener could match hesitations,,stresses, intonations, and other vocal elements with their place in the text, whether or not he understood the original language. A number of texts from my own recordings in this Nubian collection appear in the present work.[4]

In the course of subsequent field trips, the center added collections from the Nile Delta, the city of Cairo, the western desert oases, the northwestern coast area, and the Berber-speaking oasis of Siwa. Two particularly successful folktale collectors were Miss Su'Aad Hasan, who collected from the women of the eastern desert area and from Aswan Province, and Ahmad 'Aabdul-Raheem, who collected in middle upper Egypt and from bilingual informants in Siwa Oasis. Between 1968 and 1972, I listened to and read the texts of the entire narrative holdings of some 2,000 tales in the center and assigned international tale type numbers where appropriate.

A second set of archival materials developed from a course entitled "Introduction to Folklore," which I initiated in 1970 at the American University in Cairo. Students compiled forty-five collections of folktales, which varied in length from five to thirty stories. Most of these tales were written down. Because of the cultural diversity of the student body, these collections covered a range wider than that in the Center for Folklore; in addition to native Egyptian groups, the AUC collections included data from Palestinian, Sudanese, south Arabian, Greek Egyptian, and Turkish informants; one collection dealt with data from a number of Cameroonian residents of Cairo. The AUC materials also came from upper-class and elite intellectual informants whose student daughters had easy access to their repertoires. Data secured from the upper strata of society provide ample evidence that "lore," which is a cultural entity, exists also among groups who are not considered "folk," which is a societal entity.

Apart from collecting projects as a member of the CFMC, I

[4] These are tales no. 7, 10, 16, 21, 42, 61, and 62.

pursued folk narratives in their natural context. In addition to collecting on a regional basis, I attempted to secure repertoires characteristic of age, sex, and religious groups and lore on specific themes such as spirit possession, family relationships, and political hierarchies from family circles, vendors, clerks, childrens' play groups, and healers.

The majority of the tales in this volume have been chosen from among the more than 800 tale texts that I recorded mostly during the period from July 1968 to June 1972.[5] In a number of cases, some of my colleagues and I jointly interviewed an informant. Such texts are accredited to the colleagues involved as well as to myself. Archival materials other than those I collected were used *only* for annotating variant texts.

Classifications of Traditions

Folk groups in Egypt recognize four broad categories of prose narratives: serious, nonserious, and humorous narratives and undelineated narrative talk. These categories are a product of the cognitive process of grouping; items perceived to be similar are grouped together. For a listener, narratives with varying characteristics are told for different reasons; the genre to which a tale belongs is reckoned according to the story's style and content and, more importantly, according to the narrator's intent. The context in which a tale is actually told is mainly a product of these perceived characteristics.[6]

The first category includes the *qiṣṣàh* (plural *qiṣàṣ*) and the *mathàl* (usually pronounced *masàl*, plural *amsāl*). Moralistic, historical, and religious stories are known as *qiṣàṣ;* a serious narrative is always described thus: "a true occurrence," "really took place," "did not really happen, but it could have," or "a story of wisdom." Occasionally the term *qiṣṣàh* is also used to refer to a traditional story which comes from a printed source.[7]

[5] The first draft of this work was submitted in January 1972.

[6] See H. El-Shamy, "Folkloric Behavior: A Theory for the Study of the Dynamics of Traditional Culture" (Ph.D. diss., Indiana University, 1967), esp. pp. 59–81.

[7] In learned Westernized literature the terms *qiṣṣàh* and *riwāyah* stand for a novel, while *qiṣṣah qaṣeeràh* refers to a short story.

The word *mathàl* denotes a proverb or an example; the word is also used to refer to a serious story, especially when a didactic or moralistic lesson is to be drawn from it. In this respect the "proverb" and the serious story function as behavioral models to be emulated. Narratives within this category are told for the manifest purpose of education or information. Sometimes the dividing line between what is narrated with a serious intention and what is narrated for nonserious purposes is hazy. "The Contract with Azrael" (tale 17), for example, has all the characteristics of an exemplum; indeed it appears in some sources as a religious didactic story. But the narrator identified and presented this story as a nonserious tale, and the audience received the narrative as defined by the narrator.

The second category is that of the nonserious narrative; the *hikāyàh*[8] or *haddootàh*. The first of these terms is derived from the classical Arabic verb *hàkā*, which means "to narrate" or "imitate," while the second is an abridged form of the classical word *'uhdoothàh* (little event). In some rural areas the words *fazzooràh* and *hizr* (riddle) also denote such tales. These stories are narrated with a manifest intent to entertain. For the narrator as well as for the adult audience, the validity of the contents is never an issue. Narratives which folklorists label *Märchen, novelle,* simple animal tales, merry tales, humorous anecdotes, and formula tales all fall within this category. Narrative verbal puzzles which folklorists label "dilemma tales"[9] are rarely found throughout Egypt.

Humorous narratives told to elicit laughter compose the third category. The words *nuktàh* (joke) and *nādiràh* (anecdote, plural *nawādir*) are customarily used to label such narratives, especially in rural areas. Occasionally the words *haddootàh* and *hikāyàh* are also employed to refer to a humorous narrative, particularly a long, multiepisodic, and somewhat adventurous narrative, i.e., a merry tale.

[8] In various parts of Egypt the word *hikayàh* is pronounced *hijāyàh* or *hichayàh;* diminutive forms of the word, *hijjāiwàh, hijjawiyyàh,* and *hikkaiwàh,* are also used, especially in nomadic and rural communities.

[9] See notes to tale no. 7. On the problems of classifying dilemma tales, see Bascom, pp. 9–12.

The fourth narrative category is usually referred to as *kalām* (talk or chatter) or *ḥàky* (narration or talk). This category includes "telling about," "informing about," and "accounting for" events or occurrences which have newslike qualities and are told in a narrative form. Accounts with these qualities are normally narrated as matter of fact; they are not delineated or set apart from the rest of the conversation. Narratives labeled memorates and local belief legends, which have not acquired wide circulation in the community, and minor historical accounts of either a personal or communal nature belong in this category.[10]

Some belief accounts held by their bearers to be historical and factual appear only in the form of "proverb-like" references. The need to "narrate" the event as an independent story normally does not arise within the community; all the facts about the account are already well known. The "facts" may be given in a full narrative form mainly for the benefit of the outsider.[11]

Attitudes toward Narration

In each of these categories, certain cognitive qualities lead community members to assign a story to a particular group or system. This evaluative process is not only intellectual but also affective;[12] such sentiments as love and reverence as well as hate and despite characterize a social group's attitude toward a category of narratives. Every category thus finds its own position within the larger value system.

From the viewpoint of formal Islamic dogma, narrating for purposes other than expressing religious and historical truth should be negatively valued and judged inadvisable. Formal religious teachings specify the guidelines for *ideal* patterns of

[10] Cf. tales no. 40–46.

[11] See notes to tales no. 29 and 30.

[12] Psychologists differentiate between two basic kinds of affect: emotions and sentiments. Emotions "are revealed by marked bodily changes in the glands and smooth muscles," while sentiments "are feelings which rest upon past experience of training and thus have a cognitive or intellectual basis." (Paul T. Young, *Motivation and Emotion* [New York, 1961], pp. 352–54. Clearly our presentation here is concerned with sentiments.

behavior: according to the Koran, narration should follow the ultimate truth of God.[13] The religious authority Imam al-Ghazzāli (A.D. 1058–1111) stated that narratives constituted "a heretic fad" strictly prohibited by the Pious Predecessors. He permitted only one exception: "if a story deals with prophets ... concerning their religions and [if] the narrator is truthful, and with correct attributions [along the chain of transmission], I see no harm in him."[14] Such Islamic teachings have shaped Arab cultures, including those of Christian and Jewish Arab groups.[15]

The religion of Islam, like its two montheistic predecessors Judaism and Christianity, has been strongly averse to the narrative and other artistic expressions (e.g., poetry, painting, sculpture, song, dances) of polytheism. Islamic teachers, who assumed the responsibility for telling the best and most truthful narratives, considered narrating for entertainment to be an idle activity that bordered on violation of religious doctrine. The oral narrative arts encountered the same prohibition directed against poetry, music and singing, play and games, and drawing and sculpture. In spite of religious aversion to it, poetry continued to play an important role in the formal cultures of Muslim states. Meanwhile, sculpture was totally stamped out. Narration, especially for entertainment, survived in varying degrees—as did music, dance, play and games—but mainly outside the sphere of formal Islamic teachings.

Oral narrators in Egyptian folk communities are aware of these general guidelines. They regard positively the sacred and historical narratives and esteem somewhat less stories with moral or other didactic functions. Sacred narratives, exempla, and parareligious narratives are usually told freely, not necessarily within families, but often at almost exclusively male gatherings such as those which precede and follow prayers at

[13] See Koran 12:3, 18:13.

[14] Quoted in 'Aabdul-Galeel 'Aeesa Abul-Naṣr's Ṣafwàt ṣaḥeeḥ al-Bukhāri [The choicest from Bukhari's authenticated (utterances of Prophet Muhammad)] (Cairo, 1953), 4:216–19.

[15] See Morroe Berger, The Arab World Today (New York, 1964), pp. 20–41.

mosques. Women also learn and narrate these stories. Narrative reports (category 4) are generally viewed in neutral terms, while purely fictitious stories are negatively valued.

Linking a fictitious tale to a didactic or moralistic value usually moves its status toward the positive end of the spectrum. The narrator of tale no. 49, "The Partnership between Wolf and Mouse," added a series of proverbial, didactic, and moralistic issues to make his story more significant. Similarly, the point of "The Grateful Fish" (tale no. 5), according to its teller, was that "God rewards a small good deed with plenty."

Ḥawadeet, or ḥikayāt, are normally associated with women and are often called "women's stuff"; adult males, especially those who do not have the social role of raconteurs, refuse to tell ḥawadeet (Märchen).[16] Young and adult females are responsible for entertaining children, other female members of the households, and intimate neighborhood groups. It is indeed rare, or at least not openly admitted to, for a female to entertain an adult male through Märchen. I have only encountered one case, that of the narrator of tale no. 55, in which a husband asks his wife to tell him ḥawadeet. Specialized male narrators whose role and social status in the community are linked to their narrative services do occasionally tell Märchen.[17] At the present time, there are no professional tale tellers who derive their livelihood from telling secular prose narratives in Egypt.

Written and Oral Traditions

The folk keep two groups of stories separate: those which come from books and those which come from oral folk tradition. "Book stories" usually deal with religious and historical themes. Tales from The Arabian Nights, a work which is generally viewed as a "folk book," are normally not narrated; but read to listeners. Even in cases in which a printed tale has a counterpart in oral circulation, most narrators of the oral text are unaware of

[16] See informant notes to tales no. 8 and 12; see also Joseph Desparment, Contes populaires sur les ogres recueillis à Blida (Paris, 1910), 1:3–5.

[17] See informant note to tale no. 16; cf. also informant note to tale no. 10 and notes to tales no. 12 and 26.

the similarities between their own stories and printed variants.[18]
When I told the narrator of "The Noble and the Vile (tale no.
14) about the variant of his story that exists in *The Arabian
Nights*, he responded, "Yes, it is the same, but still it is not the
same. This one comes out of a book; that one is something we
just know." Another informant who was mainly interested in
songs said, "I don't know any ḥawadeet [tales], but I can tell you a
qiṣṣah [story] from *The Thousand [and One] Nights*."

The collections of tales at the CFMC contained no more than
half a dozen stories which came directly from *The Arabian
Nights*. The literate Nubian narrator of tale no. 16 claimed at
first that his tales came from books. Only one of his thirty or so
narratives, however, came out of a literary collection, the
Kaleelah wa Dimnàh, an eighth-century A.D. Arabic translation
of the *Panchatantra*. It is significant that his rendition of this
story, which belongs to type 160 *(Grateful Animals, Ungrateful
Man)*, was incoherent and that the tale was not reported by any
other members of his community.

In a number of cases, oral and printed variants of the same tale
exist side by side in a community. They do not merge, nor does
the bearer become fully aware of the duality of the tradition.
"The Noble and the Vile" (tale no. 14, type 613) appears in *The
Arabian Nights* under the distorted title "Abu-Ṣeer and Abu-
Qeer," i.e., "The Evil and the Good." Similarly, the tale which
combines types 676 *(Open Sesame)* and 954 *(The Forty Thieves)*
recurs in oral tradition without the slightest association with its
counterpart in *The Arabian Nights*, "Ali Baba and the Forty
Thieves." Even the name "'Aali Baba" does not appear in the
traditions of rural areas, where the oral variants of the tale are
normally found. Evidently the propagation of *The Arabian
Nights* through printing and radio plays has had little impact so
far upon oral traditional narratives. Stories which appear in
books with little or no circulation in folk communities, such as
Kaleelah wa Dimnàh, hardly ever circulate as oral tales (see notes
to tales no. 10, 14, and 47).

It is also evident that stories included in textbooks rarely enter
oral tradition.[19] During the course of my own search for tales in

---

[18] See notes to tale no. 12.

[19] See notes to tale no. 47.

Egypt, I asked four of my fellow students from elementary and high school for tales which had been assigned to us in Arabic and English readers.[20] All but one of these narratives, which belong to international tale types, have counterparts in the oral traditions of various Egyptian communities. When I described a specific story to any of those interviewed, they readily recognized it. Their unanimous reaction, however, was that the texts were neither *ḥikayāt* nor *ḥawadeet* but "book stories."

In his *Contes populaires de la vallée du Nil,* Yacob Artin reported a situation in which the ancient Egyptian story of "The Lost Sailor" seemed to be catching on in oral tradition.[21] As of today, almost a century later, not a trace of the story has been found in Egyptian oral tradition. None of the ancient Egyptian tales included in literary translations of hieroglyphic texts appear in oral circulation. Nevertheless, a number of traditional tales bear a remarkable resemblance to the ancient stories.[22]

Clearly, oral and written narratives belong to separate cognitive systems. Although the two systems do to some extent overlap and affect each other, the separation between the two systems is the dominant trend. This duality between formal literary and oral folk traditions seems to date back to the Middle and New Kingdom periods in ancient Egypt. Many Arabic literary works are filled with represented folk narratives. The various copiers and editors of *The Arabian Nights,* for example, seem to

---

[20] These tales included types 60, *Fox and Crane Invite Each Other;* 92, *Lion Dives for His Own Reflection;* 155, *The Ungrateful Serpent Returned to Captivity;* 214, *The Ass Tries to Caress His Master like a Dog;* 565, *The Magic Mill;* 763, *The Treasure Finders Who Murdered One Another;* 928, *Planting for the Next Generation;* 910E, *Father's Counsel: Where Treasure Is;* 910F, *The Quarreling Sons and the Bundle of Twigs;* and 1804B, *Payment with Clink of Money.* All of these narratives, with the exception of type 565 appear in the oral traditions of various Egyptian communities.

[21] P. 6; see also Dorson's foreword, p. x above.

[22] For examples of these ancient themes, see notes to tales no. 2, 3, 6, 12, 14, 47, 48, and 51. Cf. also the beliefs expressed in nos. 19, 26, 29, 30, 34, 36, 41, 44, and 45.

have expanded the book by incorporating traditional oral tales into the written collection.[23]

Occasionally a literary story does penetrate oral tradition. An example of this phenomenon is Micheline Galley's Algerian text of the ancient Egyptian tale "The Two Brothers." Galley wondered whether her oral variant was a product of continuous oral transmission or just "folklorization."[24] Taking into account the narrative traditions of the Arab-Berber area and the qualities of the Algerian text, we can assert that this tale was learned from a printed source in the very recent past.

Egyptologists confirm the existence in antiquity of folk narrative traditions. Edward F. Wente states in *The Literature of Ancient Egypt* that "the Tale of the Two Brothers is not an official version of the myth." He also proposes that "one form of the Egyptian faith was the popular story which might be told by a raconteur in the marketplace."[25] Similarly, in *Ancient Near Eastern Texts Relating to the Old Testament,* John A. Wilson points out that the tale of "The Contest of Horus and Seth for Rule" draws from "the [priestly] myth for a lusty folkstory told for entertainment rather than didactic purposes."[26]

Folklore in general and the folktale in particular seem to have existed for millennia coterminous with learned elite culture. On the whole, it seems that the emergence of lore was not dependent on the development of a specific social class, nor was the emergence of the folktale ushered in by the disintegration of priestly accounts.

Affective Elements of the Tales

Most tales, particularly recurrent *Märchen* and *novelle,* express a set of sentiments that are central to members of the community. The emotional or affective component of a tale determines a

[23] See notes to tales no. 9 and 27. Cf. also the contents of regional editions as outlined in Elisséeff.

[24] *Badr az-Zîn,* pp. 232–57, 261–62.

[25] Pp. 92–93.

[26] Pp. 14, 23.

group's attitudes toward the tale. Feelings about kinship relations; ethnic and religious groups; and significant objects, ideas,
and values are major forces around which a tale coheres. Variants
of a narrative found within a given community may differ in
some intellectual aspects, but not in the basic sentiment that
holds them together.[27]

In considering the affective elements of Egyptian tales, it is
necessary to distinguish among the age, sex, and religious groups
of the narrators. Studies on the impact of these factors upon
narrative style and content are almost totally lacking.[28] Preliminary evidence derived from archival materials suggests that with
the exception of jokes and narratives directly related to formal
religious teachings, differences between the tales told by Copts
and Muslims in Egypt are negligible.[29]

The main differences are readily observable in repertoires
characteristic of male and female groups. Children are socialized
by females: while female children continue the same roles they
have played, male children learn to play new roles when they
join adult male groups and to inhibit female roles. Thus, whereas
male members of a group undergo a process of resocialization
after puberty, female members need not go through such a process and continue to tell *Märchen* freely.

The two most recurrent *Märchen* in Egypt, types 480 *(The
Spinning Women by the Spring)* and 511A *(The Little Red Ox)*[30]
are almost invariably told by adult females and children. Although males are also exposed to these tales in their childhood,
they evidently "outgrow" the need to narrate them. Collectors
often succeed in convincing an adult male to tell such magic
tales, but under such conditions the narration is atypical.[31] It is
noteworthy that types 480 and 511A both revolve around

[27] For examples, see notes to tales no. 1, 2, 4, 8, and 9.

[28] One of the few anthropological studies which attempted to discern
the characteristics of children's tales is that of Ammar, pp. 161–82.

[29] See tale no. 2.

[30] Only a cow appears in Egyptian and other Arab and Berber renditions; an ox *never* occurs. See also notes to tale no. 4.

[31] See informant notes to tales no. 2, 12, and 55; cf. informant note to
tale no. 51. Also see El-Shamy, "Folkloric Behavior," pp. 54–59.

rivalry between stepsisters: type 511A usually involves a
heroine, her brother, and an adversary who is a stepmother or
occasionally a stepsister. In general, these themes are more
meaningful to females than to males.[32] The repertoires of adult
male narrators are more likely to avoid such themes. Their narratives tend to emphasize rivalries among male siblings and in-
laws as well as war, adventure, and other topics.[33]

In this collection, I have attempted to represent the various
groups in Egypt: females, children, Copts, Nubians, and
nomads.[34] The collection as a whole should not be considered a
"random sample" of the narrative traditions of Egypt. Although
the majority of the tales were collected at random, I pursued and
extracted from reluctant informants certain items of which I had
knowledge beforehand.[35] The stories in this book were selected
on the basis of their readability and representation of a specific
genre, social institution, or aspect of culture. Had they been
selected for their frequency alone, such tales as no. 47 would
have been eliminated. "Distorted tales" and fragments, which
may be as important for understanding the culture as fully narrated tales, would have predominated.

Formulas in the Tales

Apart from the creative vocabulary which may distinguish the
style of a narrator of an established oral tradition (exemplified by
tale 49), Egyptian narrators employ numerous verbal formulas in
the course of their communication with the audience. Normally
a narrator begins by asking, "Pray on behalf of [i.e., praise] the
Prophet," which signifies that the interactional event is off to a
good start. The listener replies, "May God's prayers be upon

[32] See also notes to tales no. 8 and 9.

[33] See notes to tales no. 1, 2, and 4; see also notes to "The Supreme
Saints Cycle" and "Imamu 'Aali's Narrative Cycle" below.

[34] Female informants told tales no. 8, 9, 28, 41, 43, 45, 50, 55, and
56; children told nos. 51, 52, and 53; Coptic informants told tales no. 2,
25, 34, 35, 39, and 64; Nubians told tales no. 10, 16, 21, 42, 50, 61, and
62; while nomadic narrators told tales no. 4, 37, and 55; see also tale
no. 5.

[35] See, e.g., introductory statements to tales no. 2 and 39.

you, Prophet." If the narrator begins by saying, "State the one-ness of God," the listener should reply, "There is no God but Allah." Both of these statements recur in social interactional situations, especially to clarify or restate a viewpoint or to sum-mon the attention of parties in a dispute. In the latter context the two sayings are a call for calm and moderation.

Coptic narrators usually begin with the statements "Glorify your God" or "Pray on behalf of Our Lady Mary." Other for-mulaic beginnings for narrative sessions are found in various parts of Egypt.

The tale itself, particularly a *Märchen* or a *novella,* commonly begins with the phrase "Once there was. . . ." Occasionally more elaborate opening formulas appear, with rhymes that vary on a regional basis. The one most frequently used in various parts of Egypt is "There was—and there was plenty." This formula is sometimes extended.

Concluding formulas are not used in factual or belief narrative or in trickster tales,[36] but they do appear in fantasy and romantic narratives. The most common ending is "I was there and just returned."[37] A sequel to this formula is occasionally added in rural areas: "Even supper I did not have. . . ."[38] Another end-ing, "And they lived in stability and prosperity," is often sup-plemented by the phrase "and begat boys and girls." This phrase, used by women and children, is eschewed by adult male narrators; in tale no. 6, for example, a young adult male's usage of this ending was considered humorous. Another formula common among females is *"Toota, toota,* the tale is over."[39]

Narrators observe the traditional rules of speech etiquette in addressing their listeners. They often employ a number of apologetic or precautionary idioms. When the conversation re-quires the use of an offensive word such as "donkey" or "shit," the narrator usually apologizes by saying, "Don't blame me" or "No offense meant." If he uses pejorative words which may

[36] Trickster tales are in a sense legendary or factual; see notes to "The Trickster Cycle" below.

[37] See tales no. 1, 5, 7, 10, 21, and 49.

[38] Tales no. 3 and 49.

[39] Tale no. 8.

seem to be aimed at the listener, such as the statement "You are . . . a homosexual" in tale no. 15, the narrator employs the precautionary idiom "away from you" or "distant one." He may also say, "away from you" at the mere mention of illness, murder, God's wrath, and similar events or objects of ill fate.

In order to state a fact without accusing the listener of ignorance, as in tale no. 29, the narrator may use the expression "You are the master of the knowledgeable." Such sayings, though not a part of the narrative per se, are important aspects of narration. They appear in the text parenthetically.

Numerous verbal formulas current in oral tradition appear in tales as a matter of course; these include truisms, maxims, proverbs, proverbial phrases, proverbial similes, and recurrent quotations from religious literature. Such formulas are indicated by single quotation marks. I have attempted to provide an accurate translation of these sayings without losing their "proverbial" or symbolic effect.[40]

HASAN EL-SHAMY

---

[40] See notes to tale no. 34, where a foreign collector translated the feminine "viper" as a masculine "dragon."

Editorial Note

Most folk narratives do not have fixed titles. The folk usually refer to a tale in a descriptive manner; a salient theme or episode serves as identifying mark, i.e., "the tale in which the magician took the boy and flew in the air" (see informant note to tale no. 6). Titles given by informants as a part of the narrative are indicated by an asterisk(*).

Most dramatic and stylistic aspects of narration are conveyed through devices of punctuation. A dash (—) indicates a dramatic pause; nonverbal aspects of telling a story are indicated whenever possible. The collector's own additions to the text and originals of key words are placed within brackets, while statements made by the narrator which do not actually belong to the text of the tale are designated by parentheses. Only grammatical changes have been made within the text itself. Most Egyptian narrators employ the present and past tenses interchangeably, sometimes within the same sentence. Although such inconsistencies are indicative of conceptual and emotional states of the narrator and the audience, they nonetheless tend to confuse most readers. In cases where inconsistencies of tense have definitely caused a confusing situation, a change has been introduced. For example, the original rendition of tale no. 2 includes this statement: "After a while she said to the boy who *is* in reality her son, 'Let's get married.'" In the present translation "was" has been substituted for "is." W. K. Simpson and the other editors of *The Literature of Ancient Egypt* found such adjustments necessary in translating ancient Egyptian texts into English (cf. pp. 11–12).

A Note on transliteration

A wide variety of Arabic dialects are spoken in Egypt. The transliteration system given in the *International Journal of Middle East Studies* deals only with classical Arabic pronunciation. I have followed that system, but with minor changes to allow for dialectical phones and for clarity in reading Arabic words:

'A (instead of ') = ع
'a and A = أ
g (instead of *J*) = ج
j = چ
oo or *ou* (instead of *ū*) = وُ
ee (instead of *ī*) = يِ

Established English spellings of Egyptian Arabic names (such as "Ibrahim" instead of "Ibrāheem") are given as they usually appear in print.

In the texts of the tales themselves, transliterated Arabic words and names are given without diacritics, except in cases where confusion may arise. A complete list of key words, terms, and names with pronunciation markings and (varied) spelling is provided in the general index.

Part I
Fantasy Tales

The Trip to 'Wag-el-Wag'

Taped in March 1969 from Ahmad 'Aumar, 46, from the village of Shattourah in southern Egypt. He heard the story twenty years before from an old villager. The narrator began his life as a farmer; after military service he remained in Cairo and is currently the guard of the Floating Theatre. He lives in a small community on the outskirts of Cairo where the majority of immigrants from his village dwell. Most of these immigrants have small jobs in government offices, factories, or businesses and at the same time carry on their old agricultural activities on a very small scale.

I first learned about 'Aumar's ability to narrate when I came upon him listening to his paternal cousin telling this tale with two other janitors in the Folklore Center (see Dorson, *Folktales*, p. 149). 'Aumar told me that "on many occasions we stay in the center after hours; some friends join us, and we chat" (see informant note to tale no. 11). The narrator stated, "Every night at home we get together after having listened to the Koran and the news [on the radio from 8:00 to 8:45] and tell tales." When I asked him, "Why don't you listen to the radio more?" he answered, "The radio has gay songs and things; most people like what is sad and 'tragic.'"

The tale comes under the native classification of *dameerah* (flood time) tale; such a tale is expected to be very long and intricate. The narrator stated, "In older times, during the months of July and August all the fields would be covered with flood water; we would put feed before the animals and have nothing else to do. This story used to take a whole night, maybe two." The building of the Aswan High Dam has changed these conditions; the fields are now cultivated year around. The *dameerah* has vanished from village life, yet narrating is still performed under urban conditions.

The tale revolves around male sibling rivalries. These rivalries concern monopolizing the favor of the father and obtaining the hand of a particular woman. There is also potential conflict between father and son over this woman (see tale no. 58). In neither case is the female a mother figure. Various social and cultural factors, such as the close living conditions within the patriarchal, patrilocal extended family, seem to give rise to such tensions in the kinship group.

Numerous supernatural entities appear, including el-Khiḍr, an omnipresent, seemingly eternal personage who helps in troubled situations. The *āf*, a winged viper that may be viewed as a modern rendition of the ancient Egyptian *Ureaus,* the viper which symbolized kingship over upper and lower Egypt, plays a minor role. Also of interest in the tale is the belief in the readily answered prayers of the poor and the handicapped. The stage for the adventures in our tale is a fictitious country called Waq-el-Waq (pronounced in southern Egyptian dialect "Wag-el-Wag"). On medieval Muslim maps, Waq-el-Waq appeared as a real country located in the same general area as modern Indonesia, Sumatra, and Japan.

ONCE THERE WAS a rich one,* 'and there is no one who is rich except God.' God did not give him any children. He had a poor water carrier who used to bring water to his household. This water carrier thought of helping the rich man. The rich man said to him, "Oh, by God, if you can help me, you will become an equal partner to my children. If I have one, you will be the second; if I have two, you will be the third."

The water carrier said to him, "I dreamed of a recipe, and I will get it for you at the spice merchants [*hannadeen*]."

No sooner had the rich man's wife used the recipe than she became pregnant and delivered one male child after another, until she had ten. The last one had hair of gold and silver, one gold hair for every silver hair.

The father said to the water carrier, "Wish anything you want!"

And the good man answered, "All I want is a mule to carry my water skins."

The father said, "That you'll have."

He also built him a house and said to him, "From now on you work for no one except me."

The youngest of the brothers was called Hasan. He was the most handsome and most intelligent of them. When they grew

---

* Toward the end of the story, this character will be referred to as a king.

up and became men, they wanted to get married. So Hasan said to them, "When our father tells us good morning, let's not reply so that he will know that we are upset."

The following day the father said to them, "Good morning," and they did not answer him.

So he went to his wife and told her about what had happened. She said to him, "Maybe they want to get married."

So their father told them, "You have to marry ten sisters or you will not get married at all."

Hasan said to his father, "We accept. Give us provisions, money, and a good she-camel for each of us." And they set out.

They kept on going and going until they became very tired, and they set up camp. At a distance Hasan saw a fire. So he said to his brothers, "Stay here until I find out what this fire is."

When he got there, he found three persons quarreling over a cap of invisibility.

When they saw him, they said, "Let's let him arbitrate."

He took a sword and said, "I'll throw this sword, and whoever can get it back will have the cap."

He threw the sword very far, and the three ran after it. Meanwhile he put on the cap and disappeared.

On his way back he came across forty robbers dividing their loot. They had forty heaps. Hasan took one. One of them said, "But I didn't get any!"

Their chief said, "How can that be? There are forty heaps, and we are forty. Let's divide again."

Hasan put the heap back, and there were forty heaps. When they divided again there were only thirty-nine! They realized that somebody was there, so their chief said, "Appear. We guarantee your safety."

Hasan appeared to them. When they saw that he was strong, they said to him, "Would you join us? Nearby is the palace of the king of China. He has gold, silver, rubies, and things like that which cannot be counted. He also has ten beautiful daughters."

When Hasan heard that, he said, "Yes" and agreed to join them.

When they got to the palace, Hasan said to them, "You wait outside for me until I climb the walls. When I call for you, climb up one by one."

They said, "All right."

Hasan wore his cap of invisibility and went up the walls. He opened the treasury in which the king stored his money and other things. Then he called for the forty thieves to enter one by one, and one by one he cut off their heads.

After that he closed the door and went up to the harem. The ten princesses were asleep. Each one was more beautiful than the next except for the youngest; she was the most beautiful of all. He fell in love with her and took his ring off his finger and placed it on hers and took hers and placed it on his finger. Then he went back to his brothers and did not tell them a thing.

Now the king's youngest daughter woke up and found the ring on her little finger. She ran to her father; "Father, father, look at this!"

At the same time soldiers came, shouting, "Your majesty, your majesty, there are forty heads in your treasury, but nothing has been stolen."

So the king ordered that all strangers in his kingdom be gathered, and he said, "Whoever can tell me what happened, I will give him whatever he asks for."

No one said, "It was not I," but no one told the real story.

Finally Hasan came with his brothers and asked to meet the king and told him the story. Before then the youngest daughter had told her father, "Father, I dreamed that we were going to be married off to the sons of the king of Egypt."

The king of China saw that Hasan and his brothers were gallant and generous, so he told them, "Wish for anything."

Hasan said, "We promised our father to get married to ten sisters, for we are ten brothers of the same mother and father!"

The king answered, "And I have what you are looking for," and the ten were married.

One day the girls' mother was asking them about how things were with them. The youngest one said, "Mother, neither is he a man, nor am I a woman!" [i.e., nothing had happened between them].

The mother went to the king and told him, and the king was very angry and shouted, "Bring me that Hasan!"

He asked him about the matter. Hasan said, "Your majesty, [with the marriage of your other nine daughters] you have had nine joys already. Don't you think my father deserves at least one? I will keep my actual marriage until I get back home."

The king said, "Right you are!" and ordered preparations for their departure and gifts of silk and gold and everything else.

He sent his youngest daughter with her sisters and their husbands and said to them, "Hasan and I will join you later."

The youngest gave Hasan a ring and said to him, "If I am in distress, this ring will become tight around your finger."

One day the ring became tight, for the group, after leaving, had traveled from one country to another. They came to the city of el-Suhsah;* el-Suhsah took them and transformed them into stone.

So Hasan left to see why the ring had become tight. On the way Clever Hasan met Sidi el-Khidr. He asked him, "Clever Hasan, where are you going?"

Hasan told him the story. El-Khidr told him, "They have been captured by el-Suhsah and have been transformed into stone. But the only one who can tell you how to free your brothers and where el-Suhsah's soul is, how he lives and how he can die, is a girl that el-Suhsah keeps as a captive. You will find her hanging by her hair from the ceiling of one of the rooms in his palace."

(El-Khidr gave him three hairs and told him, "Any time you need me, burn a hair.") Then el-Khidr left him.

Clever Hasan went on until he came to el-Suhsah's palace. He entered it and searched until he found the girl hanging by her hair. He let her down, and she asked him, "What brought you here? You are too good to die."

He told her his story and said to her, "Ask el-Suhsah where he keeps his soul and how he can be killed. If we kill him, we can both be free. I'll get my brothers back, and you can go to your people."

When el-Suhsah came, the girl played up to him; as he was

* The name "el-Suhsah" is normally associated with a character in an epic-romance entitled "Seerat al-ameerah dhat al-himmah" [The life history of Princess Dhat al-himmah; i.e., the princess with high aims and resolutions]; el-Suhsah is the heroine's grandfather. In our tale, the name is used outside its historical legend context; presumably because of its connotations of uncommonness and power, it denotes here an ogre or a wicked magician.

laying his head on her lap, she asked him, "Where do you keep your soul?"

He answered her, "My soul is in the belly of a crocodile. The crocodile is in the country of Wag-el-Wag."

When el-Suhsah left, the girl told Hasan. Hasan set fire to one of the hairs, and el-Khidr came. Hasan told him the story. He said, "This crocodile can die if he is struck with the sword only once. If he says, 'Repeat, Clever Hasan,' say to him 'A young man's stroke should not be repeated.' You will have to shave your head, for he is looking for you" [i.e., "You must disguise yourself and scar your head"].

He asked him to close his eyes and struck him lightly. Hasan found himself next to an old woman herding some animals. He was all alone there, without anything with him. So he said to this old woman, "May you stay well, mother," and she said, "May you stay well, too."

And then he said, "Couldn't you take me to herd with you?"

The woman agreed, and before she left she warned him, "Stay away from this grove. There are two *af* [a huge viper that can fly] in this grove. No one can touch its fruits!"

He got a sheep, killed it, and roasted it. The smell drew the *af*. Hasan was hiding behind a rock, and as the *af* and his mate were busy devouring the sheep, he came out and chopped off their heads. Their mouths were stuffed with half a sheep each. He hid their heads underneath the rock and went to the old woman and told her that the grove was now safe.

The old woman went to the king and said, "Hasan, my son, killed the *af* and reopened the grove."

They sent for Hasan, and when he came people exclaimed, "This scabby headed vagabond!" Everyone claimed that they had killed the *af*. Finally, Hasan brought the heads, and the king said to him, "Make a wish."

Hasan answered, "Give the grove that I freed to my mother [i.e., the old woman]."

The king asked, "Is that all?" and ordered the grove to be given to the old woman.

Now we return to the crocodile for which Hasan originally went there.

Each year they had to throw a bride to the crocodile. It

chanced that for that year it was the turn of the king's daughter.
Everyone was much sadder that year. Hasan said, "Send me with
her, and I will rid you of this crocodile."

When the time came, they took Hasan to the girl on the bank
of the Nile. She was all tied up and covered with gold and
jewelry. He said to her, "I am tired, and I will rest my head on
your lap for a while. When the crocodile comes, wake me up."

The crocodile came, and the girl tried to rouse him, but he
wouldn't wake up. The crocodile was very happy, for he thought
he was getting two instead of one this year. One of the girl's tears
fell on Clever Hasan's cheek; the warmth of the tear woke him
up. He took his sword and struck the crocodile once. The
crocodile said to him, "Second it, Clever Hasan."

He replied, "A young man's stroke should not be repeated."

The crocodile died, for if Hasan had repeated his stroke the
second would have revived him. Hasan split it open and found a
can in its belly. He took it.

The girl returned home, and the people rejoiced. But some
were envious and were saying, "He is scabby headed, a son of a
dog."

But the king said, "The girl is for the one who freed her from
the crocodile."

Clever Hasan asked them to keep the girl for him until he
returned. He burned another hair, and el-Khidr appeared. He
said, "Take me back to el-Suhsah." In the blink of an eye, he was
there.

When he opened the can he found three eggs in it. He took
hold of the first egg and struck it on the ground. As you might
say, the roof of a house had toppled down. El-Suhsah appeared
with one half of himself all broken up. He appealed to him: "By
your honor, Clever Hasan!"

Hasan replied, "By my honor, what? Get me my brothers
back and I will let you go free, just for God's sake."

El-Suhsah said to him, "All right, take some of this sand and
scatter it like this."

He answered, "All right." He took the sand and scattered it; it
became people. Plenty of people appeared, but he said, "My
brothers haven't appeared!"

He said to Hasan, "Try the black sand."

When he scattered the black sand, black people appeared. His brothers didn't appear. El-Suhsah said, "Try the red sand."

When he scattered the red sand, red people, like the English, appeared. But his brothers did not appear.

El-Suhsah said, "Try the white sand!" He said to him "Try the white sand."

When he scattered the white sand, his brothers appeared. El-Suhsah said, "Now let me go, for God's sake!"

Hasan replied, "Let you go, for God's sake! Have you got many more people?"

He replied, "Yes."

He struck the second and the third eggs and el-Suhsah died. He kept on scattering the sand, and people kept on appearing until all of them were free. Hasan said to them, "Go back to your homes."

He took his brothers and his two brides and left. They kept on going through the hills for about a month. Of course the hills, or the desert, are full of desert wells ['Audood]. They came to one well but found that their rope was a little bit too short.

They said, "Clever Hasan, why don't you go down? Our rope is too short. Why don't you go down a foothold [margiyyah] or two because our rope is not reaching?"

He said to them, "Will do."

He went down two or three footholds and brought water, watered their animals, his brothers, and the women who were with them. . . . After they were all satisfied, they pondered, "Now what? Clever Hasan has done it all! If we go back, our father is an old man, and he will say the kingdom is for Hasan. Now we need to get rid of him."

The eldest of them said, "Leave this to me."

He said to him, "Clever Hasan, give me your hand."

He gave him his hand [to lift him out], but he [the brother] let go of it. He [Hasan] went tumbling down the well. Whether he has stayed in the well a day or two [doesn't matter]; there came a group of Arabs to water their animals. When they let their bucket down, he got hold of it. They inquired, "Are you a human or a a jinni?"

He replied, "I am a human of the best humans. Pull me up. I am fatigued."

They pulled him up. The Arab girls found him sweet and handsome. They kept on feeding him: eggs, pigeons, butter, and I don't know what else until they made him brim with vigor again.

He said to them, "With your permission, I'm traveling." He stayed with them a number of days and left. He went to his country and found. . . . He came close to the city of his father and found a man selling lupine [*tirmis,* eaten for snacks]. He said to him, "Paternal uncle, may I stay with you and work and you just feed me?"

The man replied, "There is no harm in that."

He stayed with that man. After the man had been preparing only one measure he started preparing two [i.e., his business picked up]. Every day he improved by one measure until he became rich. He 'denied the favor' of Clever Hasan [and mistreated him]. Hasan said to him, "Even you, lupine vendor? You degrade me!"

He left the man, and to whom did he go? He went to a goldsmith, one of the best known in the city. He said to him, "Paternal uncle, I am poor and tired. May I stay with you? Can you teach me the craft and [just] feed me?"

The goldsmith said to him, "There is no harm in that, son."

Now he wanted to know the news of the country. He inquired and learned that his father had asked his sons, "Where is your brother, boys?"

They answered, "We went to get some water. As we were coming back with the brides, the man [the brides' father] was generous to us by giving us one extra girl." (They had not said that it was Hasan who brought the girls; when they were returning they had warned the girls, "Don't you dare say, 'Hasan brought us from the country of Wag-el-Wag.' Say that it is we who brought you from the same country; if you don't we will kill you!")

They [lied] to their father, "After we brought back the girls, the man was generous to us and gave us the extra girl as a servant for the others; we stopped for some water, and Hasan went down the well, but the well collapsed. It was a deep well, about sixty meters deep. We tried, but we couldn't [get him out]. From where were we going to get men in the desert to help us dig? By the time we had done that, Hasan would have died a hundred times. Now he is dead and buried."

Their father [lamented], "Now Hasan is dead!"

They replied, "He is dead."

He moaned, "May God compensate me for Hasan. Had he come back, he would have been more blessed than all of you [put together]."

The man mourned for several days, but he looked and saw that the girls whom Hasan had brought were beautiful. All of the other brothers had one each, and there were still Hasan's two.

The vizier said to him, "Are we going to mourn for the rest of our lives? Why don't you take one for yourself, and I'll take one?"

He replied, "By God, this is an idea. Until when will we be in mourning? Let us."

Now Hasan learned all that and knew that the king and the vizier were going to take the two girls. The girl who was the daughter of the king of China knew that Hasan got out of the well; she had what you might call a secret [*sirr,* i.e., intuition].

They said to her, "The king will marry you."

She replied, "There is nothing wrong with that."

They went to get the marriage shiek [*ma'zoon*] and to invite all the people and big crowds; the minister did the same thing. The first girl said to the king, "You are going to marry me? Before you do, you must get me a bracelet like this one."

The second girl also said, "And I want a bracelet like this one before I marry the minister." (For the daughter of the king of the country of Wag-el-Wag had also given Hasan a bracelet.)

They took the bracelets and went to the goldsmiths and asked them, "Can you make bracelets like this?"

"Oh no, by God."

"Can you make bracelets like this?"

"Oh, no, by God."

Until they finally came to our friend. He also said, "No, I can't, by God."

Hasan said [to the goldsmith],* "Effendi, let me see. Yes, I can."

* The full narrative situation here can be understood only through its kinesic-visual components. The narrator conveyed the idea that the

"You can?"

"Yes, I can!"

[The goldsmith went out to the king and the vizier and told them that he, himself could make them.]

They said, "Wish for whatever you want, and just make us ones exactly like them."

Hasan replied, "This is a very simple matter. Give me a fifteen-day period and five hundred pounds."

"All right, here are the five hundred pounds, and take as long as twenty days."

[The goldsmith went back to the king and vizier and told them that he could.]

Hasan put the money in his pocket and kept on eating out of that money and spending it until the period of the twenty days that they had given him passed. [Meanwhile he pretended to be working on the bracelets.]

When they returned, he [Hasan] gave them both [the original] bracelets.

The girls looked and found that the two bracelets were the very same. They said, "One more thing! Bring the man who made these two bracelets here. Kill him before our eyes, and we will marry you."

He pleaded, "It is not I! I did not make them. The one who made them is that scabby head, that son of a dog! It's not I. Oh, people, help! Come here, scabby head!"

He came and said, "What do you want from me?"

They said, "They want to kill you."

He said, "Here?"

They answered, "No, at the palace."

He said, "All right, I will go to the palace and die there."

When he went there he asked, "Why do you want to kill me? Is that the reward for one who made you such a fine piece of work? To be killed! Is this the reward, king, for the person who made the bracelet for you so that you could marry the fiancée of Hasan your son?"

storeowner shuffled back and forth between the king and the hero—who was sitting in the work area in the back room—by turning his face to the listener when the goldsmith was speaking to one party and away when speaking to the other.

The king said, "And how do you know?"

Hasan asked him, "Don't you have a sign (by which you can recognize Hasan your son)?"

He replied, "I do. His mark is that he was born with his hair, you might say, one silver and one gold."

Hasan said, "Like this?" [Taking off his head disguise].

He exclaimed, "You are Hasan." He hugged him and married him to the two girls at the same time.

Of course the lives of all his other brothers, because of their wives, were spared. But they were put under his hand.

And I was there and just returned.

· 2 ·   *The Black Crow and the White Cheese*

Recorded in July 1970 from I. Ḥ., 64, an Orthodox Copt from Cairo. Soon after the death of his first childless wife, Ḥ. remarried; now he has four children. He works as a public scribe; for a small fee he writes personal letters and petitions for the illiterate and assists others in dealing with bureaucratic regulations. He jocularly referred to himself as "a spare scribe" because he is one-eyed. Tilib (see informant note to tale no. 11) described Ḥ. as "never ceasing to narrate" and arranged for me to meet with him. At first Ḥ. refused to tell any folktales but was perfectly willing to instruct me about narratives from the Bible and other "true things," mainly his own personal experiences with the supernatural. However, at a later date he told me this tale as a piece of wisdom. The story reflects some of Ḥ.'s attitudes toward females.

I asked him whether he told folktales at home, and he explained, "How can I? My son has twice failed his junior high school admission test! He has no time for anything except the radio, movies, and quarreling with his mother. I can't tell him such things. I have to help him with his school work. His [female] teacher [does not teach him a thing]. . . . You ask me whether I narrate to him? How can I! The boy would lose his respect for me."

He joked, with a streak of bitterness, "My wife [who is much

younger than he is] tells the youngest child, 'Call him *a'Awar*
[one-eyed], and the girl says it to me. What a man needs is
respect."

Ḥ. learned the tale in his home village of el-Sheen, in the
northwestern part of the Nile Delta, from a man named Sheik
Ahmad.

Predestination and distrust of females are the two basic themes
expressed in this narrative. According to religious beliefs, all
there was, is, and ever will be is written on a tablet in heaven. An
Arab adage states, "What is written on the forehead must be
witnessed by the eye," i.e., what is predestined will happen. The
first portion of our story gives a vivid, concrete illustration of
this belief. Weakness and ingratitude, two traits usually ascribed
to women, characterize the conduct of the hero's mother in our
tale. Two interesting symbols appear: the crow, which stands for
the evil male, and the cheese, which stands for a luscious female.

'THERE WAS, and there was plenty; [may your lot in life be]
either happiness or generosity;* talk will not be sweet without
mentioning Our Lady Mary; upon her may there be the best of
prayers and greetings.'

Once an old man was walking in the cemetery, cutting across it
to go home. It was about sunset. He looked at the graves and
saw something luminous. He wondered, and he walked to the
thing and picked it up. He saw that it was a human skull, just
bone. The man looked carefully and saw that on its forehead
there was some writing. He tried to read it (for as you know,
there are people who can read 'what's written on the forehead').
There was written, "Alive I killed forty, and dead I will kill as
many."

The man said, "What's that? This skull, this dead skull, will kill
forty!" He said, "By God, I must prevent this from happening."

He took the skull home and ordered, "Light the oven," and he
put the skull inside until it was white hot. Then he took it out,
put it in a mortar, and pounded it until it became powder. He
put this powder in a jar and put the jar in his cabinet, locked it,
and put the key in his pocket.

---

* This is one of a number of possible meanings of the middle clause of
the opening formula.

Now this man was a merchant. He traveled everywhere. Time passed, and it became pilgrimage time. He set out for Hejaz. Before he left, he told his wife, "No one should touch this cabinet."

She said to him, "No one will come near it."

The man left. A week passed and a second, and the man's wife left her home for some urgent business (to visit her sick mother or something; for as you know, women of older times never left their homes except for the grave).

When she was out, her daughter—the man's daughter—was cleaning the house. As she was cleaning, she came across the jar. She looked at it like this [with a scrutinizing eye], and she wondered, "What brought that jar here?"

She opened the lid, smelled it: "It doesn't smell like coffee or anything else!"

She wet her finger like this and dipped it in the jar and tasted what was inside. She did not know what it was. She put the lid on again and left it where it was. After a while the mother returned, and the girl forgot to ask her about the jar.

Days went by, and finally, after two or three months, her stomach began to rise. Her mother hid her inside the house and brought midwives to check her because the girl had told her, "No human touched me!" The midwives found that she was still a virgin.

The mother realized that the girl was innocent and thought, "We must wait until her father returns." Some time later she delivered a baby boy, after she had completed her nine months of pregnancy.

No sooner had this happened than the man returned. When they told him the story, he asked, "Has anybody touched or come near the jar?"

They wondered, "Which jar?"

He answered, "The jar in my closet."

The girl said, "As I was cleaning, I found the jar and I took a lick from it to see what it tasted like."

The father knew what had happened and realized that 'what is written on the forehead must be witnessed by the eye.' He named the boy 'Ailm-el-ghaib [knowledge of the unknown].

The boy grew up fast and did amazing things. The man was a

jewel merchant. When he had returned from Hejaz, he had with him hundreds of jewels. 'Ailm-el-ghaib said to him, "Grandfather, these jewels are fake."

The man wondered, "How come? I have been in this business for maybe fifty, sixty years. Impossible!"

'Ailm-el-ghaib scattered the jewels in front of him and pointed out, "This one is genuine, and that one is genuine. The rest are worthless."

The man started examining his jewels, took them to his prominent jewel dealer friends, and they realized that what the child had said was true. The story became famous, and the boy 'Ailm-el-ghaib became known throughout the country.

Now it chanced that the king of that country had a dream. He woke up horrified and called on his vizier. "Counsel me, vizier."

The vizier said, "Counseling is God's, king."

The king said, "In a dream I saw a black crow pecking at a disk of white cheese. What is the interpretation of that?"

The vizier answered, "The religious sages ['Aulama] and those who interpret dreams can tell you."

They called them, but no one could interpret the dream to the satisfaction of the king. Finally they said, "The only one who can interpret this is the child 'Ailm-el-ghaib."

The king ordered, "Call him." They sent for him.

The boy came with his grandfather, and the king told him his dream. The boy said, "Assure me of my safety."

The king said, "Your safety is assured."

The boy said, "Assure my grandfather of his safety."

The king replied, "And your grandfather's is assured."

The boy said, "Then do as I tell you. Take me to the harem, the wing of women."

The king took him. The boy started with the queen: "Take your clothes off."

The king became furious. The boy said, "You promised to do as I tell you." Then the king ordered the queen, "Take your clothes off. I'm your husband, and he is only a child."

The queen took off her clothes, and then the boy said, "All the maids should take off their clothes too."

They all did. They finally came to a black maid, and she said, "No, I cannot."

The king said [furiously], "The queen has taken off her clothes and you can't? Undress!"

She refused. The king took his sword out and said, "By God, if you do not undress, I'll split you in two!"

She began undressing, and with the last piece the king saw that she was a man disguised as a woman who had been living with the queen for years. 'Ailm-el-ghaib [pointing at the man] said, "King, this is the black crow, and that [pointing at the queen] is the white cheese!"

The king called his guards and his executioner and said, "Chop off the head of this man and all the guards and maids who have known about it and not told me."

When the executioner was through, there were exactly forty heads. The grandfather of 'Ailm-el-ghaib knew that what he had read on the skull came true to the letter.

The king called his son and said to him, "Clever Muhammad (for example, or Clever 'Aali, whatever his name happened to be), this is your mother and this is what she has done! You choose either her or me."

The boy said, "I will choose her."

The king said, "All right, take all you need from the palace and leave before sunset prayer time."

The boy saddled his horse and loaded it with everything he needed and took his mother with him, and they left. They went through deserts and forests until they finally came to three roads. The first road was called the road of safety, the second road was called the road of sorrow, and the third was called the road of no return. He kept on going and going until he finally came to a cave.

This cave had a boulder blocking its entrance that could be moved only by forty strong men. The boy was very strong, and he alone moved the boulder. When he looked inside the cave, he saw a palace with a garden and a water fountain. In the palace he found gold, silver, and everything that could occur to your imagination. The cave belonged to forty thieves who lived in it, and they were away robbing somebody or killing somebody else.

The boy rested his mother and his horse inside the cave, and a while later they heard the thieves coming. As they entered, the boy chopped their heads off one by one. Only their chief managed to escape inside the cave. He hid there until Clever

Muhammad went out looking for something, food or something.

While Clever Muhammad was away, his mother heard a sound—something groaning. She started looking around and found the chief of the robbers, who had managed to escape. He was wounded by a blow from Clever Muhammad's sword.

When this broad [*mara*] saw that man, she acted as if she had known him for a hundred years. Oh, many a greeting, and "How are you?" and all that! She bandaged him, and the wound was not serious. He recovered right away. The woman took to the chief robber and started playing up to him. Of course the man was horrified, for he had seen how her son Clever Muhammad took on his forty men. He said to her, "I cannot do anything of the sort. If your son finds out, he will kill me as he did my friends."

The woman said, "Let's get rid of him. Find a way."

The robber said, "Pretend that you are sick and about to die; and when he returns, tell him that you must get the water of life. He will be gone for a very long time, and if he does not die on the way, there will be lions that will eat him there."

When the boy returned, his mother started. "Ahhh, my head! Ahhh, my back! Ahhh, my heart! Ahhh, my liver! Ahhh, my gizzard!" and all that.

He said, "What's the matter? I wish you better health, mother."

The woman said to him, "O son, I must have the water of life. Without it I will die."

The boy replied, "May this be after a long life, if God wills."

The woman said, "The water of life! For I am dying."

He said, "I'll get it even if it happens to be at the end of the earth," and immediately he set out.

He kept on going and going until he finally came to a place where there was an old man.

"Peace be upon you."

The man replied, "And upon you be peace. What do you want?"

The boy said, "I want the water of life."

The old man said, "What for?"

"It's for my mother"; and he told him the whole story.

The old man said, "Clever Muhammad, your mother wants to send you to your death."

The boy replied, "Don't say that!"

The man said, "There is a hundred years of travel between you and the water of life, and I will help you get there, but when you get the water come back here."

The old man called, and three of the jinn appeared. He asked the first one, "Clever Muhammad wants to get the water of life. How long will it take you to take him over there?"

The jinni answered, "A year."

The man said, "That's too long."

The second said, "I'll do it in a month."

The third said, "I'll do it in a day."

So the third jinni took Clever Muhammad and flew him to the fountain of the water of life. He set him on the ground at the outskirts and said, "I'll wait for you here."

As soon as he [Clever Muhammad] came close to the fountain, he heard the roaring of the lions. He wasn't afraid. He walked steadily and finally came to the lioness. She was in labor, and he helped her deliver. The lioness, after having been in great pain, came to feel the utmost comfort and contentment. She said to him, "What do you want, Clever Muhammad?"

He answered, "I want to fill this skin with the water of life, because my mother is dying and she needs it."

The lioness said, "Oh, your mother wanted to send you to your death. Go and fill the skin and get what you want."

After he filled the skin, the lioness gave him two of her cubs and said to him, "You will need these. They will be of help to you at the time of distress."

He took the two cubs and the water; the jinni that was waiting for him carried them back to where he started.

The old man, Sheik Mahmoud, said to him, "You are back. Sit down and rest."

While Muhammad was resting, the old man took the water of life, poured it in a pot, and filled the skin with regular water. After the boy rested, Sheik Mahmoud said to him, "Safety be with you." And he started back to his mother.

When he got there, his mother's heart sank to her toes when she saw him, for she had been sure that he would never come back. She took a sip of the water and said, "Ahhh, I feel much better. Thanks to God."

When the boy went out again, the chief of the robbers said to her, "See, he came back. He is like a cat with seven souls!"

She said to him, "We have to find another way to get rid of him."

The chief of the robbers said, "Send him to get grapes from the garden of the Ogre. The Ogre has forty dogs. If the Ogre does not eat him up, the dogs will tear him apart."

When Clever Muhammad returned, his mother said to him, "I need grapes. If I don't get them, I will die."

And the boy said, "But this is not the season for grapes."

His mother said, "I'm ill and I need grapes to be cured, and I know that there are grapes in the garden of the Ogre."

So [accompanied by his two lion cubs] Clever Muhammad set out to look for the garden of the Ogre. Sheik Mahmoud met him and said, "Where to, Clever Muhammad?"

He replied, "To the Ogre's garden to get grapes."

Shiek Mahmoud said, "But this is in the country of Waq-el-Waq."

Clever Muhammad said, "My mother is ill, and I need the grapes right away."

Sheik Mahmoud said, "The Ogre is ferocious. He steals maidens, and after taking their virginity, he throws them to his forty dogs. The forty dogs have become rabid. When you get there, strike the Ogre [only] with his wooden sword. If he asks you to strike again, do not, for this would bring him back to life."

Clever Muhammad said, "Thank you, and peace be upon you."

When he got there, the forty dogs sniffed his odor and ran toward him to attack. The two lions which the lioness had presented to him came down on the dogs and shredded them. All this while the Ogre was still asleep.

Clever Muhammad went into his room and found two swords on the wall, a steel one sharper than a razor and a wooden one. [One of the audience: "As sharp as Uncle Haggag's razor!" Roars of laughter from the audience: Hagagg is the hamlet barber.]

He took the wooden one and said, "In the name of God," and struck the Ogre once.

The Ogre opened one eye and said, "Repeat it, Clever Muhammad."

Clever Muhammad answered, "A young man's stroke is not to be repeated." As soon as he said this, the Ogre fell dead.

Clever Muhammad got the grapes and left.

On his way back he came to a town. The town was all lit up and decorated: Half the people were making trilling cries of joy [*yizaghrat*], and the other half were wailing and crying. He asked, "What's the matter?"

They told him, "Every year a crocodile comes and takes a virgin girl from town. We dress her well, beautify her, and set her on the bank so the crocodile will come and take her. Without this, the crocodile will come and parch the city. This year it is the turn of the king's daughter. One half of us must celebrate for the beast, [while] the other half must lament for us!"

So Clever Muhammad went to the bank and found the girl sitting all alone crying. She was very beautiful. Her beauty was indescribable. As soon as she saw him, she said, "You are too young to die. Go back."

He replied, "Never mind." He said to her, "I'm very tired, and I'm going to lay my head on your lap and go to sleep. When you see the crocodile, wake me up."

After a while, the crocodile appeared, splitting the water in two. The girl was so horrified that she forgot to wake Clever Muhammad. Her tears came running down her cheeks, dropped on Clever Muhammad's face, and woke him up. He took his sword, and as the crocodile opened its mouth to grab the girl, he said, "In the name of God," and cut him in two. He took the girl back to her father (just like Mari Girgis [i.e., St. George]).

The streets of the town were empty, and when people realized that he had the girl with him, they started shouting, "Take her back! The crocodile will kill us!"

He said to them, "The crocodile is dead."

They did not believe him. They finally went out and saw the body of the crocodile lying on the bank.

The king was very happy and said to him, "Make a wish."

He answered, "I wish for nothing except the girl I saved."

They held festivities for forty days and forty nights, and after that, with the king's permission, he took his wife and left.

On his way back, he stopped by Sheik Mahmoud's. He asked, "What's this, Clever Muhammad?"

He told him the story. Sheik Mahmoud said to him, "Leave your bride here, and come back for her later."

He left his bride and went. When he reached his mother and

she saw him coming, she said to the chief of the robbers, "What are we going to do with him? He is like a cat; he has seven souls!"

The chief of the robbers said to her, "When he comes, play checkers [*seega*] with him and say, 'The winner should tie up the loser.'"

When Clever Muhammad came back, his mother said to him, "Welcome back; *ahlan wasahlan* [welcome, welcome]." And after he rested she said, "Let's play *seega,* and he who wins should tie up the loser."

Clever Muhammad won three times and tied her up very loosely, and finally he lost to her deliberately, for it would not be polite for him to win all the time. She tied him up in a fiery way and called, "So-and-so, come out."

He came out, and she said to him, "There he is in front of you. Slice him up."

The boy stared at the chief robber, and the man dropped from fear. His mother became very angry, took the sword, and killed him [her son]. She and the chief robber cut him into a hundred pieces and put him in a box and threw it into the river.

The mother was pregnant when she asked for the grapes, and she had a baby boy by the chief robber.

Now we return to what? To the box. When the box was thrown into the Nile, his [Clever Muhammad's] bride whom he had saved from the crocodile, the daughter of the king, chanced to be promenading.

She went out to the river and found a fisherman. She said to him, "Throw your net once to see what my luck brings me." The box came out.

She took the box to Sheik Mahmoud. When they opened it, they found Clever Muhammad inside in pieces. They put him together piece by piece, and when he was all put together, they poured the water of life which Shiek Mahmoud had hidden away into his mouth and splashed it all over his body. With God's power, he came back to life.

They took care of him, and Sheik Mahmoud told him what had happened. After a while, when he gained his strength back, he said to them, "I have to go and see about these two" [i.e., his mother and the chief of the robbers].

He got a black robe and a rebec *(rababa)* and went around singing like a bard *(maddāḥ)*. When his mother saw him, she did not know who he was, for he looked different. She saw that he was young and handsome and had a beautiful voice and sweet words. She fell in love with him.

She called on him and said, "Sing some for me," and he sat down and sang.

The chief of the robbers said to her, "This man looks like your son, Clever Muhammad."

She replied, "God creates forty of each face."

After a while she said to the boy, who was in reality her son, "Let's get married."

He answered, "What about your husband?"

She said, "May a catastrophe find him!"

He asked her, "Would you kill him?"

She replied, "And a hundred like him."

The boy saw his mother as she really was and remembered the black crow eating the white cheese. He threw his rebec away and revealed his true identity. He drew out his sword and killed her. He also killed the child who was begotten by the chief of robbers.

When the chief of the robbers saw all that, he came out and said to him, "Kill me too."

The boy said to him, "You have done nothing wrong in all this. Go away, for I have granted you your life."

The man said, "I have only one thing to ask of you."

The boy asked, "What's that?"

The chief of the robbers said, "I would like to live the rest of my life as your servant."

He answered, "That would be all right."

He went back and took his wife, who was waiting with Sheik Mahmoud, and they all went back and lived with his father.

Taped in April 1969 from 'A. Abu-'Aashoor, 55, illiterate peasant from Gharbiyyah Province in the Nile Delta. He is married
and has several children going to school, some of them at high
school level. He does not narrate to them, but they may hear
him narrating to other men. Abu-'Aashoor did not remember
when or from whom he learned the tale. He explained, "We, I
mean a group of fellahin, get together, and each one of us would
say something, and that is all." His narrative style is austere.

The recording took place in the home of another villager; a
number of other adult males and children were present. The
wife of our host stood by the doorway to the room which was a
sitting room as well as a bedroom, for according to custom she
was not supposed to be seen by strangers (see informant note to
tale no. 56). She commented, "I know this story; the wife of the
fisherman was from the river," i.e., a *jinniyyah*.

Marriage or a similar type of association between jinn and
humans is believed to be possible and is often reported. The
theme of the speaking newborn baby is common in both formal
and folk religious literature, especially in saints' legends. According to the Koran, the infant Jesus Christ spoke to the critics
of the Virgin, thus providing the proof of her truthfulness.
However, our tale is for entertainment, not for belief, although
its contents may be viewed as factual in a different context.

PRAY ON BEHALF OF the Prophet.
One time the king was going through the town with his vizier.
He saw a woman who was truly beautiful. She appealed to him
very much, so he turned to his vizier and said, "Vizier, counsel
me."

The vizier answered, "Counseling is for God, king."

The king said, "What do you say? I admire this young woman
very much."

The vizier wondered, "What next?"

The king replied, "I want you to investigate and see whether
she is married, widowed, or what is her story."

The vizier asked around and found out that she was the wife of a fisherman. He went back to the king. The king asked him, "What did you do?"

He replied, "By God, the matter is very easy. Her husband is a poor man. As long as your conscience agrees to it, of course we can find a way to get rid of her husband or find another solution."

The king said, "All right."

Then the king sent for the fisherman. When he came, he said to the king, "Yes, sir!"

The king said, "I'm going to ask something of you. If you don't do it, I'm going to chop off your (distant one) head!"

The fisherman replied, "Whatever you order, your majesty."

The king said to him, "Tomorrow I want you to come here riding-walking."

The man went home very sad and puzzled. He went to his wife and said to her, "The king did to me such-and-such things."

She replied, "Never mind."

She went to her sister; it happened that her sister was close to the sons of the jinn. The sister said, "We have (do not blame me) a she-ass who has just given birth. We have her foal. Let him ride it. His feet will be dragging on the ground, while his bottom will be on the ass's back."

In the morning he went there astride the foal. The king said, "Ahhh! You beat me! But guess what? I'm going to ask you another thing. Tomorrow I want you to come to me dressed-naked."

The fisherman went home very sad. His wife went to her sister, who said to her, "There at home he has his fishing net. Let him wear it."

The following day he went to the king wearing only his fishing net. This time the king set him aside for awhile and said to his vizier, "This time we have to find him something that he can't solve."

The king said to the fisherman, "Now, listen. This time I'm going to ask you something. If you don't get it, then your death (distant one) has become legitimate."

The fisherman said, "All right; tell me, your majesty."

The king said, "I want you to get us an infant who is seven days old to tell us a story that is lies through and through."

He left and wondered, "This is the one thing that no one at all can do!"

Of course he went home extremely distressed. He told his wife, and she went to her sister. Her sister said to her, "Give me a little while."

She went out and came back with a seven-day-old infant. The sister gave her [the wife] the baby, and she took it to her husband. Her husband exclaimed, "Is this the thing I'm going to take with me?"

She answered him, "That's none of your business. You just go."

"Lady, I'm going to die tomorrow!"

She replied, "Just go."

The following day he left sadly; he was not convinced. He entered the king's presence; the ministers and everybody else were present. As soon as the fisherman with the infant stepped into the hall, the baby said, "Peace be upon you, your majesty the king."

Naturally our friend's heart quieted. Everybody wondered and looked at him like this [with astonishment].

He put the infant on a chair, and the king asked sarcastically, "Is that what's going to tell us the story?"

Immediately the baby shouted, "Pray upon the Prophet, king."

The king immediately answered, "Upon him be prayers and peace."

"Fifty years ago I went out to get myself some dates from a palm tree. I didn't find any on the ground, so I picked up a few pieces of adobe and started throwing them at the bunches of dates [at the top of the tree]. The pieces of adobe stuck together, and in a short while I had about an acre of land up there."

[The king replied,] "That's reasonable."

The boy said, "I ran home and got the plow and two cows and twelve ardebs of sesame seed. I took them all up the palm tree. I plowed the land and divided it into sections and prepared it 'twenty-four carats' [i.e., perfectly]. Then I sowed the sesame. After I finished, and as I was just coming down with the animals, some man asked me, 'What are you planting this season?'

"I answered him, 'Sesame.'

"He replied, 'But this is not sesame [planting] season.'

"I went back and started picking out all the seeds. I got eleven ardebs full. As for the twelfth, there is still one seed missing [from it]. What do you think? Should I leave it?"

The king replied, "What else, clever one!"

The baby said, "Never! I have been looking for it for the past fifty years. I have not been able to tolerate losing that one seed."

The king said in amazement, "Ohhh, my! You have got back all twelve ardebs; nothing left except that seed for you to find! Why don't you do without it?"

The baby answered, "Why don't you do without the fisherman's wife? You have got all these ardebs of other women, and you still want this one!"

The king replied, "Right you are!" and turned to the fisherman and said, "May God bless what he has given you. Take your son and go home."

I was there and just returned; even supper I did not have [there].

· 4 ·   *The Magic Filly*

Taped in March 1969 from H. Ghanim, a 16-year-old Bedouin. Originally his family lived in Sinai, but they had to move because of the June War of 1967. Now Ghanim resides in a little hamlet on the eastern outskirts of Cairo, where a large number of nomads have settled recently. In their new environment some of the newly settled nomads carry on with their old pastoral activities in the eastern desert, while others have begun new urban undertakings.

A unique economic pattern, which we may refer to as urban pastoralism, has developed. Lacking sufficient vegetation in the desert, nomads drive their herds through the streets of Cairo's suburbs to feed on lawn grass and city garbage. I met Ghanim while he was grazing his small camel herd (about seven young animals) on the lawns of the exclusive district of Maadi, and he agreed to tell me some tales. The tape recording took place on the front porch of my house, where he could watch over his camels at the same time.

Ghanim's active repertoire is fairly small; he readily narrated eight tales, but his stories lacked the description and the details which give a story its "fullness." This is probably due to his youth and the fact that he had been for the most part a listener, not a narrator. He learned his tales mostly from his paternal grandmother, who narrates *Märchen* to a group of household youngsters "almost every evening." He also learned some serious tales from his maternal uncle and other men in the family.

The problem of the hostile relationship of a child and a stepmother has been particularly salient in Arab lore. Conditions of polygyny and high mortality rates especially among young mothers, which were very dominant in Arab societies until relatively recently, contributed to the magnification of this problem. This narrative reflects a young person's view of this type of relationship. In addition, it demonstrates the rivalry among brothers-in-law (*'Aadayil;* i.e., husbands whose wives are sisters). The conflict here is essentially a power struggle to win the recognition of the father-in-law and to succeed him in power.

I'LL TELL THE STORY of Clever Muhammad—Clever Muhammad of olden days. Clever Muhammad was a king son-of-kings. His stepmother was full of hate for him, and she couldn't wait to kill Clever Muhammad. Then Clever Muhammad was king son-of-kings.

When he was still little, his mother died. When she died his father married again. Then Clever Muhammad—Clever Muhammad had a young filly. This filly—Clever Muhammad was a king, and his stepmother hated him because he was king son-of-kings. He had this young filly. The young filly discovered that the stepmother was putting poison in his [Muhammad's] food. While coming back from where he worked, the filly said to Clever Muhammad, "Do not eat the bread, for your stepmother has poisoned it."

So the boy did not eat the bread. The woman, then: "How could it be that he did not eat the bread? Somebody must be telling him!"

Then she put poison in the blueing used to wash his clothes. The filly told him again.

One day she discovered that it was the filly that was telling him about everything. She started thinking of a way in which she could get rid of, kill the filly so that she could complete her crime. Now this is what she did (do not blame me)—she got dry bread and wrapped it around her back; she wrapped the bread over her back. When her husband came, [he heard] crack, crack. Of course her lover had told her about the bread and said to her, "You do the bread, and I'll pass by and say, 'A healing doctor, who'll cure all ailments.' Then you say that only the young filly will cure you."

Now this man was wandering around crying "A healing doctor, who'll cure all ailments."

So she called him. They said, "This woman has a cracking back!"

He said, "Her cure is very easy: a young filly to be slaughtered."

Her husband said, "The filly that we have!"

The filly heard that and became sad and cried. Clever Muhammad said to her, "Filly, why are you crying?"

She said to him, "Such and such and such. After that, today they will slaughter me."

He said, "Never mind."

He took the filly and dressed her from end to end in gold and said, "Father, you are going to slaughter the filly when I have not enjoyed or promenaded with her yet."

He said, "Son, ride her and go around as slowly as you like."

The boy ran the filly back and forth once, twice, and fled. When he fled, she—the filly—said to him, "Take three hairs from my mane. Whenever you rub them together, you will find me underneath you."

After that, he went on his own. He got to a king's palace and sat down. There came an oil vendor, and he said to him, "Take my shiny clothes and give me yours—" [narrator cuts his statement short].

He found that oil vendor who was all oily and dirty—he was begging. He said to him, "Take my clothes and give me yours."

He said, "You are a king son-of-kings. What are you going to do with my dirty clothes?"

He answered, "Never mind."

He put on the dirty clothes and looked very shabby. If you

were to see him, you wouldn't say that he was a king or son-of-kings.

He came next to an apartment building [palace] that belonged to a king; that king had seven daughters. These seven daughters were of great beauty, none more beautiful in the world. He sat beside the palace. The girls were looking out like this—they saw him. They said to him, "Would you like to come and work for us? Sweep, do chores and such?"

He said, "Might as well."

They said, "You can work in the garden and sweep the tile and so on."

He said, "I might as well."

One day at noon time—that king had a beautiful, really marvelous garden. He was a king whom all his subjects loved. Now he [Clever Muhammad] got to a corner of this garden and rubbed the three hairs. There he was king son-of-kings. The filly came, and he mounted it. As he was turning around the shrubs, the king's youngest daughter—the youngest—saw him. She saw that he was king son-of-kings and fell in love with him. He said to her, "Do not tell."

She said, "All right."

She kept the secret.

In the morning her father was saying, "Who broke that shrub, who broke the shrub?"

The youngest daughter said, "I broke it."

He disregarded it. Now the youngest daughter said to her father, "Father, all girls have been married, but we haven't yet. 'Had we been wheat we would have been moth-eaten by now'!"

So he said, "Tomorrow I'll collect the country's young men, the best young men. Each one of you should select one of them."

They gathered all notable young men and lined them up like this. Each girl cast her shawl at the one of her choice. Each one threw hers on somebody except the youngest. She threw hers on the poor boy who was actually a king.

When she did that, her father said, "You daughter of a dog! By God, I'm going to put you in the dung with him. You will be washing floors."

Her father hated her for that.

In the morning there came horsemen and fighters and took

away all whose money? Her father's. And all the horses. Now he
(the young king) was mounted on a small jackass, a lame jackass,
while all his brothers-in-law were mounted on horses and holding swords—really tough men. The king looked and saw him and
said, "You go to hell with your jackass! Do you think you are
going to do something?"

He followed them with his jackass. When they did not notice
him, he rubbed the hairs, and there underneath him was his fine
filly.

After he had been at the rear, he got ahead. They [the
brothers-in-law] were frightened of the battle and ran away.
Only Clever Muhammad and the king were left.

Clever Muhammad kept on hitting them with his sword until
he defeated them. After his victory over them, the king was
swinging his sword like this. It hit Clever Muhammad's arm. The
king took out his kerchief and bandaged his wound. After this
the king got a good look at him. Of course it was he [Muham-
mad] who brought back all the [king's] possessions. When the
king was not paying attention, he rubbed the hairs, and the filly
disappeared. And he got back on his donkey. All the others
started returning.

The king said, "I know who brought back my possessions for
me. For I have injured his arm by accident."

Now he started checking his sons-in-law and his own family;
there was nothing. Nobody was left except the poor boy, who
was sitting alone looking pitiful. The king said, "Bring the pitiful
thing. Maybe."

Now everybody was laughing, thinking, "Nobody left but
this! Who could return the kingdom?"

The king looked at his [the boy's] arm and found his handkerchief. He said, "It's true, you are a king son-of-kings," and took
him along.

He divorced his daughters from all the others and took them
away, married his youngest daughter to Clever Muhammad, and
made the best celebration in the world. He [Muhammad] went
back to his father, and everything was fine.

This is the end of the story.

Narrated in November 1969 by S. Ghunaim, a 54-year-old policeman of Bedouin origin from Fayyoum Province. He is married and has several children; normally he does not narrate to them. He can read and write "very little." I met Ghunaim during a saint's birthday celebration. He stated, "I heard this story several years ago from a 'brother' [i.e., friend] who visits this celebration every year. I still remember it, because it shows how God rewards a small good deed in plenty."

When I asked him whether the story is true, he stated, "It may have happened, and again it may not have; but this is not the point."

This "story with a deep meaning" imparts the same kind of experience as Sufi mystic practices. The actual hero is a dervish—a Muslim hermit sometimes called a fakir. Dervishes are viewed as austere, enigmatic, and above all capable of performing supernatural feats. Through their mystical visions and interpretation of sacred dogma, dervishes play an important role in the popular and folk religion of all Muslim countries.

Some sociologists regard Sufi brotherhoods, each with its own distinctive garb and chanting dances, as providing one of the very few means for voluntary associations in traditional societies which are organized mainly around kinship.

AFTER YOU HAVE PRAYED on behalf of the Prophet.

Once there was a poor fisherman who lived only on whatever fish he caught. He used to catch three fish a day—one for himself, one for his wife, and one for his son. Once he spent all day without catching anything. Finally, before sunset, he caught one small fish. He gave it to his son to carry. The son looked at the fish and saw that it was very small and looked like no other fish he had seen before. He said to himself, "What is the use of this fish?" and he threw it back in the river. When his father saw that he shouted at him, "You son of a dog! By God, you will not eat tonight."

The same thing happened the following day and the day after. This time the father said to his son, "Go away! Don't ever come back!" and the son went away.

The boy's name was Hasan. He had only a little bread and a
little water with him. At midday Hasan got his bread out and sat
down to eat. A poor dervish came to him and said, "Son, would
you give me a drink of water?" Hasan split his bread with him
and gave him all the water he wanted. After the meal, they sat
and talked. The dervish asked Hasan, "Where are you going?"

Hasan said, "I'm drifting 'from God's countries to God's
peoples.'"

The dervish said, "Then we will walk together."

They went from one town to another until they came to a
large city. The dervish said to Hasan, "I'm going to the market to
get something for us to eat. You wait for me at the coffeehouse."

Hasan said, "All right," but instead of going to the inn, he
started looking at the people and the shops. It was all strange to
him.

As he was looking around, soldiers came around shouting,
"Go to your homes! Go to your homes! The sultan's daughter is
going to the bath."

Everybody in the street ran to his home except Hasan. He had
no place to go to. He saw the sultan's daughter coming down the
street, and servants and maids were all around her. She was so
beautiful that he could not move. When she saw him there star-
ing at her, she was very angry and said to her guard, "Arrest
him!"

They took Hasan and threw him in prison.

When the dervish returned, people told him what happened.
He waited until it was night, took out two of Hasan's hairs that
he had with him, and recited the Kursi chapter [of the Koran].
Immediately Hasan came through the window.

Hasan told him the story, and the dervish could see that he
was sick with love. A few days passed, and Hasan's condition was
getting worse. He couldn't eat any food or enjoy any drink. No
medicine helped him. Finally the dervish told him, "I will let
you see the sultan's daughter."

The dervish opened a small can that had kohl in it. With the
dip stick, he put some kohl on Hasan's eyelashes and wrote
some magic words on his eyelashes and forehead. When he was
finished, he said to Hasan, "Now you can go see her."

And Hasan wondered, "How can this kohl make me see her?"

The dervish answered, "Now you are invisible. You can do whatever you want, but remember that God can still see you. Don't do anything to make him angry at you."

Now Hasan left for the sultan's palace. When he got there and saw the soldiers and guards, he could not believe what the dervish told him. He came close to one of the guards and pushed him. The guard looked around and shouted, "Who? Who?"

Now he realized that nobody could see him, so he ran directly to the harem quarters. The sultan's daughter was lying on her bed. She could feel his presence, but she could not see him.

When food came, he sat down next to her and ate as much as he could. The sultan's daughter knew that there was somebody there, but she could not see any person. He spent two or three days in her room until finally the girl told the sultan.

The sultan ordered all the doors and windows closed, and they searched every corner in the palace, but they did not find anybody. At last an old woman said, "If there is anybody hiding here, I can bring him out."

The sultan gave her permission: "Do all you think is necessary."

She said, "Bring me some green corn cobs and some buffalo dung."

She lit a big fire in the girl's room and put the cobs and dung into it. Smoke came out. 'It was [thick] enough to blind the afreet.' Hasan's eyes began to water, and the water washed away the kohl from his eyelashes. The words the dervish had written were all wiped away. Now everybody saw him.

They arrested him and threw him in prison. And they sent a crier with a drum through town saying, "Hasan will have his head chopped off tomorrow for having entered the harem of the sultan."

Now the dervish sent a message to the sultan, saying, "Hasan is my son, and I want your daughter's hand in marriage for him."

The sultan got very angry and shouted at the vizier, "You go get me that man."

The vizier left, having said, "I heard and I'll do, master!"

When the vizier got to the dervish, he said to him, "The sultan wants to see you."

The dervish answered, "I'll go with you after you have had some tea with me."

They drank two or three glasses of tea, and they left together. On their way the dervish made a palace appear, a magnificent palace!

"Whose palace is this?" the vizier asked in amazement.

"Yours!"

"Mine?"

"Of course!" said the dervish. "Let's go in."

This palace was second to none. The vizier said, "It's so cool in here, I'm going to take a nap. But be sure not to be late for the sultan." And he went to sleep.

Now our friend the sultan waited—and waited—and waited! Nobody came. He sent his soldiers to see what happened. After looking everywhere, they finally found the vizier lying underneath a mule. The vizier was wet, for the mule had urinated over his head.

The vizier told the soldiers, "By God, keep my secret!" They promised him, "Nobody will know."

When the sultan saw the vizier he asked him, "Where have you been?"

The vizier answered, "Your majesty, he would not come with anybody but you."

The sultan shouted, "Go back and get him, or you'll have your head (away from you) chopped off!"

The vizier said, "Let's both go, for he is going to have much more respect for you."

So the two of them went.

When they got to the dervish's, he received them with *"ahlan wa sahlan."*

The sultan said, "Neither *ahlan* nor *sahlan;* you come with me now."

The dervish asked, "Where?"

The sultan answered, "You will know later."

The dervish said, "I leave my affairs in God's hands," and all three of them left.

On their way back to the sultan's palace, they came across a palace that was more beautiful than any they had ever seen. It was built of alternating bricks of gold and silver. The sultan wondered, "I've never seen this palace before. Whose palace is it?"

The dervish answered, "It's yours, your majesty. Let's go in."

The sultan inspected the palace until he came to the bath. There was a marble bathtub, filled with glittering water. The sultan said, "I'm going to take a dip." Of course the vizier could not say anything.

The sultan took off his clothes and stepped into the tub. As soon as he went underwater, he found himself changed into a woman standing by a river bank. A Bedouin came by and asked her, "Where are you from?"

She answered, "I don't know." (That is the sultan who became a woman).

When he [the Bedouin] realized that she was 'a limb cut off from a tree,' he ordered her, "Come with me," and he grabbed her.

She shouted, "Take your hands off me! I am the sultan!"

"Sultan who, crazy woman! Come with me," and he dragged her behind him.

When they reached his tent, she found that he already had three wives and fifteen or twenty children. They all started ordering her to do this and that. They kicked her and punched her, and at the end of the day they fed her only crumbs.

The following day they piled up all their dirty clothes and said to her, "Take these to the river and wash them."

When she got there, she looked around and found nobody. She took her top garment off and took a dip in the river. As soon as she went underwater, she found herself changed back into the sultan. The dervish and the vizier were waiting for him at the edge of the tub.

The vizier asked him, "How was the bath?"

The sultan said, "Nothing like it! You've got to take one too. You will like it very much."

The vizier said, "Your majesty, I feel cold. I don't need a bath" (for he knew from experience what could happen).

The sultan said, "You are not cold. It is midsummer! I order you to get in the tub!"

So the poor vizier took his clothes off, and as soon as he went underwater, he found himself changed into a woman standing at the river bank.

The Bedouin came with a stick in his hand and started whipping her, shouting, "You daughter of sixty dogs! You take all day to wash some clothes!" Beat, beat, beat!

She jumped into the water, and as soon as she went under, she found herself changed back into the vizier standing in the bathtub.

When he got out he said to the sultan, "Your majesty, I think we should marry your daughter to the dervish's son."

The sultan answered, "This is the best counsel you have ever given."

The marriage took place, and they celebrated it for forty nights and forty days. And before the dervish left, he said to Hasan, "Remember that fish you returned to the water three times? That was I."

And I was there and just returned.

· 6 · *The* Maghrabi's *Apprentice*

Recorded in April 1969 from M. Abu-Zaid, a 19-year-old farmer from Sharqiyyah Province in northern Egypt. As a young boy, he was sent to the village *kuttāb* where he learned to recite the Koran, but he did not go beyond that stage. He can neither read nor write, but as he described himself, he has "been around and seen a lot."

I met Abu-Zaid while he was visiting one of his relatives in Cairo. A discussion on magicians reminded him of the story; he identified it as that "in which the magician took the boy and flew in the air. . . . The boy would say, 'I see . . . the world like a matchbox.'" Abu-Zaid used to tell tales to his playmates when he was younger; he stopped doing so when he "became a man" (about 13 or 14 years of age). Abu-Zaid could not specify his source for the present story; "I just know it," he stated. For him, the tale is a *Märchen;* it has no manifest moral or didactic functions.

In our tale a *maghrabi* magician plays a dual villainous role: that of a child's instructor and that of the young hero's adversary. Because of the use of severe punishment, resentment of teachers is widespread, especially in traditional schools, and is expressed in a number of folk narratives. The story also reflects the general attitude of young boys in Arab society toward the paternal uncle, who is feared and respected but not loved.

The symbolic association between the opening and closing of scissors and the female is common in folk literature; it appears in our tale in this symbolic connection (see also tale no. 57). Similarly, the rooster *(deek)* and the mongoose *('Airsàh,* i.e., the ichneumon, the Egyptian species of mongoose) play roles congruent with the attitudes Egyptians have toward them in actual rural life. It is believed that a jinni may assume the form of a rooster; an ancient Arab belief portrays *deek al-jinn* (the rooster of the jinn) as a powerful, usually evil spirit. The mongoose is viewed with a considerable amount of mystery, especially as a snake killer. This view dates back to ancient Egypt, where the mongoose was venerated in many areas for that very reason (see Ions, p. 118.)

The tale has its roots in ancient Egyptian religious narratives.

STATE THAT THERE IS no god but God [Allah].

Once there was a man who was married, but he had no children. The man and his wife prayed to God to grant them a son, but the woman never became pregnant. One day a *maghrabi*— one of those who 'open the book,' make amulets, and write magic, a magician, I mean—passed by their house. The woman said, "Let us call him. Maybe he can do something!"

Her husband said, "All right."

So they called him, and he went upstairs to see them. He said to the woman and her husband, "What is your story?"

They said, "We have no children, and we are getting old. We are afraid we might die without leaving somebody behind us. Without offspring."

The *maghrabi* answered, "All right, I will give you what you want, but on one condition."

They asked, "What is the condition?"

He answered, "If it is a girl you keep her, but if it is a boy I take him when he is seven years old."

They asked him, "Why?"

He answered, "I will teach him and raise him to be knowledgeable."

They implored him [to be more merciful to them]. "May God lead your path. May God satisfy you!"

He said to them, "It is no use. Either you agree to my condition, or there will be no child."

They said, "We leave our affairs to God. As you wish."

The *maghrabi* opened his book, took out a piece of paper, and wrote on it—he wrote magic of course—and gave it to the woman. He said, "Put it under your pillow for six days, and on the seventh soak it in water and drink it."

No sooner had she done this than she became pregnant. Day in and day out her stomach rose, and after nine months, she gave birth to a baby boy. He was so beautiful that one could not stare directly at him.

Go time, come time, the boy whom they called Clever Muhammad grew up and began going to school. A while later—of course his father and mother had forgotten about the *maghrabi* and everything—a man came to the boy and said to him, "Clever Muhammad, say to your mother, 'The time has come.'"

The boy forgot. This happened once, twice, three times, many times. Every time the boy would forget. Finally the man put some stones in the boy's pocket and said to him, "Say to your mother, 'The time has come.'"

When the boy went home, his mother took his clothes to wash them and found the stones. She asked, "What is this?"

The boy answered, "Oh, yes! A man met me and said to me, 'Tell your mother, the time has come.'"

When his mother heard this, she became horrified and ran to the boy's father to tell him. They locked the boy in his room and said to him, "Don't open any windows or doors!"

The *maghrabi* came. When they refused to give him the boy, he said "All right," and left. He went downstairs and sat next to the staircase, took his book out, and began reading. He looked and found the boy in front of him. He took the boy by his hand and flew up in the air.

After a while he asked the boy, "What do you see?"

The boy looked down and said, "I see my mother and my father crying over me."

They kept on going up. Again the *maghrabi* asked him, "What do you see?"

The boy answered him, "I see our house and our neighborhood."

They kept on going up. The *maghrabi* asked him, "What do you see?"

The boy answered, "I see the world like a matchbox."

They finally reached the home of the *maghrabi*. They went in and the *maghrabi* gave the boy a book to read. He also gave him forty keys, less one key, and said to him, "You can open all these rooms except the last one. Now I will go out tending my work. When I get back, I will find that you have learned the whole book."

The *maghrabi* departed, leaving the boy all alone. The boy was very frightened, but he was also very intelligent. He learned the book inside out in one day and waited for the *maghrabi* to get back. When he did not, the boy became restless. He said to himself, "I shall see what's in these rooms."

He got the keys out and began opening the rooms one after another. In the first room he found food and drinks, roasted chicken, roasted pigeon, and everything. He sat down and ate until he was full. In the second room he found all kinds of fruits—bananas, apples, pears. He had his dessert and when he was full, he said, "Thanks to God."

In the third room he found silver and gold. In the fourth he found rubies and emeralds. Each room was fuller than the previous one. He kept on opening all the rooms until he got to the last one. Then he remembered that the *maghrabi* had told him not to open it. He started thinking, "Boy, should you open it or should you not? . . . Should you open it, should you not? Should you open it, should you not?"

He finally said to himself, "There is only one life span, and there is only one God. I will open it and see."

When he opened the door, he looked and found a girl hanging down from the ceiling by her hair. She was in the middle of the room. He became frightened. He ran out, but before he closed the door, she called to him. "Clever Muhammad, come here. Don't be afraid. I'm predestined for you."

He returned and looked. The girl was very beautiful. 'No one is beautiful except Muhammad [the Prophet],' may the best of prayers and greetings be upon him.

The girl said to him, "Let me down."

He said to her, "How? There is no ladder, there is no knife. How am I going to get you down?"

She said to him, "On that table over there in the corner you will find a pair of open scissors. Shut them and that will bring me down."

As soon as he shut the scissors, he found the girl on the floor. She said to him, "Bring me some water."

He went and got her some water. After she drank, he asked her, "What's your story?"

She answered him, "My story is exactly like yours," and then she began to tell him about what happened to her with the *maghrabi*.

She said to him, "I'm the daughter of the king of such-and-such a kingdom. My father and my mother had me when they were very old. The *maghrabi* used to come and tell fortunes to my father. He saw me and wanted to take me away. When my father refused, he brought me here by magic. He wants to use me in his magic, but I refuse. He said to me, 'I will hang you by your hair until you say yes.'"

After this, the girl asked him, Clever Muhammad, that is, "Have you learned the book which he gave to you?"

He answered her, "Yes."

She said to him, "If he asks you, 'Have you learned the book?' say 'No!' Because after you have learned it, he is going to kill you."

Day after day, the boy and the girl waited for the *maghrabi*, until a whole year passed. One day the girl said to him, "I feel that the *maghrabi* is coming today. Put me back where you found me."

He took her to the room and opened the scissors again, and once again she was hanging down by her hair as before. He locked the door and went out. A short while later, the *maghrabi* came and asked him, "Did you learn the book? Can you recite what's in the book?"

The boy answered, "Learn what? What book?"

The *maghrabi* became angry and said, "The book I gave to you!"

The boy answered, "Oh yes, that book. Yes!"

With every question the *maghrabi* asked him, the boy answered, *"La kani wala mani wala dukkan izzalabani"* [no ifs, no buts, and no Zalabani's shop: a nonsensical statement].

Every time the *maghrabi* asked him, "What did you learn?" he answered, I learned *la kani wala mani wala dukkan izzalabani."* The *maghrabi maddu* [paddled him, gave him a beating on the bottom of his feet].

The *maghrabi* thought, "Maybe he did not have enough time," so he left him and went away for another year. But when he got back, the same thing happened. The boy told him, *"La kani wala mani wala dukkan izzalabani."*

He paddled him again. A year later,

"What did you learn, boy?"

"La kani wala mani wala dukkan izzalabani."

The *maghrabi* was astonished, for he knew—through his [magic] books—that the boy was very clever and that he was going to become something very important. Finally he said to himself, "Maybe I made a mistake. The boy is an idiot." He said to the boy, "Get lost! Go home to your mother!"

When the boy went home to his mother, her eyes had been torn off from crying over him. He knocked at the door.

"Who? Who is it?"

"It is I, Muhammad."

"Muhammad who, son? Muhammad must be dead now."

"Open, mother, I'm Clever Muhammad."

His mother thought that it was the children of the neighborhood playing tricks on her. She took a can full of water to splatter it on them. When she opened the door, she found that the smell was like that of her son.

The two of them embraced, and immediately she regained her sight. She asked him, "Where were you, my son?"

He told her the whole story, 'from hello to good-bye.' After he was rested he said to his mother, "Listen, mother. I'm going to turn myself into a water buffalo."

His mother said, "Water buffalo, what? Is this what you learned?"

He said, "Just wait. I'll turn myself into a water buffalo, and you take me to the market and sell me to the merchants there, but don't you ever sell my rope."

In the morning the mother woke up to find a water buffalo [so large that it] filled her cattle pen. The woman exclaimed and said, "Praise be upon the Prophet!"

She took the water buffalo—it chanced to be a Monday.

She took it to the Monday animal market. One merchant said, "I'll pay seventy-five pounds."

Another one said, "I'll pay eighty."

A third said, "Ninety."

Finally it was sold for a hundred pounds. The merchant paid the money and took the water buffalo. Before leaving, she said, "Give me the rope."

The merchant said no.

The woman said, "Then 'may God open another door' [i.e., bring another deal]. I'm not selling it."

People around her started saying, "What's the rope to you, lady?"

She said, "It was my late husband who braided it."

People said to the merchant, "Brother, you can buy another rope for three piasters."

The merchant gave her the rope and took the water buffalo. After a while he looked behind him. He found that there was nothing but his rope. He almost went crazy. He couldn't find the water buffalo anywhere and finally placed his loss in God's hands.

The following day the boy said to his mother, "Today I am going to turn myself into an ox, and you sell me like the last time."

The same thing happened, and the mother of the boy became rich. Signs of comfort started showing. They bought more land, more farm animals, more ducks, geese and chickens, and everything. The boy's *'Aam* [paternal uncle] noticed all this. He became jealous. He came to her [the mother] and said, "What's the matter? Where did you get that money? Did you find a treasure or something? I will have to report you to the police."

She said, "No, by God! We found nothing."

He said, "Then it is my brother's money. I am the one who
should take care of it!"

The boy's mother told him the story. The boy's paternal uncle
grabbed him and said, "Next market day, I will take you."

The boy said [in despair] "All right. I'm going to turn myself
into a very swift Arabian stallion. I'm going to have on a beautiful saddle with silver and gold. You may sell the stallion, but you
may not sell the reins. They're going to be of silver."

His uncle said, "Good."

The following day the boy turned himself into a stallion, nothing like it anywhere! His uncle mounted it and went to the
market. The stallion neighed and displayed itself. It was flying on
three hooves. It went like this . . . and came like that. [Narrator
indicates the swift motion with his hands.] All of a sudden the
market was over, for everybody went to look at the stallion.

Merchants started bidding, "Two hundred!"—"Two hundred
and fifty!"—"Three hundred!"—"Three hundred and fifty!"—

At this time the *maghrabi* came, looked the stallion over, and
recognized it. The *maghrabi* said "Five hundred pounds!"

All the other merchants withdrew. Then the boy's uncle said,
"I'm selling only the stallion, not the reins.

The *maghrabi* said, "Another five hundred for the reins."

The boy's uncle immediately agreed and said, "Give me the
money. May God bless your deal."

The moment the boy heard this, he turned himself into a
pigeon and flew into the air. The *maghrabi* made himself a falcon
and chased the pigeon. They flew after each other until the
falcon almost overtook the pigeon. The pigeon made itself into
a pomegranate; it fell into the king's garden.

It chanced that the king was sitting in his garden, and the
pomegranate fell into his lap. The falcon turned itself into a
hudhud [hoopoe bird] and dived at the pomegranate, striking it
with its beak. The pomegranate split in two, its seeds scattering
all over the place. The hoopoe made itself a rooster and began to
pick up the pomegranate seeds. He gulped down all the seeds
except one underneath the king's chair. The rooster did not see
it; this seed contained the boy's soul.

Suddenly this seed became a *'Airsah* [mongoose]. It darted at the rooster and caught it by its neck. It kept on biting and biting until the rooster was dead. After this, the mongoose turned itself into a boy again. All this happened in front of whom? The king! The king was very astonished. He said to the boy, "You're not leaving here until you tell me the story."

The boy told him the whole story about how the *maghrabi* kidnaped him and took him to his palace and how the girl was hung by her hair, and he told him about everything.

The king asked him, "Does this girl look like such-and-such?"

The boy said, "Yes."

The king said, "She is my daughter, and this *maghrabi* kidnaped her."

They went and got the girl from the house of the *maghrabi*. The boy and the girl got married.

And they lived in happiness and prosperity [one of the audience, jokingly: "And what else?"] and begat boys and girls." [Laughter, for this ending is commonly used by female narrators.]

· 7 ·   *The Royal Candlestick*

Taped on the eve of Tuesday, October 28, 1969, during the celebration of the *moulid* of the "Five Grandfathers" of the Nubian nation. The narrator was 'A. 'Aawadalla, a 65-year-old Kenzi Nubian from Dahmeet village. Presently 'Aawadalla is a farmer, but he has also worked as a licensed "health barber," a boatman, and a merchant. During his early life he immigrated to Cairo and then to Alexandria. He worked as a truck driver until he was laid off because of his poor eyesight.

I did not meet 'Aawadalla until almost midnight of that Tuesday. The Nubian folklorist 'Aumar Kidr, a native of this area, drew my attention to him. At first 'Aawadalla refused to narrate for me and stated that he had already given what he knew to Mr. Khidr and that he was also tired. He finally agreed to tell one tale, "to compensate you for your trouble," he said. Afterward he volunteered another story, stating, "So that you don't feel turned down."

The recording took place under a shedlike tent set up as a coffeehouse for the annual occasion. A large number of customers listened to the stories. 'Aawadalla was an active narrator and explained, "I have narrated all my life. Wherever I went, I narrated . . . the last time was just today." He heard this tale for the first time "more than fifty years ago," he assured me. He narrated in Arabic with great efficiency, without hesitation, pauses, or gaps in his story, and proved to be an able raconteur, probably the best I have encountered.

One curious motif found in this tale is that of the creation of a living person. According to formal Islam, only Jesus Christ may bring a dead person back to life and create lesser living creatures; God provided Christ with such miracles so that he may prove his prophecy. In folk religious beliefs these and similar miraculous accomplishments are argued to be within the realm of the possible for a saint; however, their occurrence in oral traditions is extremely rare. Originally formal Islam considered the production of a lifelike creature by carving, painting, or sculpture a form of idolatry, because it attempts to match God's acts of creation. It was not until recently that a formal Islamic viewpoint permitted painting and other related artistic activities, provided that the finished product does not produce a shadow.

ONCE THERE WAS a merchant who had a single son. Every day he gave him fifty pounds or twenty-five pounds and said to him, "Spend, son! When you are finished, come back to me for more."

One day the boy said to himself, "Is my father making this money or what? Every day he gives me twenty-five or fifty pounds to spend."

He went to his father and said, "Father, I want a hundred pounds to go away and start a trade."

His father said, "Son, there's nothing that you are missing. You are getting everything. Why do you want to go away?"

The son answered, "Impossible; I must go and start a trade."

The father gave him a hundred pounds, and the boy's mother also gave him her necklace and said, "Any time you need more money, take it out of this necklace."

Now the boy took the hundred pounds and spent it immediately in one day. He spent it immediately, not on sinful
things but on the poor. He had nothing left with him except the
necklace. He said to himself, "Now that I have wasted all the
hundred pounds without starting a trade or anything, what am I
going to go back and tell my father? The best thing is to run
away."

He readied himself and walked along the bank of the river.
He walked and walked and walked. Finally he met a fisherman.
He said to the fisherman, "Fisherman, cast your net once for me
to see my luck."

The fisherman cast his net and pulled. There was nothing in it
except a small brass box [narrator points to a match box].

"Give it to me."

"By God, I will not give it to you except for a hundred
pounds!"

"A hundred pounds for this box!"

"Yes, a hundred pounds."

"I have nothing except a necklace. This necklace."

The fisherman said to him, "All right, give it to me."

He handed the hundred-pound necklace over to him, took the
box, and now had nothing at all with him. He took the box and
walked away.

He walked and walked and walked until he came to a deserted
place. The boy was very hungry. He said to himself, "Already
you have wasted your two hundred pounds, and now you haven't
even got the price of a meal. What are you going to do?"

He thought, "Why don't I open this box and see what's in it?"

He opened the box, and inside he found an exact replica of a
human being, whose size was the exact size of the box. The
moment he opened the box, the thing said to him, "I am at your
command."

"'At your command'! What's this?"

It answered him, "I came out to you because of your luck. Ask
for anything and you'll get it."

The boy said to it, "I'm hungry."

It answered, "Close your eyes and then open them."

He closed his eyes, and when he opened them he found a
table with every good thing on it. He sat down and ate. When he

was finished, he folded his table, put away the things, took his box, and went on.

He walked and walked and walked until he came to a different country. On the border of this country he came to a town. At the edge of this town there was a palace. From the foundation up this palace was built of human skulls.

"What's this?"

Every time he asked somebody, "Why is this palace this way?" no one would answer him.

Finally he went to a tobacco seller. The tobacco seller said to him, "I have Cotarelli, Belmonts [brands] and this and that."

The boy asked him, "Tell me, why is this palace the way it is?"

The tobacco seller answered him, "Ask this old woman."

He asked the old woman who was sitting nearby. (Of course 'old women are catastrophes' [i.e., extremely sly]). He said to her, "Maternal aunt, tell me, why is this palace the way it is?"

She answered him, "By God, son, our king has a daughter who does not speak. The king has offered his daughter to the young men of the country. He gave them the condition that he who stays with her for three days and makes her talk will marry her at the end of these three days. But he who fails will have his head cut off."

"All these people died because of that?"

"Yes," she answered him.

He went to a corner, took his box out, opened it, and said to our friend inside it, "This is your day. They say that the king's daughter does not speak. Will you be able to make her speak?"

He said to him, "Yes! When you get inside, put me underneath the candlestick" (for in the old days they did not have electricity; they had only candles).

Now where did the boy go? He went to the king. The boy said to the king, "'I'm asking closeness to you.'"

The king said, "Son, you are too young. It is a shame that you should die; traces of good living still show on you. Why don't you go away? Look at all these heads."

The boy answered him, "I am just like those to whom they belonged."

"Is that so?"

"Yes, that is so."

"All right, get the witnesses. Get the judge. Write."

He wrote, signed, and said, "Put your seal on it."

The king put his seal on it and said, "Take him to her."

They took him to the room of our lady. Before she entered, he put his box underneath the candlestick.

He said to her, "My lady, daughter of kings."

She did not utter a word.

"Peace be upon you. How do you do? Queen. You who are this. You who are that."

She was just like a piece of stone sitting on a chair.

He said to her, "All right, if a human being cannot keep me company, then maybe the candlestick will."

He turned to the candlestick and said, "Peace be upon you, royal candlestick."

The candlestick replied—that other one from beneath the candlestick replied, "And upon you be God's peace and his mercy, son of kings."

The boy said to him, "Why don't you tell us a story instead of this sad time we are having?"

He answered him, "All right, I'm going to tell you a story."

"What's the story, candlestick?"

"Once there were three brothers. They had one *bint 'Aam* [paternal uncle's daughter]. This one said, 'I'll marry her!' And that one said, 'No! I'll marry her! The third one said, 'No! I'll marry her.'

"People in their country decided, 'All three of you will take a trip. He who brings back the most precious things will marry her.'

"So the three got their things and left. Finally, the road branched out into three different roads: the road of safety, the road of sorrow, and the road of no return. Each one of the three went down one of these roads.

"The one who went down the road of no return finally came to the spring of the water of life. He took some.

"The one who went down the road of safety found a carpet which when struck would fly.

"The third one found a mirror. This mirror could show him anything in the whole universe.

"Finally, all of them met on the same road. The one with the mirror said to them, 'Brothers, our cousin is dying.'

The one with the carpet said, 'Let's go!'

Immediately they were there. The girl was almost dead. They were dripping water into her mouth drop... by... drop. The one with the water of life gave her some, and immediately she got up, as if she had never been sick."

Now all of this was told by the candlestick to the boy. The candlestick asked the boy, "Who should marry the girl? If it weren't for the mirror, they wouldn't have seen her. If it weren't for the carpet, they wouldn't have reached her in time. If it weren't for the water of life, she wouldn't have been revived. Now who should marry her?"

The boy answered, "Of course the one with the water of life."

Now the one who was completely dumb spoke eloquently. She said, "Glory be to God, how strange natured we are! If it weren't for the one with the mirror, they wouldn't have seen her dying, they wouldn't have reached her, and they wouldn't have revived her. She should go to the one with the mirror."

The moment the girl spoke, the boy pulled the [loose sofa] cover over his head and said, "Ekkk! You have a bad mouth odor!"

The judges who were watching them were surprised. The king's daughter, who hadn't spoken a word all her life, was now talking like a rattler! No, that couldn't be! They had better wait until tomorrow.

The judges left, and the boy pretended to be asleep. Now the girl started talking to the candlestick. Wanting what? Wanting the candlestick to converse with her as it had with the boy.

"Peace be upon you, royal candlestick! ... Peace be upon you, royal candlestick!"

Nothing. The girl was furious, and hit, hit, hit, she broke the candlestick.

In the morning our friend took his box out from beneath the broken candlestick. He said to it, "Now where am I going to put you?"

The box answered, "Put me underneath the chair."

He put it underneath the chair.

At night the girl entered the room again. The boy started talking to her. The more the boy talked, the more the girl remained silent. The boy finally said, "All right, since the human cannot keep us company, maybe the chair will. Peace be upon you, royal chair."

"And upon you be peace, king's son."

"Tell us a story to keep us company, royal chair."

The chair said, "All right, I will. Once three persons were traveling together—a carpenter, a tailor, and a sheik, an *'ustaz* (a religious savant, I mean). Finally they came to a lonely area. By night they divided themselves into three shifts. Two would sleep, and the third would stay on guard.

"The first third of the night, who was awake? The carpenter. While the sheik and tailor were asleep, the carpenter found a piece of wood. He made a doll out of it.

"At midnight he went to sleep, and the tailor took over. The tailor found the doll; it was almost human, but it was naked. He took out his sewing machine, and tick, tick, tick, tick, tick—he made her a dress.

"At the end of the night our friend the worshiper saw the girl before his eyes, almost perfect and dressed, but with no soul. He prayed to God to give a soul to this girl. God accepted his prayer and, the doll became a human being.

"Each one of the three said, 'She is mine!'

"Now, son of kings, who should marry the girl?" (That's what the chair was asking the boy.)

The boy answered, "The *'ustaz,* naturally."

The girl said, "Praise be to God, how strange you are. Had it not been for the carpenter who made the doll in the first place, there would have been no girl. The carpenter should marry her!"

The boy turned his face away and said, "Ekkkk! Your mouth has a bad odor." [Narrator turns his face away and covers his nose to indicate disgust.]

Now the judges who were standing by went to the king.

"King, now for two nights your daughter has spoken."

"My daughter?"

"Yes."

"Well, let's see what's going to happen on the third night."

Now after the girl had spoken, the boy pretended to be asleep. The girl spoke to the chair. "Royal chair."

The chair did not answer.

"Honored chair."

The chair did not answer.

"Our property. . . ."

The girl became furious and broke the chair into pieces.

In the morning the boy took his box out and asked it, "Now where am I going to hide you?"

The box said, "Hide me underneath your turban. She can't do a thing to it."

That night when the girl came, he spoke to her, but still she did not answer. "Our dear daughter. Our dear friend. You have spoken for two nights; speak now."

She didn't utter a word. The boy said, "All right, the first night they broke the candlestick. The second night they broke the chair. These were their property. Now my very own turban, peace be upon you."

The turban replied, "And upon you be God's peace and mercy, master. What do you want?"

The boy said, "Tonight why don't you put on a show? We want stage shows and dances."

From underneath the turban came seven girls. This one was playing the castanets, this one the drum, that one dancing. All of them were wonderful, *gi-n-a-a-a-n* [cr-a-a-azy]!

The boy watched all night. Finally the girl, the king's daughter, threw herself at the boy. The boy pushed her away and said, "Go away. Don't you see I have got all those who are better than you are?"

[A listener: "She has become jealous!"]

She became jealous; these girls were very beautiful.

The judges went to the king and said, "King. Now for two days your daughter has been speaking. And now she is just dying over the boy. She is throwing herself on him."

The king wondered, "My own daughter? Spoke two nights! And now is throwing herself on the boy! I have to see this with my own eyes."

"Come along."

The king went to find his daughter naked. [He screamed in amazement.] "What are you doing, daughter! What's this?"

She answered him, "The whole world is like this. I hadn't seen the world, nor have I entered it yet."

The king ordered celebrations to be made. They gave wedding parties and beautiful celebrations. The king married his daughter to this boy. The boy took over the kingdom, and they lived in stability and prosperity.

And I was there and just returned.

· 8 · *Louliyya, Daughter of Morgan**

Narrated in March 1969 by K. Seliman, 65. She first heard it from her mother, a native Cairene, and told it repeatedly to her brother until he grew up (see informant note to tale no. 12). She had not told it for several years. Commenting on the contents of the tale, K. said, "In olden days parents, especially the father, used not to be as [lenient as] they are today. A girl could not even look out of a window. If a father saw his daughter even looking at a man, he would make her day a black one. A girl wouldn't go out of her parents' home except to her husband's."

K., however—like many urban women—has had a considerable amount of personal freedom; she was described by her relatives, especially sisters-in-law, as a forceful woman "who did what she wanted." Her autonomy was achieved after the death of her father and the development of complications in her married life. K. was not able to recall many of the *hawadeet (Märchen)* she used to know. She had a wealth of information, however, on the cult of possession *(zar)* which she used to practice.

A young woman's resentment of her father's confining, overprotective measures toward her and of her role as homemaker in her parent's house is symbolically expressed in this fantasy story. A paternal figure as an ogre, or ogress, is a common theme in folk literature. A number of important social practices, including the *nàdr* and wet-nursing, are mentioned. A *nàdr* is a pledge a person makes to God that if a wish is granted, the person will do certain things (usually give away money or food or perform certain religious rituals for a long time). The now abandoned practice of wet-nursing presented social problems; children breast fed by the same woman were considered actual brothers and sisters and therefore ineligible to marry one another.

The ogress, a maternal figure, with breasts of unusually large size may be a survival from older Middle Eastern religious beliefs. The ancient Arabian goddess al-'Auzza was described in older sources as "having her breasts thrown over her shoulders"; see Ibn al-Kalbi (d. A.D. 826), p. 25; see also al-Ālūci, 2:204.

ONCE THERE WAS a king and his wife who did not have any children. One day the queen prayed to God, "O God, my God, who hears my prayers, be kind to me and grant me a child. I will name him Yousif."

She made a *nadr* [pledge]: "If I have a child, I will make three wells and fill them, one with honey, one with butter, and one with rosewater."

Time passed. One day went and one day came, and she became pregnant. She had a boy whom she called Yousif. The king and his wife almost flew with joy.

One year after another, Yousif grew up, and he was going to school. With time, while the king was asleep he heard a *hatif* [supernatural voice] saying, "King, fulfill your pledge. Fulfill the pledge that you owe."

This happened three times. Every time the king forgot. Yousif became ill. They got him all the kingdom's doctors and the sheiks. No one could cure him. Finally they said, "Maybe there is an unfulfilled pledge. Think! Have you made a pledge, king?"

The king and the queen remembered their promise. Immediately the king ordered that three large wells be dug and lined with china tile and filled to the top—one with honey, the second with butter, and the third with rosewater. And he dispatched a crier to announce in town, "O God's people, people of this town, he who wants honey, butter, and rosewater should come tomorrow to the king's palace."

That was it. With [the appearance of] the morning star, everyone in town was rushing to the king's palace. This one carrying a saucepan, that one carrying a wash tub, and this one and that one! They clustered around on the three wells, and [almost] immediately they were empty. After a short while there was nothing at all.

A while later, an old woman came leaning on a cane. She had three cans on a tray which she carried on top of her head. When she found that the wells were empty, she took out a little piece of sponge and began sponging the drops off the walls of the wells. After a very long time, she had hardly filled her three small cans, and she turned back to go home. Now the king's son, Yousif, was playing with his ball. He threw his ball like this—and it hit the old woman. She fell on the ground, and everything was spilled. Yousif ran to her and said, "Never mind, old mother. I am wrong."

The woman answered, "With what can I curse you? With what can I curse you, son? You are too young. I am going to curse you with Louliyya, daughter of Morgan," and she left.

He went to his father and mother and asked them, "Who is Louliyya, daughter of Morgan?"

They answered him, "Son, you are too young. You should have nothing to do with these things."

Everytime he asked someone, the answer was, "You have nothing to do with these things."

Finally an old servant said to him, "She is a beautiful girl that you have to find yourself."

That was it. He went to his mother and father and said, "Prepare rations for me. I'm going out into the world. I have to find Louliyya, daughter of Morgan."

When they heard this, their 'hearts sank to their toes.' They kept on crying and imploring him, "Don't do this, son. Stay away from her. No one has gone to find her and come back. We have no one else but you."

He answered them, "It is no use."

He finally took a horse, food and water, and some money and left. He kept on moving 'from God's countries to God's peoples.' One town carried him, and another town put him down, until the inhabited part [of the world] ended. He kept on traveling in the desert. After a while, he saw dust coming from a distance. It came closer and closer. He looked to find a ghoul [ogre] coming toward him. The moment the ogre was by his side, he greeted him, "Peace be upon you, father ogre."

The ogre answered, "Had your greeting not preceded your speech, I would have devoured your flesh before gnawing on your bones. What do you want?"

He answered, "I'm looking for Louliyya, daughter of Morgan."

The ogre said, "Son, keep on going. You will meet my brother. He is one day older than I am and a year more knowledgeable."

Yousif kept on going until he saw another cloud of dust, larger than the one before it. It came closer and closer, and finally when the ogre was next to him, he said, "Peace be upon you, father ogre."

The ogre replied, "Had your greeting not preceded your speech, I would have devoured your flesh before gnawing on your bones. What do you want?"

He replied, "I want to know how to reach Louliyya, daughter of Morgan."

The ogre said to him, "Keep on going. Ahead you will meet my brother. He is one day older than myself and a year more knowledgeable."

He kept on going until he met the third brother. He was much larger and much more fearsome [than the first two]. Yousif said to him, "Peace be upon you, father ogre."

The ogre replied, "Had your greeting not preceded your speech, I would have devoured your flesh before gnawing on your bones. What do you want?"

He replied, "I want to know how to reach Louliyya, daughter of Morgan."

The ogre said to him, "Keep on going. Ahead you will meet my brother. He is one day older than myself and a year more knowledgeable."

He kept on going until he met the third brother. He was much larger and much more fearsome [than the first two]. Yousif said to him, "Peace be upon you, father ogre."

The ogre replied, "Had your greeting not preceded your speech, I would have devoured your flesh before gnawing on your bones. What do you want?"

He asked him about Louliyya and said, "I want to reach Louliyya, daughter of Morgan."

The ogre said, "Ahead of you you'll find my sister, and she is the only one who can tell you how to reach her. When you get there, if you find her with her red chicks around her and her hair combed and groomed, don't you dare say a word or make her feel your presence; but if you find her with her hair messed up and her green chicks around her and her breasts thrown over her shoulder [narrator giggles and explains, "This is the way it is said!"], you can talk to her, for she is going to be in a good mood."

Yousif left and kept on going and going. When he reached the ogress's house, he hid and peeped. He saw that her hair was well groomed and her red chicks were hopping up and down around her. He did not say a word and remained in his place. After a while, about sunset, she messed up her hair and started catching her red chicks and eating them. She let out her green chicks from the pen and threw her breasts behind her back [narrator laughs] and started singing. Yousif tiptoed behind her. The chicks saw him and shouted, "Somebody's coming!" but she was singing so loudly that she did not hear them. Of course she was in a good mood.

When Yousif reached her, he suckled each of her breasts once. She shouted [in rhyme], "Ahhh, now you are my 'milk-son.' You suckled my right breast, you became like my son Isma'Aeen; you suckled my left breast, you became like my son 'Aabdel-'Aal! What do you want?"

He said, "Louliyya, daughter of Morgan."

She said to him, "Why, son? You are too young to die." 'Even if his head was against a thousand swords,' he insisted and said, "Never! I have to find Louliyya, daughter of Morgan."

She said, "Well, take this ball and this racket. Hit the ball with the racket, and wherever the ball goes, you follow it. They will take you to the place you want to go."

That was it. Yousif got back on his horse and struck the ball with the racket. The ball flew into the air, landed on the ground, and kept on rolling. Mounted on his horse, Yousif followed it. He kept on hitting the ball and running after it, hitting the ball and running after it, hitting the ball and running after it. Hit and run, hit and run, hit and run, until finally he found himself in

front of a huge palace in the middle of the desert. This palace
was high, high, high; it had neither windows nor gates.

He went around it, and finally he saw one small window at the
top of the palace. As he stood wondering about this palace and
thinking who it might be who owned it, he saw a huge dust cloud
coming from far, far away. He heard a dog barking and a big
commotion. He hid himself behind a big boulder and peeped
out (like this). He saw an ogre much larger than all the ogres he
had met. The ogre came to the palace and shouted, "O Louliyya,
daughter of Morgan, let down your long hair and take your
father the ogre away from the heat of the hills."

Yousif saw the little window open, and out of it appeared a
young woman whose beauty was indescribable. Glory be to the
creator for his creation! She swung her hair out of the window,
and it came down until it reached the ground. 'Our father' the
ogre climbed up on her hair. Pull, pull, pull, he was up there. He
got in, and the window was closed.

When he got inside, he asked her, "What have you cooked for
us today?"

She said, "Such-and-such," and served him what she had
cooked.

He ate, and after that he rested his head and went to sleep.

Now to whom do we return? To Yousif outside! He kept
himself hidden until the morning of the following day. The window opened, and the hair was let down from it, and the ogre
climbed down on Louliyya's hair.

Yousif waited until the dust disappeared. He came out of his
hiding place and shouted, "O Louliyya, daughter of Morgan, let
your long hair down and take Yousif, for whom you have been
predestined, away from the heat of the hills."

The window was opened, and he looked up and saw her looking
down. When she saw him, her heart softened for him; she fell in
love with him. She said to him, "What brought you here? Get
away with your skin [still on your body]! For if my father sees
you, he will 'kill you and drink from your blood.'"

He said to her, "Before I go, lift me up, and I will tell you my
story."

She swung her hair out, and he climbed up. He told her his

story 'from hello to good-bye' and said to her, "You are pre-destined for me, and we must get back to the house of my father and mother. We must escape from here."

She said to him, "Escape to where? The distance we could cover in a day my father the ogre will cover in one step."

As they were talking, they heard a big commotion and heard her father shouting, "O Louliyya, daughter of Morgan, let your long hair down and take your father away from the heat of the hills."

She was frightened and said [narrator strikes her chest with her hand], "What a catastrophe! My father the ogre is back. Where shall I hide you! Where shall I hide you!" She trans-formed him into a pin and pinned it on her chest. When her father came up, he asked her, "What took you so long?"

She said, "Nothing; I was just in the bath."

The ogre started sniffing around, saying, "I smell the trace of a human not of our race."

She said to him, "There is nothing."

He looked all over the place and did not find anything. He asked for his food, and after he had eaten, he went to sleep.

The following day the ogre left as usual. As soon as he was gone, she pulled the pin out of her collar; it became Yousif. She said to him, "We must go now!"

She got some henna and tinted everything in the house [with rose coloring]. She overlooked only one thing, the tambourine. It hid from her underneath the sofa. She took her comb, her sewing needle, and her mirror, and she went out with Yousif.

When 'our father' the ogre returned, he started calling "O Louliyya!"

Nobody answered.

"O Louliyya!"

Nobody answered.

Finally, when he became impatient, he started calling on ev-erything in the house. "O chair!"

The chair said, "She is sitting on me!"

"O bed!"

The bed answered, "She is sleeping in me!"

"O bathtub!"

The bathtub answered, "She is bathing in me!"

Finally the tambourine started dancing and singing. "Tumm ti
dum, tshshsht, tshshsht, Tumm ti dum, tuu, tuu, Yousif took her
and flew! Tuu, tuu, Yousif took her and flew."

That was it. 'Our father' the ogre heard this, and he went
mad. He got his dogs to sniff around, and they flew after them.

Now we return to whom? To Yousif and Louliyya. They kept
on going until they finally saw the cloud of dust coming from
afar. It kept on getting bigger and bigger until it blocked the sun;
it was just like nighttime. Louliyya took out her needle and
threw it back over her shoulder. Immediately it became a field of
thorns. The ogre and his dog went right through it; the thorns
pierced their feet.

The ogre kept saying to his dog [narrator pants], "Pluck out,
my dog, and I'll pluck out with you. Pluck out, my dog, and I'll
pluck out with you."

Meanwhile Yousif and Louliyya were far away. After a little
while 'our father' the ogre drew very near to them again.
Louliyya threw her comb back over her shoulder. Immediately
the comb became a thick hedge of bamboo. They got lost in it.

The ogre kept saying to his dog [panting], "Chop down, my
dog, and I'll chop down with you. Chop down, my dog, and I'll
chop down with you."

Yousif and Louliyya got a little bit farther away from them.
Again the ogre drew very close to them. Louliyya threw her
mirror back over her shoulder. Immediately it became a lake.

When the ogre got to it, he and his dog started drinking it.
The ogre would say, "Drink, my dog, and I will drink with you.
Drink, my dog, and I will drink with you."

They kept on drinking and drinking and drinking until they
exploded. Before the ogre died, he threw some pins at them. As
soon as the pins struck them, Louliyya became a she-dog, and
Yousif became a lark. He flew away.

Louliyya kept on going until she reached Yousif's parents. She
lay down in front of the doorstep and kept on barking. No one
paid any attention to her. Yousif kept on coming back and hovering over the house and singing, "How are you, how are you,
Louliyya, in the house of my father and mother?"

Louliyya would answer back, "Over me is dust, underneath
me is dust, just like a dog's place of rest, Yousif!"

One day Yousif's mother heard her saying, "Yousif."

She and Yousif's father had become blind from crying over their son. She asked the dog, "What did you say?" It repeated what it had said. Yousif's mother took her inside and made a bed of straw for her in the stable."

The following day Yousif hovered over the house singing, "How are you, how are you, Louliyya, in the house of my father and mother?"

She answered back, "Over me is straw, and underneath me is straw, just like a mare's place of rest, Yousif."

Yousif's mother heard this, and she said to herself, "Something must be the matter with this dog." She took her upstairs and put her in a room with a bed with silk sheets and covers.

The following day, when Yousif hovered over the house singing, "How are you, how are you, Louliyya, in the house of my father and mother?" she replied, "Over me is silk, and silk is underneath me, just like a prince's place of rest, Yousif."

Yousif's mother was listening this time. She heard the whole thing. She entered the room and called the dog to her. It went to her. She kept on feeling its body and caressing it with her hand (like this). As she was passing her hand over its head, she found three pins pierced deep in it. She pulled them out, and immediately, with the omnipotence of the Omnipotent, she [the dog] became a beautiful young lady again. She told Yousif's mother and father about all that happened, how her father imprisoned her, how Yousif came to her—everything that happened. She said to them, "Get me some sugar, and I will get Yousif back."

"How?" they asked her.

She answered, "Just wait and see."

The following morning Yousif came back hovering over the house and said, "How are you, Louliyya, in the house of my father and mother?"

She said, "I have some sugar for you," and she put her hand with granulated sugar in it out the window.

The lark perched on the palm of her hand to have some sugar. Ooops! She caught it! She found three pins stuck in its head. As soon as she plucked them out, the lark—with God's omnipotence—became Yousif again. He went and embraced his father and mother; their sight was restored by God's will. Yousif and Louliyya got married! The celebration lasted for forty days and forty nights. 'They lived in stability and prosperity and begat boys and girls.'

Now *toota, toota,* the tale is over. Was it sweet or dragging? If sweet, you owe a song, if dragging, you owe a story.

· 9 · *The Promises of the Three Sisters*

Recorded in November 1969 from Sayyida, a 55-year-old woman from the village of Aghoor al-Kubra, in the Nile Delta. She heard it from her mother and other women in her family when she was a little girl. She used to tell this tale to her own younger brother before she got married. Currently she narrates rarely to her grandchildren; this story is one of their favorites. The narrator stated, "The tale shows how a brother must be kind to his sister and look after her, no matter what; and the sister more so!"

Two major sentiments underlie the plot of this tale: affection between brother and sister and conflict among sisters over the same man; these sentiments are highly pervasive and stable in Middle Eastern cultures. The story also expresses hostility between female children and their maternal aunts which is a product of the conflict among sisters (i.e., the children's mothers). The belief that God automatically provides for every newborn child, which appears in our narrative, is one of the main factors behind the problem of overpopulation in the Middle East.

ONCE THERE WAS a king. He wanted to see if his subjects loved him or not. He said to his vizier, "Vizier, send criers throughout my country to tell people not to have any lights on tonight."

The vizier carried out the king's order.

That night the king said to the vizier, "Let's go out and see who loves me and who does not."

They disguised themselves as merchants, wearing merchants' clothes, and went through town. It was very dark in town, for nobody had any lights on.

The vizier said to the king, "Now you can be sure that everybody loves you." and they started back to the palace.

At the edge of town, they saw a very faint light coming from a small distant hut. The king was very upset and said to his vizier, "Let's go and see what's the matter with those who have disobeyed my order."

When they arrived at the hut, they found three girls weaving inside. The eldest girl was pretty, the middle girl was prettier, but the youngest girl was the prettiest. The king and the vizier listened to them talk as they wove.

The first one said, "If the king were to marry me, I would bake him a cake that would be enough for him and his army."

The second girl said, "If the king were to marry me, I would weave him a carpet that would seat him and his army."

The third one said, "If the king were to marry me, I would bear him Sitt el-Husn [mistress of beauty] and Clever Muhammad. Their hair would be of gold and silver; for every golden hair there would be a silver hair."

The king listened to what they said and went home. In the morning he sent for them. When they came he asked them, "Why did you disobey my orders? Didn't you know that I ordered that no lights would be lit last night?"

The girls replied, "We knew, king."

"Then why did you disobey my orders?" asked the king.

They answered, "We are orphans, and we have to weave all night so that we can sell what we weave in the morning for three piasters. If we didn't weave, we would die of hunger."

The king said, "I forgive you," and he gave each one of them something (a present) and said to the eldest, "Will you marry me?"

"Yes!" Of course the girl agreed.

The day following the wedding night, the king said to her, "Now bake me the cake that will be enough for me and my army."

The girl laughed and said, "Did you believe this? 'Night talk is covered with butter; it melts when the sun rises.'"

The king divorced her and married the middle sister.

Again on the day following the wedding night the king said to her, "Now weave me the rug that will seat me and my army."

The girl laughed and said, "Did you believe this? 'Night talk is covered with butter; it melts when the sun rises.'"

The king divorced her and married the youngest sister.

God was kind to her, and on the day following the wedding night, she was pregnant. After nine months she gave birth to twins, a baby girl and a baby boy. Her sisters, who were living in the palace as servants, had fires of jealousy ignited inside them. They agreed with the midwife to substitute a [male] puppy and a [female] kitten for the boy and the girl. They put the infants in a box and nailed down the lid and threw it into the river.

When they told the king, "Your wife gave birth to a puppy and a kitten," the king was sad, but he replied, "God's grant is always good. Take the children to her, and let her feed them."

He sent her off with her sisters and stayed alone sadly.

Now we go back to the box. It drifted with the current until it got caught in the weeds. A fisherman who had nobody but himself and his wife was fishing nearby. God had been sending him two fish a day, one for himself and one for his wife. He saw the box, picked it out of the water, and ran home to his wife.

His wife said to him, "Take it back to where you found it, for it is either money that we don't need or evil that we don't want at this old age. We are seeking only a good end."

Her husband said to her, "Woman, this was sent to us by God, and we have to accept it."

They opened the box and found the two beautiful babies. The girl had her thumb in the boy's mouth and the boy had his thumb in the girl's mouth. They were suckling each other. They took them in and called the boy Clever Muhammad and the girl Sitt el-Husn. The woman immediately had milk in her breasts, and that day the fisherman caught four fish.

Folktales' children grow quickly. The boy and the girl loved each other very much. When the girl cried, it rained, and her brother [if absent] would know that she was unhappy. When she smiled, the sun shone, and her brother would know she was happy.

One day the fisherman called his son and said, "Son, I will die on such-and-such a day. Under my pillow you will find two hairs from a horse's mane. If you need anything, just rub them."

The boy went out fishing in his father's place that day. After a while it started raining, and he realized that his sister was crying and that his father had died. He went back and did what needed to be done and buried his father.

The following day when he was out, the mother called the girl and said to her, "Daughter, I'm going to die on Friday. Under my pillow you will find a purse. Every morning when you open it, you will find ten pounds in it."

A few days later, when the boy was out fishing, it started raining, and again the boy knew that his sister was crying and that his mother had died. He went home and did what needed to be done. He called an old woman who was there. "Mother, won't you help us wash my mother!" And he buried her.

The boy and his sister left the hut and went to town. With every sunrise the girl found ten pounds in the purse. She saved all the money she found and finally bought a plot of land opposite the king's palace. She got builders and said to them, "I want you to build a palace exactly like that of the king."

One day the king was passing by and saw the new palace. He asked, "Whose palace is this?"

People answered him, "Clever Muhammad and his sister Sitt el-Husn's."

The king met Clever Muhammad and found him to be very generous and polite. He liked him very much, and they spent most of their time together. They ate together, drank together, sat together, did everything together.

Now the boy's maternal aunts, his mother's sisters, recognized him because of his gold and silver hair. They kept on inquiring about him and learned also about his sister. Now they said, "Surely they are the two babies that we had thrown in the river."

They went to visit this sister. They said to her, "Sweetheart, your palace is beautiful, and it is complete except for one thing."

She asked, "What is it?"

They answered (they were mischievous), "It is very hard to get, and your brother would not be willing to get it for you."

She said, "Just tell me, and my brother will get it for me."

They said to her, "Your palace lacks the dancing bamboo."

While her brother was sitting with the king, it started raining. He realized that his sister was crying. He asked the king's permission and left. When he got home he asked her, "Why are you crying, sister?"

[In tears] she told him, "I want the dancing bamboo."

Clever Muhammad said to her, "Don't worry; you will have it."

They prepared rations for him, and he set out 'from God's countries to God's peoples' asking about the dancing bamboo.

One old woman told him, "Between you and the dancing bamboo is three years' travel. It is in the garden of 'our father' the ogre. The ogre sleeps for seven years and is awake for seven years. Hurry, may God will that you catch him during his sleep, the seven years of his sleep."

Clever Muhammad went in the direction that the old woman showed him; he finally got to the ogre's garden. He heard neither sound nor word. He climbed the walls, and inside the garden he saw the bamboo, dancing just like humans, even better. When he got close, the bamboo started dancing very hard. The birds started screaming, and the roses shouted, "A stranger! A stranger! A thief!"

He quickly pulled out a bunch of bamboo, wrapped the roots in his mantle, and fled. Meanwhile, it was time for 'our father' the ogre to wake up; the noise and the shouting awakened him, and he came out to look. He saw Clever Muhammad escaping. But before he could do anything, Clever Muhammad was gone. He went back to where he came.

When his sister Sitt el-Husn saw the bamboo, she became very happy. They planted the bunch in the garden. It grew and prospered and kept on dancing.

Her two maternal aunts came and saw the bamboo which dances. They knew that Clever Muhammad had returned safely. They said to Sitt el-Husn, "That [bamboo] is nothing! Still your garden lacks the singing water!" And they left.

Sitt el-Husn cried, and it rained. Her brother saw it and came back in a hurry. "What is the matter, sister?"

She answered [in tears], "I want the singing water!"

He said, "Never worry. I will get it for you."

Like the first time, they prepared rations, and he set out 'from God's countries to God's peoples.' He took the same road that he had taken before and came to the same old woman. She said to him, "Clever Muhammad! Now what?"

He answered, "I need to get the singing water."

The old woman said to him, "Between you and the singing water is seven years' journey. It is in the garden of Mother Ogress. She is like her son and sleeps for seven years and is awake for seven years. Take this road."

Clever Muhammad took the road which she showed him. He kept on traveling until he came to a beautiful palace with walls as high as ten men's height. He climbed the walls and got in. What happened in the garden of Father Ogre happened in the garden of Mother Ogress. The water started shouting, "A stranger! A thief!" and so did the birds and the roses and the fruits, everything.

He filled a bottle which he had with him, and before the ogress woke up, he was on his way home. He returned to his sister, and they put the water in a fountain. It started singing! Now they had two wonders in their garden, the dancing bamboo and the singing water.

Their two aunts came to visit Sitt el-Husn. Of course they had thought that Clever Muhammad was gone—that [maybe] he had died, or a beast had eaten him or something—but when they heard that he had returned, they thought of another disaster into which to throw him and his sister Sitt el-Husn.

They went to Sitt el-Husn and said to her, "Now your garden will be perfect, perfect if only you get the talking lark.

They left, and Sitt el-Husn cried. Her brother came. She said to him, "Our palace—is lacking—the talking lark. I want it."

He said to her, "Never mind. I'll get it for you."

He set out with his rations and took the same road which he had taken before. He got to the old woman. She said to him, "Now, Clever Muhammad, what next?"

He said to her, "I need the talking lark!"

The old woman said to him, "All but that! Someone wants you destroyed. You go back home and settle down, for no one knows where the land of the talking lark is."

Her [Sitt el-Husn's] brother, Clever Muhammad, did not know what to do. While he was sitting and thinking, he remembered the two hairs which his father had given to him. He rubbed them, and there in front of him he found a horse; this horse was the son of the king of the jinn.

The horse said to him, "I'm at your command. Order and you will find."

Clever Muhammad told him the story. The son of the king of the jinn said, "Between you and the talking lark there are a thousand years. It is in the garden of the palace of Um-ishi-'Aoor [the long-haired lady]. I can only take you there, but I can't go in with you. When you get there, you will find sheep grazing there. Take one and cut it in four pieces. In front of her palace you will find two lions. Give each one a [sheep] quarter. They will say to you, 'Hello, Clever Muhammad. You have honored us.' Do not answer them at all, because if you do, you will find yourself changed into stone. At the second gate of the palace, you will find two dogs. Give each one a [sheep] quarter. They will say to you, 'Hello, Clever Muhammad. You have honored us.' Do not answer them at all, because if you do, they will tear you apart. Inside the garden you will find Lady Um-ishu'Aoor. She will say to you, 'Hello, Clever Muhammad. I love you, Clever Muhammad. You are predestined for me, Clever Muhammad.' Do not dare to answer her or to utter a word or even to say, 'What is one third of three?' [i.e., the simplest thing]. If you were to speak, she would transform you into stone."

Clever Muhammad did as the son of the king of the jinn told him. As he entered the garden, trees spoke to him. "Hello, Clever Muhammad." And roses spoke to him. "Welcome, Clever Muhammad," and finally he found the long-haired lady before him. There were many stone people all around him; they had wanted to get the lark but had not kept silent [and so were turned to stone]. Wherever he looked, there were stone people.

The long-haired lady said to him, "I love you, Clever Muhammad. I know why you are here, Clever Muhammad. I know what your mother's sisters have done to you and to your sister." But he did not pay any attention to what she said. He walked to the middle of the garden and found a golden cage on a marble pedestal. The talking lark was sitting outside of its open door. The lark kept on saying, "Clever Muhammad, you whose father is a king—you who—you who—"

Clever Muhammad did not utter a word. Finally, when the lark got tired of talking, it said, "I am tired! Isn't there someone who will say to me, 'Rest!' Isn't there someone who will say to me, 'Sleep!' Isn't there someone—isn't there someone—"

Finally Clever Muhammad shouted at it, "Why don't you be

quiet! Why don't you sleep, brother, and get it over with?"
Immediately he was turned to stone.

Now, to whom shall we go back [with our tale]? To his sister,
Sitt el-Husn. His sister's heart felt that her brother was in danger. She put on men's clothing and prepared rations and left.
She kept on going—one country carries her and one country
puts her down. She finally saw a huge dust cloud reaching to the
sky; it kept on coming nearer to her, and finally she saw herself
in front of a ghoul [ogre]. Before the ogre said anything, she said
to him, "Peace be upon you, Father Ogre."

The ogre replied, "Had your greeting not preceded your
speech, I would have munched on your flesh before your bones.
What brings you here?"

She said, "I am looking for the talking lark."

He said to her (he didn't know that she was a woman), "Son,
why don't you go back. You are too young to die."

She said, "I must go."

He said to her, "Keep on going this way; you will meet my
brother. He is one day older and one year more knowledgeable
than myself."

She kept on going until she met the brother of the ogre. She
said to him, "Peace be upon you, Father Ogre."

He said to her, "Had your greeting not preceded your speech,
I would have munched on your flesh before your bones. What
do you want?"

She said, "I want to go to the country of the talking lark."

He said to her, like the first one, "Go back" and all that.

She said, "I must go."

He said to her, "Keep on going. You will meet our eldest
brother. He is one day older and one year more knowledgeable
than myself or my younger brother whom you have met."

She kept on going until she finally came to the third ogre. He
was the biggest of them all. She said to him, "Peace be upon
you."

He answered, "Had your greeting not preceded your speech,
I would have munched on your flesh before your bones. What
do you want?"

She said, "I want to go to the country of the talking lark."

He said to her, "It must be very important to you. Take this ball and this racket. Hit the ball with the racket and follow it. It will take you there in no time."

She took the ball and the racket and kept on hitting the ball with the racket and following it until she finally found herself in front of the palace of the long-haired lady. She did as her brother did. She killed a sheep and gave each lion a quarter. They let her pass through the gate. When she met the two dogs, she gave each one of them a quarter and found herself inside the garden.

She looked around, and there were whole nations of people petrified, nations upon nations of people. She came to the lark and found that he was standing outside his cage with her brother, a stone, right next to him. The lark kept on saying, "You, Sitt el-Husn, whose father is the king and whose mother is such and such and such and such—"

She did not say a word. Finally the lark did to her exactly what he had done to her brother. The lark started saying, "Oh, I am tired. Isn't there somebody who will say to me 'Sleep!' Isn't there somebody who will say to me, 'Rest!' Isn't there somebody—isn't there somebody—"

She was more clever than her brother. She did not say a word. Finally the lark entered his cage. Immediately, she closed the door after him and picked him up. At this very moment, as soon as she closed the cage, all the people who were stone came back to life. They went to their homes. Her brother did not recognize her. She was dressed in men's clothing then. He said to her, "Thank you, brother," thinking she was a man like himself.

She answered, "I am your sister. What made you this way? Why did you speak to the lark?"

He answered, "God's command" [i.e., predestination].

Together they went outside the palace from whence they came. They found the horse, the jinni, in the same place where her brother had left it before. Her brother mounted it, and she mounted behind him, and in the blink of an eye they were back home.

The lark said, "I want you to give a party for the king. Ask the king to invite all of his ministers, all of his army, all of his people, and ask him not to forget his dog and cat children and also the midwife and his two previous wives."

They all came. The king had the dog and the cat all dressed in

silk and seated on golden chairs. When everybody was there, the
king asked Clever Muhammad, "What is the party for?"

Clever Muhammad answered, "For this lark."

The king wondered, "A party for a bird? It is only a bird."

The lark spoke to the king, "Peace be upon you, king."

The king was amazed. "And upon you be peace, lark."

The lark said [pointing to the cat and the dog], "What is this,
king?"

The king replied, "It is God's grant, lark. Whatever God
grants must be good."

The lark said, "Is there a king who would beget dogs and cats,
king?"

The king replied, "It is God's will, lark."

The lark said, "Bring the midwife."

They brought her. She came trembling, with her face as blue
as indigo. As soon as she saw the children, she immediately
shouted, "I didn't do it! It was their maternal aunts! Their maternal aunts said to me, 'Give us the children, and we will give
you the dog and the cat to put in their place.'"

Now, everyone in the kingdom was there, and everyone heard.
The king said to his people, "He who loves the Chosen Prophet
should set fire to the midwife and the aunts." And they burned
them. The king restored his wife.

And they lived in stability and prosperity and begat boys and
girls.

Part II
Realistic and
Philosophical Tales

Recorded in Arabic in October 1969 from Kenzi Nubian Sheik A. 'Aali, 73, ex-assistant to the 'Aùmd̀ah (mayor) of Girshah village. 'Aali can read and write. He heard this tale from his grandfather, who had learned it from "the Bisharis [a branch of the Beja people] themselves." However, 'A. Isma'Aeel, an able narrator (see informant note to tale no. 16), confided to me, "This story is mine! He heard it from me. He couldn't narrate it correctly and was about to add another tale to it at the end." Isma'Aeel told me a tale identical except for one detail—his tale involved a "'Aabbādi Arab" (a member of an Arabic-speaking branch of the Bejas who had originally spoken a Cushitic language) instead of the less Arabized Bishari.

Our narrator spoke with the serenity and dignity expected from a village notable like himself. He did not view himself as a raconteur and stated, "I am not a *kummaji* [from the Nubian name for a tale, i.e., *Märchen* teller] but will narrate only as a part of a *wanasàh* [a conversational get-together]." He labeled this story a *mathal,* i.e., an example or a piece of wisdom. "It is true," he assured me.

Mastery of the Arabic language, the glories of nomadic life, and distrust of urban females are the basic themes of this story. The tale illustrates the Nubian view of the Bisharis, a non-Arab group (evidently because of their nomadic life, the Bejas are called "Arabs," i.e., nomads). Commenting on the story, the narrator and some of his friends described the Bishari as "honest...more courageous in the hills [than the Nubians], especially with the sword and the shield,...and never capable of treachery or betrayal." They added, however, "We [Nubians] surpass them in the use of firearms; the Bisharis say, 'Beware of the fire spitter [i.e., Nubians; see notes to tale no. 48] controlling our women, knowledge of the Arabic language, and religiosity." Nubians usually cite an alleged Bishari custom of trial marriage to test the fertility of a girl as an example of the shallowness of their understanding of Islam. Resocializing the *sons* into allying themselves with their father, instead of mother, underlies the plot. (See p. lii above.)

PRAYERS ON BEHALF OF the Prophet, whose characteristics are perfect. Once there was a Bishari. This Bishari traveled on the road until he reached a village. In this village there was a king. The king was sick. His vizier said to him, "King, I have your remedy."

The king answered him, "Well, vizier, let's have it."

The vizier said, "You have to eat the livers of two persons—a foolish one and a wise one. If you eat the liver of a foolish person and that of a wise person, you will be cured, and the illness will go away."

The king asked him, "Is that so?"

He answered him, "Yes, that is so."

The king said to him, "All right, find someone who is foolish and someone who is wise."

The vizier looked around and found the Bishari. He had his men arrest him. They took him to prison until they had found a wise one. He said to the king, "King, we found the foolish one; now we have to find the wise one."

The king looked around, and the vizier looked around also. Then the vizier said to the king, "King, we have the wise one right here! We have the judge. the judge is the wisest man in the whole kingdom."

Immediately the king ordered, "Take him! Put him in prison, with the other one."

They took the judge and put him in prison. Now the Bishari was shouting, "Why am I here? What do you want of me? Why did you put me here?"

The judge was weeping; he said to the Bishari, "Tomorrow they are going to kill us. They will take our livers, mine and yours, and feed them to the king so that he may be cured."

When the Bishari heard this, he started beating on the door and shouting, "Get me out of here! Get me out of here! Take me to the king! Take me to the king! King! King!"

They took him out and took him to the king. He said to the king, "Why did you bring me here? What do you want of me?"

The king answered him, "You are here so that I may eat your liver and that of the judge so that I can be cured."

The Bishari said to him, "Why?"

The king answered, "I have to eat the liver of a foolish man
and that of a wise man so that I can be cured."

The Bishari wondered, "Who said this to you?"

The king answered, "The vizier; and you are the foolish one,
and the judge is the wisest one in my kingdom."

The Bishari asked, "And who told you that?"

The king replied, "My vizier."

The Bishari said, "As for foolishness, I am not a fool. I know
that there is only one God, and I know the number of days and
months in the year. I know the calendar, and I know the stars. I
fare inside the desert without any guide; I know my directions. I
say all the prayers; I fast and I know my religion well! Now, why
is this man here?"

Meaning whom? Meaning the judge.

They answered him, "Because he is wise. The judge is naturally
wise."

He replied, "No, he is not wise. His parents and his masters
have taught him by the rod and insults. Knowledge was forced
into him through beating and insults. [He did not learn on his
own, as a Bishari does.] He is not wise. As for being foolish, I am
not. As for being wise, the judge is not."

Then the king asked him, "Then who is wise, and who is
foolish?"

(Now it was the king who was asking the Bishari this question). The Bishari replied, "The foolish one is the man who is
still living with a sterile wife, still living with a sterile woman who
does not give birth to children. What is he waiting for! This is
the real foolish one."

The king said, "All right, now we know who's foolish. What
about the wise one? Who is the wise one?"

The Bishari said, "The wise one is the person who sits at the
coffeehouse and fashions speech. He is the man who fashions
speech from memory. The wise one is the *labeeb,* the man who
makes up words; the man that recites poetry." [i.e., the impro-
vising oral poet].

The king said, "All right," and he looked around.

He did not find any foolish man except his vizier. The king
ordered, "Take him!"

He pleaded, "But—my lord!"

The king replied, "No buts! You are the foolish one. For years you have been with a sterile wife." They looked around outside. In a coffeehouse they came upon a man who was making up songs and singing. The man, an artist, was saying, "Ohhhh, my night, ohhhh, my day," etc.

They said to him, "What night! What day! Come!" and they took him and put him with the vizier.

Whether the king ate the livers or not, whether he was cured or not, does not concern us here. What concerns us is that the judge took the Bishari man home. Of course the Bishari saved his life. The judge said to him, "I have three daughters. You choose the one that appeals to you the most. I will marry her to you."

The Bishari man consented and selected one of the three. The judge married them, and they lived together. [She bore him three male children.] One day the Bishari man said to the judge. "'A boat does not float except on water,' 'watermelon does not ripen except on its vine,' and 'he who seeks his home lives.' I want to go to my home; I want to go to my home. If your daughter comes with me, she is welcome. If she does not, I would like to take my children and go back to my home."

He took his wife and his children and left. They covered a distance as far as from Cairo to El-Minya [about 150 miles]. They came to a valley. It was full of cattle. The Bishari man said to one of his sons, the eldest, "Boy, this is your home. All these cattle are yours."

For this Bishari man had very much money and property.

After this they kept on going. After they covered a distance as far as from El-Minya to, say, Asyout [about 100 miles], he said to his second son, "This is your home. You stay here."

Now there remained only himself and the [third] boy and the boy's mother, his own wife. They went as far as from Asyout to Aswan [about 300 miles]. He said to his third son, "This country is your home. You stay here."

Of course all this was his, for he was a very rich man. Then he took his wife and went far away from his children.

When the man and his wife reached their home, his wife kept on boasting about her father, the judge; "my father is . . . , my

father is. . . ." He said to her, "I would like to send you back to
your father, the judge. You go and ask the judge, your father,
'What is the fattest, what is the heaviest, and what is the lightest
of things?'"

The woman went, and her father asked her, "Why did you
come back?"

She replied, "My husband sent me back to ask you, 'What is
the fattest, what is the heaviest, and what is the lightest of
things?' When I have received the answers to these questions, I
should go back to him and tell him your answers."

Now what did the judge do? The judge filled a pillow with
ostrich feathers and gave it to her and said, "This is the lightest
of things."

He filled another case with lead and said to her, "This is the
heaviest of things."

He also brought a very fat young sheep [*bargi*] and gave it to
her and said, "And this is the fattest, the richest of things."

The woman took these three things and set out for home. Her
husband had told her, "Do not stop to visit my sons."

She came to the first valley, where the first son was. She
stopped to visit her son and said to him, "Your father asked me
to go to my father, the judge, and ask him these three things:
'What is the richest, what is the heaviest, and what is the lightest
of things?' My father gave me these three things—the sheep, the
lead, and the ostrich feathers."

Her son said, "That's right. What my grandfather said is correct."

The same thing happened with the second son. He also told
her, "My grandfather is right."

Now she went to the third son. He asked her, "What brings
you here, mother?"

She told him the story. He took the feathers and blew them in
the wind and threw the lead away and slaughtered the sheep. He
said to her, "The lightest is the cheerful, generous person. The
heaviest is the villainous miser. The richest is the [well] water of
the month of *ṭooba* [December]. You go and tell my father that
these are the lightest, heaviest, and richest of things."

The woman left. When she reached her home her husband
received her. "Welcome, welcome, wife. Have you seen your

father? Have you asked your father about the three things I
asked you?"

"Yes husband."

"What did your father say?"

"He said, 'The lightest is the cheerful, generous person. The
heaviest is the villainous miser. The richest is the [well] water of
the month of December."

"Well, well, well! That's good! Did your father say that?"

"Yes, husband."

"Well, well, well, he is right. . . . Have you seen my sons, wife?"

"No, husband."

He knew that these were not the answers of her father. Now
these three sons were named Muhammad [Praised], Hasan
[Nice], and Sadiq [Truthful].

The father rode his horse to see the first son. "How are you,
Muhammad?"

"I'm well, father."

"How are things going, Muhammad?"

"They are going well, father."

"Has your mother been here, Muhammad?"

"No, she hasn't, father."

The man said to him, "Well, son, I'm glad."

He went to the second son. "How are you, Hasan?"

"I am well, father."

"How are things, Hasan?"

"Things are well, father."

"Has your mother been here, Hasan?"

"No, she hasn't, father."

The man said, "Well," and left.

He went to the third son, "How are you, Sadiq?"

"I am well, father."

"How are things, Sadiq?"

"Things are well, father."

"Has your mother been here, Sadiq?"

"Yes, she has, father."

"What did she say? Did she have anything with her?"

"Yes, father. She had a sack full of ostrich feathers and
another full of lead and a fat sheep. She said her father had told
her that these three things were the lightest, the heaviest, and
the richest of things."

Then the father asked him, "And what did you do, Sadiq?"

The son answered, "I blew the feathers in the wind. I threw away the lead. And I killed the sheep. I told her, "The lightest is the cheerful, generous person. The heaviest is the villainous miser. The fattest is the [well] water of the month of December."

The father smiled and said, "Your name is Sadiq, and you are truthful. Come, Truthful.

Then the father said, "Your other two brothers, Muhammad and Hasan, are now among your possessions. You can sell them or buy them as you wish."

And he said to him, "Peace be upon you, Sadiq," and left.

He went back to his wife. He again asked her, "Wife, have you seen my sons?"

"No, husband."

He didn't say anything. A short while later, he began yelling, "Woman! Woman! Get me my gun! Get me my spear! Our property has been stolen; our sons have been raided. Hurry! Hurry!"

The wife said, "Calm down; none of this happened."

He replied, "No, no, the children have been raided."

The wife replied, "I have just been with them."

"Aha! Then you are a liar! Like your father the judge, who is ignorant."

He made the youngest son head of all the rest. He realized that the woman and her two sons were liars and treacherous and their grandfather the judge was ignorant and foolish. That was a test that he made to prove all this.

And I was there and just returned.

· 11 ·   *The Man Who Put His Mother over His Shoulder*
         *and Rode His Father**

Taped from M.A. Tilib, janitor at the Folklore Center in Cairo. Tilib was born in 1926 in el-Bargi village, in the middle of southern Egypt. He left the village when he was drafted into the army and remained in Cairo after leaving the service. Tilib is

very hard working and honest. He and a number of other friends
get together to chat; tales usually come up during these gatherings (see informant note to tale no. 1).

He proved to be an especially good narrator of novelle,
humorous anecdotes, and religious and historical legends, as
well as a reliable source of information on the local history and
beliefs of his village and neighboring areas. Although the
Folklore Center undertook field trips to Tilib's village, he was
never asked to assist in any capacity. I was the first to view him as
a tradition bearer. He often came to my office in between chores
to declare, "I've just remembered a story for you!"

Tilib can barely read and write; he heard most of his folktales
in the village from an old narrator named Sayyid Ahmad. He
states, "I haven't told this story to anyone before.... It 'fills my
head' [i.e., I admire it]; that is why it can never be forgotten,
even twenty-five years after having heard it." For him it is a
mathàl, a story of wisdom. Tilib presented all the basic episodes
in the tale. As might be expected from a person who has not
used a story for a long time, he tended not to elaborate on
actions or situations.

A major issue underlying the plot of the narrative is the problem
of being in debt. An Egyptian adage states, "Debt is grief by
night and humiliation by day!" Borrowing or lending money
with interest is sinful; the word *ràhn,* pawning, is synonymous
with being a hostage. This story is based on themes which are
central to religious value systems, especially those related to the
doctrines of *ḥalāl,* that which God has legitimized for man, and
ḥarām, that which God has prohibited to man. Islam prohibits
the consumption of meat from a dead animal or fowl (see introductory note to tale no. 47).

Riddling wagers between a man and woman in which either
the woman's hand is won or the suitor is disgraced are very
common in folk narratives. Similarly, riddling contests appear in
"historical" reports from the pre-Islamic period and were also
reported to have constituted a powerful marriage custom among
the Arabs of Libya until the 1930s and 1940s.

The importance of a woman's hair underlies the climactic
event in our tale. According to Islamic traditions, an adult
female's hair, unlike her face, hands, or feet, must be covered

and concealed from all but immediate relatives. The loss of a braid is symbolic of the loss of chastity.

ONCE THERE WAS a sultan [i.e., a rich man] who had an only child named Clever Hasan. Things went bad for the sultan until he had nothing. Clever Hasan wanted to go out into the hills to work as a hunter or something. He went to the gunsmith and said to him, "I want a rifle [on credit],"

The merchant replied, "Why should I give you one? The time I would have readily given you a gun is long past. Now you will have to pay for it." And he refused to give him a gun.

Now the merchant's mother was friends with Clever Hasan's mother. Clever Hasan went to his mother and said to her, "Mother, I went to So-and-so and asked him, 'Give me a gun,' but he refused."

Now Clever Hasan's mother went to the merchant's mother and said to her, "Mother of So-and-so, would you do the good deed of making your son give my son a rifle, for Hasan, as you know, is my only son?"

The merchant's mother spoke to her son, and he replied, "Will she be liable for him?"

His mother said, "Yes."

He replied, "All right," and gave Clever Hasan a rifle.

Clever Hasan went to buy a horse. The horse dealer also refused to give him one until he got his father to be his guarantor. Now Clever Hasan has pawned his mother for a rifle and his father for a horse. He strapped the rifle across his shoulder and mounted the horse's back.

He rode off into the hills. There he found a gazelle. He chased it, but it ran away, and he kept after it for a very long distance. He finally shot it, and it fell. He went to it in a hurry to mention the name of God while slaughtering it, but he was late and it was dead. Now eating it would be sinful—he cut open its belly and found a baby gazelle there, which he slaughtered according to creed. He roasted it and ate it. Now he was very thirsty. There was no water to be found anywhere, for it was a desert with neither rain nor wells. His horse was sweating from running so hard. He scraped the sweat off the horse's skin with one hand into the palm of his other hand and drank it.

Now he had put his mother over his shoulder, ridden his father, eaten the pure out of the profane, and drank water that came neither from heaven nor from earth.

He gathered himself together and traveled until he came to a town. In this town there was a palace, and there were heads hanging in front of it. He asked a woman selling radishes—one of those poor people who sit around—"Lady, what's the story behind this?"

She replied, "Son, it is the emir's daughter. She gives and receives riddles. If you give her a riddle that she cannot answer, you will marry her; and if she gives you a riddle that you can answer, you will marry her. If she can answer your riddle or you fail to answer hers, your head will be hung along with the others."

He went in and asked to meet the princess.

"What do you want, fellow? What's your name?"

He answered, "My name is Clever Hasan. I want to riddle you."

She asked him, "First, have you seen what's hanging outside?"

He answered, "Yes, I know about it all."

"Will you give me a riddle, or shall I give you one?"

He replied, "No, I'll give you one."

She said, "Give it."

He said, "What about somebody who put his mother over his shoulder, rode his father, ate the pure out of the profane, and drank water that came neither from heaven nor from earth?"

She listened, thought for a while, and said to him, "Clever Hasan, come back tomorrow."

He said, "Will do."

He went to an old woman in town and said to her, "Please let me spend the night here."

She said, "You are welcome, son."

The following day he went back to the princess. She said to him, "Clever Hasan, again, tomorrow."

He went back to the old woman's house. [The following day he went back to the princess].

"And again tomorrow!"

"Again, tomorrow."

"Again, tomorrow."

One tomorrow, after another, until a month had passed.

The princess inquired about him until she learned that he was staying at the old woman's. She went to her and said, "I'm So-and-so."

The woman replied, "I know."

The princess said to her, "I want you to tell Clever Hasan that I am your daughter and that I came to visit you. I'll change my looks. He will not know me, and I will pay you so much or whatever you ask for."

The princess put on a peasant dress, and later she said to Clever Hasan, "Hey, Clever Hasan, I heard that you gave the princess a riddle that she can't solve."

— [No reply.]

She laughed with him and teased him. In short, 'the west became east' [i.e., things went too far], and she spent a whole week with him in the house.

"Oh, please, Clever Hasan! Tell me, Clever Hasan!"

He finally said to her, "I'll tell you, but you will have to spend the night here with me in my room."

She agreed.

During the night while she was asleep, he got a pair of scissors and chopped off part of her braid. He wrapped the hair in a handkerchief and put it in his pocket.

In the morning he told her the whole story: "I pawned my mother to get a gun and my father to get a horse. I got a living gazelle out of a dead one and drank the sweat of my horse."

She said to him, "Fine!" And she left.

That day he went back to the palace. The princess announced, "I am ready. Summon the court."

Everyone came: the king, the vizier, and the courtiers; and she gave him the answer that he had just given her that morning.

The king shouted, "Executioner, chop off his head!"

The executioner went to him, and Clever Hasan shouted, "Wait! I have another riddle for the princess. If she can solve it, my blood will be legitimately hers. 'A bird left its nest, with a stranger to rest. When it came back, one wing it did lack.'"

The princess—[here the narrator reaches to the back of his

head and bites his lower lip to indicate the princess's action]. She could not utter one word. She admitted that she had gotten the answer from him and that he had won.

The king said to Clever Hasan, "Do you want her in marriage, or will you name your own reward?"

Clever Hasan chose to marry her, and the king gave him half his kingdom. After a while he took his wife, went back to his father's home, and reopened his father's guest house; things went back to the way they were, and his father became a sultan again.

· 12 ·   *"It Serves Me Right!"**

Recorded in March 1969 from S. Seliman, 55, businessman from Cairo. He learned the story about twenty-five years earlier from his tutor; the tutor had heard the story in his native village in Monoufiyyah Province in the Nile Delta. He told it to Seliman to illustrate that "every person has his lot in life coming to him" and that "greed and interference in what has been forbidden brings nothing but sorrow."

Seliman received several years of schooling, but he decided, against his family's wishes, to quit and go into business. Currently he runs and co-owns a shoe-designing and making operation which caters to upper-class women. Seliman sometimes narrates to his children. His repertoire of a few simple animal tales is reserved only for the youngest, an 11-year-old girl (see tale no. 51). Seliman refused to tell any *Märchen* and stated, "No! No! Tales such as 'Louliyya. . ., lower your hair and take your father the ogre away from the heat of the hills' [see informant note to tale no. 8] and stuff like that are not for me; K. [his sister] is the specialist in this kind of tale."

Seliman's practice of telling his children a certain kind of tale reflects urban middle-class familial attitudes. Unlike families in rural and nomadic areas, the urban middle-class family has relaxed rules for maintaining social distance between age and sex groups.

This wisdom story portrays life in a utopian two-class society in which each member knows his social rank and role, earning and spending power, and marries only his social equal. The symbolic associations found in the story between a water jug and a female, a tree and life, a river and earnings, and a boathouse and worldly life are recurrent in all aspects of culture. Sycamore trees in particular have a considerable ritual and magical aura in Egyptian folk belief systems. The tale also discourages inquisitiveness into the supernatural and promotes belief in predestination.

So powerful is the theme of this narrative that it pervades various aspects of social and individual life. Sami Zaghloul, a folk dance specialist at the Folklore Center, told me the following: "When I was young, there was a man in our village [Meet Kinanah, Qalyoubiyyah Province, in the Nile Delta] who roamed about hitting his chest with a large stone, shouting, 'It serves me right! It serves me right!' When I grew up I asked about the reason behind this man's strange action. They told me this story and said 'He was there!'" Zaghloul told a very close variant of our narrative. Two other folklorists had witnessed the same occurrence in other parts of Egypt. Saber el-'Aadily reported a similar incident from a district of Cairo; also 'Aadly Ibrahim stated, "There was a man in our village [in southern Egypt] who did the same thing." These occurrences of emotional disturbance demonstrate that this story, like numerous other aspects of folk culture, sets a pattern for behavior which includes mental and emotional disorder. These patterns are normally not explicable in Western psychiatric terms and are usually lumped together under the heading of "exotic syndromes."

ONCE THERE WAS a man who was sick and tired of his life. One day he walked down a road (similar to the Muqattam Road). He found a side track and followed it until he came to a cave. In this cave he found people, nine persons. Each one of these nine was slapping his own face, crying, "It serves me right! It serves me right!"

Our friend watched them for a while and was surprised: "What is 'it serves me right'?"

What did our friend do? He joined them and started saying,

"It serves me right!" without knowing for what reason or what purpose. He just stood among them doing as they did.

While they were doing this, noontime came, their food time. "They" [mystical agents] gave them nine loaves of bread, a loaf for each one. He snatched a loaf for himself. They found that one loaf was missing, for they were nine persons, and they always received nine loaves.

They started looking around; they found our friend, the stranger. They said, "Come here! What brought you here to us?"

He answered, "By God, I came upon you and saw you slapping your faces and crying, 'It serves me right!' I came among you and did as you were doing."

They said, "No, your place is not here. Your place is this way."

They got him by the hands and feet and tossed him. He found himself landing in a place about which he knew nothing at all. They tossed him into a well. He landed in a town in which he did not know anybody, for he was a stranger.

What should our friend do? He found no place to go. He just kept walking down the streets, here and there, until it was sunset [prayer time]. He entered a mosque. He said his sunset prayers, and [about two hours later] he said the late evening prayers. He tucked himself away in a corner. The keeper of the mosque realized that he was a stranger, so he let him sleep there.

The following morning he got up, performed the prayers, went out, and came back around noontime for the noontime prayers. He kept on going out, wandering around, and coming back to the mosque. The mosque keeper noticed this and said to him, "Respectable sir, come here. You are not from this town! Are you a stranger?"

He answered, "By God, I am a stranger."

The keeper said to him, "So I have noticed. Where are you from?"

He said, "By God, I'm from Cairo."

He asked him, "What brought you here?"

He answered him, "I was walking depressed . . ." and told him what happened with the people who tossed him into the well.

He replied, "All right, son. Whoever lives here can get anything and everything on account. You pay with prayers upon the Prophet [i.e., blessings earned]. Any restaurant or any other shop that you enter, if you need to eat or to drink, all you have to say to the keeper after you have eaten and drunk is, 'Add it to the account,' and pay with prayers upon the Prophet. He will let you go and will never ask you for money."

He said, "Fine, let it be."

Our friend gathered himself together and left the mosque. He was too frightened to go to a kebab place or a famous restaurant or anything like that. So he went to a *falafil* [fried bean patties] place, just in case, so that the beating would be fairly light [since shop owners usually thrash those who do not pay].

So our friend entered a simple restaurant selling *fool* [fava beans] and *falafil* and ate. When he was going out, the keeper said to him, "Pay the bill, please."

He answered him, "On the account, prayers upon the Prophet."

The keeper answered, "You have been good company and have honored us."

Evening came; now, with a bolder heart, he entered a good restaurant. Now he ate pigeons and everything a soul could desire and also desert. And he did not stint himself. When he was going out, they asked him, "The bill?"

He said, "On the account," and paid with more prayers upon the Prophet.

He spent about a week just like this. He was very happy with things. He said to the mosque keeper, "My clothes have become soiled."

He [the keeper] said to him, "Go to a department store (like Cicurel or Sidnawi or one of those famous stores). Choose whatever appeals to you, and tell them 'On the account' and pay them in prayers upon the Prophet."

He went and chose several good caftans, several turbans, a few *gibba* [ankle-length top coats], and a couple of pairs of shoes. As he was going out he said to them [the sales clerks], "On the account," and paid them with more prayers upon the Prophet.

They answered him, "You have been good company and have honored us."

Now this man longed for marriage and longed for a house in

which he could live. He was still sleeping at the mosque. So he said to the mosque keeper, "By God, uncle sheik, I would like to find myself a good wife."

He replied, "All right; the way we go about it here is that you go outside the town. You will find tents, white tents and green tents. Do not enter a green tent; they are for the upper [-class] people. Find yourself a white tent. There you will find young women, 'glory be to the Creator for his creation' [i.e., of startling beauty]! And they will be holding water jars. In this case they will all offer their jars for you to drink from. Whoever appeals to you, take her jar and drink from it. This will be your choice; pay her her dowry."

Our friend thought, "What a grand opportunity!"

He gathered himself up and ran out of the town. He saw the tents pitched. There were the green ones and the white ones. He became greedy and said, "By God, I am not going to enter a white tent. I'm going to enter a green tent!"

He entered the biggest green tent, where he was met by a girl, 'glory be to the Creator for his creation!' He took the jug from her and drank. He began to leave; she said, "No, now you can't. Now you have become my husband, according to God's creed and his Prophet's. You have to come with us so that we can sign the marriage contract."

It happened that the girl he chanced to get and whose water he drank was the daughter of the sultan of that country. She took him to her father. They signed the contract, and our friend paid the dowry, so many thousand prayers upon the Prophet, and they made all the celebrations and they lived together 'twenty-four carats' happy.

One day he came to her and said, "So-and-so, by God, I would like to go out and promenade a bit."

"Gladly," she said, "but there is one condition in this country that you have to know. The first condition is never to inquire about anything, anything! That is, anything that happens in this country. Do not ask, "Why is this?" or "What is that?" Anything you see you merely regard with your own eyes, and that's it."

He said, "Will do."

She said, "For if you went out and asked anybody, 'Why are

you doing this?' I would be divorced. For one divorce oath of the three permitted would have been made.*

He said, "Will do."

He gathered himself up and went out. As he was walking down the street, he became very tired, so he sat under a tree. He looked up to find somebody feeling the fruit of the sycamore. He left some ripe ones and ate some unripe ones. Our friend became upset: "Is there anyone who would eat a bad sycamore and leaves a good one?" So he shouted at him, "You! Brother, up there!"

He [the man in the tree] answered, "What do you want?"

He asked, "Why are you leaving good sycamores and eating bad ones?"

The man answered him, "It's none of your business."

"Ahhh," he moaned, "I'm sorry. She said to me, 'Do not ask about anything you see,' but I did," and he returned home to her.

When he got there she said to him, "You asked about something. You have actually sworn the first divorce oath. Do not enter my chamber."

He begged her, "For God's sake! For God's mercy!"

She finally consented and said, "All right, we will revoke the oath."

They brought the sheik and did this. He [our friend] stayed at home for a while. But then he got bored and said to her [his wife] "I would like to go out."

She answered him, "All right," but warned him again, "The condition is not to ask about anything."

He answered, "Will do."

He gathered himself up and went out. He walked until he got to a big river. There he saw a young man with two buckets of water (hanging at the ends of a cane across his shoulders). The young man repeatedly went down to the stream, filled his two buckets, went up to the bank, and poured the water there. He went down, filled, went up, and poured. He went down, filled,

---

* According to Islamic law, a husband may divorce his wife and remarry her twice; a third divorce is final (see introductory note to tale no. 15).

went up, and poured. Meanwhile right next to him there was an
ancient man with a bucket full of holes. He dipped his bucket
into the stream [below], and by the time he reached the top of
the bank, it was empty. He wasn't getting anything. He [our
friend] felt sorry for the old man, so he shouted at the young
one, "Hey, brother, you ox! Why don't you help this old man
and fill for him two or three buckets?"

The old man snapped at him, "None of your business!"

He said, "Ahhh, I'm sorry!"

He gathered himself up and went back to his wife. She said to
him, "Now the second divorce oath has been sworn. Do not
enter my chamber."

He implored her and said, "Repentance! This is the last time!"

She said, "All right."

They brought back the sheik, and she was restored. He stayed
at home for a period of time, and again he wanted to go out
walking around. Now she warned him, "'The third time is the
sure one.' If you talk to anyone, if you ask anybody anything, I'll
be illegitimate [as your wife], and that's according to the religious law!!"

As he was strolling along the river again, he saw a ship in the
middle of the river, and he saw people, some on the eastern
bank and some on the western bank. What were they doing? He
found that this group was pulling the ship by ropes this way
[toward itself], while that group was pulling it that way [toward
itself]; the ship was moving neither to the east nor to the west
bank. He got very upset. "You people! Either these should let
go so it can go this way, or those should let go so it can go that
way!"

They answered, "It's none of your business."

He said, "Ahh, that is it!"

He gathered himself up and went back to his wife. She met
him at the door and said to him, "Now to approach me would be
sinful. Do not enter!"

And he said, "All right, but before we are separated and go
away from each other, explain to me these three things which I
saw, the three events concerning these people."

She said, "Will do." She said, "The first event is that of the
tree; it is [the tree of] life spans. When a lifetime is up, its

sycamore fruit dries up; and the sycamore fruit of those who still have time looks fresh, but when the time is up, death takes all, young and old."

He said, "Fine."

"As for the second event, of the old man filling water along with the young one, it is that everybody is getting his predestined livelihood; this one gets much, that one gets little, exactly as God, glory be to him, has willed it."

He said, "Fine; how about the third?"

She said, "The third event is the world. The ship is just like the world. Each one hangs on to it for a while wanting to bring it to his own side. It smiles at each one for a while, but nobody gets hold of it."

Now she got hold of him and thre-e-ew him; he landed with those who are saying "It serves me right," and he became the tenth.

(Of course when they received their food, there were [now] ten loaves of bread.)

· 13 ·   *"I've Seen [It] with My Own Eyes;
Nobody Told Me!"* *

Recorded in March 1969 from S. Seliman (see informant note, tale no. 12). He heard the tale from a friend "more than twenty-five years ago." At the time of recording, he had not told this tale to anyone in his family since he first heard it.

It is believed that everyone's past, present, and future were already preordained at the time of the creation of the universe. Attempts to alter one's lot in life will never meet with success unless success itself has already been predestined. Challenging predestination can only result in total failure and disaster. Before a person may express any hope or future plan whatsoever, it is necessary to declare, *"Insha'allāh"* (If God wills).

THERE WAS A MAN. This man dreamt that there was a water faucet in front of each one [who was washing for prayers]. In the morning in the mosque while washing for dawn prayers, each person had a water faucet in front of him that was really pouring out water. His faucet was fully turned on, but it went "drip—drip—" He became angry. What did he do? He got a nail and a hammer. He drove the nail inside the faucet and hammered it in, to unclog it.

Now the water faucet was completely blocked. Before it had only been giving out drops; now it was completely sealed.

In the morning when he woke up (for it was a dream that he saw), he went down the street, slapping one hand against the other [a sign of despair and wonder] and murmuring, "I have seen it with my own eyes; nobody told me!"

One day as he was walking, he passed by a house. The sultan's daughter was living in the house, and the sultan's wife was in it too. It happened that day that the sultan's wife was getting out of the bath, and she was, as you might say—naked, and her body was showing. She heard this man saying, "I have seen it with my own eyes; nobody told me!"

So she thought that this man saw her. This man had stopped at the garden fence, for he was tired, saying, "I have seen it with my own eyes; nobody told me!"

So she ordered her servants to call him and said, "Give him a hundred pounds," so that he wouldn't go out and say, "The body of the sultan's wife is such-and-such."

She did not tell her husband; she just said, "Give this man a hundred pounds."

And so they did.

Now our friend took the hundred pounds, gathered himself up, and went on a spending spree and had a good time. All the hundred pounds were gone. He saved nothing; he invested nothing. After the money was gone, he returned to the fence, to the same place, and this time he started yelling, "I have seen it with my own eyes; nobody told me!"

They called him again: "Man, take this hundred pounds again. Do not say that you have seen anything."

He gathered himself up, took the hundred pounds, and ran out. Just as he had spent the first hundred, so he spent the second. He returned for the third time, yelling, "I have seen it with my own eyes; nobody told me!"

The sultan's wife became very unhappy and went to the sultan and told him, "It seems that this man saw me getting out of the bath, and it seems that I was naked. Now he is going to disgrace us by saying, 'I have seen it with my own eyes; nobody told me.'"

The sultan was very angry and ordered, "Call him!"

The sultan intended to do him harm, to kill him. (May this happen to the distant one.)

"Come here, man! What are you saying? You are saying 'I have seen it with my own eyes; nobody told me.' What have you really seen?"

For the sultan wanted to test him.

The man said, "Your majesty, I dreamt that I was washing for my prayers, and this one was washing for prayers, and that one was washing for prayers, and this one, and that one. Everybody's faucet was gushing except mine; water was only coming out of it drop by drop. I tried to get more water, so I got a nail to widen the faucet. Ooops, it was blocked completely. So I realized that that was my predestined livelihood, and for that reason I have been saying, 'I have seen it with my own eyes; nobody told me!'"

The sultan said to him, "All right! I will make you happy. Go to the top of such-and-such minaret. Take a ball with you, and throw it from above as hard as you can. From the place where the ball lands, I will grant you all the land for that same distance in a circle around the minaret. It will all be your property, and you will be a rich man. Your situation will improve."

He said, "Will do, your majesty."

Our friend gathered himself up and went to the top of the minaret. Being so greedy and wanting to change what had been predestined for him, he threw the ball with such force that it plucked him off the minaret. He landed down in the street. His blood formed the following: "I [God] made him poor; you [the king] wanted to make him rich. I took his life; now you give it back to him!"

Recorded from Tilib (see informant note to tale no. 11) in March 1969. He heard the story in his childhood from Sayyid Ahmad, the village's raconteur.

Conflict between personified good and evil, which harks back to ancient Egyptian religion, is the focal point of this story. A modern Egyptian belief is expressed in a truism: "Truth and falsehood are brothers," meaning that they are closely related and are always present side by side.

The narrator stated, "This is a story of wisdom. As far as I am concerned, it could actually have happened; why not?" He added, however, "But it is told as a tale, not as something that really took place."

ONCE THERE WAS a man, el-Aṣeel (the Noble), who was sick and tired of his life. One day he put some bread in a handkerchief and made a parcel, filled a water jug with water, and set out as a wanderer. A neighbor of his, el-Khasees (the Vile), met him. He said to this neighbor, "By God, I am fed up. I'll pull myself together and leave this town."

His neighbor said to him, "Wouldn't you take me with you?"

He answered, "Well, go get yourself some rations and a water jug with water and come—and let us do what? Move 'from God's countries to God's peoples.'"

The two of them left. The Noble was talking to the Vile and saying to him, "Let's eat."

The Vile answered him, "Let's eat your food first. Later we will eat the food I have."

So he [the Noble] answered him, "Why? It's better that each one eats his own rations."

The Vile said to him, "It's better that we eat one ration first and drink all the water in one jug, then turn to mine."

(The Vile was telling the Noble, that is.) The important thing is that the Noble opened his parcel, and they ate breakfast. At noon, of course, they sat down to rest and ate dinner, and at supper time they sat down and ate supper. This went on until all his food was gone. The food and water of the Noble were all gone now.

The following day they wanted to eat breakfast. Now the Noble's food was all gone. The Vile sat down and untied his bundle and started eating. The other one came to reach out for some food, but the Vile shouted at him, "No! Don't you dare touch it! If you (may this happen to the distant one) eat one morsel, I'll pluck out your (may this happen to the distant one's) eyes."

He asked unbelievingly, "Why, my friend? We have already agreed."

He answered him, "There is no agreement! That's final! You eat with me, I'll pluck out your eye."

'Now east became west.' Our friend (the Vile) sat down, ate, drank water, tied his parcel, gathered himself together, and left. At noon it was very hot. He sat down again and ate while the other remained without breakfast and dinner. He [the Vile] sat down and ate while the other one watched him eating. After this he tied his food in the parcel and got up and left. At supper time the Noble said to him, "I'm very hungry now, and I can't keep on going any longer."

He answered him sharply, "Make your choice! I pluck out an eye, you eat with me!"

"Oh no, my friend, I am—" He answered him, "Impossible."

Naturally his eye was dear to him. The other one tied his food into the parcel and left. Three days went on like that. The Noble had tightened his belt around his stomach so that he would not feel his hunger.

The fourth day came; now he could not walk. He needed to eat and drink some water. The important thing is that he [the Noble] said to him, "Well, my friend, let me have one morsel of bread to keep myself alive until we get to a town."

He answered him, "It's final! I pluck out your eye, you eat with me!"

Later on, he [the Noble] said, "This affair is in God's hands. Pluck out my eye, and let me eat."

Now our friend immediately plucked out his eye and let him eat.

Now as he was eating he choked and grabbed hold of the water jug. The other one quickly snatched it away and said to him, "I pluck out your other eye."

He implored him, "Do me a favor."

"Never!"

The important thing was that the morsel was going neither down nor up. The Vile plucked out his other eye and relieved his choking. He took him by the hand, and the two of them went on together.

As they were walking they came to a well by the road. The Vile—for the other one could not see now—brought him to the edge of the well and pushed him in. He left him there and went away.

Our friend was now at the bottom of the well, and midnight came. The fact is that this well was predestined for the gathering of the four *aqtab* [arch-saints] of the world (such as el-Sayyid el-Badawi, and el-Mitwalli). When they gathered, one of them said, "Above this well there is a tree whose leaves will cure blindness—for those who have lost their sight. One needs to get a green leaf, rub it in the palm of his hand, and apply it to his eyes like this. And then, God willing, he will be cured."

Our friend heard these words and kept silent. He stayed there until the morning.

There were people who left their villages to pasture their (do not blame me) animals around this well and in the hills. One of them looked in the well and was startled. He exclaimed, "In the name of God the merciful and compassionate!"

This child called to that child, and that child called to another. "Afreet! Afreet!"

At the bottom of the well the man yelled to them, "Children, I'm human, and my name is So-and-so."

The children took the ropes from around the (do not blame me) animals' necks, tied them together, and lowered the rope into the well. All the children, twenty or thirty of them, pulled the rope and pulled him out.

He said to them, "Children, may God increase your livelihood for that."

He sat underneath the tree until everything quieted down. He hugged the tree and climbed it. He picked some leaves and put them in his bosom and climbed down. He sat underneath the tree, rubbed one of the leaves in the palm of his hand like this, put some on his eyes, and found out that they had opened wide.

He gathered himself up, put some leaves in his pocket, and left happily.

He walked and walked until he arrived in a town. In this town there was a palace, and there were heads hanging in front of it. He inquired and was told, "Sultan So-and-so has a princess whose eyesight has gone. Whoever cures her may ask whatever he pleases, but if he fails he will be killed."

The important thing is that whoever entered to treat her was given the conditions first: "Are you willing to take the risk of going in?"

"Yes, I am."

"If you don't cure her, we will take your head off with a sword and hang your head [outside] for others to learn from."

"Understood!"

When our friend came and stood before them, they saw that he was pitiful and his clothes were torn. The guards sent him away and said to him, "Can't you see what's happening?"

He left. He became very impatient to get in, for he had the means which he himself had tried. Now one of them thought, "By God, cure might come at the hands of this pitiful thing."

So he shouted, "Hey you! Yes, you."

He [the Noble] went to him.

He said, "Go up!"

They took him up, and he entered her room. He got a leaf out of his pocket, rubbed it in the palm of his hand, and put it on her eyes. To her astonishment, she found out that her eyes were as sharp sighted as they could be. The king [i.e., the sultan] ruling this town had nobody else but himself and his daughter; himself, his daughter, and his wife, that is. He lived with them in the same palace. The sultan was an aging man. After a short while, he died. After he died, the Noble reigned after him with the sultan's daughter next to him. The two of them ruled the town.

Days passed by, and fortunes were reversed. Now the Vile, roaming the streets wearing a blue *galabiyya* [the characteristic garment of poor peasants], was very miserable. Now our friend was sitting on the balcony, I mean the terrace of his palace. He saw our friend coming at a distance. He called the guards and ordered, "Bring that man here."

They brought him.

"Where are you going, man?"

He answered humbly, "Oh, by God, your highness the sultan, I have no aim but 'God's door.'"

The sultan said, "Put him in prison," and they did. Shortly after that, he ordered the guards to take him, bathe him, tailor some clothes for him, and put him in shape. The guards took him, bathed him, and put good food for him on the dining table; and every day they fed him well and changed his pitiful clothes. In short, he was extremely happy inside the prison.

Now our friend was thinking, "Why is the sultan doing this? They must be up to something."

You know, he was afraid. Good food, good clothes? Later the sultan got the keys and entered his room and said to him, "Brother, do you know me?"

He answered, "No."

He [the sultan] said to him, "Not at all?"

He said, "No."

He said, "I am your friend and companion who has eaten bread and salt with you on the road. I ate with you for one eye, and you eased my choking for the other. For that, God has been generous to me. However, in turn, I will not be a miser with you; ask me something that is big. Ask me for money, for land, ask me for big authority in the palace; I'll give it to you in a second."

When that other one realized that he was really his companion, he became intimate with him and asked boldly, "What did you do?"

He answered, "By God, after you had thrown me into the well the four arch-saints gathered and said that the tree over the well had leaves that cured blindness. In the morning child shepherds gathered to pasture their animals. [They shouted], 'Afreet! Satan! This and that!' I said to them, 'I am human, and my name is So-and-so.' They pulled me out. I got a leaf and put it on my eye. I found out that my eyesight had returned to me."

He [the Vile] said to him, "I don't believe you."

He said, "By God, this is what happened."

—[the Vile still did not believe the Noble.]

The Noble gave him many details about the food and the town and things they did together and finally said to him, "Now do you believe that I am So-and-so? Can you live with me in the same town?"

Now our friend the Vile replied in hate, "No! It's impossible to live with you. I don't want anything from you. Here are your clothes, and here is your food.

He took off his clothes and put his hand in his mouth and "Ghauuu," vomited all the food. He put on his dirty rags and went out running until he got to the well, where he threw himself in. At midnight four (away from you) jinn gathered there. One jinni was saying, "You know it was I who built this well."

The second said, "No it was I who built it!"

The third said, "No, it was I who carried its bricks on this shoulder of mine!"

The fourth said, "All right, this well must be divided four ways!"

Another said, "No, no, neither this nor that. It must be torn down!"

Boom, boom, boom! It was turned into a heap of dust!

· 15 · *Sultan Hasan**

Recorded in January 1970 from 70-year-old H. Mitwalli, nicknamed "Abu-'Aabbas," from 'Aizbat Bilal, a hamlet on the eastern outskirts of Cairo. Until his retirement about four years earlier, Mitwalli worked as a cook for a *firashàh* (catering service).

Mitwalli can barely read and write and is viewed by his friends as a good narrator. He narrates slowly, in a soft tone. His profession took him "to many a place and many an occasion where narration and interesting social talk is needed: weddings, funerals, saint's birthdays, circumcision occasions, and others and others," he said.

Mitwalli is currently living near his eldest son, a teamster; the son's wife looks after him. He sees similarities between his own life and that of the hero of the story: "We both suffered in our youth. Now I am comfortable. My son is providing all the rights due me in my old age."

In Muslim jurisprudence, unless otherwise specified at the signing of the marrige contract, the right to instant divorce is the man's alone. A husband may divorce his wife and "restore" her only twice. After the third divorce, restoration of the wife is permissible *only* if she has already been married to someone else and divorced from him. As a legal trick, so that a man may marry his ex-wife for the third time, a short-term marriage between her and another person may be arranged. The man involved in such an interim marriage is called *muḥallil,* literally, "legitimizer." The hero of our story was forced to play this role. The temperamental mayor, the well-treated second wife, the powerful "Arab" family, and the village's blessed old man are all true-to-life representatives found in typical Egyptian villages.

Belief in dreams as instructive of future events and belief in predestination are central to the plot. Our story has an implicit etiological function as the source of the adage, "When it departs it will sever the chains, and when it comes, it comes on a hair." That is, when predestined, neither can bad fortune be averted, no matter how hard one tries, nor can good fortune be lost, no matter how careless one may be. Sultan Hasan's mosque, mentioned at the end of this narrative, is considered an architectural feat representing a revolution in Muslim architecture. It is one of the main tourist sites in Old Cairo.

THIS IS A STORY about Sultan Hasan whose mosque is in the Citadel district. State that there is no God but God.

Sultan Hasan had geomancers. Every day they read the future in the sand and told him how things were going in his kingdom.

One day he sent for a geomancer and said, "Geomancer, I had a dream. It's a bad dream. Read your sand and tell me what it means."

The geomancer read his sand and wept. Sultan Hasan asked him, "Geomancer, why are you weeping?"

He replied, "Promise me safety."

Sultan Hasan said, "Safety is yours."

The geomancer said, "Reassure me."

The Sultan said, "Again, safety is yours."

The geomancer told him, "The world will mistreat you for seven years. If you leave your children alone, it will mistreat only you. If you take them with you, it will mistreat all of you, and the kingdom will no longer be yours."

The sultan asked, "'Has anybody seen the camel?'" [i.e., "Will you tell anyone else about what happened?"]

The geomancer replied, "'Nor the camel man'" [i.e., "As far as I'm concerned, I have seen nothing"].

Sultan Hasan said to him, "Keep this story a secret between you and me," and asked, "Have I got much time?"

"You have got a week, seven days!" he replied.

One day before the week was over, he gathered his children and said to them, "I'm going to the el-Sham countries [Syria, Lebanon, and Palestine] for a tour. No matter how long it should take me, one year, two, four, five, make no effort to find me."

He left by night and no one saw him except God, 'glory be to him.' He took nothing with him but a mule with a saddlebag full of money.

He came to a river and found a ferryman. He called to the ferryman, "Take me across." (The dawn of the eighth day was about to break).

The ferryman said, "All right. Bring your mule and step aboard."

Sultan Hasan got hold of the mule's chain and pulled it on to the ferry. The mule bolted, broke the chain, and leaped into the water. It sank on the spot.

The ferryman shouted to him, "Haven't you got any brains?" and slapped him on the side of the face.

Sultan Hasan crossed the river and left the man alone. On the other bank he met a good old man sitting under a tree. The man called to him, "Peace be upon you, Hasan."

Hasan replied, "And upon you be peace."

The man said to him, "Take off your costume, your shoes, and your headdress, and put on this *galabiyya* and this skull cap [the garb of peasants].

When Hasan did, the man said to him [signaling with his hand for him to go], "May safety be with you."

He kept on going until he reached a little town. He met a man driving an animal loaded with corn stalks and said to him, "Paternal uncle who is passing by, couldn't you bring me some stalks?"

The man answered, "Will do, paternal uncle. What's your name?"

He replied, "My name is Hasan," and did not say, "I was a king," or anything like that.

The man gave him some stalks, and he built a little hut for himself there. From that time on people sent him things. Maybe a woman would send him some milk, another a loaf of bread. They believed he was a blessed man and did this for his blessings.

He stayed there until the seven years had almost passed. The *'Aumda* (mayor) of this village was a ferocious man (away from you) and he was married to two [women]. He loved one of the two very much, as much as his eye. The other one he didn't love as much as the first one. He had a palace built for his favorite wife outside the village so that she could be by herself. She was exclusively for his pleasure. But unfortunately he was a man who swore divorce too many times. He swore her divorced once, twice, and the third time it was all over. Now he could not restore her except through a *muḥallil* [legitimizer].

The girl's family were Arabs who were strong and generous. They were even more powerful than the mayor's family. The mayor went to the judge to restore his wife.

The judge said to him, "This will not work out unless you get a legitimizer to spend one night with her and divorce her in the morning. This will solve your dilemma, and without this it will not be solved."

They thought about somebody for the job: "Who? Who? Who?"

They remembered the sheik who happened to be Hasan. At that time he was (away from you) looking like an ogre. His beard was not cared for, water had not touched his body for a long time, his nails were that long [as long as two joints on the index finger]!

The mayor sent one of his guardsmen to call him. Hasan refused and threatened to leave the village if they made him come. When the guardsman went to the mayor and told him this, the mayor slapped him and said, "You are (away from you) a *khawal* [homosexual]," and he sent another one.

He said to this next one, "Drag him on his face."

When Hasan found that there was no escape, he said, "I leave my affairs to God," and went with him.

They took Hasan and two witnesses to the judge. When they explained the matter to him, he said, "I'm not fit for marriage or for women."

They answered him, "You'll do it by order, or you'll die."

They wrote the marriage contract and took him to her villa, which had two stories. Before that, the mayor had ordered Hasan to be given a bath, shaved, and cleaned up quite a bit. Hasan walked into the first story and stayed there.

The lady sent her servant to say to Hasan, "I would like to see you upstairs."

Hasan refused to go upstairs. The lady herself went down and said to him, "Aren't you my husband according to God's law and his Prophet's?"

—[No reply.]

She led him upstairs, and he sat down with his face to the floor all the time. She spoke to him; he did not reply.

"Would you drink tea?"

He did not reply.

"Eat this bite?"

He did not reply.

As she (do not blame me) was caressing his hair, she found the mark of the crown and the royal seal. She realized that he was a king. She begged him to go to bed with her, but he refused to come close to her.

In the morning the judge and the mayor came. She would not open the door to them and spoke to them from her window. "What do you want?"

"We want Hasan."

"Will you go away, or do I have to pour dirty water on you?"

The mayor implored her, "So-and-so, this is not nice."

She answered him, "You are not my husband, nor do I even know you."

They implored, "So-and-so, this can't be."

She said, "I've said what I have to say, and that's final."

They couldn't do anything to her, for her family was greater than the mayor's in wealth and power.

Now the mayor went to her brother and told him the story.

Her brothers were decent people. They said to him, "Our youngest brother is getting married two days from now. We also have two boys to be circumcised on the lap of the bride in her bridal array. On this occasion we can invite them, and we will discuss the matter."

In the morning her brother went to invite her to the wedding. Hasan told her, "I will not go," and she answered him, "If you do not go, I will not go."

Finally, he said to her, "If I go, I will go on foot as your squire."

Until now, he hadn't really touched her!

At the wedding celebration, horsemen were playing the *birgas* [polo]. Enthusiasm seized him, for he was a horseman—in olden days a person could not be a king without being a good horseman. He jumped on a horse and flashed, whooosh-sht, whooosh-sht, back and forth. The spectators were petrified. His wife was looking out of a window on the upper floor. After the game was over, he returned to the crowd.

At a wedding like this, they take great pride in the gifts given to the couple. A scribe was registering who gave what. Sultan Hasan, coming triumphantly from his game, shouted, "Scribe, take this down: if things go back to the way they were, there will be a bushel of gold for the bridegroom. And take this down, scribe: if things go back to the way they were, there will be a bushel of gold for the circumciser. And scribe, take this down: if things go back to the way they were, there will be a bushel of gold for the scribe."

Now the brother of the lady became very angry. He came to Hasan and said, "What's this, liar! You are truly a liar! Bushel what? And gold what? and he slapped him on the face.

And Hasan said, "Scribe, take this down: if things go back to the way they were, the arm that carried the hand that slapped me will be cut off."

When the slap landed on Hasan's cheek, his wife was watching, and it was as if it landed on her own face. She went down immediately and took him by the hand. They mounted on the horse, and they left.

When they got home, he said to her, "Listen, you are my wife, and I am your husband. You stay here where you are, and when things return to the way they were, I will be back for you." For the seven years were about over.

He left and took the same road home. When he reached the spot where he had met the sheik who took his clothes, he found him still sitting there. The sheik called to him, "Hasan, take your clothes."

He put his clothes on and went to the ferryboat. He looked into the water and saw a hair [from a mule's mane] floating on the surface. With the tips of his fingers, he pulled the hair, and out came the mule with the saddlebag full of gold.

He turned to the ferryman and slapped him.

The man asked in astonishment, "Why did you slap me?"

Hasan answered him, "Seven years ago you slapped me 'when it severed the chains and went away. Now that it is coming, it comes on a hair!'" (That is how life is.)

He reconciled himself to the man by giving him some money and made him content. The man forgave him, and he left.

Now he came to Cairo and found somebody else ruling in his place. He went to a friend and told him the story. The friend said, "Remain here until we can arrange things."

They got two hundred good men and gave them arms and formed a small army.

Now the man who was taking his place used to give the sermon for Friday prayers in the mosque. He spoke of nothing but how bad Sultan Hasan was.

On a Friday, Sultan Hasan, his friend, and all their men went to the mosque. As the man ruling in his place went up to the pulpit, he said nothing but "Sultan Hasan is evil. Sultan Hasan is this; Sultan Hasan is that."

Now our friend Hasan was infuriated. He walked up to the man and chopped off his head. He fought this man's army—some were killed, and some ran away; as for those who had nothing to do with what happened, they were left in peace.

He went back to his palace and was reunited with his family. After he had done this, he went back to the el-Sham countries and made good all his promises. He brought his wife back, and they lived in stability and prosperity.

If you don't believe me, go to Sultan Hasan's mosque. You will find blood stains still on the pulpit.

Recorded in October 1969 from Kenzi Nubian Sheik 'A. Isma'Aeel, 63 years old. He is literate and has recently retired from his post as the head of guards of the village of Girshah. Isma'Aeel has traveled widely within Egypt and held numerous minor jobs in Cairo and other major cities. He is considered a raconteur and is referred to as *kummaji.* He usually narrates in Kenzi Nubian (locally referred to in Arabic as *ruṭān,* which means rattling), but he spoke to me in Arabic. Like all Nubian males of his age and travel experience, he is perfectly bilingual. Isma'Aeel does not narrate to his children. When he was about to tell me a story with an overt erotic episode, he asked his 18-year-old son to leave the room and stated, "I just want to spare him the bumps" (i.e., the shock of being exposed to erotic motifs).

Isma'Aeel had the tendency to claim that he either "composed" or "got from a book" his "stories of wisdom," but no such claims were made concerning other types of tales. Evidently he considered most of the serious stories to be his own (see informant note to tale no. 10) but thought it prestigious to attribute them to printed sources. He could not name his published sources, however, and finally stated, "What I really meant was that they deserve to be in books."

Nomadic values and skills are portrayed in this story. Two types of skills which were referred to in early Arabic writings as "sciences" are those of *qiyāfah* (tracking) and *firāsah* (physiognomy or judging of character). The belief that legitimacy of birth produces a good character while illegitimacy produces a bad character is an essential aspect of folk theories about personality. The importance of hospitality in nomadic communities is clearly projected in the tale. Failure to observe the strict rules of courtesy are indicative of a person's bad character and hence illegitimate birth.

Muslim jurisprudence frowns upon willing more than one-third of one's property and sets specific rules for inheritance among all members of the family of the deceased. A folk saying states, "He who deprives an heir of his [legitimate] share will have God deprive him of his share in paradise." Our story goes against this rule of inheritance.

PRAY ON BEHALF OF the Prophet. Once there was a rich man, I mean a millionaire. When he was about to die, he said, "I want to make a will."

So everybody gathered around him. He said, "I have three sons, all of whom are named Muhammad. One of them will not inherit anything from me."

Immediately after the man had said this, three days later, he died. His sons were grown up, and each one of them was more intelligent than the others. They said, "We would like to execute the will of our father."

They did not know which one of them should not inherit or which one the father meant. They said, "Let's go to the judge of the Arabs to judge among us. After he has made his judgment, 'the full ones will pour into the empty one'; that is, we should not deprive him."

They said, "Fine."

They all agreed and said, "Let's go."

They went to whom? To the judge!

As they were on their way to the judge, they met another Arab. The Arab asked them, "Fellows, haven't you seen a lost camel?"

The first son, that's the eldest Muhammad, said, "Your camel is one-eyed."

The middle Muhammad said, "Your camel is tail-less."

The third Muhammad said, "Your camel was loaded with sugar. We haven't seen your camel."

The man was surprised and said, "Oh, now you have made my camel one eyed, tail-less, and loaded with sugar, which it is, and you finally tell me you haven't seen it! Undoubtedly you stole it!"

There had only been three of them going to the judge; now they had become four. Our friend, the owner of the camel joined them.

They reached the home of the judge at a late hour. It was about half past nine. Of course the judge was an Arab. He was already asleep. He had to meet them well. He ordered his maid to prepare food for them. He did not meet them himself. There was a little window, a concealed window, from which the judge overheard the conversation that went among his guests.

Now these four persons sat down to eat. After the food was served and the table was set, the three brothers said, "By God, we will not eat. We cannot eat this food."

The eldest Muhammad said, "This judge is 'son of sin!'"

No, no, no—What's this!

The middle Muhammad said, "Not only is he 'son of sin,' but this meat was originally a dog."

The third Muhammad said, "Even this bread is profane. The woman who prepared the dough (no offense, do not blame me) had her period."

Now what? They found fault with the meal from all sides. Now the fourth person, the Arab who joined them, said, "I can't eat profane food," and he too left.

When the judge heard this, he entered the room and said, "Now, what have you said?"

The eldest brother said, "I said that you (distant one) are 'son of sin.'"

The second brother said, "And I said that the animal is a dog."

The third one, the youngest son, said, "And I said that the woman who prepared the bread had her period. She was profane."

The judge looked at the fourth man and asked, "Haven't you said anything?"

He said, "No, your honor, I'm just coming for something else. I just have a question for you."

The judge asked them, "How come? How were you able to say that I'm 'son of sin,' and that the meat I served you was a dog, and that the woman who prepared the dough was having her period?"

They answered him, "Investigate and you will find out. That is, investigate inside your house, and you will find out."

Immediately the judge went inside to his mother and said, "Mother, my body is feeling itchy. Would you please light up the stove and heat some water for me?"

When the water was boiling, he said to his mother, "Mother,

would you please—even though this might be rude—hand me the towel from the bath."

His mother went to get the towel, and he ran inside after her and said, "By God, if you don't tell me the truth of the matter about my birth, I'm going to push you into this boiling water!"

She said, "I swear by glorious God that I've never been touched by a human being all my life."

Then he answered her, "Then from where did you get me! [sarcastically] From the angels?"

She said, "No, I mean anybody other than your father. Your father was a sheik. He was a very good man but the day, I mean the night he slept with me, he said to me, 'Today I ate from the dates of So-and-so without having asked him.' Therefore you are actually 'son of sin' but not a bastard. You are not illegitimate."

The father realized that he had eaten something that belonged to someone else without having his permission. Therefore the son was actually only "son of sin."

Then the judge said, "Ahhh!"

He really realized that he was "son of sin" and that the boys were right.

Now about the meat. The judge, of course, had bought the animal from So-and-so. He went to him and said, "So-and-so, this morning I bought an animal from you. Did you raise this animal in your own pasture?"

The man said, "No, but I got it from Haji Moustafa."

The judge went to Haji Moustafa and said, "Haji Moustafa, did you raise that animal that you sold to So-and-so in your own pasture?"

Haji Moustafa said, "Yes, it was born here, but the day it was born its mother died. We had no way to keep it alive except that we had a dog that had given birth recently, and then we were forced to let the lamb suckle the milk of the dog so that it would live."

Ahhh, the lamb got the smell of the dog.

Now the last, and a really sensitive spot. The blood in the bread. The judge went to his wife and said, "How did you dare let me have intercourse with you last night? You did not tell me you were having your period. You have made me sin."

She answered, "No, my husband, I was not."

Then he said, "How come the bread had traces of a period in it?"

She said, "My dear husband, the one who prepared the bread is our maid and not myself."

He went inside to the maid and said, "Murgana, do you have your period now?"

And she said, "Yes, master, streams, streams, streams."

"Oh, may God take you and your streams!"

Now he realized that all that they said was true. He went to the three wise ones and said to the eldest, "Muhammad, come here. How did you know that I am 'son of sin'?"

Muhammad said, "You have gone to great trouble to be courteous and generous. After having gone to the trouble of fixing us food , meat, jam, and honey, you sent all this with the maid. You did not trouble yourself to come and welcome us. You were inflated by the devil's spirit [i.e., conceit]. Had you come to us and said, 'Fellows, I have already eaten, and if I eat any more it will upset me; you go ahead and consider this house yours,' then we would have known that you were legitimate. But with this inflation, with the spirit of the devil, we realized that you were 'son of sin.'"

He [the judge] went to the second and asked him, "How did you know that this animal was a dog?"

He said, "The moment we sat down to eat, the smell of dog struck my nose."

As for the third, he asked him, "How did you know that the person who prepared this meal had her period? Did you see any blood in it?"

He said, "No."

Then the judge asked him, "How did you know? Nobody can tell."

The boy answered, "During period time, if the woman does not wear something over her head tightly, her hair falls down and gets into everything she does. There were plenty of hairs in that bread."

The judge said, "Fellows, you are right, for I have investigated and found out that the truth corresponds to all you have said.

Now I would like to know why this man is complaining against you."

The eldest son said, "This man asked us, 'Have you seen my camel?'; and I told him, 'Your camel is one eyed.' My younger brother said, 'Your camel is tail-less.' My youngest brother said, 'Your camel was loaded with sugar.' We also told him that we hadn't seen his camel. He accused us of having stolen it."

Then the judge was surprised and said, "Well, how come? If you tell him that his camel is one eyed, tail-less, and loaded with sugar, then you must have seen it."

The eldest said, "No, we didn't. It's just that as we were going down the road I saw its traces. I found out that the camel had been eating only from the right side of the path. Had it had two eyes, it would have eaten from the left as well as the right, and the left side had some good things growing on it."

The judge said, "All right now, you second Muhammad, how did you know the camel was tail-less, for a camel does not see with its tail?"

Muhammad said, "No, it does not, but—as the camel was going down the road, it made droppings. Had it had a tail, it would have scattered the droppings to the sides of the road, but since it did not have a tail, all its droppings fell down right over its tracks. This is how I knew it did not have a tail."

The judge said, "You are right. Now how about you, third Muhammad. How did you know the camel was loaded with sugar?"

Muhammad said, "Later, down the road we found out that the camel got tired and knelt down to rest. When it stood up, it shook itself. This scattered some sugar on the ground, and this is how we knew that the camel was loaded with sugar."

The judge called the man and said to him, "Man, go home. Your camel is not with these three. And you had better not say much, for if you do they are going to make you a 'son of sin' as they did me."

The man went away without saying a word.

Now the judge asked them, "What do you want of me? Why did you come to me in the first place?"

They said, "Our father, may God be merciful with him, passed

away. Before he did, he made a will and said, 'I have three sons
whose names are Muhammad; only one of them does not inherit
anything from me.' We would like to know which one he meant.
We all really know the one he meant and the one he meant
actually knows himself. But we don't want to offend anyone. We
would like to hear the judgment from you, and after that 'the full
one will pour into the empty one.'"

The judge said, "All right," then he took the eldest into a
room, far away from his brothers. He asked him, "Did you know
your father well?"

He said, "Yes."

He said, "Were you there when he died?"

He said, "Yes."

He asked, "Do you know where the grave is?"

He said, "Yes."

Then the judge said, "Well, if you really knew where his grave
is, then you could get me a sign from it. Could you get me
something from his grave so that I'd know that you really know
it?"

He answered angrily, "May God prevent this from happening!
Do you really want me to dig out my father's grave? My father
has given us everything, and now we can't even let him rest in
peace in his own grave!"

The judge told him, "You may go back."

The judge asked the second son to come. He asked him the
same thing. The answers of the middle one were exactly like the
answers of the first one. The judge told him, "You may go back."

Now—he went and got the third son and asked him the same
thing. The third son said, "Of course, I can get you anything, you
just name it."

Then the judge said, "You are the one who will not inherit."

Now they knew which one of them should not inherit. They
went back to their home, 'and they lived happily together until
they were met by the destroyer of every pleasure and the dis-
perser of every group, glory be to the one who is ever living and
never dies.'

And I was with them and just came back.

Part III
Tales Based on
Religious Themes

Taped from Tilib (see informant note for tale no. 11). He heard this tale from Khaleefah, an old peasant in his village.

Our tale contradicts formal religious dogma, which states that a human being may not know when or where he will die and that he may not witness or converse with the angel of death.

Although this tale is based on religious themes and characters, it should not be viewed as a religious legend. It is "just a tale"; it "didn't happen or anything like that, but it still has a [significant] meaning," stated the informant.

ONCE THERE WAS somebody who borrowed from everybody in his town. People disliked him very much, and he got tired of his life. He went to another town, and the same thing happened. Nobody trusted him with anything. He wanted to commit suicide, for there was nothing else in life for him.

He went to the top of a high mountain and threw himself off; he found himself sitting down at the foot of the mountain, unharmed. He got a knife and plunged it into himself, but he found that the blade had become as soft as dough or paper. The same thing happened several times.

One day as he was sitting down thinking to himself, he found Azrael sitting next to him. Azrael said to him, "Brother, you are trying to kill yourself, but your life must last until you are forty."

The man said, "I'm sick and tired of this world."

Azrael said to him, "What do you think of this: I will befriend you. Will you be my friend and be honest with me? Or will you betray me?"

The man exclaimed, "Be friends? What can you do for me?"

Azrael said, "Pretend to be a doctor and go through [different] countries. Now you can see me. If you see me at the head of a patient, you will realize that his life span has elapsed and that he is gone. If you find me sitting at the patient's feet, you will realize that his life span has not elapsed and that he will live. Then you can say, 'I will cure him.' Do anything for him! No sooner will I have left than he will sit up and get well, and you may ask for whatever fee you wish."

The man replied, "That's great!" And they agreed.

Now our friend Azrael left, and the man started wandering about, shouting, "A curing doctor who can cure all ailments." [Narrator laughs.] No one paid any attention to him.

One day he came to a town where there was a princess who was ill. All the doctors had failed to cure her, and they had had it advertised all over the place—on walls, trains, and everything—that whoever cured her would be granted an estate and this and that and would marry her. He tried to enter her palace, but the guards kept him away. He tried to force his way through, but they beat him up and sent him away.

Finally somebody said, "Why don't you let him in? Maybe he is a 'man of God.'"

They let him in, and he went up to see the princess. He saw Azrael sitting at her feet. He asked for some milk in a cup and said to them, "Close the door and ask everybody to leave us alone." Maybe he drank the milk himself, maybe he gave it to the princess; it didn't matter. Azrael left, and the girl got well immediately.

They gave him a big celebration and the sultan asked him, "What do you ask for?"

He said, "Nothing."

"Nothing! This can't be." The sultan ordered, "Give him a farm!"

They gave him a forty-acre estate with all its servants and animals. From that time on he became famous. His name changed from "Sheik So-and-so" to "Doctor So-and-so." Everybody heard of him; he became rich and owned farms and servants and guards. It was [like] a second kingdom. Of course all these days counted against him, for they were being deducted from his forty years.

One day when life was still blossoming before his eyes, he found Azrael sitting next to him. Of course he was surprised and asked him, "What are you doing here?"

Azrael answered, "We had agreed that you would not betray me and I would help you. Now your time is up. You have four hours left. What do you want to do during that time?"

The man said, *"Ya salam* [Oh, my]! Four hours! All these years went by so fast?"

They argued with each other until he had only ten minutes left in his life. The man asked Azrael, "Would it be possible to let me have a short prayer for God?"

Azrael said, "Not only a short one, take twice as long."

The man said, "I'm afraid of you."

And Azrael said, "On my honor, I will not take your soul until you have prayed."

The man still said, "No, I'm afraid. Swear by God that you will not touch me or touch my soul until I have finished my prayers."

Reluctantly, Azrael swore to that. As soon as Azrael finished his oath, the man who was standing up ready to perform the prayers turned his back to him saying [rudely], "I swear by your mother, I will never pray!"

Now Azrael had sworn, and his oath [because of its gravity] would make God's throne shake. Now Azrael followed him. Of course he had to take his soul away, but he could not break the oath with which he had trapped himself.

The man mounted on one of his horses and said "Escape!" [That is, he escaped as fast as he could.] He spent days on the racing horse, but whenever he looked behind he would find Azrael right on his tail. He would spur his horse and go faster. This went on for as long as it did. Every time he looked back, there was our friend Azrael. Of course there is no escape (you know that in the Koran [4:78] God says, "Wheresoever ye may be, death will overtake you even though ye were in lofty towers").

Finally, one time the man looked behind him and did not see Azrael. He thought that it was because of a trick or the dust from his horse, so he kept on going. He looked back again, but no Azrael. He stopped to catch his breath. This time he looked around him. Still no Azrael. So his heart quieted a little, and he went slower, but still he was not completely secure. He kept on looking back; still no Azrael.

Now he was very thirsty, tired, and hungry. His horse also was exhausted and about to perish. He looked behind him; still no Azrael. When he looked ahead up the road, he saw a beautiful palace with a garden the like of which an eye had never seen. He went to it and saw a beautiful girl, 'glory be to the Creator for his creation,' a stunning beauty. But there was not a human soul around her. He asked her for some water; she gave him water and food for himself and for his horse. He looked around; still there was no Azrael.

He strengthened his heart and asked the girl, "Who are you? What are you doing here all alone?"

The girl looked as if she were a houri from paradise. She answered, "My father wished me to fulfill a promise, to be the reward for the man for whom I'm predestined. When I grew up and people in the kingdom learned about my beauty, everyone wanted me. All the young men of the kingdom wanted to marry me. But my father said, 'No! She has been predestined for one man; none of you is the one.' Finally he decided to build this palace in the desert with everything an eye had seen and an ear had heard except men, to keep me pure for the one for whom I've been predestined."

Now our friend looked at the girl; she appealed to him, naturally, for she was so beautiful—a houri from paradise! He said to her, "Here I am; I am the one! Will you marry me?"

She replied, "Yes!"

He said, "But where will we find a marriage judge and two witnesses [as required in legal practice]?"

She answered, "We are both of legal age. Witnesses are required in case of malicious intent. Do you intend to deny having been my husband?"

He exclaimed, "No! God forbid!"

He said to her, "Give me yourself in marriage according to God's creed and his Prophet's."

She answered, "I've given you myself in marriage according to God's creed and his Prophet's."

Now for the consummation of the marriage. The girl went to bed, and he followed. When he wanted to start things, she said, "Hold! I am a virgin; this is our first time. Aren't you going to perform the prayers? [as traditional practices require on a wedding night]?"

As soon as he heard the word "prayers," he jumped out of bed. He exclaimed, "It is not required. It is only a preference—"

She said, "No prayer, no consummation of marriage!"

Our friend became confused. He looked around; there was no Azrael. He looked at the girl, under the bed covers. She looked—(you know) everything was there! He had 'one eye on paradise and one eye on hell.' He started the prayers [narrator raises his hands to the sides of his face to simulate the event]: "God is greater . . .," but still his eyes roved about the room; still no Azrael. So very hurriedly he finished the "two kneelings" prayer and took off his clothes (you know) and jumped into bed. When he lifted the covers off the girl, the houri from paradise, he did not find the girl. Instead he found Azrael! He was sitting beside him on the heap of dirt where he first saw him. Azrael jumped at him [snatching away his hand] and said, "Got you!" and left him lying there. (For Azrael had set up the palace and made himself look like a houri from paradise to get him; naturally, he did.)

· 18 · *When Azrael Laughed, Cried, and Felt Fear*

Recorded from Abu-'Aashoor (see informant note to tale no. 3). He heard this story "while traveling about, maybe ten years ago." Abu-'Aashoor does not remember who told him the tale and states, "just someone [male] like you or me, that's all."

Predestination and a nonfuturistic world view are expressed in this didactic religious story. The tale also illustrates the friction between formal legal rules and informal traditional practices. Usually the imposition of a formal contract upon a binding verbal agreement is considered alien to ideal folk community practices. In most cases, the formal contract itself will not be morally binding. The three emotions found in the title are interesting in that, although crying and experiencing fear are not alien to an angel's nature as perceived by Muslims, laughing is.

ONE DAY God asked Azrael, "Did you ever laugh, Azrael?"
   Azrael answered, "Once, God."
   God asked, "When?"
   He answered, You are more knowing than I."
   "Of course," God said, "I want to see if you remember."
   Azrael said, "One time you ordered me to take away the soul

of a landlord who had some tenants. They were going on year-by-year contracts, when all of a sudden the landlord said, 'I want three-year contracts!'

"The tenants implored him, 'May God lead your path. May God satisfy you' [i.e., change your mind and let things be the way they are].

"But he said, 'Never!'

"They said, 'Why? No one can guarantee his own life until tomorrow. We are doing well on a year-by-year basis.'

"He said, 'It's final. Three years, and three years it will be.'

"So, my God," said Azrael, "I went to take his soul, and he was imposing a three-year contract! I laughed at his foolishness! Here he was going to die in an instant, yet he was thinking about himself for three more years!"

"God said, "All right, and did you ever cry?"

He answered, "Yes, once."

And God asked, "When?"

Azrael said, "You ordered me to take away the soul of a woman. When I went to do so, I found that she had just given birth to a baby. It was only a few minutes old. I cried for the infant, but I had to take her soul away according to your command. I wept for that baby."

And so God said, "Did you ever feel fear?"

Azrael answered, "Yes, once."

God asked, "What made you afraid?"

"Once I went to take away the soul of a king. When I got there, to his palace, the whole world was standing in awe of him, while he sat there in a way that would turn a young man's hair gray. A falcon could have stood on the tip of his mustache! To tell you the truth, I was afraid."

And then God said, "The king was that infant for whom you cried."

So Azrael wondered, "What made him king?"

And God answered, "I ordered angels to carry him and set him in front of the door of a good man. When the man got up for his dawn prayers, he found the child. He took it to the king, for the king's wife could not bear children. And there he was, as you saw him."

[A listener comments, "God forgets no one. They say, 'God may give respite, but never neglect.'"]

Recorded from Abu-'Aashoor (see informant note to tale no. 3).
He heard it from a religious sheik, a preacher, several years ago.

One of the most serious preoccupations for the good Muslim is
the hereafter. It may be said that a true believer lives so that he
or she may die; meeting the creator after a life of virtue is what
life is believed to be for. The existence of some sort of life
inside the grave, found in our story here, is a strong belief
among modern Egyptians. Although references to this idea are
found in Islamic literature, it certainly harks back in both belief
and practice to ancient Egyptian religion.

Prayer is one of the five "pillars" of Islam. Formal religion
states that starting at the age of puberty, those who do not
perform their prayers will have to perform whatever they have
missed at the edge of hell. Our narrative gives a concrete example of this doctrine.

The story also deals with grave robbing, which seems to have
been a problem ever since the time of the pharaohs; it portrays
the robber as a compulsive thief, a kleptomaniac. The notion of
"mania" is expressed in folk tradition through the belief that a
part of a person—especially the hand and the tongue—may act
independently of that person's will.

ONCE THERE WAS a very money-minded man. He spent all his
life not performing his [five] daily prayers. When he grew old,
God did not enable him to perform his prayers at all, and he
wanted to do something to make up for all the prayers he had
missed. He came to a heavily traveled road, drove a water pump
into the ground, and set next to it two large water jugs. He stood
there himself serving whoever came. He who came (do not
blame me) riding was not permitted to get off the back of his
animal, and he who came walking was handed the water.

All this was not sufficient for him. In his village there was a
man who stole the shrouds of the dead; that is, if a person died, it
was inevitable that he would take the shroud off the dead person. He sent for that man. When he came, he asked him, "How
much do you get for these shrouds?"

The grave robber answered, "They are not all the same. A

poor man's sells for two, maybe three pounds, and the best sells for five pounds, whereas it's owner might have paid thirty or forty for it."

The man said to him, "From this moment on, when any person dies, even if he happens to be a child, come to see me, and I'll give you twenty pounds. And do not rob the dead. As long as I'm alive and on the surface of this world, whenever a person dies, come and get twenty pounds from me. After all, I have plenty of money, and I would like to redeem my sins, for I do not perform my prayers."

The man answered, "All right."

They carried out their agreement, and whenever somebody died, the grave robber went to the rich man and received his twenty pounds. Time passed and this man—what? God took back his deposit, and the man died. Meanwhile, the grave robber had prospered, for the village was large, and many of its people had died. When the rich man died, of course, he (the grave robber) went and witnessed his burial preparations. He also saw the luxurious shrouds that were on him. When everything was over, he went home and sat down sadly. His wife asked him, "What? Are you sad because of that man? Of course he was a good man, and he was . . ., and he was . . ., and he was . . .!"

He answered her, "By God, there is something on my mind."

She answered him, "What something? The man died after having taken his share of this world. He also left us plenty. It will be a while before we finish the money he has given us."

He replied, "I'm restless."

In short, she learned from him that he wanted to go and get this man's shroud. She warned him, "If you do this evil deed again or go on that trip, I'm going to scream and gather the whole village and cause a scandal."

He quieted down for a while; then the idea came back to his mind. It obsessed him. As he started to leave his home, she blocked his way. He swore, "The distant one will be such-and-such [*] thrice, if you don't step out of my way [i.e., you will be divorced thrice], and I will strike you down and finish you off. I must go and get this shroud, for I won't be able to sleep without it." [A listener: "'His hand has disowned him.'"]

---

* The narrator is avoiding the word "divorce." See introductory note to tale no. 15.

He went to the cemetery. When he got there, he looked into all the graves, but he could not find the door to the one he wanted.

"I was here! I attended the burial, and I know it was a good large grave with a large door. Now where did that door go?"

He did not find it. He went around seven or eight times, and finally he saw a hole with light coming out of it. He looked through it, and inside he saw on that side (the righthand side) a chair; of course it was one of those beautiful things (not just an ordinary chair). In the middle there was a fountain of pure water. On the other side there was a fire pit. He also saw a group of angels standing by, holding that man, the rich man. At prayer time, as soon as the call to prayers was given, they took him and dipped him in the fire. He would spend the five or ten minutes which is the time necessary to perform the prayer in the fire pit. Afterward they would take him out and dip him in the water fountain. When he was taken out, he would be as he had been before. Then they would dress him in beautiful clothes and seat him in the other corner (where the chair was).

This happened five or six times while our friend was looking. One of the angels came [to the grave robber] and asked him, "What do you want?"

He replied, "I'm only looking."

The angel said, "What you see is the prayer time; he has to spend it in the fire. The fountain is for his water service, and the silk that he's wearing is the shrouds of the dead that he ransomed."

And he looked to see no door, no hole, no light, only himself standing out there. He went back home, redeemed his sins, and lived well.

· 20 · *The Beast That Took a Wife*

Recorded from Tilib (see informant note to tale no. 11). He heard this story in his home village. Tilib described his source as "a regular man, not a [religious] sheik," and added, "As far as I am concerned, these things really happened."

Reports on different types of interaction believed to have taken place between Prophet Muhammad and his companions offer a virtually infinite cycle of religious legends. Two important supernatural beings of folk extraction appear in this story: el-Khidr, a human being who attained immortality (see tale no. 23), and the *burāq,* a winged angel-horse with a human face (similar to Pegasus). The *burāq* appears in folk paintings and tattoos as a mare. According to religious tradition, Prophet Muhammad ascended to heaven mounted on the *burāq.* He ascended from the spot enshrined by the Dome of the Rock in Jerusalem. (See notes to tale no. 5).

The legend also refers to the important Islamic doctrine of intercession. According to this belief, Prophet Muhammad will plead with God on behalf of Muslim sinners, thus gaining for them a lighter punishment and eventual admission into paradise.

ONE TIME the disciples [of Prophet Muhammad] were sitting, and the Prophet was sitting in their midst. They saw a beast coming down from the hills. The beast went through them until he reached the Prophet and put his mouth over the Prophet's ear and whispered something. After that, he left.

The disciples became uneasy, and they said, "Muhammad, what's the matter? This is our enemy. How could he cut across us like this and whisper in your ear?"

The Prophet said, "Disciples, this snake, this beast wants to marry. Who has a daughter to give to the beast?"

They wondered, "Muhammad, would it be sensible for anybody to give his daughter to a beast? Of course he would devour her. We are always afraid he may attack and wound us. Who would throw away his daughter like that?"

The Prophet said, "This is what happened. However, I will vouch for him. You think it over and let me know."

Omar, the Leader of the Believers, had two daughters, one older and one younger. He entered his house and said, "Children, you have a suitor."

They were very happy and cried out with joy. The older one was especially enthusiastic, because naturally the suitor would be for her.

They asked, "Who is he? Do we know him?"

"No, you do not know him."

"Who is he?"

"A beast."

Of course his wife and elder daughter cried out and quarreled with him, and they made a great commotion. The younger daughter said, "Father, who will vouch for this beast?"

He replied, "Muhammad."

She said, "I will agree."

"Is that so?"

"That is so."

She put on her clothes and went with him. They went to the Prophet, and Omar said, "Messenger of God, my youngest daughter agrees to the marriage."

"Do you really agree, daughter?"

"Yes, I really agree."

The Prophet said, "I vouch for the beast."

A little later the beast came down from the hills. He had a howdah on top of a camel with him. The beast was holding the camel's rope in its mouth. They made the camel kneel, placed the girl inside the howdah, and the beast held the rope in its mouth and went away. Nobody knew what it was! But who was the one who had vouched for it?—the Prophet.

A month went by, and another and another, until it had been a year. Nobody heard anything [about the girl]. The disciples started reproaching Omar: "Is there such a man who would throw his daughter into the hills as you did? What kind of a man are you?"

Similarly, he would go home and his wife would quarrel with him. Finally he went to the Prophet and said, "Muhammad, I would like to see my daughter. You vouched for the beast and you are responsible."

The Prophet said, "Why don't you go out and wander around, and maybe you will meet them."

The Leader of the Believers left and continued into the hills. The first day passed, and the second. On the third day at noontime he came to a very high palace. He sat underneath it. His daughter happened to be looking down from above. He ran inside, and they met. "Oh, daughter, are you happy? Are you comfortable?"

She answered, "Father, this palace has a hundred rooms. I can

go into ninety-nine of them. As for the hundredth, I have its
key, but I am not supposed to open it. I am married to Master
el-Khidr."

They inspected the palace. Of course it was a palace from
paradise. After they had seen all ninety-nine rooms, Omar said,
"Daughter, what happens if we go into this last room? Let's open
it!"

She replied, "Father, my husband warned me and advised me
not to do so."

Her father said, "Never mind, he's not with us."

As soon as he put the key into the keyhole, the earth trembled
and the skies thundered, and he found Master el-Khidr getting
hold of his hand which had the key.

"What made you do this? This room has the *buraq* in it. This is
Muhammad's *buraq;* he has to ride it to the heavens to intercede
on behalf of his nation on the day of resurrection. This room
must not be opened before that day."

Of course Omar found that his daughter was living happily.
He took her to visit her home and her family, and she returned
to her husband.

· 21 ·   *The Three Robbers and el-Khidr*

Recorded from Isma'Aeel (see informant note to tale no. 16).
He heard this story in Nubia "from other wise men who already
passed away." Isma'Aeel states this tale is a *qiṣṣah,* a serious
narrative: "It could happen, and it might have happened, but it
really did not."

The importance of "a good wife" for the prosperity of the
household is expressed here. Although it is generally thought
that Arab women have no power over their families, the influence a woman exerts within the household is usually much
greater than is believed at first glance. A recurrent adage states,
"If a man is a sea [i.e., a spender], a woman must be his dam."

An interesting motif here is the supernatural effect of a saint's
spittle, which grants the recipient the power of speaking well.
Eloquence and proper speech are highly valued in Arab culture.

THREE PERSONS were predestined to meet with el-Khidr. They were three robbers. El-Khidr came walking down the road. He was wearing a *gibba* [ankle-length topcoat] and a caftan [the garb of sheiks]. They thought, "This is an old man. We could hit him a couple of strokes with our cane, and he would drop dead."

They approached him. El-Khidr said to them, "Hey! What do you think you are doing? You are robbers! Do you think 'there is a sheik under every dome'? I haven't even got a *ta'Areefa* [a small coin worth about a nickel] on me. I am el-Khidr. I have been predestined to meet with you. Your repentance is going to be at my own hands. Make a request, and you will find that God will make it come true for you."

They said, "All right, are you really el-Khidr? Peace be upon him."

He replied, "Yes."

One of them said, "Then give me plenty of money, for I would like to enjoy my life and live diligently. I would like to be a big merchant (like Abu-'Aoaf' or Benzion) with large department stores."

El-Khidr said to him, "You take this *ta'Areefa*. You want money?"

The robber replied, "Yes."

El-Khidr said, "You take this *ta'Areefa* and use it as yeast for your capital."

He took the *ta'Areefa* and went away.

The second said, "I would like to be a great savant."

El-Khidr said, "Well, open your mouth."

Itfooo! He spat into his mouth, and immediately the man started saying nothing but Koranic verses and citing not only *hadeeth* but also *Qudsi* [attributed to God, but not a part of the Koran]. A trivial word would never be uttered by him.

The third one said, "I want a woman who is 'twenty-four carats' legitimate."

El-Khidr replied, "Uh, you have me! Where am I going to get you a purely legitimate woman? This request of yours made me give up!"

The man asked, "Why? Why is that so?"

El-Khidr replied, "In all this universe there is no female who is purely legitimate, but I know of someone who is a whole one-fourth legitimate. Only six carats legitimate, that is six carats out of twenty-four carats that you are asking for. Let me tell you where she is; you go and get her."

He went and married her.

Later el-Khidr wanted to stop by the houses of each of these three men. He wanted to see how they were after all these changes. He went to see them in a completely different condition. He went in the form of a beggar, not in the form in which he had met them in the hills.

The first man, who had become a very big and rich merchant, was just opening his store in the morning. El-Khidr approached him and begged, "Master, give me some of what God has given you. Give me a *ta'Areefa.*"

The man replied, "Now, what a way to start a day! So early in the morning? Here is a *ta'Areefa,* and get out of my sight!"

He threw the coin at him. It turned out to be the *ta'Areefa* of blessings. A little later the store caught fire. The fire consumed the good and the bad. It finished up everything. It even took away some of what he had had earlier. He turned out to have nothing at all. He became the way God created him.

Now he [el-Khidr] went to the savant. Now this savant was situated in a little mosque where the pashas and beys and all big and important and knowledgeable people went. This one was learning new things, and that one was receiving instructions, and this one was receiving interpretations and answers to his questions. El-Khidr also went to him as an old man walking with a cane, looking clumsy and not very tidy. He asked, "Master sheik, I have a religious problem. I have a friend who died leaving behind him a wife and two daughters and that much money. What should be the share of each one of them?"

The sheik looked at him in disgust and went, "Itfooo!"

He spat at him and shouted, "Go into a catastrophe! Do you think I am for the likes of you? I instruct only the very knowledgeable and the very important."

Now, after having been saying nothing but the holy and the truthful, he uttered nothing but the blasphemous and the profane. Instead of saying, "There is no God but Allah," he started saying, "Jesus is the son of God." People gave him a good beating, the like of which he had never seen in his life, and drove him away.

Now who remains with us? There remains the third man, the

one who wanted a twenty-four-carat legitimate wife. El-Khidr wanted to get into the house without raising any suspicions in the husband's mind concerning his wife. (Of course, if I saw a young man in my house, I would think evil, but if he were a very old man, who was very weak and could hardly move, of course I would not have any evil thoughts.)

El-Khidr looked as if he were a hundred and fifty years old. He went to this man's house and was received by his wife. She performed all the duties due a guest. When her husband returned, he found this man. He greeted him and said to his wife, "Get us supper."

The wife said, "By God, the only thing we had was a loaf of oat bread. I fed it to our old guest."

Reluctantly, the husband said, "All right."

His wife looked here and there for a few things that she gave him to eat. Of course he was thinking that this old man would stay for a short while and leave in the afternoon.

When it was sunset, they had to send him to the guest house. It was the month of *tooba,* and it was very cold. The wife thought that if this old man was to go to the bath, he couldn't stand the cold water. So she heated some water and sent it with her husband. She said to her husband that if he needed more warm water, he should wake her up.

Now the husband took the old guest to the guest house. Our Master el-Khidr went to the bath and used up all the water. Just as soon as our friend went to sleep and began to snore, the guest went, "Hey! Hey! More warm water!"

So he got up and went home and had his wife heat water and brought it. Just as soon as he was about to drowse off again, the guest went, "Hey! Hey! Get up! More warm water!"

The man went and did everything and got back. Just as soon as he was about to drowse off again the guest went, "Hey! Hey! Get up! . . . Hey! Hey! Get up!"

The host started mumbling to his wife, "Oh, this is an old dying man. He has diarrhea. Let us send him away."

His wife rebuked him and said, "It is not you who is doing the work. It's me. He is our guest."

The husband said, "All right, it is one night, and it will soon be over."

The following day when he returned home, he found him still

there. He said to himself, "'What an impalement!' All night last night, ordering water. 'Oh I want to go to the bath.' All day today at work, I couldn't do anything, and now this."

El-Khidr had awakened him fourteen times the night before, and he was determined to wake him up another fourteen times this night. Everytime he was just about to doze off, he went, "Hey! Hey! Some warm water! Hey! Hey! Some warm water!"

The man started complaining to his wife, "He is a rude man! He is a sick man! He is a dying man!

His wife calmed him down and said, "Father of So-and-so, it is I who have to do most of the work. I have to get up and light the kerosene stove and get the water and wait. He is our guest."

The night passed, and in the morning the man went to work. When he got back home, el-Khidr was still there, and the same thing happened all over again.

"Hey! Hey! Heat me some water! . . . Hey! Hey! Heat me some water!"

Except this time, the last time the man went home to heat the water at dawn, el-Khidr went along with him. He said to him, "Listen, I know what you have been saying about me and what you wanted to do to me; and by God, it is only for your wife's sake that I am sparing you. Had it not been for that one-quarter legitimate wife of yours, you would have caught up with your friends, because you have been saying, 'This man has diarrhea. This man has come to die here. This man is making me sick.' Now, because of your wife, may God bless you and bless the things that are yours; and from now on you and your family will find your gift [i.e., money] underneath the rug, and you will live the rest of your lives happily." And he left.

And I was there and just returned.

· 22 ·   *The Killer of Ninety-Nine*

Recorded in November 1970 from 60-year-old Haji M. el-Sayyid, nicknamed "el-Emiri" ("the princely"), from the village of Aghoor al-Kubra, in the Nile Delta. He heard this story from other Egyptian friends during one of his nine visits to Hejaz for pilgrimage.

Although illiterate, el-Sayyid is a well-to-do farmer. His travels and involvement in various social activities have given him broad experience. He is married and has a number of children. His three older sons tend the farm, thus enabling him to lead a fairly comfortable life. Shortly after the recording of this story, el-Sayyid traveled for his tenth pilgrimage to Hejaz, where he died; that had been one of his most cherished hopes in life, to die in Mecca (see introductory note to tale no. 19).

According to formal Muslim doctrines, God forgives all sins for the mere asking except for disbelief and premeditated murder. The Koran states that he who kills a believer without legitimate cause will be consigned to hell. The following belief narrative expresses a different viewpoint. In both formal as well as folk religious doctrine, long periods of penitence are not necessary for redemption and forgiveness. The principle of divine forgiveness is usually expressed in the following adage, "He who forswears his sins is like him who is sinless."

THERE WAS A MAN who had killed ninety-nine persons with his staff. He went to the "Judge of Islam" and said to him, "Master, I have killed ninety-nine souls with this staff, and now I would like to do penance. I want to know whether God will forgive me and whether I'll go to paradise, or what? From this moment I am following the straight path."

The judge said to himself, "Now he has killed ninety-nine; if I tell him, 'God will not accept your penance and you will go to hell,' I'm going to be the hundredth!"

So just to send him away, the judge said, "Go and plant your staff in the cemetery, and return to it the next day. If you find that it has bloomed, then God has accepted your penance."

Of course what else could he have said to him?

This man, the killer of ninety-nine, went to the cemetery and took his staff and drove it into the middle of the beaten track. When he was at the cemetery and in the middle of the graves, a funeral arrived. They buried somebody and left. A short while later a man came looking around to see whether someone was there or not. He dug the grave and went inside. Our friend the killer of ninety-nine was watching all this. He knew that the dead person was a woman. He snatched his staff out of the ground and went in to see what was the matter.

Our friend looked in from outside and saw what was happening. The man was (I resort to God for protection from Satan) trying to undress the corpse. Every time the man tried to take her shroud off, the woman, with God's omnipotence, would pull it back on again, that is, the dead woman. Our friend the killer of ninety-nine became very angry, and 'blood boiled in his veins.' He shouted at the man, "You, cursed one! what are you doing?"

The man was horrified and told him, "By God, this woman . . . I spent half of my life seeking this woman and couldn't reach her while she was alive. Now—"

The killer of ninety-nine shouted, "You couldn't have her during her life, and you will not have her during her death! Here, take this! You will be the even hundredth!" He struck him with his staff on the head and smashed it; he closed the grave on the two of them and planted his staff—right through the top of the grave.

The following day he went back and saw that life had not only gone through the staff but that it had become green as clover. He pulled it out and ran to the sheik. When the sheik saw this, he wondered, "How could this be possible? This one has killed ninety-nine, and now his staff is green and he is going to paradise!" [He said to the man,] "Tell me the story."

He said, "I found a man who could not have a woman while she was alive, so he tried to have her when she was dead. Every time he tried to undress her, she pulled her shroud back to cover herself. It was something from God. I struck him with my staff, and with him I had an even hundred. I drove my staff into the ground, and this morning I went back and found it was green."

The sheik said, "It was your protection of that woman that redeemed all your sins. Go, God has blessed you with what he has granted you!"

Part IV
Etiological Belief Narratives

Recorded from 'A. Hasan, age 64, a native of Cairo and owner of a notions shop. He is literate and used to head a shadow-play troupe. Hasan stated, "I heard the story from several people, especially from our learned sheiks." This story was collected jointly with Saber el-'Aadily.

The planet Earth is thought by the folk to be divided into four quarters—the Ruined Quarter, the Dark Quarter, the Empty Quarter, and the Inhabited Quarter. However, only the first two quarters appear in active usage; the latter two are simply known, but do not recur in oral traditions. El-Khidr is a supernatural personage whose characteristics are similar to those of the four arch-saints, but he is not one of them. It is believed that at the mere mention of his name, el-Khidr appears and greets the person who uttered his name: "Peace be upon you." By saying, "And upon you be peace," as the narrator in this tale does, one is returning el-Khidr's greeting.

EL-KHIDR ('And upon you be peace and god's mercy and his blessings') was a relative of al-Iskander Zulqarnain (Alexander the Dual-Horned). He was his maternal cousin and also his minister. Al-Iskander was a very pious man; he had an angel who kept him company every evening.

King al-Iskander was saying to the angel, "By God, I would like to worship God until the day of resurrection. Don't you know of something that would prolong my life until that day? For I would like to pay God back for his goodness."

The angel answered him, "Iskander, by God, I have heard of something called the Spring of Life. Whoever drinks from it or washes in it will never die."

Al-Iskander asked him, "Where is this spring?"

The angel answered, "I've heard that it is in the Valley of Darkness."

"Do you know the road to it?"

"No!"

Al-Iskander gathered all of his philosophers. Among them was a man who had read the heavenly Scriptures and learned them by heart. He said to al-Iskander, "It is beyond the Ruinous Quarter [of the earth] which is inhabited by Master Ahmad el-RifaʿAi. It is in the Darkness Quarter."

"How long is the distance between us and it?"

"Twelve years of traveling."

Al-Iskander prepared his army; el-Khidr ('And upon you be peace') was with him. They all set out after the Spring of Life.

Before they left, the angel had given al-Iskander and each member of the army a bead that made a warning sound and said to al-Iskander,

"If one of you gets lost in the darkness, throw this bead. It will make a warning sound, and thus you can all find each other again."

They traveled until they reached the Darkness Quarter, and the whole army spread out to look for the spring. "Uncle" el-Khidr stumbled on it, by God's will. He bathed in it and drank from its water until he was 'twenty-four carats' satisfied.

When he joined the rest, he said to them, "Hey, we have to get out of here, for we can't find anything."

They got on their horses and set out on their way back. As they were riding, the hooves of the horses hit against something strange and solid. It was too dark for them to see what it really was. Al-Iskander asked the angel, "What is this?"

The angel answered him, "This is something: he who takes from it will regret it, and he who does not will also regret it."

A while later "Uncle" el-Khidr emerged from the Darkness Quarter with his hands full of emeralds and rubies. Jewels! Those who had not taken any wished they had, and those who had taken some wished they had taken more! So both groups regretted it!

God had willed for Master el-Khidr to drink from the Spring of Life [and thus to live until the day of the end of life]. Whenever you mention his name, he will pass by you and greet you, saying, "Peace be upon you," and you should answer, "And upon you be peace, God's mercy and his blessings.' He is everywhere, especially at road intersections.

This is why our brothers the Christians call him Mari Girgis. It means *marr* ("passed"), *giri* ("ran"), *gis* ("feel"); which means that he is passing, running, and feeling things everywhere

Recorded in January 1970 from H. Mitwalli (see informant note to tale no. 15) and 'A. Hasan (see informant note to tale no. 23). They heard this "fact, not story, from many people who are knowledgeable and also from many friends." Mitwalli added, "I was told that it exists in books."

In Egyptian folk culture the Turk is stereotyped as uncompromising, brutal, extremely neat, light-complexioned, handsome and clean, and also arrogant without justification. A proverbial simile, "Like a Turk: 'Give me alms and [don't forget that] I am your master!'" represents this view of the Turk (see tale no. 57).

WHEN AL-ISKANDER ZULQARNAIN was returning with his army from their trip in search of the Spring of Life, he reached the people of Ya'goog wa Ma'goog [Gog and Magog]. They were very evil, and all the neighboring tribes complained to al-Iskander: "Save us from them! Do something for us!" He then built that iron wall around them which is mentioned in the Koran.

Up until now Gog and Magog have been trying to get out by licking the wall through. They lick it all night long and come so close to licking it away that they can see daylight through it. But as soon as the sun rises, the wall goes back to the way it was. They will not get out until the day of resurrection. If they were to come out today, the day of resurrection would be tomorrow.

Now, when al-Iskander was building that wall, some of Gog and Magog were away herding their animals. So they were left out. That's why the Turks were called "tùrk." It really means those who were left out.

· 25 · *Why the Copts Were Called "Blue Bone"*

Narrated in May 1971 by N. R., 54, a clerk in a government office in Cairo. The informant, a Copt, is originally from Asyout, a town in upper Egypt. He heard this account from other Coptic friends in Cairo.

The color blue plays an important symbolic role in Egyptian culture. Until recently, the blue garment used to be the distinguishing mark of the Egyptian peasant; the expression "wearers of blue garments" stood only for the poor inhabitants of the Egyptian countryside. Other stereotyped sayings which include the word "blue," such as the proverbial expression "blue fang," denoting an uncompassionate person, appear frequently in the Egyptian dialect. The following story accounts for the origin of one of these expressions.

ASYOUT is the Coptic center of Egypt. The Copts there are very prejudiced against Muslims. The Muslims in Asyout are a minority, and they are [also] very prejudiced against Copts. The cemeteries of the two groups were opposite each other, separated only by a country road. The important thing is that some time, a long, long time ago, it rained in torrents. The rainwater destroyed the graves and swept what was inside of them down the road. The important thing is that the two cemeteries got mixed together, and the bones of the dead mingled.

The Copts became very upset and said, "It is impossible that we let our dead be buried with the Muslims!"

The Muslims got very upset as well and said, "It's sinful that we would be buried with Copts!"

The Muslim sheik and the Coptic priest got together. They said, "Muslims are put directly into the earth with nothing but shrouds, and therefore the earth absorbs blood from their bones. As for the Copts, they are buried in caskets. Their blood dries inside their bones, and they therefore become blue."

And out of this the division came: the white bones for the sheik and the blue bones for the priest. And from that time on, the Copts have been called "Blue Bone."

Recorded in January 1970 from H. Mitwalli (see informant note to tale no. 15). He heard it from "Many people" and "had known it and told it for years and years."

There is virtually no community whose members consider it to be the proper size that does not have its own enshrined saint. One such saint who appears in numerous areas is Sidi el-Arb'Aeen, "Saint the Forty." The following etiological tale is based on the theme of contests in manipulating the supernatural; it is the *kahin*'s *sihr* (magic) versus the saints *karāmā* (miraculous manifestations). The tale also reflects, as did its counterpart in ancient Egypt (see notes to tale no. 6), the state of accommodation between the religious majority and the opposing minority. Such conflicts, historians have observed, are never totally resolved by destroying the opponents; instead, the victory of the majority is limited to one situation, and coexistence continues.

A KING, such as the king of Egypt, for example, had a vizier, but this vizier was a Copt. There were forty robbers who used to visit the king disguised as sheiks [pious men]. The king treated them well and asked them for blessings.

One day the vizier, who was a Copt, said to the king, "Every time these people come, you are very generous to them and give them a thousand pounds. They don't seem like sheiks. They seem to be robbers.

"I have a *kahin* [a coptic magician] who can [narrator moves the palms of his hands toward each other] merge two walls together by magic. Why don't you invite them, and I'll invite my man and let us see who will show the proof over his brother. Either the Muslims will win over us, or we will win over the Muslims."

The king sent a messenger to call them from the hills. Actually, they were not sheiks or anything like that.

Now at that time, the arch-saints el-Badawi, el-Kilani, el-Rifa'Ai, and el-Disouqi were still around here [i.e., living], but now each one of them is staying in his isthmus, carrying the world at its four ends.

Now el-Sayyid el-Badawi met Master el-Rifa'Ai and said to him, "Hurry, our path is going to be exposed! The Christians will win over us!"

Now as the forty thieves were coming down from the hills, el-Rifa'Ai was waiting for them. He asked them, "Where are you going?"

They answered, "To see the king."

He warned them, "Now see, you will follow me. Not one of you will utter a word. You will not make a sound, neither from above nor from below. I'll be in charge, if God wills."

They went to the king, and the king welcomed them. The king said to the vizier, "Send for your *kahin*, and let him show us his proof."

This *kahin* had money that could not be measured or counted. There was a big celebration in the middle of the king's garden. And a big crowd was everywhere.

El-Rifa'Ai said to the king, "Let him be first."

The king said to the vizier, "Let your man show us his proof."

The *kahin* spread a rug on the floor, sat on it, and hit it with a stick. It flew into the air, up, up, up, until it disappeared.

Master el-Rifa'Ai (may God accept him as such) took off one of his slippers and ordered it, "After him!"

The slipper flew over the *kahin* and kept on hitting him on the head until he came down in the middle of the crowd in pieces. Everybody applauded.

And (your enemy) the vizier was lost, for he had lost his man. And the Muslims emerged victorious in this encounter.

The vizier said to the king, "This man that died has money that can neither be measured nor counted. Let's open his safe and let them have what's in it."

The king said, "I'm not a poor man myself. I will reward them out of my own treasury."

He gave them four thousand pounds and said, "May God bless you. You truly made Islam victorious, and may safety be with you."

Saint el-Rifa'Ai took them to the hills and said to them, "If you work as robbers again, I'll send you where even the blue flies [of the graveyards] can't find you. Now you have four thousand pounds; divide them among you. Each one of you should find himself something to toy with—[be] a grocer, a vendor, anything!"

They repented of their sins, and they became true sheiks and spread over the whole country. And this is why there is a "Saint the Forty" in each town.

· 27 · *"Blow for Blow"* *

Recorded in July 1969 from S. Seliman (see informant note to tale no. 12).

During a visit to Seliman's shop, I made a jocular remark about his job, which required handling the feet of his all female clientele. He assured me that as a family man he must remain faithful to all its members in both thought and deed: "Life is 'Blow for blow!'" Seliman's business partner fully agreed.

Seliman heard the narrative repeatedly from his friends; "As for the proverb," he explained, "I hear it and use it almost every day!"

An important aspect of the world view of Egyptians and all other Arab groups is that all elements in the universe are inherently interconnected. The following moralistic story explains the cause-and-effect relationship between two apparently independent acts (see also story no. 33). This unitary view climaxes in the philosophy of Sufi mystics who regard the entire universe as fused with God.

In traditional Arab homes, no adult male other than a close relative may be admitted inside while the man of the house is not present. The water carrier and the Koran recitalist seem to be exempt from this rule, the first out of necessity and the second out of trust.

ONCE THERE WAS a good-hearted sheik who had a *kuttab* [a one-room religious school] where he taught little children the Koran and how to read and write (you know). He was married; he had a wife and a house, for he lived comfortably on what people gave him for teaching their children: corn, wheat, clothes, eggs, money, and everything they had in their fields or houses. He also went every day to several homes of well-to-do people in the area to recite a few verses of the Koran to bring blessings. He lived contentedly like this, thanking God for his blessings.

One day as he was going out of one of these homes after having recited [some verses from the Koran], he noticed that the door of the bedroom was ajar. Of course it was about ten or eleven o'clock in the morning, and the man of the house was at his work. He did not look for long and left.

The following day he saw that the same door was open. Satan whispered in his ear [i.e., tempted him]. This time he glanced at the door and left in a hurry.

The day after, the same thing happened. This time he stopped and—what? He looked inside. He saw the woman, that is, the wife of the man of the house, lying in bed. She did not notice him. He stared his eyes full as long as he wanted and left.

The day after, he became more bold; he strengthened his heart and went into the room. He found the lady lying down, half asleep. All this while Satan was encouraging him, buzzing, buzzing in his ear. He put his hand on the woman like this [gently]. She moved in the bed but did not wake up. He recoiled and *ran* outside this time.

When he got home, his wife was waiting for him. She had been crying. She said to him, "Sheik So-and-so, what did you do today? What have you been doing the past four days?"

He answered her, "Nothing."

She said, "No, something must have happened. You must have been doing something evil."

He was about to swear, "By God—

She interrupted him: "Do not swear, so that your oath will not be perjured. I will tell you what happened here."

She asked him, "Do you know 'Uncle' So-and-so?"

He answered, "Of course; he is the *saqqa,* a good man who has been carrying water to our house for thirty, maybe forty years. What about him?"

She said, "Three days ago he 'raised his eye' [off the ground] and peeped at me. The following day he stared at me. The day after that he came and spoke to me. Today he wanted to get hold of my hand and touch me."

The man said to himself, "Ahhh! That is because I have betrayed the trust in So-and-so's house and have been looking at his wife."

He knew that God was not going to let him get away with that. The water carrier, who was a very good and honest man, who had never 'raised his eye' to the mistress of the house for thirty or forty years, was doing to his wife the same thing he had been doing.

The sheik said, "Ah! Now I understand. 'Blow for blow. Had I gone further, the *saqqa* would have too.'" (From that time on this statement has become a proverb.)

He repented of his sin and said, "May God dishonor you, Satan," and returned to his previous path. Consequently, the water carrier became as he used to be before.

· 28 · *Why the Kite Always Attacks the Crow*

Recorded in September 1970 from Galeelah, 24, a housemaid. She lived with her family near Maadi, where she worked. Originally Galeelah came to the city from a village in the delta, where the rest of her family still resides.

The narrator heard this etiological tale from her parents while still in the village, about fifteen years earlier. She has not heard it since then. She still narrates tales to the children of her married brother.

The crow and the kite are both found in great numbers in Egypt. These two vultures are particularly disliked because of their raids on household fowl and other small animals. Unlike the hoopoe and the ibis, for example, the crow and the kite are not considered "friends of the farmer," and hunting them is legal. Only the crow is associated with ill omens. Among the folk a crow's cawing, like an owl's hooting, is believed to indicate an approaching disaster and must be answered with prayers requesting that God make the news heralded by the appearance of these two birds into good news. The narrative clearly falls outside the Islamic belief system concerning death.

IN THE BEGINNING people were very few and there were not very many newly born. The dead represented a great loss, for they were not replaced. People thought, "If it goes on like this, we will be finished, and we will never grow."

They got together and decided to send a message to God, asking him to permit the dead to return to life after three days. They looked for someone to take the message to God and did not find anyone except the kite, because she knew how to fly.

In the middle of the way, the crow met her and asked her, "Where are you going?"

She answered, "I am going to God with a message."

He asked, "What is the message?"

She told him, "People want God to let the dead return to life after three days."

The crow said to her, "You have done what you could; I will do the remaining half. You give me the message, and I will carry it." She agreed.

The crow took the message and went to heaven. There he said, "People want the dead never to return!"

God accepted the people's request, and the dead never came back. This is why every time the crow caws, people say, "[May it be] good, if God wills," and they know that there is going to be a death.

That is why whenever the kite sees the crow, she attacks him, for he had tricked her.

Part V
Axes, Saints, and Culture Heroes

The Supreme Saints Cycle

There are thousands of enshrined saints who belong to all three religions—Islam, Christianity, and Judaism—strewn over Egyptian villages, towns, cities, and even desert roads. The overwhelming majority of these once average humans are not known outside their immediate locale; several have regional and occasionally a little national importance, but only a few enjoy nationwide eminence. In a number of cases, belief in the powers of a national saint cuts across religious lines; Saint Theresa and Mar Girgis, for example, are two Christian saints who are also revered by Muslims.

The powers of saints and their ability to mediate with God in behalf of man influence every aspect of Egyptian life. Saints aid a smooth childbirth, help a student get good grades on a school examination, drive away invaders, and absorb the brunt of natural disasters in lieu of the rest of mankind. Certain saints tend to be associated with specific functions in which they are believed to be particularly effective.

For Muslims, saints are stratified in a hierarchical structure according to their powers and national eminence. At the top of their crowded community is a special class called *aqṭāb* (singular, *qùṭb*), which literally means "axis" [of the earth] or what we may label, "arch-saints." They are superior to all the rest in power but possess differing amounts of it. From an ideal viewpoint, there are only four arch-saints, one for each of the four quarters (sometimes called corners) of the earth. When asked to name the four arch-saints, most informants will cite the names of more than four. Also, a saint may appear in different roles in different folk belief systems held by the same individual. To the outsider such beliefs may seem contradictory, but for the believers no contradiction is experienced, and each belief makes sense. In most cases each account of the supernatural represents a semi-independent cognitive system. These systems overlap but do not totally merge with one another.

Narrated in January 1970 by A. Mahmoud, a 54-year-old farmer from Manoofiyyah Province in the Nile Delta. He can read a little "but only if necessary, as in [the case of] a deed, a price list, and things like that." When asked from whom he learned the story, the narrator answered, "This is something that the old and the young know [i.e., everyone]! But I still can tell you 'from others who are around us.'" Mahmoud visits el-Sayyid el-Badawi's shrine yearly during the saint's birthday. He also narrated a number of el-Sayyid's miraculous deeds of a serious nature.

In this belief narrative with a humorous twist, the arch-saints act like average humans. They tease, boast, and challenge one another. El-Badawi is acknowledged to be the most powerful of all axes. He combines the performance of a wide variety of roles ranging from intimate household functions to national tasks. He is perceived as being a joker as much as a war lord. Numerous episodes from a folk epic about el-Sayyid are alluded to in our present account.

AS YOU KNOW ('and you are the master of the knowledgeable'), each one of the arch-saints has his own post and his own job. They carry the earth each from his own quarter. They used to get together and discuss things. One time they started boasting to one another (they were just joking). El-Sayyid [el-Badawi] said, "I am the one who beat you all and defeated Fatima Bint-Birry." El-Mitwalli said, "I am the 'Burden Bearer'; I carry as much as all of you put together." El-Kilani [actually "al-Jilani"] said, "I made the lion in Baghdad turn my water wheel instead of the ox it ate!" and el-Rifa'Ai said, "I control all snakes, vipers, and creatures like that."

El-Sayyid said, "Everyone calls on me for help," and el-Rifa'Ai said, "I . . .! I . . .! and I . . .!" Everyone started saying, "My position is such and such." Of course with every sunrise God sends [only] four catastrophes down upon earth. The axes bear them all, except for a quarter of one. El-Mitwalli bears half of the four, that is two; el-Kilani bears half of the half, that is one; el-Rifa'Ai bears half of the [remaining] half, that is one-half; while el-Sayyid bears half of the half of the half, that is a quarter. Only one quarter of a catastrophe hits earth. All the mishaps (away from you) that happen, somebody killing somebody else, somebody stealing from somebody, a car running over a woman, a man leaping off a tall building [suicide], a person burning himself to death, and things like that, are [the result] of one-quarter of the quarter of the original [catastrophes] which were supposed to happen.

So el-Mitwalli said to el-Sayyid, "You are saying 'I do and I do!' why don't you wear my mantle [i.e., sit in my place], and I'll sit in your place, and let us see who will do a better job than his brother?"

El-Sayyid said, "Come on, sit! Do my job, and I'll do yours."

Now, when a man was trying to lift a heavy—and I mean ve-e-ery he-e-eavy—load, that man would shout [as he lifted the load], "Ohhh, Mit-wal-li!" So el-Sayyid would go to him and help him lift his load. But this only happens every once in a while. As for el-Mitwalli—[narrator giggles], every woman who was giving birth [and having labor pains], would scream "Ooooh, Sayyid!" Of course, now el-Mitwalli had to go to help. When a teamster was pushing his cart uphill, he would shout, "Ohhhh, Sayyid!" Even those who would go (don't blame me) to the restroom and had constipation would shout,"Oh, Sayyid!" El-Mitwalli said, "Up to this point and that is it! Sayyid, come and take over. You do what you usually do, and I will do what I usually do!"

They were just joking with one another.

· 30 · *An Arch-Saint's Attempt to Punish Sinners*

Narrated in June 1972 by Shakir, 45, originally from the village of el-Fashn in southern Egypt. He is a retired shaman and is literate. Currently he works as a janitor in a government office in Cairo. He narrated this "event" in the company of six other persons. All those present except myself had heard of this incident before.

The folk consider the sacred power which God grants to religious figures such as prophets, saints, and religious leaders as the *real* power; they refer to it as *bāṭin* rule. Secular power as represented by kings, presidents, and premiers is not real; the folk refer to it as *ẓāhir* (facade) rule. One of the most important agencies which administer the affairs of humans and oversee the dispensation of power is a council of saints called the Diwān. The most important component of the council is a triad formed of a sister and her two brothers. They are Prophet Muhammad's grandchildren: Zainab, the sister who presides over the council, and her brothers al-Hasan and al-Husain. Unlike their father 'Aali, they represent domestic and nonmilitary supernatural personages.

The concept of the Diwān harks back to the ancient Egyptian Ennead, a council of gods also headed by a triad of one female and two male deities. The role played by the modern Islamic triad corresponds to that of Isis, Osiris, and Horus, the ancient Egyptian trinity (see Budge, *The Gods,* 1:114).

The belief that God defers punishing human sinners for the sake of other innocent beings, including animals, is a formal Islamic religious doctrine.

[EL-SHAMY: "What is the Diwān?" Shakir: "They say that

> Al-Husain is the Kingdom,
> Al-Hasan is a sultan,
> El-sayyida Zainab is the sovereign;
> She rules through wardens and guards

She has wardens and guards; these are all the sheiks (the lesser saints). The four arch-saints are part of the Diwan, like consultants, I mean."]

During the celebration of Lady Zainab's birthday, of course there were thousands upon thousands of people there (you know). A man got together with a woman. He took her around and around in the hills, and finally he brought her to the celebration grounds of the Lady [Zainab] and committed adultery with this woman.

One of the axes, who are the guards of el-sayyida, passed by (they are the invisible guards, each one assigned to a sentry).

The axis saw what was happening. He went to the hills and picked a boulder as large as a house; he lifted it up above his head (and arched his back) to throw it at these two. He was about to squash the entire celebration because of these two fornicators.

The Lady aimed the divine electricity at him; it froze him in that position. She said [in a maternal, instructive tone] to him, "Come here, silly! Axis, what are you going to do!" He answered, "I am going to throw this boulder at those two." She said, "Because two persons went astray, you would kill thousands! Forgiveness! God forgives and defers punishing the sinful for the sake of the innocent. God even defers punishing the sinful for the sake of innocent animals that may get hurt! Forgive."

"Imamu" 'Aali's Narrative Cycle

Imamu 'Aali ibn abi-Talib is Prophet Muhammad's parallel paternal cousin (*ibn-'Aam*) and son-in-law. His life history is fraught with outstanding events. These include being the first youth to embrace Islam in its early stages, being the Prophet's companion, sustaining the suffering of early Muslims, participating courageously in religious wars, being the fourth calif (A.D. 656–661) and then becoming prey to a deceptive arbitration that forced him out of the caliphate and led to the split of Muslims into warring camps, and dying at the hands of an assassin in the year 661. Imamu 'Aali's person and history are attractive topics for the creative religious imagination.

Historians agree that 'Aali was neither an accomplished military strategist nor an outstanding politician, yet in folk tradition his image is that of a chivalrous warrior: mighty but humble, extremely generous, pious, eloquent, and learned. Stephan and Nandy Ronart argue that 'Aali's image as "the gallant and blameless knight" was taken over by "Arabic folklore at the times of the crusades...[from] European chivalry ideals." (1:34). This view seems to be an oversimplification of a complex religious phenomenon. 'Aali's manners are cited as the model for ideal behavior with equal frequency in semiliterary religious exempla as well as in the lore of traditional communities.

Two supernatural objects are associated with Imamu 'Aali's heroic adventures: his stallion, nicknamed al-Maymoun, and his sword, Dhul-fiqār. (Motifs: B184.1.3, "Magic horse from water world"; see also Chauvin, 7:7; D184.1.10, "Magic horse makes prodigious jumps," controlled by the sight of his rider; and D631.3.3, "Sword large or small at will.")

In addition to the religious prose narrative cycle, a number of heroic, epic-like stories, which were until relatively recently performed by bards but are currently mostly available in print, are also known in oral tradition. Three such heroic accounts exist: *Rās el-Ghoul (The Ogre's Head), The Wars against the King al-Haddām,* and *The Battle of the Flag Well.* The first, *Rās el-Ghoul,* has been translated into Swahili (see Harries, pp. 29–49).

From a psychological standpoint, 'Aali's deeds contrast sharply with the nonmilitary, mainly domestic deeds of his children Zainab and al-Husain. The father on one hand and the children on the other represent different cognitive and emotional systems which rarely overlap.

· 31 ·   *"Imamu" 'Aali and 'Aantar*

Narrated on April 7, 1969 by M. A. Tilib (see informant note to tale no. 11). He heard it frequently in his village in southern Egypt and also in Cairo.

In the following supposedly historical story, two culture heroes of contemporary lore, both of whom belong to a distant past, are said to have met. The then living Muslim 'Aali meets the pre-Islamic pagan 'Aantar, already dead. In Arab lore the black 'Aantar is the hero of a much admired *seerah* (an epic-like bard tradition; see Dorson's foreword, pp. xxxiv–xxxvi above), in which he plays the role of the invincible warrior who defends his tribe and suffers because of his love for his white parallel paternal cousin, 'Aabla, who has been promised to him in marriage. Our story points to the moral of humility and the unpredictability of wars, for 'Aantar started by fighting the enemies of his tribe and ended by having to fight his own kinsmen.

In the realm of supernatural beliefs, a person's identity is determined by his relation to his mother, not to his father; maternity is indisputable, whereas paternity is not. Because of this doctrine, 'Aali must first call 'Aantar by his mother's name and not by his father's.

ONE TIME the Prophet and Imamu 'Aali were walking. They saw that the disbelievers had built a citadel with walls around it so that they would be safe. The fence had an iron door which could be opened only by forty mighty men. Of course they thought they were safe, for if forty mighty persons could open their gate, neither Muhammad nor anybody with Muhammad could open it. They were all inside asleep.

The door had a small hole in it through which they could look outside. Imamu 'Aali put his little finger in this hole and pulled. There it [the door] came, out of the wall. He flung it into the air, and no one could find any trace of it. 'Aali wondered, "Where is the gate?"

The Prophet answered him, "'Aali, it traveled to the Ruined Quarter of the earth."

'Aali wondered, "*Ya salam!* Muhammad, had there been one ounce of food in my stomach, this gate would have kept on traveling until the day of resurrection!"

They finished their rounds and went home. 'Aali said, out of conceit, "Muhammad, no one in the whole world is stronger than I am."

Muhammad warned him, "'Aali, wombs produce, and as long as there are women who can give birth, there will be stronger people."

'Aali insisted, "No one is stronger than I am!"

Muhammad said to him, "All right, go to the cemetery and call, 'O 'Aantar,' and see what happens."

'Aali went and shouted, "'Aantar!" The whole cemetery arose, for they were all 'Aantars [i.e., mighty men].

'Aali went back to Muhammad and said, "Muhammad, I shouted, 'O 'Aantar!' and the whole cemetery answered me."

Muhammad said, "You go back and call, 'O 'Aantar-son-of-Zubaida' [Zubaiba].

When he went back and shouted, "'Aantar-son-of-Zubaida!'" 'Aantar rose and shouted [the war cry], "Ḥa-a-a-as!" (That is 'Aantar-ibn-Shaddad who shouted.)

'Aali said to him, "Let's go fight the disbelievers."

He readily answered, "And the rest of the world, for if I wake up, I'm not going to leave anybody, believers or disbelievers! I'm going to war with everyone!" 'Aantar then shouted,

> Ḥa-a-as! The God of the Throne is my aim.
> Paradise with humiliation I will not accept,'
> While hell with pride is my home;
> I have fought the jinn underneath the earth,
> And this [being beneath earth] is my abode.
> The iron has decayed, whereas we have not.

Imamu 'Aali left him lying inside the tomb and went back to Muhammad and said, "True, Muhammad, the womb produces!" (That means no matter how mighty you may be, how smart you may be, how, how, and how, there is always someone who is mightier or smarter—so never be conceited. As they say, 'Conceit is from Satan.')

· 32 · *The Twelfth Month*

Narrated in February 1970 by 'A. 'Aaql, a 54-year-old farmer from Kafr el-Sheikh Province in the western part of the Nile Delta, during his visit to a shrine in Cairo. 'Aaql heard this "true account" in his village from his peers. "I was grown up then . . . these are things which are told in religious gatherings such as the *ḥaḍrah* or the *zikr* [a folk religious ritual dance]," he added.

Although formal Muslim instructions contain teachings which promote both futuristic thinking and forethought, as well as nonfuturistic thinking and abstention from reflecting upon the future, it is the latter that is almost universally stressed. The following religious legend illustrates the powerful ethos of fatalism. It is the salience of this doctrine that may account for the severity of the punishment which was considered for the future-oriented farmer.

A FARMER planted his land. Every year the land produced enough crops to last the farmer and his family until the next year's crop. One year the land yielded only eleven of the twelve measures it had always yielded. The farmer became distressed. "What am I going to do! How can I and my family last for a whole month without food!" Someone told him, "Go to Imamu 'Aali and sue Earth. He will get you your rights back from it.

The farmer went to the imam's house. He found him sitting on a rug in front of the house with two plates before him, one full of grapes and the other full of figs. Imamu 'Aali would take one bite of the fig and follow with a grape, one bite of the fig and follow with a grape. The farmer wailed to him, "My land did not yield enough except for eleven months for me and my family to live on. What am I going to do?"

The imam looked at him and said, "Did you see what I have been doing? I have been eating grapes and figs at the same time because I don't know whether my life will be long enough [to last] until the next bite, while you have guaranteed your own life for eleven months and are worrying about the twelfth!"

The imam struck him with the back of his sword and said, "Go! Had you not been my guest, I would have decapitated you! A new life span had been predestined for you. Go!"

· 33 · *The Betrayal*

Narrated by 'A. 'Aaql (see informant note to tale no. 32). He heard this story from the "same people as in the previous story."

It is believed that all parts of the universe are interconnected in a cause-and-effect relationship (see introductory note to tale no. 27). Our narrative illustrates in an unusual way how the disruption of one aspect of life results in chaos and loss of justice. Imamu 'Aali, however, is not assumed in this belief legend to be

the agent that established the universal code. He is only the one
who supervised its proper maintenance.

A MAN USED TO TRAVEL to Hejaz [on a pilgrimage] every year
on foot. On his route he used to stop at a Bedouin's camp and
rest. The Bedouin had one sheep which he milked. He lived on
its milk, and at the same time he also had a wolf. Both wolf and
sheep lived side by side without either one transgressing against
the other. The man was surprised and asked the Bedouin, "How
can a sheep and a wolf be kept together like this?"

The Bedouin said to him, "They understand and know that
the universe has a controller and rules! They know."

One year later that *haji* [the traveler] was resting at the Bedouin's tent. He looked outside and saw the wolf attack the
sheep. The wolf killed the sheep and ran away. His friend the
Bedouin did not do anything; he just sat there and lamented,
"Only God is everlasting! Only God is everlasting!"

The *haji* asked the Bedouin, "Why did this happen? Why did
you not try to save your sheep?"

The Bedouin answered him, "What happened is beyond my
control and yours. The system of the universe has mal-
functioned, and a betrayal has taken place! Only God is everlasting!"

Before they left their places [where they were seated], a mes-
senger came, declaring that Imamu 'Aali had been killed. The
Bedouin said, "That is why! It was he who kept the order. Only
God is everlasting!"

"Mari" Girgis's Belief Legend Cycle

Among Egyptian Copts a saint is commonly referred to as a
qiddees, a word which denotes affiliation with that which is holy;
such an association is not part of the Muslim concept of "waliy,"
yet both titles have been translated into English as "saint." A
number of Coptic saints are also referred to as martyrs, or
shuhada. The most important figure of this category of saints is
Mar Girgis ("Mari Girgis" in folk pronunciation). His martyr-
dom as an early Christian at the hands of the Romans is reported

in both Muslim and Christian historical and literary works (see al-Tha'Alabi, pp. 242–46; Amélineau, pp. 166–273; Jullien, pp. 230–31; and Basset, *Mille et un contes,* vol. 3, no. 117).

Mar Girgis's legend cycle, especially his role as the "dragon slayer," is recurrent among Christians and is also known to Muslims. The Mar Girgis belief complex is used in a church ritual to exorcise evil spirits possessing the bodies of humans. This event takes place during the annual mass service performed at the Mar Girgis church at Meet Damsees, a little town in the Nile Delta. Many Muslims participate in this healing ritual as well.

Hanauer (pp. 52–54) reports a similar practice from Palestine. Although Hanauer states that the shrine where the "mentally deranged" are treated is dedicated to el-Khidr, it is evident from the rest of his description that it is a Christian establishment headed by a Greek priest.

In Egypt the church healing ritual is the Coptic counterpart of the *zar* cult prevalent among Muslims but abhorred in formal Islamic circles. Although the Vatican has recently decanonized Saint George, strong belief in his sainthood and miracles remains unaffected among Egyptian Copts.

· 34 · *Mari Girgis and the Beast*

Taped in July 1970 from I. Ḥ. (see informant note to tale no. 2).

One of the current native Egyptian folk festivals is that of the annual rise of the Nile *('Aeed wafā' el-neel),* which literally means "the festival of the Nile's fulfillment [of promise]." On this occasion a wooden doll dressed in bridal clothes is thrown into the Nile. This practice has declined since the completion of the Aswan High Dam, which regulates the flow of water year around (see introductory note to tale no. 1). The modern folk practice seems to be a survival from ancient rituals in which an actual human sacrifice was made. Al-Nabhāni (1:158) cites a miraculous manifestation reported by Al-Subkī (d. A.D. 1370), according to which the Nile refused to flow when the sacrifice was stopped, but resumed its flowing upon receiving an order from Calif 'Aumar. (See Dorson's foreword, pp. xxxi–xxxii above).

A HUGE SERPENT lived near a village. It threatened the people of this particular village. They had to give him a virgin maiden every year, or he would throw himself into the "sea" [i.e., the Nile] and prevent water from reaching the village. At the same time, he horrified the village, for he was awesome, and his body was huge. Naturally, every year the people chose one of the village maidens to be the sacrifice for the serpent.

One year the daughter of the king himself was drawn by lot; it was her turn for the serpent to get her. The king became very sad, for he had no other children but her; she was his only child. When his daughter was chosen he was very distressed, for she had to be offered to this dragon (of course "dragon" means a huge serpent), and she was going to die, but he could not say no.

On the appointed day, the girl was dressed in a bridal gown, all white and adorned with jewels, and taken to the Nile, to that river. Of course there were music and drums and pipe sounds and a large crowd of people. When they reached the bank, they left the daughter of the king there for the serpent to come and take her away.

It chanced that Mari Girgis was passing by; God had sent him to save the girl. He saw the girl sitting on the bank waiting. He got off his horse and asked her, "What are you doing here?"

She told him the story and asked him to go away, so that the serpent would not devour him also. He said to her, "Do not be afraid. I will rid you of it."

A while later the water of the Nile boiled and became very turbulent. It parted and there was the serpent! Mari Girgis, very composed, drew his sword out of his scabbard and waited. Of course the beast thought, "What is this little thing?"

It kept on coming toward them. When it was very close, Mari Girgis struck it once and didn't need to strike again. The beast became a heap of meat at his feet.

He made the girl carry the serpent (they say); it was a horrible serpent, and they went through the town. Of course everybody was hiding in his house with his door locked. They were all afraid. When they saw them coming, they ran out in the streets and rejoiced. The king wanted to give his daughter in marriage to Mari Girgis and give him his kingdom, but Mari Girgis did not accept. Because for us [Copts], saints do not marry; they don't have worldly desires.

· 35 · *The Golden Signature*

Recorded in June 1970 from N. Tanyoas, a 50-year-old clerk. He is from middle southern Egypt, but he currently lives and works in Cairo.

The theme of a saint responding to a cry for help is recurrent in all religious traditions. In the following "true" account, Saint George functions as a police officer; he must also observe bureaucratic procedures. The image of Saint George as a government official in uniform is perhaps derived from historical reports and other legends stating that he was originally an officer in the Roman army.

YOU KNOW that in southern Egypt roads are deserted at sunset, and traveling becomes dangerous. One woman who was visiting some relatives in a neighboring town was returning home; for some reason, time slipped away from her, and she looked up to find herself midway between her home and that of the people whom she had been visiting. She had no male escort. Night fell upon her, and she was afraid, especially since she was wearing many gold bracelets from here [the wrist] to here [below the elbow].

Suddenly a bunch of robbers came out of the cornfields and stopped her. "Who are you?"

"A lone woman."

"What are you doing here?"

"Going home."

In short, they saw that she had no one to protect her and heard the [tinkling of] gold under her sleeves. They grabbed her and stripped the bracelets and the necklaces off her. She shouted and screamed, but who would hear her out there?

She screamed, "Oh, government! Oh, district attorney! Oh, police!" No answer.

Finally she screamed, "Oh, Mari Girgis!"

A police officer appeared and took the whole bunch to the little police station of the region. It was very late, and only the night-shift sergeant was there. That officer said to him, "Put these in jail, for they robbed this woman. Here is the gold they took from her."

The sergeant said, "Sir, you must sign the book before I can do anything."

The officer said to him, "Just lock them up! That's an order! I will sign."

The sergeant got up from behind his desk and took them to lock them up. When he looked back, he didn't see the officer. He called, "Sir! Sir!" but he was gone. Of course he couldn't do anything to those, the robbers, without an "arrest report." He went to look at his register. He saw the name of the officer signed in gold, "Mari Girgis."

· 36 ·   *Letter to the "Justice of Legislation"*

Told in August 1969 by 'A. A., a 48-year-old man from Qalyoubiyyah Province in the Nile Delta. Currently he works as a stock clerk for a contracting company in Cairo. His family is still in the village.

Sending letters to the dead is a practice dating back to ancient Egypt. Imam al-Shafi'Ai (A.D. 767–820) was a jurist and founder of one of the four orthodox schools of Islamic jurisprudence. Because of his pious life and distinguished role as a legislator, many Egyptians think of him as still presiding over the execution of justice. The role the deceased imam currently plays among the living resembles that played among the dead by the "still living" ancient Egyptian god Osiris.

For the majority of Egyptians, gold ornaments and copperware are among the most valuable possessions within a household. In most homes they represent a family's savings that can be converted into cash quickly without much depreciation.

WHEN I GOT MARRIED, [since] my in-laws are very good people, they brought for their daughter copperware the like of which the village had never seen. The mortar alone weighed over ten pounds: pure brass! That was during the midst of the period for low prices for copper. Now things are expensive. The price of copper [burns like] fire. The mortar alone is worth five or six pounds. Now everyone buys aluminum; those who can afford copper are rare!

Some people, whom I will not name—but you know them—stole all the copper: pots, pans, strainer, even the mortar and the pestle! How? I don't know. After asking around with no avail, we finally went to Sheik Muhammad (he took over after the government ordered Sheik Ḥ. to stop his practice). Sheik Muhammad did what he could; he said, "I can tell you who took it, but they are people among you. If I tell you who took it, I may be starting a feud, and this will bring grief to the village. But I can tell you that the copper is still in the village, and whoever took it is from the village.

Some said to go to the police; we went, but they said, "Theft of copper is difficult [to track]," and they did nothing. I thought of reading the Ya Seen section [Sura 36 in the Koran] at them, but again I thought that would be too drastic.* Now! Forty or fifty pounds worth of copper lost like that!! Someone of legitimate descent [i.e., good] said, "Write a letter to Imam el-Shafi'Ai." We said, "By God, we will!"

We wrote the letter. "In the name of God the merciful, the compassionate. Justice of Legislation, Imam el-Shafi'Ai: Someone has transgressed against us. We don't wish those who have transgressed against us evil, but we plead by the right of God and his Prophet that you restore justice and return the property to its legitimate owners." We addressed it to the imam in Cairo. That was all. I swear by my children, within a week, seven days, those who stole the copper—one of them came to me and said, "So-and-so, I want a word with you." I said, "May it be good, if God wills."

He said, "I am a messenger, and 'a messenger is responsible only for conveyance [of the message].' I've been asked by some to tell you that your copper is awaiting you. You may pick it up or have it delivered to your door. If you insist on knowing the name, I will tell you, but—

I said to him, "I only want what is mine. We know who did

---

* It is believed that reading this sura at someone produces severe harm to him. The informant thought that such punishment was not warranted by the crime of simple theft.

it! Names don't concern us. May God protect everyone from defame."

The following morning we found the copper, clean and polished—to the last little saucepan cover, right at our front door. We later heard that the imam [in a dream by the thief] summoned those people to his court and told them, "God's law states, 'He who steals will have his hand cut off.' You have been condemned on the basis of evidence and witnesses."

But I forgave them.

· 37 ·   *Sidi 'Aabdul-Rahman*

Narrated in June 1970 by Bedouin Ṣāfi 'A., 40, of the 'Aazayim clan, a branch of the Awlād 'Aali el-Abyaḍ tribe. He settled near the 'Aagami beach area in western Alexandria, where he was working as a middleman. He is married and has a number of children. He states, "I heard this story for the first time from my grandfather, my father's father."

Regrettably, when I returned to the area about a year later, I was informed that Ṣāfi had been shot to death in a vendetta. When I asked about the reason, my source stated, "His family owed blood; he had nothing to do with it. He was considered the proper compensation for the murdered person [from the other tribe]. They took him for their own man."

The following saint's legend accounts for how Sidi 'Aabdul-Rahman, after whom a small town is named, acquired sainthood. An important symbol in this narrative is the watermelon which reveals that a murder has been committed. In numerous contexts the watermelon is associated with a number of female functions, especially as enveloping human life or as a birth giver.

SIDI 'AABDUL-RAHMAN was a merchant. He was traveling one time with one of his friends. They reached a deserted area and made camp. After they rested and ate and drank tea, they sat down chatting together. His friend said to him, "If I were to kill you and take all of your half [of our money], who do you think would tell about me?"

Sidi 'Aabdul-Rahman replied, "The flying air would."

He said, "Air what? and flying what?"

He killed him, took his money and all he had on him. He went—of course it was money that he didn't earn, and it belonged to some one else—he bought fine clothes and a good mare and spent [lavishily].

A year later, as he was going back home on the same route he took with Sidi 'Aabdul-Rahman, he remembered [the event]. He thought, "I'll go and see what's happened. I'd like to see how the flying air will tell."

When he got there, he could not find anything except a watermelon vine. It had a single watermelon on it, a watermelon growing out of season. He thought, "How strange!" He took it and put it in his saddlebag.

The sheriff in the police station in el-Burg, or a town like it, was a very good friend of his. He was from Alexandria and from a good family. He went to him in the police station and said, "'The Prophet has accepted the gift.'"

The sheriff answered, "And I, also, have accepted [your] gift."

He said, "I have something wondrous for you!"

The sheriff asked, "What, if God wills, is it?"

He said, "Here it is."

He pulled the watermelon out of the saddlebag.

A watermelon out of season. Everyone gathered.

"A knife." And someone took out a pocketknife and cut the watermelon. The moment he drove the knife into it, it bled. Inside was the head of Sidi 'Aabdul-Rahman!

"What is this?"

"By God! I don't know!"

"Seize him!"

They caught him. The sheriff, his friend, interrogated him. "Q— and A—" [i.e., question-and-answer formal interrogation]. He confessed.

A shrine for Sidi 'Aabdul-Rahman was built on the spot where he was killed, and the watermelon vine grew. Now there is no one who doesn't visit him.

Recorded in March 1969 from H. Ghanim (see informant note to tale no. 4). He heard about this "event" in the environs of Helwan, a southern suburb of Cairo, from his maternal uncle. The narrator also heard his mother and his friends tell about this "occurrence."

Before burial it is believed that a dead person can make his or her wishes known in a number of ways. Among these, the corpse may become immovable, as is the case in our present account, or the bier carrying the corpse may become unmanageable, making it impossible for those carrying it to choose their direction or path; in such a case, the bier is thought to be "flying." The people in the congregation will do whatever they think the deceased wants done; normal conditions will be restored only when the actual wishes of the deceased are met.

THIS STORY TRULY HAPPENED here in Cairo. A merchant-vendor of skullcaps and clothes and things like that went around until he came to some poor people and spent the night at their place, as a guest, I mean. He saw that the woman was sick, so he gave her one pound and said, "Dress yourself with that amount of money."

He also gave each of the children a pound. He gave the father some money and said, "Buy clothes and be happy."

The man, who was really ungrateful, said to him, "I've got to kill you, for I need the money."

The merchant said, "Man, take everything I've got! I don't need it, and God will make it up to me. And if I were to say a word to anybody outside [about your robbing me of my property], then I deserve to be put to shame!" The merchant swore that he would never mention anything about it to anybody outside. The man said, "No! I must kill you, and that's final."

He killed him and took his money and cloth and everything else. After that he carried him to the mosque and left him there. The government came in the morning [and asked], "What killed this man? Who brought him here inside the mosque?"

Nobody knew. They tried to remove him, but they couldn't.

The corpse just would not move [narrator imitates their pulling movement].

Now the man who killed him said to himself, "I'll go and see." The people saw him coming and called on him for help [in moving the corpse]. Of course they didn't know that it was he who had killed him.

They said, "You! Good man, come and help."

As soon as he touched the corpse, it went along with him very nicely. People carried it to the cemetery. They said, "This is a blessed man, for the corpse is moving with him."

At the cemetery they wanted to dig out a grave, but the ground would not dig. They dug, dug, dug; nothing dug. So they called on the man who moved him, the corpse. When he tried, the earth dug very nicely, and the grave was ready in no time.

Now they tried to put the corpse in the grave, but it wouldn't go. They said to the man, "Step in and pull."

As soon as he stepped in the earth closed up on him, up to his neck. God is capable of everything. They said to him, "Tell us, what have you done in your lifetime?"

He replied, "It was I who killed this man for his money, and I don't know why."

They put a glass box around him so that everybody would see for himself, and they charged money for people to see. This really happened. Everybody in the world says it's true . . . but I didn't see it. It happened in a village called Ghammaza, near Helwan [a southern suburb of Cairo].

· 39 ·   *The Mountain That Moved*

Narrated in July 1971 by I. H. (see informant note to tale no. 2). He heard this belief narrative first "at home," then from his friends and later in church. He states, "It is also in Coptic books; it is a fact that everyone knows."

The Muqattam hills mentioned in this narrative are a high ridge, mostly lime and sandstone, surrounding the east flank of Cairo. Previously they represented the easternmost borders of the city and were regarded as a strategic natural barrier against invasion. This Christian religious legend expresses the traditional rivalry between Copts and Jews. By implication, the king in this account had to be a Muslim.

HERE [i.e., in Egypt], there used to be disbelieving kings. One of them had a Jewish vizier. One day he said to the king, "We want to drive those Christians out of the country; they should not remain here with us."

The king answered him, "We have to find them something, a *fatwa* [religious opinion], to drive them out."

The minister answered, "Their book says—there is a verse: 'He who has as much as a mustard seed's worth of faith will order the mountain, "Move!" and it will move.' They have to prove that they have faith. Either they move the mountain, or we cut their throats, or [we] get them out of here. Then they will have three choices."

The king said, "This is very good advice."

Naturally [this was] the advice of a Jew, for they have hated Copts all their lives.

They, the Jew and the king, agreed on this; they called the patriarch and informed him that either the Copts would have to move the mountain, or their churches would be torn down, or they would have to leave the country. They were given three days.

Priests prayed and did all they could. One priest entered his church to pray asking God's mercy— The Virgin from the picture spoke to him. She said, "Why are you sad?"

He answered, "Sad? Don't you know the situation?"

She said to him, "All right, you go to a cobbler called Sam'Aan." (A man who mends shoes, for God may place his power in the weakest of his creatures—and also as the proverb says, 'There is no rag on the dirt pile that has not seen a [good] day.' I mean, one should not have contempt for the weak creature. You don't actually know the person in front of you; maybe he is more acceptable to God than yourself.)

In short, she told him, "Go to such and such a place. You will find such and such a person. He is the one that will move the mountain for you."

The priest went to the patriarch and said to him, "The Virgin told me such-and-such."

The patriarch answered, "Fine."

They went to Sam'Aan and told him the story. He was frightened, but they quieted him down and asked him to have faith in God. (Of course the Virgin, the mother of God, had told them to do so. You see, everything we [Christians] have is according to faith in God. No man can help you.)

They took this Sam'Aan to the patriarch. Sam'Aan said to him, "You can tell the king yourself, for I don't want to see him."

The patriarch went to the king and told him, "We have your order. We will present it at such-and-such an hour."

The whole world turned out that day: the people, the Muslims, the king, the Jewish minister, and everybody. Sam'Aan instructed the patriarch, "Say *'Keri ya laysoun'* [*Kyrie eleison*] forty-one times after having read that section in the Bible in which moving the mountain is mentioned. Read, publicly and loudly!" That was Sam'Aan the cobbler, who mended shoes, telling the patriarch, for God plays no favors; 'God is God of hearts.'

The patriarch did as Sam'Aan instructed him. He read that section of the Bible and said, *"Keri ya laysoun"* forty-one times. Slowly the mountain moved—this [pointing toward the ridge] Muqattam mountain! It went up, and up, until the sun could be seen from underneath it. The king became frightened and said to him, "What is this!" (This is something that really happened, three or four hundred years ago.)

Sam'Aan the cobbler feared that he would be famous for this and that people might worship him instead of God. He ordered the mountain to land on him so that he wouldn't become famous in the world.

The king saw all this, and he became convinced, and he and his minister started fighting. Whether the king shot his minister or imprisoned him does not really matter.

Part VI
Local Belief Legends and
Personal Memorates

Told in March 1971 by 55-year-old "Uncle" 'Aabdu, a shoe-maker from Cairo. 'Aabdu is married and has a number of children. I paid a business visit to 'Aabdu's workshop, which lies directly across the street from his apartment; his 14-year-old daughter came to see him. He noted that she had not been feeling well lately and reminisced about her previous illness, then told me this story.

The notion that the jinn assume the forms of different animals is central to the folk belief system. In the household the jinn are believed to dwell in bathrooms, under staircases, and in other isolated places. Beating or being otherwise cruel to cats or dogs, especially at night, is always feared and strongly discouraged, for they may be jinn. Supernatural sickness is a widespread phenomenon on all social levels and is treated by sheik and priest shamans of local and national fame. In many cases folk healers rival established physicians and psychiatrists in practice.

In our present account the shaman receives advice from a female jinni with whom he has developed a friendly brother-sister relationship; she is called his "sister." This type of bond is typical of the category of healers who use their supernatural aids to diagnose and prescribe a treatment. In this respect, the healer is unlike the magician, who claims to have the power to control and coerce the jinn.

ABOUT SEVEN, maybe five, years ago when my daughter Loula—whom you have seen here in the workshop before—was about ten years old, something wondrous happened to her. One day, it was a *moosim* day [seasonal celebration], we had a male duck slaughtered. As my daughter was going into the bathroom, she saw a great big she-cat holding the thigh of that male duck and eating it. Loula took (do not blame me) the wooden clog off her foot and threw it forcefully at the cat. It hit the cat in the stomach. The cat howled, "Awwwuuu...," left the thigh, and attacked Loula and bit her big toe (this one, the right toe). She fell ill. I took her to all doctors until I grew dizzy [from going around], but to no avail.

Finally a friend of mine (a good man like yourself) told me

about a man called Sheik Muhammad in Monoufiyyah Province, in a village called Megiryeh, or something like that, and said, "This is the one who will cure her."

I said to myself, "Let us see; maybe God will cause recovery at his hands."

On Sunday [because of business requirements, several shops close on Sunday instead of Friday, the Muslim sabbath] that friend of mine and I and our wives, who came along, took the bus. We got there right before the time of afternoon prayers. We asked, "Where is Sheik Muhammad's house?" They showed us his house. As soon as we knocked at the door, it was ajar, and the sheik called from inside, "Come in, *haji* [i.e., honorable] 'Aabdu!" (By God, it happened just as I am telling you right now. How did he know my name? I don't know.) He was sitting on a mat, leaning against one of those stiff rectangular cushions used in the countryside. We sat next to him. He said to me, "Open that door over there." I opened it. I found there a pitcher of water. My! What water! Sweet, cool, and fragrant! As I was drinking, I looked around and found neither a window nor a hole in the wall. I took the pitcher for the others to drink. He asked us, "How are you?" and things like that. A short while later, maybe five or ten minutes later, he said to me, "*Haji* 'Aabdu, open that door again." I opened the door. I found there one of those large round trays full of all God's gifts. I ate soup that tasted like no soup I have ever had before; bread, rice, meat, fowl, everything! We were hungry, so we ate 'until we thanked God.' After we drank tea, as we were drinking it, Sheik Muhammad said, "That duck's thigh, was it absolutely necessary?"

When I heard that, I was astonished! How did he know? How did he know my name! From where did that food come? How did he know about the duck's thigh! I answered, "A mistake! She is only a little girl; she doesn't know [any better]."

He said, "Was it that necessary? Why! Why!"

The girl's mother said to him, "By God, master sheik, ask them to forgive her." She gave him one [of Loula's] handkerchiefs which she had brought along.

He said to us, "Spend the night here," but I said to him, "We must return to Cairo, for I have to open my shop on Monday; customers and things, you know."

He said to us, "Well, peace be with you, but come back 'like today' [i.e., a week from today]."

Next Sunday I went alone. He had consulted the lady whom he had "bebrothered." She told him, he said to me, "Listen, I want you to buy three young ducks of the highest quality. Slaughter them as you mention God's name this time. If they [the jinn] are Muslims, they will take them, if they wish to do so. [The implication here is that if they were not Muslims, he would have to repeat the procedure without using God's name]. Fry them in pure clarified butter, put them in one large plastic bag, and go to Maadi near Sheik—" I forgot his name—"and bury them in the hills. Don't let anybody see you. Then go back the following day and see what happened. If they are gone, then they [the jinn] have accepted our offering. If not, God forbid, come back to me."

I did exactly as he told me to do. The following day I went back. I had marked the spot with a few bricks. When I dug the sack out, by God, the ducks had become nothing but dry bones. Every speck of meat and fat was gone. Not a single bone was out of place. I swear by God, it happened just as I am telling you. When I returned home I found Loula recovered and better than ever.

· 41 ·   *The Possessed Husband and His* Zar

Recorded on July 9, 1972 from 45-year-old Fatima I. 'A. She is a widow and the mother of two grown sons and a daughter. She lives in the rural part of Manyal, a district of southern Cairo. After the death of her husband, about fifteen years earlier, she had to go to work in order to support herself and her children. She works as a door-to-door vendor, selling primarily eggs. She can neither read nor write.

Our story illustrates some sources of conflict between husband and wife; it also shows how an emotionally disturbed person— who is, among other things, a transvestite—is treated through belief in jinn. *Zar* spirits, unlike ordinary jinn (which appear in tale no. 40) represent a different type of emotional illness and require a specialized ritual, including a sacrifice, to be appeased; they are hardly ever totally expelled.

The *zar* ritual has been commercialized lately, and in some instances it resembles Western rock festival cults or night clubs with psychedelic music and dance. Formal Islam considers the *zar* cult sacrilegious, and the practice of the ritual has been outlawed since the mid 1950s. However, the belief and its practice not only persist but are spreading.

This report on the experience of a close relative is one step removed from a memorate; it is also not quite a local legend, for this report per se does not circulate within the community. Such a report may be labeled a "postmemorate" or a "prelegend."

HAJI D., the owner of the district butcher shop, is the husband of my sister Karam. My sister married him while he was, I swear by God, working only for seven piasters per day. When my sister entered his life, she entered accompanied by good fortunes. He used to work for a [small contractor] beside the Nile before the building of the Nile Boulevard. We used to plant [the strip of land] between the river and the bank. We always planted watermelons. Those who worked around there used to stroll by. He saw my sister Karam. She is very beautiful, very, very beautiful. He said, "I'll marry this girl." Then my mother said to him, "You are a Cairene, and we are *fellahin*. If you marry her, you will not be able to live [the way you are used to]." He said, "No! I will marry her." Circumstances deemed it so, and he took her for a wife.

When he took her, his daily wage was very little, seven piasters [the equivalent of seventy cents]. My mother never let them rough it on their own. She always took [foods and other stuff] to them. He was able to stand on his own feet, little by little, and became rich—for she [Karam] came to him along with good fortune. He bought a piece of land and built a house, and [they] stayed in it. She first had Ibrahim [a boy], then 'Aali, [another boy]; then she slapped [her husband] with five girls in a row [this apparently depressed him].

When my mother went to visit, during the height of his wealthy period, he would say to my sister, "Listen, I will make you swear on the Koran not to take anything [from my house] and give it to your mother. If your mother comes, feed her and make her tea and make her comfortable, but she should not take out anything from my house. If your head scarf wears out, show it to me [before you give it to her]." That was the husband of the daughter talking about the mother-in-law who supported him when he was in the midst of poverty! Now he was saying [to his wife], "If your slip wears out, show it to me before you give it to your mother."

Now, when the distant one [i.e., the husband] became rich and stood on his [own] feet and 'carried and put down' [i.e., went through much interaction], you might say his body became possessed. He remained at home for about three years without opening his shop or selling. He would lock behind him (in his home) a door like this one [in the editor's home] and not open it at all. He asked for neither food nor drink, nor tea, nor tobacco, nor anything. Did he last long [in this mood]?—For about six months. They tested his "trace" [something that belonged to him] and said he was "visited" and needed a "beat."

They went ahead, invited men and women [a team of *zar* exorcists]. They got him candles and said to him (don't blame me), "You need a ram and six pairs of pigeons [to be slaughtered and offered to the possessing spirit; the blood would be used to rub the body of the possessed person]. He got all that, and God alleviated his affliction. Before, when my sister would enter his room, just as soon as she got to the doorstep, he would say to her, "God's line [separates] between you and me. Stay out!"

That one who was from underneath the earth [a female jinni] had put a barrier between him and his wife. He wouldn't talk to her for three years. When they made the "beat" and quieted down the one who was possessing him, things were better and are better now, thank God.

They found that she [the possessing one] was an Arab [i.e., Bedouin]. She laid down her conditions (don't blame me), that he should wear rings and wear clothes that she liked. When he responds to the "beat" [by doing the ritual dance climaxing in dissociation], he must wear an Arab woman's garb (don't blame me); he should hide his face with a red veil, wear an ankle bracelet, wear [female] rings, silver arm bracelets—those thick

silver ones—and some chain necklaces. He does the dance until
he is exhausted and hits the ground. After that he takes this
costume off [and leads a normal life until the next ceremony].

He was very much interested in marrying someone else in
addition to my sister, but the one who is possessing him
wouldn't let him. She could bear neither the old [wife] nor the
new [prospective wife]. So she seized him and arrested him [i.e.,
his power]. He has to do the "beat" three times yearly, just to
get some comfort. For "the distant one" [that is, the narrator's
brother-in-law] has no comfort; he can't sleep or even 'catch a
glimpse' of sleep [without the *zar*].

· 42 ·   *The Only Murder in Girshah*

Told on October 30, 1969 by 'A. Isma'Aeel (see informant note
to tale no. 16). He narrated this account of a "true event" in
response to my inquiry about it.

Belief in magical practices which render a man sexually impotent
is widespread and strongly feared. This process is called *ràbt,*
tying or fastening (its counterparts which cause infertility in
women are called *mushahràh* and *kàbsàh*). The following "event"
was told to illustrate the nature of Nubians, who live in the
southernmost portion of Egypt and are well known for their very
peaceful nature and their honesty.

A LONG TIME AGO someone was getting married. We had a
person in the village who performed magic. One of the things
that he used to do was to "tie" grooms on their wedding night
and go to them the following day and ask for something: money,
food, clothes, anything of value, to "untie" them. He used to do
his magic using a fish, an animal, or a bird. The most difficult is
the magic written on the stomach of a catfish, for once it is let
loose in water, it is gone forever.

One time he tied a person using a star in the sky. Of course
the groom was in utmost distress; he became a woman before his
bride. Our friend wanted to check the star before telling the

goom that he could untie him, but he could not find it. He lost track of it.

Twenty years later—(all that time he had been looking for the star)—twenty years later he found it and undid his magic. He went to that groom; he was getting to be an old man by then. The groom was sitting among a group of people. He said to him, "So-and-so, by God, forgive me, for I've done such and such. Only today was I able to find the star and untie you."

The man did not say a word. He stood up and left. A short while later he came back with a gun. He shot the sheik [the magician] and killed him. That is the only murder I can remember ever happening here in our village.

· 43 · *The Changeling*

Taped in January 1971 from Galeelah (see informant note to tale no. 28). She heard this particular account of the incident from her father; however, she has always been quite aware of the changeling belief and knows numerous other reports about other people's experiences with it. The informant states, "I hear stories like this every morning while I am waiting for the bus [the route cuts across an old cemetery]. Women say they take their babies [believed to be changelings] to the cemetery and leave them for fifteen or twenty minutes. . . . Then they return to find out whether they [the jinn] have returned the real child."

The belief that the jinn may steal a human infant and put their own infant in its place is widespread in numerous parts of Egypt. This belief may account in part for the maximum attention given to children during the early years of their lives. Parents, especially mothers, abhor letting their newly born children cry, especially when unattended. Thus a child's wants are immediately satisfied, and the child is constantly in the company of adults and under their supervision. Such child-rearing practices are probably responsible for the formation of some basic personality traits characteristic of the Egyptian.

MY FATHER SAID that there is a man in our village who was married and had a son; it was only forty days old. His wife had left the little boy in a room by himself and gone off to do something and left him to cry. When she returned, the little boy was sick. They took him to everybody, to no avail. They took him to doctors and sheiks. They took him to visit el-Sayyid el-Badawi and all the saints, to no avail. The boy's stomach was like an open irrigation canal. He ate everything, and nothing showed on him, neither food nor days [age].

One day his father looked in his mouth and found that [the supposed] forty-day-old infant had teeth! He knew it was a *badal,* changeling. He got his cattle whip and said to it, "Where will it hurt you [most]?" Taaakh! taaakh! taakh! (hit, hit, hit) until the baby spoke and said to him, "I'll bring your son back." They found their own son in the room, and the other one disappeared in the ground. Of course they [the jinn] (may God make our talk light on them) had exchanged one of their own for the boy!

· 44 · *El-Muzayyara*

Narrated in July 1968 by M. el-Sayyid (see informant's note to tale no. 22). He states, "This event took place about thirty or so years ago. Everyone in the village has heard of it. People still talk about it." A number of other villagers confirmed that the event really did happen and added a number of similar encounters between the *muzayyara* (water spirit) and other men.

Belief in water spirits is very strong in all parts of Egypt. There are numerous categories of water spirits, each with its own characteristics and specific types of relationships that may develop with humans. A *jinniyyah* (female jinn), for example, may marry a man, but he must keep their relationship secret; children from such a marriage belong to the mother, never to their human father. In a number of cases in which a man who is believed to be married to a *jinniyyah* mysteriously disappears, his disappearance has been interpreted to mean that his wife took him into the water.

ONE NIGHT Idrees was returning from Barshoom, which is about three kilometers from here. He was riding his mare. He took the main road. There at the bridge he heard a voice calling, "Oh, Idrees; oh, Idrees."

He looked around and did not see anyone. He thought that it was the wind or something and kept on going. The voice called again, "Oh, Idrees, come and help me."

He looked toward the voice and saw a woman standing by the canal with a water jar in front of her; she couldn't raise it to carry it over her head.

Idrees dismounted and walked to her. He saw that she was not from our village. He asked her, "What are you doing here at this hour?"

She answered, "I am from over there," turning her head toward the eastern part of the village. "We are neighbors. I just had to get water, and time passed and it became too late. Wouldn't you let me mount behind you and ride to my house?"

Idrees said, "All right."

He put her behind him on the mare and went on. A short while later, he noticed that she was restless. He looked behind him, only to see her getting her breast out. It was an iron breast, with fire glowing at the nipple. He immediately realized that she was the *muzayyara*—her hair came down to her knees (they are beautiful)—and she was going to kill him. He poked his mare with all his might and caused it to rear up, while he held tightly to the reins. She (the *muzayyara*) fell to the ground, and he flew away like the wind.

As he got farther away, he heard her biting her [index] finger and grumbling, "Akh! Son of a dog, you got away from me!" Her eyes were sparkling with fire.

・ 45 ・   *The Stone in Bed*

Recorded in October 1969 from Nabawiyya M. Y., about 45, from the Geeza district in southern Cairo. Nabawiyya was looking for a job as a housemaid when I met her. She was being introduced to a prospective employer by a 68-year-old woman who may be called a service-broker. Both women wore amulets against the evil eye.

The belief in the power of the evil eye is universal in all parts of Egypt as well as all other Arab countries. Practices associated with the prevention of the evil eye are visible in all walks of life. The belief in the evil eye has an extremely important psychological function. Among other things, it makes every individual the sole owner of something unique and very valuable which is unobtainable by others. Thus a person's self-concept is never lacking in positive assets.

THERE IS A WOMAN in our neighborhood who has got an eye that is evil. No one or thing she looks at escapes the harm [her eye causes]. One time one of my neighbors gave birth; her baby boy was very big. Of course we neighbors and friends went to visit. I wasn't there, but I heard from the others. While they were sitting around her, for she was still in bed, they told her "So-and-so," meaning that woman, "is coming." Immediately she said, "Her eye is evil!"

Of course her son who had just been born was beside her, covered with a bedcover. She said, "Take the boy to the other room, and get me the stone from beside the front door."

It was a big piece of limestone to sit on. She put the stone beside her in bed and covered it with the bedcover. That woman walked in, looked at the baby and said, "My! Your son is big. He is as big as a calf." After a short while she left.

When that woman, the mother of the boy, took the cover off the stone, it was split in two!

I overheard this narrative in December 1970, while waiting in a medical doctor's reception room in Cairo. Two adult males, about 35–40 years of age, were involved in a conversation. One of the men told this account of the evil eye event to the other. From titles used in the conversation, it was evident that both men were graduates of an engineering college.

The following account demonstrates the effectiveness of the belief in the evil eye as a defensive mechanism. The person who parked the car without applying the emergency brakes did not consider himself to be at fault. It was the "eye" of the envious friend that caused the accident, not the negligence of the owner.

A FRIEND OF MINE from college days had his brother, who is in Spain, send him a car. He took his wife and his forty-day-old son for the first ride in the car. He met another fellow from work and said to him, "Come with us."

The whole time they were driving, that friend of his did not take his eyes off the car. He kept on saying, "How beautiful! How neat!" How this! How that!

My friend did not pay much attention to what he was saying. After they finished their ride, his friend stepped out, and he drove the car to the garage.

The following day when he went to the garage, he found that the car had rolled down a steep slope and crashed against the wall. He immediately remembered what his friend had been saying the night before and how he had eyed the car. He said, "Thanks to God that it was not my child or my wife that his eye hit!"

Part VII
Animal and Formula Tales

Narrated in February 1970 by 'Aaql (see informant note to tale no. 32). He heard the tale from "older people" in his village about forty years before. He referred to the tale during a discussion of two current political events, stating, "As they say, Son-of-Adam [i.e., a human being] can be outwitted only by another Son-of-Adam like himself!" When I asked him to explain his statement, he first outlined the tale and later agreed to tell it.

'Aaql later stated a series of truisms: "See, 'no man can outwit a woman', 'a woman outwits Satan', and 'only death defeats Son-of-Adam!'" All of these proverbial statements are common themes in expressing "folk wisdom" and are also associated with a number of recurrent folk narratives (type 2031, *Stronger and Strongest*).

Folk views of the relationship between Son-of-Adam and other animals follow formal Islamic teachings. God has made man superior to all worldly creatures by virtue of his intelligence. Man may utilize other creatures only for purposes which God has legitimized, mainly as food to sustain his life and as beasts of burden to help him in his daily activities. As long as these rules are observed, man remains the rightful master of all beasts.

Besides the crocodile, four domestic animals—the camel, the water buffalo, the cow, and the donkey, all of which are a standard part of village life—appear in the tale. Of these four only the camel—the symbol of patience, strength, and dependability—and the donkey—the symbol of stubbornness, stupidity, and deception—play roles congruent with their nature as perceived in folk culture.

Both the cow and the crocodile played sacred roles in ancient Egyptian religion; it was considered the greatest of honors for a person to fall into the Nile and be devoured by a crocodile. Evidently subsequent religious changes have deprived the crocodile of the opportunity to be so magnanimously accommodating.

ONCE THERE WAS a camel man who was going about his work. As he was walking, he found a crocodile that was left behind after the river water had receded. The crocodile was left on the dry land, and the sun was what—it was like fire!

The crocodile said to the camel man, "Paternal uncle camel man, would you take me to the river and soak me in its water, for I am getting dry? Let me moisten my mouth. May God reward you."

The camel man said to him, "But you will eat me!"

The crocodile answered, "After you have done me such a favor, would I eat you? Do you really believe this?"

He said to it, "Surely, you would eat me!"

"Son-of-Adam, after you have carried me and taken me to water, to eat you would be a disgrace!"

The camel man said, "All right; I will take you there, and let us see what you will do."

He let his ropes down, dismounted, wrapped the crocodile, lifted it up, and put it on top of the camel. Everything was done 'twenty-four carats.' The camel kept on going until they reached the river bank. The camel man made the camel kneel down, loosened the ropes around the crocodile, carried the crocodile to the water, and let go of it.

The crocodile struck the water with its tail like this—boom! boom!—and drank. Now his strength came back to him. He turned to the man and said, "Come here! where are you going?"

The man answered, "Going home to my children!"

The crocodile said, "I have been starving for the past three days. Now it is either you or the camel."

The camel man said, "Is this my reward? I have carried you and brought you and—"

The crocodile [interrupted], "I haven't eaten for three days! It is either you or the camel!" He came closer to him.

The camel man said, "Wait, here comes the water buffalo. Let's ask her to be the judge."

The crocodile said, "All right."

"Water buffalo," said the man, "This crocodile was left behind on dry land, and he was about to die. I brought him here. Now he wants to eat either me or my camel."

The water buffalo said to the crocodile, "Eat Son-of-Adam; he takes my milk and beats me too."

The man said, "Let us disregard this. We will wait for the cow; here it comes."

The man said, "Cow, I brought this crocodile here from dry land; now he wants to eat either me or my camel."

The cow said to the crocodile, "Eat Son-of-Adam. He makes me turn the water wheel and beats me too. Eat Son-of-Adam."

The camel man became very sad. What was he going to do?

The crocodile said, "Camel man, you have heard with your own ears."

The camel man saw a donkey coming. He said, "Wait, here comes the donkey; let us ask him."

He said, "Donkey, I carried this crocodile from dry land. He couldn't walk. I carried him and brought him here to safety. Now he wants to eat either me or my camel."

The donkey said, "Eat Son-of-Adam. He works me to death. What wrong has the camel done?"

The man said, "Wait; here comes Son-of-Adam. Let us ask him."

The man said, "Son-of-Adam, the crocodile was on dry land; he was unable to walk. I carried him and brought him here. Now he wants to eat either me or my camel."

Son-of-Adam said, "You are a liar. You such-and-such. Were you really able to carry a crocodile and bind it with ropes?"

The man said, "Yes."

Son-of-Adam asked the crocodile, and it also said, "Yes."

He said, "Before I can judge, I have to be sure. Now," Son-of-Adam said, "let me see."

The man made his camel kneel down and tied up the crocodile with ropes. Son-of-Adam said, "Was the camel able to get up?"

The man made the camel get up.

Son-of-Adam said, "Was the camel able to walk to that place? If you are a real man, let me see if you will be able to do so."

The camel kept on going until they reached dry land.

Son-of-Adam said, "Will the camel be able to kneel down?"

The man made the camel kneel down.

Son-of-Adam said, "Could you really untie the ropes?"

The man untied the ropes.

Son-of-Adam said, "Now were you to carry the crocodile you would die! Could you really carry it? You would certainly die."

The man carried the crocodile.

Son-of-Adam said, "Were you able to gather your ropes and make the camel get up?"

The man said, "Yes!" And the camel got up.

They took the camel and went away, leaving the crocodile to crack in the sun. Son-of-Adam said, "Let him die. After having been saved, he wanted to eat you up. What ingratitude! And as for the buffalo, cow, and the donkey, we use them only for what is legitimate!"

· 48 · *Son-of-Adam and the Lion*

Recorded in April 1969 from Abu-'Aashoor (see informant note to tale no. 3). He heard this tale when he was about 15 years old. "It was first told to us as a *nuktàh* [i.e., joke or humorous story]. But sometimes we use it to describe a man who puts his brains to work," he stated.

Our story demonstrates the folk's awareness of the empirical effects of what psychologists term "conditioning." The climactic episode, in this tale in which the lion flees, may be viewed as a conditioned response. It is man's intelligence and knowledge that assure his mastery over other beasts.

The contents of the story, as explained by the narrator at the end of the tale, may be referred to by the code name "Pour, Fatma!" This saying "means that someone is getting frightened because of something which hurt him in the past. It may also mean that something is a bluff," he stated.

THE LION asked the mouse, "Is there anyone stronger than I am?"

The mouse answered, "There is."

The lion roared at him, "Who?"

The mouse said, "Nobody but Son-of-Adam."

So the lion said, "Show him to me."

They walked until they came near a small village. There was a farmer plowing his land. The mouse said, "Do you see this man plowing? He is stronger than you are."

The lion asked [in amazement], "This?"

The mouse said, "Yes."

The lion walked up to the man. The man's knees became

loose.' [i.e., he became very frightened]. The lion said to him, "Are you Son-of-Adam?"

The man answered, "Yes."

The lion asked, "Would you wrestle with me to see who's stronger?"

The man replied, "But my strength is not with me! I left it at home."

"Go get it," the lion said.

The man asked, "How do I know you will not run away?"

The lion said, "I will not. I'll wait for you."

The man said, "To be sure you will not run away, let me tie you here until I come back."

The lion answered [with indifference], "Tie me."

The farmer got a sturdy rope and tied the lion tightly. He got the whip with which he drives his animals and asked the lion, "Where will it hurt you the most?" Takh! takh! takh! (strike! strike! strike!), until the lion's skin peeled off. Then the farmer took his animals and went home.

After a while the mouse came and said, "Eh? Didn't I tell you?"

The lion said, "Do me a favor! Let me loose!"

The mouse gnawed the rope and freed the lion. The lion still said, "I'll never let go of that Son-of-Adam!"

So he went to the village. The farmer was outside and saw the lion coming. He ran inside his home, closed the door, and said to his wife, "Fatma, boil some water."

The lion came and started ramming the door with his head until the door was about to break. Meanwhile the water was good and bubbling. So the wife took it to the top of the house, right above the lion. The lion was just about to ram the door in when her husband shouted, "Pour it, Fatma!"

The hot water fell on the lion! It peeled the lion's skin for a second time. Our friend the lion 'hoisted his sails in full' [i.e., ran away as fast as he could].

Still the lion wouldn't let go of the farmer! A few days later the lion went to the field. This time he had his relatives with him, about a hundred! The farmer didn't know what to do. He ran to a palm tree and climbed it. The lions stood one on top of another, until they were just about to reach him. By chance the lion on the bottom was the one previously skinned. The farmer shouted, "Pour it, Fatma!"

Our friend, the lion at the bottom, 'put his tail between his teeth' and *ran* away. They all fell down and scrambled over one another. The lion finally realized that Son-of-Adam was stronger.

[The audience laughs. The narrator adds, "Sometimes we say, 'Pour, Fatma!' This means that someone is getting scared, because of something which hurt him in the past. It may also mean that something is a bluff."]

· 49 · *The Partnership between Wolf and Mouse*

Recorded in April 1969 from 35-year-old M. 'A. 'Aatiyyah from a village in Gharbiyyah Province. He is literate and works as the village's switchboard operator, but he is also a farmer. Occasionally he narrates humorous anecdotes and animal tales with a humorous twist, but not *Märchen,* to friends.

Our present text is an excellent example of the kind of creativity which a narrator exercises within the limitations set by an established text. 'Aatiyyah narrated with pleasure; he dwelt on details and used allegories, puns, and proverbial sayings to enhance his presentation. He also added a realistic dimension to his fantasy tale by correlating the tale's characters and actual village personages. He heard this tale from Abu-'Aashoor, who was present at the time of the recording (see informant note to tale no. 3) several years before. "It was shorter than this, but I have 'inlaid' it," our present narrator stated. Several other persons from the village were present during the recording; they participated with comments and explanations.

"The strong are abusive" is a folk adage which appears in the context of our tale. It presents the view which the powerless peasant holds of those with power and how they must be accommodated. For millennia the Egyptian peasant has been both exploited and despised by foreign rulers. Even native urban and nomadic groups have looked down on the peasant and consid-

ered him to be stupid and at the same time tricky. In the face of
the overwhelming odds which the peasant has faced, he has
relied on fatalism, suspicion, and trickery for survival. The narrator and his audience, who are members of a farming community, openly identify with the weak, submissive mouse which
triumphs over the powerful and abusive wolf.

The tale portrays a number of economic concerns and values;
the scarcity of agricultural land, the rule that the partner who
divides a joint property does not have the right to first choice,
and the need for cooperation.

THE WOLF AND MOUSE planted some onions together [Listener
(teasing): "Where did they get the land?" Narrator (jokingly):
"They rented a piece of land, the two of them, from Mahmoud
S.," a landlord in the village; "they rented eight *qirat*"—one-
third of an acre—"from somebody like Mahmoud S."] They
planted onions. At the end of the year, after the onions grew
and—prayers upon the Prophet—were fully ripe, the wolf said
to the mouse, "Brother, come! We want to reap our crop," and
things like that.

The wolf, with his strength over the mouse, said to him, "Let's
divide now so that each one of us will work for himself."

Of course the mouse said to him, "Yes, sir," for he is a weak
man. What can he do, compared to the wolf?

The wolf said, "I will divide!"

The mouse replied [submissively] "Paternal uncle, divide."

The wolf said, "And I will choose."

The mouse replied, "And you choose too! Paternal uncle, you
divide, you choose, and you leave me whatever you wish not to
have."

The wolf said, "Fine. Mouse, I am going to choose what's
above the ground. What is underneath the ground is yours.
Whether it is good or bad, I have nothing to do with it." That
was the wolf [talking], for he had seen the leaves of the onions.
They were very large and shooting up, for the land was very
productive (he didn't know what's inside the ground. Of course
he is not a *fellah*.)

The wolf went and got all his relatives and gave them sickles;
they charged on the onion crop and "castrated" it—takkk, takkk,

takkk, takkk—it was all cut down and divided up into bundles. They took the leaves to the wolf's threshing ground, and in two days they were dry and reduced to nothing.

Meanwhile the mouse went and got his friends and relatives. All the *ci-ci* family [squeak-squeak family, i.e., mice] (we have a family named Cici here in our village too)—he said to them, "I have a crop of onions that I planted in partnership with the wolf, and I need to have it reaped."

Of course they were poor people. They did not have the necessary tools. They borrowed a hoe from 'Aabd el-Fattah [one of the audience] and an axe from me and another from Sheik Ameen [one of the audience]. They worked for two-three-four days. They pulled out very good onions. Each head was—prayers upon the Prophet—that large [spreading his arms]! They had a huge heap. They wanted to take it home and store it in their own threshing ground. They found somebody like myself on the back of his donkey coming back from his field. They said to him, "By God, would you be generous enough to lend us your donkey so that we may take these onions home?"

They borrowed a large rope sack from another person. They suspended the sack on the donkey's back with two forked sticks, and they loaded their onions and took them home.

The wolf had nothing but the leaves. When he tried to sell them, they brought him only three ten-piaster pieces. The Sheik-of-the-Mice [honorific title for the mouse] and his relatives sold their onions for no less than three hundred pounds! The wolf was extremely sorrowful. He couldn't go back to the mouse, for he himself was the one who made the division.

He said to himself, "My boy, you have it in for the mouse! The next crop you get the root."

He understood that it is the root that has the good things, all the benefits.

The following year, "What are we going to plant?"

"We are going to plant wheat."

So they planted wheat. Later the wheat—prayers upon the Prophet—grew and ripened, and they wanted to reap it. The wolf said to the mouse, "Listen, mouse. We are going to divide the crop in the field."

The mouse said, "All right."

The wolf said, "Last time you chose, and I did not want to use my force over you. We have to divide now so that each one of us will go and attend to his own business."

The mouse said, "Father-of-Wolves, whatever you say!"

The wolf said, "From underneath the spike downwards all the way to the ground will be mine. The spike will be yours." For the wolf had learned that the tips or leaves of a plant were no good.

He ordered the mouse, "Tomorrow morning you chop off the tops of the wheat and leave the rest in the field for me."

[Sheik Ameen, a listener comments: "'And the evil plot encloseth but the men who make it,'" Koran 35:43.]

The Sheik-of-the-Mice called his relatives, the relatives of his relatives, his in-laws, and all his acquaintances. They flew to the field and trimmed the spikes of the wheat off, and they left all the stems and the roots for the wolf.

The wolf is naive; he doesn't know about agriculture. The mouse stored the wheat in his threshing grounds, and the wolf got his relatives and they reaped the stems and even plucked out the roots.

The mouse threshed and strewed [the wheat]. His crop yielded pure wheat, for he had no stalks at all. The wolf went and got his relatives. They threshed and strewed and had camel loads of nothing but chaff. His field looked almost like a *wesiyya* [communal threshing ground]. There was no wheat at all. It did not even yield enough to pay for the sweat of the camel driver who had carried the crop to the threshing ground. The wolf went and walked around the mouse's heap of wheat, which was almost equal in size to the chaff that he himself got.

The wolf thought, "If I want to sell my share—" [Listener interrupts: "It will not be worth more than two or two and a half pounds at the most"] "Two and a half pounds!"

He looked and saw that the mouse had wheat that was worth almost a hundred and fifty pounds. Naturally, these are predestined livelihoods, for the mouse is weak and God is with the weak. The wolf said to the mouse, "Listen, this division will not do. I can't even pay for the sweat of the camel driver. This cannot be!"

Of course, 'the strong are abusive.' The wolf is strong. The mouse said in despair, "Sir, whatever you say. I leave my affairs to God. As you wish."

The wolf said, "Tomorrow we are going to have a race. He who reaches the heap of wheat first will get it all. We will stand at two or three hundred meters away from the heap, and as soon as I say, 'Hoop!' we race. He who gets there first will get the heap."

The mouse said, "Whatever you order."

The Sheik-of-the-Mice was sly. He ran to his relatives and friends and said to them, "Listen, we are in danger. The wolf wants to get our wheat. What should we do?"

They answered him, "Whatever you tell us to do."

He got fifteen or twenty mice and went to the threshing grounds. The mouse said to them, "The wolf and I will stand at the starting line. One of you should stand on top of the wheat pile, and the rest of you scatter between here and there."

When the wolf shouted, "Hoop!" they started running. The mouse fell behind. Every time the wolf shouted, "Mouse?" one mouse would reply, "Here I am ahead of you."

"Mouse!"

"Here I am ahead of you!"

"Mouse!"

"Here I am ahead of you!"

The wolf ran very hard and fast. Ten meters before the heap, he called, "Mouse!"

The mouse replied, "Here I am on the top of the heap! You can't take it from me. You have used all your tricks, and it is no use."

The wolf said, "You are right; I will leave my affairs to God." And that's it!

And I was there and just returned; even supper I did not eat.

· 50 ·   *The Sparrow**

Recorded in March 1969 from Zainab G., a 70-year-old widow originally from the Kenzi Nubian village of Girshah. After the death of her husband, she stayed with her married son and his

family. I was introduced to the narrator by the Nubian folklorist
'Aumar Khidr, who also comes from Girshah. We went to her
one-room residence at the top of an apartment building in the
early afternoon. She was pleased to receive us and welcomed the
opportunity to tell tales. Zainab had not told tales since she came
to Cairo; she remarked, "No one asked me to narrate. [Folk]
narratives are good; no one objects to what you say or gets mad
at you . . . [but] the children of my son are foolish, for they don't
show interest in tales."

Because of her old age, Zainab did not object to my presence
(as an adult male who was not related to her), and she commented, "you are like my son's son." She also stated, "When I
narrate, my mind gets relieved." However, she was still careful
not to expose materials which she considered unsuitable for an
outsider. When Mr. Khidr asked her, "Tell him the story of the
man who wanted to marry his daughter" (as told in Nubia, this
narrative is composed of types 510B, *The Dress of Gold, of Silver,
and of Stars,* and 410, *Sleeping Beauty*), she retorted in a rep-
rimanding manner, "No! I wouldn't tell it. . . . 'Away from you!'
Is there a man who would marry his own daughter!? I wouldn't
tell it [now]; it is disruptive to good relations and defamatory!"
Mr. Khidr proceeded to tell the tale himself, and she was upset.
The two of them disagreed over the contents in a number of
spots.

Although, as the narrator stated, she had not told tales to
others for about thirty years (probably an exaggeration), she had
meanwhile been thinking of them. Zainab stated, "When I am all
alone, I think of these stories of our parents and grandparents;
they set my mind at ease." Therefore we may conclude that she
has been practicing "solitary tale telling" subvocally. The following tale was collected jointly with 'A. Khidr.

Gift giving is an important aspect of Arab folk economic systems. In an oasis area in the western Egyptian desert, people
differentiate between two types of gift giving, "planting" and
"reaping." The first stands for giving a gift to a person or a group
for the first time, while the second stands for reciprocating for a
gift received or given earlier. A gift given with no expectations
of reciprocity is often viewed as being "for God's sake." Gift

giving follows very strict rules of etiquette which prescribe
when, where, and what to give. Our narrative dramatizes the
expectations of a false gift giver who gave the right thing at the
right time in the right way but expected the wrong repayment, at
the wrong time, in the wrong way. It is this hyperbole and contrast that give the tale an implicit sense of the type of humor
associated with trickery.

A BOY BEWITCHED HIMSELF into a sparrow.

[Khidr:] No! They say he was born in response to a prayer—

[Narrator:] No! A boy—

[Khidr:] Once there was a woman who could not give birth to
any children. She prayed to God and said, "God, give me a child,
even if it happens to be a sparrow."

God responded to her plea, and she became pregnant. When
delivery time came, she gave birth to a sparrow.

One day after the other [i.e., a while later], this sparrow flew
away.

[Narrator continues:] He found some people sowing barley.
He stole a seed from them and flew away. He found a woman
grinding grain on her grinding stone and said to her, "Would you
like to have this one seed of barley?"

She answered him, "It will not hurt."

She took the seed and put it with her own. She finished
grinding, and the sparrow was still waiting. He said, "Lady, I
want to go."

She replied, "Go! what's keeping you?"

He said, "I want my barley seed."

She answered, "It's already ground."

"I want it back!" he said.

But she said, "From where?"

He answered, "A fistful of flour for my barley seed!"

To get rid of him, the woman gave him a fistful of flour. He
took it and went away. He came to some women baking. He sat
next to them and said, "Would you like a fistful of flour?"

They answered, "It will not hurt."

He said, "Take it and bake it along with yours." So they did.

He said, "I'm going."

They said, "Peace be with you, go."

He answered, "No! I want my flour. I found a barley seed; a fistful of flour for the seed. Now a loaf of bread for the flour."

They gave him the loaf and said, "Go away."

He took the bread and went to some people gathering onions in a field. He said, "Take this loaf and eat it. It's fine; it is even still warm."

"Thank you," they said.

They got some onions and ate them with the bread. After they finished eating, he said to them, "I'm leaving."

They answered him, "Peace be with you."

He said, "I want my bread."

"Where are we going to get you your bread?" they asked.

He replied, "I found a barley seed; a fistful of flour for the seed; a loaf of bread for the fistful of flour; and now onions for the bread."

They gave him a sack of onions and shouted at him, "Go away!"

He took the onions and kept on going until he came to some people herding goats. It was noon and they were eating.

He said to them, "Take these onions and eat them."

They said, "Thank you," and they ate the onions.

Now he said, "I'm leaving."

"Peace be with you" they said.

He said, "I want my onions!"

They asked him, "Where will we get them?"

He answered, "I found a barley seed; a fistful of flour for the seed; a loaf of bread for the flour; some onions for the loaf of bread; and now a goat for the onions."

They gave him a goat and shouted, "Go away!"

He came to some people herding cows and said to them, "I'm spending the night here. I'm going to kill my goat, and you will have supper with me."

They said, "Fine."

They killed the goat and cooked it and had supper and sat down. He said to them, "I'm leaving."

They answered, "Peace be with you."

He replied, "I want my goat."

"From where?" they asked.

He answered, "I found a barley seed; a fistful of flour for the seed; a loaf of bread for the fistful of flour; a sack of onions for the bread; a goat for the sack of onions; and now a cow for the goat."

They begged him: "May God lead your path; may God satisfy you."

He said, "Impossible! I want a cow for the goat!"

They gave him the cow and shouted, "Go away!"

He took the cow and left. He walked until he came to some people celebrating a wedding. He tied his cow outside and joined the dancers. He made a lot of noise until people started wondering, "Where did this one come from?"

Finally, he said, "I must slaughter my cow in your honor and feed you all."

They slaughtered his cow, and they all ate. The procession started moving toward the bride's house. He *ran* to the door and sat on the doorstep.

"What's the matter? What's the matter?"

He started singing, "I am the green sparrow; I walk pompously. I found a barley seed; a fistful of flour for the seed; a loaf of bread for the fistful of flour; a sack of onions for the loaf of bread; a goat for the sack of onions; a cow for the goat; and now the bride for the cow."

[The people implored him]: "What? Oh, sir, may God lead your path. May God make you satisfied."

"Never," he replied; "the bride for my cow."

They said, "May God compensate you."

He took the bride and left. He kept on going until he came to the graveyard. There they were burying an old woman. He went and put a belt around his waist and mud and dust over his head and face. He tore his clothes from the chest down and wailed, "Only God is everlasting!"

Now they were lowering the corpse into the grave, and he said, "Stop! What are you going to do to the dead person? If you bury her, she is a loss. You take the bride and give me the corpse."

They said, "Fine," and gave him the corpse and took the bride.

He carried the corpse and went to the Nile. At the bank there were seven loaded ships anchored at the dock. He got some yarn, put it on top of that dead old woman's head, and pinned a

spindle to her sleeve. He stood her up at the dock. Then he went
to the boatmen and begged them, "Oh, do me a favor. This is my
grandmother; she wants to cross to the west bank, to visit her
daughter. Please take her across. I'm in a hurry, and I have to go.
My grandmother is a bashful woman. When the boat comes
close to her, just give her a push with the oar."

They said, "All right."

As soon as the boats reached her, they called, "Woman come
down; woman, come down!" but she didn't. One tapped her with
the oar, and she fell on her face.

The sparrow up there started shouting, "The boatmen killed
my mother! The boatmen killed my mother!"

People came running to help him. The boatmen became
frightened and jumped off their seven boats and ran away. The
sparrow took the ships and went back to his village.

[Khidr:] It does not end this way. They say: "As the sparrow
stood arrogantly on the mast of the lead ship, he started singing,
'Seven loaded ships for a dead corpse. A dead woman for a living
bride.' As he was bragging, an ant—one of those big black
ants—saw his red rear, his anus. It bit into it and would not let go
until the sparrow died."

· 51 ·   *The Biyera Well**

Recorded on March 9, 1969 from 11-year-old Nadya Seliman.
She was aided by her father, who had told her the story often.
The father (see informant note to tale no. 12) would not tell me
the story, for it is "for children only." He in turn had heard it
from his mother. Little Nadya, who was somewhat tense, narrated well; her father encouraged her and at the same time kept
her 13-year-old brother from interrupting and mimicking her as
she told the story.

The donkey as a trickster appears in this children's animal tale.
He not only steals the share of his partners but also swears
falsely. In actual life swearing as a testimony of truth is supposed
to be only "by God." However, all types of oaths are recurrent
in folk culture.

Wells which are believed to have supernatural powers are common in Egypt. Many wells are believed to be the abode of jinn and other supernatural beings.

ONCE A DONKEY, a she-goat, and a duck agreed to become partners. They said, "What shall we do? What shall we do? Let us plant clover."

They planted a field of clover. They all participated in preparing the land, sowing, watering and taking care of the clover until it became [Nadya's father adds, "as God willed"] that high [about two feet]. They agreed on going to the field early the next morning to eat the clover together.

The donkey was greedy. He sneaked behind their backs by night and went to the field. He landed on it and *ḥatatàk, batatàk* [hmmmm, hmmm], and what? He finished it off. He went home unable to move; his belly became that high.

In the morning the she-goat and the duck went to waken the donkey, but he was very sick. He said to them, "Eat your share, and leave mine for me. I'll eat it later."

They got there. "Oh, my! Where is the clover? Where is the clover? There is no clover!" They said, "No one did this but the donkey!"

They returned home. This one said, "I didn't eat it!" The donkey said, "I didn't eat it!" The duck, "I didn't eat it!" and the she-goat said, "I didn't eat it!" Who then?

"Then let us got to the Biyera Well [literally, "Welly-well"] and swear by it."

They all went there.

The duck said,

> Quack, quack, If I've eaten it,
> Quack, quack, if I've drunk it,
> Quack, quack, Biyera Well, may I fall in you
> And remain there for two months and one night.

And she jumped to the other side. The She-goat said,

> Baa, baa, if I've eaten it,
> Baa, baa, if I've drunk it,
> Baa, baa, Biyera Well, may I fall in you
> And remain there for two months and one night.

And she jumped to the other side. The donkey came and said,

> Haa, haa, if I've eaten it,
> Haa, haa, if I've drunk it,
> Haa, haa, Biyera Well, may I fall in you
> And remain there for two months and a night.

He tried to jump, but he fell in the well.

[Here Nadya's father asked her: "Why?" She added the following statement:]

Although he was much stronger and more able to jump, he was swearing falsely, so God pointed out the truth.

· 52 · *The Little, Little Woman**

Narrated in May 1970 by Kamal, a 10-year-old boy from a middle-class family living in a Cairo suburb. The young narrator was telling the story to a group of small boys on a street corner. He stopped his narrative when I approached him. Kamal was hesitant to tell me the story because it had "dirty" words in it. He finally agreed to tell it but used the word "dirt" instead of "shit," which I had heard him use in telling the tale to his friends. I restored the original.

An Egyptian folk proverb goes as follows: "'Master judge, the wall [of the house] has been pissed on by a dog.' He replied, 'It must be torn down seven times and rebuilt seven times [before it becomes pure again].' They said, 'But it is the wall between our house and yours.' He answered, 'The least amount of water will purify it!'" This image of a judge as being able to rationalize or justify any decision according to his whim occasionally dominates the folk's attitudes toward human justice. This view seems to be implied in our story (see introductory note to tale no. 54). In our narrative the judge speaks in classical, dissonantly inflective Arabic, which adds to the humor of the tale.

ONCE THERE WAS a little, little woman. Everything she had was little, little; the house, the wardrobe, the chair were all very little. Every day she swept the floor. Every day she found a pound which she put in the *taqah* [a small niche in the wall] to buy meat. Every day the burglar came and took it.

She went to the kadi and said, "Master kadi!"

He answered, "Yes."

She said, "Every day I sweep my house."

He [readily] answered [in classical Arabic], "Because of your cleanliness."

She said, "Every day I find a pound."

He answered, "Because it is your predestination."

She said, "I save it in the niche."

He answered, "Because of your cleverness."

She said, "I want to buy meat with it."

He answered, "Because of your appetite."

She said, "Every day the burglar comes and steals it."

He answered, "Because of your naiveté."

She said, "What shall I do?"

He answered, "Arrange your affairs on your own!"

She went home and put shit in the niche, stuck pins in the wall, put a rooster on top of the house and a donkey behind the door.

The burglar came and when he put his hand into the niche to get the pound, his fingers got dirty. He tried to wipe his hand on the wall, and the pins pricked him. He opened his mouth to curse, and the rooster made a dropping into it. He went out running, and when he opened the door the donkey kicked him.

· 53 ·   *Once There Were Three*

Narrated in July 1970 by a 12-year-old girl. She heard the tale from her classmates in an elementary school in Cairo. The narrator's father immigrated from his Arab village in Aswan province several years earlier; he works as a doorkeeper. Neither the narrator's father nor her mother had ever heard the story; her younger brother knew about it but couldn't tell it.

The following story is considered an exercise in linguistic dexterity; it is similar to tongue twisters and other verbal puzzles which show "cleverness." It is composed of a series of contradictory sentences which, in the original Cairene dialect, show use of some poetic meter and end rhyme. The story is also considered humorous and is sometimes referred to as a "joke."

ONCE THERE WERE three sheiks; two were blind, and one could not see. The one who could not see found three millemes [pennies]—two were defaced, and one would not spend. The one that would not spend bought three sheep; two were empty [skin and bones], and the third had no meat on it. The one with no meat on it filled three pans; two were empty, and one had nothing in it. The one with nothing in it fed three men; two who were already full, and the third could not eat. The one who did not eat went to feed the cattle; two were not acquired yet, and one wasn't there. He found a thief opening doors; two were already open, and one had not been closed. He shouted three times; two cries made no sound, and the third was not uttered. The robber dealt him three blows; two were not delivered, and the third did not hit. That is it!

Part VIII
Humorous Narratives and Jokes

Recorded in April 1969 from Tilib (see informant note to tale no. 11). He heard the story in his village in southern Egypt.

The capricious character of a judge is portrayed in this humorous tale (see introductory note to tale no. 52). Actions in the story are based on two fundamental norms in early Muslim society and in a number of contemporary nomadic communities. The first is the doctrine of compensation for personal injury, which perceives justice as the redressing of a wrong rather than the mere administration of punishment to the guilty. The second doctrine is the hierarchical arrangement of the old Muslim community into social categories according to piety, sex, and age; the pious adult Moslem male is the most valuable.

The expression "My donkey had no tail [to start with]" is often used proverbially. It refers to a person who denies his rights because of fear.

A BAKER had the judge for a friend. One day, as they were sitting on chairs in front of the bakery, a man brought a male duck on a tray. It was big and fat.

The man said, "Master baker, will you please bake this male duck for me?" and he left.

After a while, the smell of the duck was everywhere. The judge said, "Oh, my, master baker, the aroma of this male duck is piercing. What do you think? Why don't we eat it?"

The baker said, "This can't be."

So the judge said, "Why can't this be? I'm the judge of this town, and I've just sentenced this duck to be eaten by us!"

The baker asked, "What about its owner? What should I tell him when he comes?"

The judge answered, "Don't worry about it; just send him to me. I'll do what I see fit."

"That's impossible!" said the baker.

The judge replied, "All you have to do is just pick a fight with him and bring him to court."

They got hold of the duck, and the two of them finished it. The judge then left for his own business.

After a short while, the owner of the duck came to the baker to claim it. The baker handed him the tray.

The owner said, "There was a duck here. What happened to it?"

The baker said, "Oh, the strangest thing happened to your duck. It fought with me, bit me and scratched me, and it flew away."

The man said in amazement, "Flew away."

The baker answered, "Yes, it flew away."

One word here and one word there, and they got hold of each other. "Let's go to the judge! Let's go to the judge!"

As they went down the road on the way to the judge, someone came to intervene, saying, "Oh, good people, not like this!" As the baker was waving his arm, his finger pierced the man's eye.

"Oh, my eye! Oh, my eye! Let's go to the judge!"

Now the fight was among the three. As they continued down the street, a man and his pregnant wife tried to solve the problem. The baker was still waving his hands, and as he was going like this, he hit the woman, and she aborted on the spot. Now she and her husband got hold of the baker, and all of them were going to the judge.

The baker saw that things were getting much worse. He never thought the affair could go that far. He pulled himself loose from those holding him and ran into a mosque and up into the minaret. And oops! He jumped!

He landed on somebody performing his prayers, and the man did not take a second breath. The praying man's brother was nearby, and he came running, calling, "My brother! My brother! The baker killed him!"

Now all of them went to the judge. Just before they reached the judge, a man riding a donkey saw the big commotion. He dismounted and started asking, "What's the matter? What's the matter?"

The baker was still trying to get away and began to dodge his pursuers by running around the donkey. He got hold of the donkey's tail—oops! It came off in his hand.

The owner started yelling, "Oh, my donkey! Oh, my donkey!" and he followed them to the judge.

When they all got to the courthouse, the judge realized that it was the case of the male duck, so he summoned the case.

The first to go in were the baker and the owner of the duck. The baker told his story and said that the duck had flown away. The owner replied, "Your honor, this is truly a strange affair. Would you believe that a duck, after having been killed, dipped in hot water, plucked, and put in an oven until roasted, would get up and fly?"

The judge simply replied, "'God is able to do all things' [Koran 29:20]; 'God resurrects bones after they have decayed'" [Koran 36:77]. For doubting that, you are fined five pounds.

The man started to open his mouth, and the judge said, "Are you disputing my word too?"

The man answered, "No, your honor, I was just about to agree. 'God resurrects bones after they have decayed,'" and he left.

The second man was called in. the judge asked him, "What's your complaint?"

He answered, "I was only pulling them apart, and the baker put out my eye."

The judge replied, "Ahhh . . . What's your name?"

The man said, "Ḥanna [John]."

The judge said, "You have a right—a Muslim's eye is worth two of a Copt's. Let him put out your second eye, and then you put out one of his."

The man said, "No, I don't want to do that."

The judge said, "For consuming the court's time, I hereby fine you five pounds."

The judge called for the next person to come in. The man and his wife walked in. The judge asked him, "What is your complaint?"

The man answered, "Your honor, in this affair 'I had interest neither in the [mill] ox nor in the grain [to be ground].' I was just passing with my wife, and the baker hit her and caused her to abort."

The judge said, "Hmmm, you have a right. I hereby order the baker to take your wife and return her to you when she is loaded again."

The man said in amazement, "May God make me do without this!"

The judge answered, "You should have thought of that in the first place. A five-pound fine!"

The judge called for the next person to come in. The brother of the dead man walked in.

"Your honor, the baker jumped off the minaret and killed my brother who was praying."

The judge said, "Hmmm, you have a right. 'An eye for an eye; a tooth for a tooth.' I hereby sentence the baker to go and pray in the mosque and for you to climb up the minaret, leap on him, and kill him as he did your brother."

The man said, "May God compensate us for losing him; I don't want anything from the baker!"

The judge said, "You should have thought of this in the first place. A five-pound fine!"

The judge called in the next person, and the man and his donkey were ushered in.

The judge asked him, "What's your complaint?"

Having heard with his own ears and seen with his own eyes what had happened to those before him, he replied, "Nothing! By God, 'my donkey had no tail [to start with]!'"

· 55 ·   *Stingy and Naggy**

Recorded in April 1969 from 'Aazeezah 'A., 38, a Bedouin from a district of Maadi bordering the eastern desert. I asked her husband, a middleman, to help me find a Bedouin woman who told tales. He explained that no Bedouin man would allow a female member of his household to converse with a male stranger. The husband offered to introduce me to a man, his own father, who was well versed in poetry. I explained, "I want to hear stories which a woman has learned from her *maternal aunt,* for example." He evidently internalized this specific fact; after several months he offered to have his wife narrate to me, "since we have become 'like a family.'" He agreed to let me record her tales but not to let me take pictures.

'Aazeezah narrated in my home in her husband's presence and at times told specific tales which he suggested but could not himself narrate. She learned most of her tales from her mother and so stated. However, her husband, apparently influenced by his desire to give me exactly what I asked for as his profession and rules of courtesy both required, often interjected: "She learned it from her maternal aunt." At the beginning of the recording session, 'Aazeezah repeated what he said. Toward the end of the session, however, 'Aazeezah gave "other women" only as her source. Her husband interrupted: "Say 'From my maternal aunt!'" 'Aazeezah snapped, "I haven't got a maternal aunt! From where shall I produce a maternal aunt who would have told me the story!" She defiantly stated, "I heard it from my mother" (in Dorson, *Folktales,* p. 159, I erroneously reported "maternal aunt" as her source). She went on to explain, "My father would go out some place, then our mother would tell us these things."

'Aazeezah enjoyed telling the tale and was vividly ego-involved in its events. However, she did not elaborate or give background descriptions.

Glimpses of traditional funeral practices are seen in this humorous story. The graveyard as a hiding place for robbers is a common theme in traditional narratives. The names of the main actors represent two opposite personality patterns (see tale no. 14) which are usually referred to by the names of the main characters in this tale. See also Dorson's statement on "spongers," p. xxxiii above.

'STATE THE ONENESS of God.' [Listeners: "There is no God but God."]

Two brothers, one Shaḥooḥ [stingy] and one Laḥooḥ [a nag]. Stingy went to his brother Naggy and said, "Brother, for the Prophet's sake, lend me a pound until tomorrow?"

Naggy said, "From where? 'I haven't even got the air with me.'"

Stingy implored, "Oh, by the Prophet! Oh, by the saint!"

Naggy said, "All right, but only until tomorrow morning."

Stingy took the pound and ran home. Naggy went home and started thinking, "Now, he got my pound. How do I know he's going to return it? Well, am I going to wait until tomorrow?"

Before Stingy reached home, Naggy began running back after his brother. When he got to his place, he said, "Now, dear brother, give me my pound back." [Narrator laughs.]

Stingy said, "But you promised to wait until tomorrow. I don't have it."

And they started arguing. This one wants his pound, and that one does not have it. So Stingy said to his brother, "I have an idea."

His brother said, "what?"

He said, "I'll pretend to be dead. You start crying, 'Oh, my dear brother! Oh, my beloved brother! Oh, shroudless brother!' and things like that. People will take pity on us and will give you some money so that you can bury me. You get your pound, and the rest is for me."

Naggy said, "All right," for he was going to get his pound back.

They went to a place where there were good people. Stingy laid himself down on the ground, and Naggy started screaming, "Oh, dear brother! Oh, you who have died before your time! Only God can make it up to us! Oh, my beloved brother! Oh, shroudless brother!"

People gathered and started saying, "tchhh, tchhh," and "Only the Almighty is everlasting."

But they said, "Why should we give him money? He is so much in grief. What we should really do is prepare the late brother for burial." [Narrator laughs.]

And they sent after the person, the undertaker, who was going to wash the body.

Now the washer came; he had a handkerchief full of dates with him. He set it on the windowsill. He was a blind man. As he was feeling his way around, he hit Naggy's hand reaching for the dates. He took the dates and put them right next to the dead body.

[The narrator addresses Stingy directly:] Now, you dead one, get up and do what? Eat all the dates! Now, there, the handkerchief is empty! How are you going to fill it up? (Do not blame me) He [Stingy] defecated in the handkerchief and tied it up as it was before.

Now the blind washer was feeling his way like this, reaching for his dates. His fingers got stuck in it. So he said, "Dead? Dead one, you son of a dog! By God, I'll show you; right now your wash water is going to be boiling!"

He went out and said to the man at the fire pit, "Make the water boiling!" [Narrator laughs.]

Our friends heard him, and the dead man said to his brother, "Our blind friend is going to scald me with boiling water!"

Naggy went to the washer and said, "May God lead your path. May God reward you. Forgive him," and things like that.

They washed him and wrapped him in shrouds and took him to the grave. They put him in his grave and put the dirt back in. They all left except Naggy, who hid somewhere.

Now in the night, one-hundred-less-one robbers who had just made a big robbery came to the grave. They dug up the grave so that they could hide in it to divide the loot. They divided everything among them. There remained only a sword. Each one said, "I want it! It's mine!"

The chief said, "Whoever can split this corpse through in one blow will have the sword."

They said, "Fine."

The first one was raising his hand like this. He, the corpse, shouted at him, "Hold it!" [Narrator laughs.]

The man dropped the sword and ran away like the wind. The rest followed him, shouting, "The dead are resurrected!"

Now Naggy came in to take his brother out. He too saw the sword and said, "I want it."

Meanwhile the chief of the robbers said to his assistant, "Go find out about the story." The assistant looked through and found the two quareling. He ran back [frightened] to his chief and said, "All the dead are up. They are preparing to fight us."

The chief said, "Minus one piece of loot! We will make it up next time. We can't go back there."

They left their things in the graveyard and went home.

Now Stingy and Naggy took the money and everything else home to their wives, and they are still fighting over how to divide it. [Narrator laughs.]

Narrated in April 1969 by a 30-year-old housewife and mother from a village in the Nile Delta. She heard her mother tell the story to some female friends about twenty years before. The informant's husband was my host during a recording session in the village (see informant note to tale no. 3); he invited a group of villagers and myself to move from our earlier host's to his place. According to Arab rules of modesty, our present narrator was not supposed to be seen by me, a stranger. She stayed away while her husband and others participated in the recording. After finishing her housework, and lacking a place to go, she lurked at the door of the room and showed considerable interest in the tales. She briefly commented on some and indicated that she also knew them. Finally, ignoring her husband's warning looks, she stepped into the room and declared that she had a "little tale." After a brief appeal from me to her husband, he agreed that she would tell the story, but it was not to be recorded. He stated, "We are fellahin; this would be too serious [an offense] in our community." After the wife finished telling this anecdote, the husband commented, "I've been married to her for fifteen years, and I've never heard her tell this tale." However, he was quite amused and added jokingly, "My wife puts it to good use."

On the wedding night the groom and the bride each receive advice from the elders that he or she should establish patterns for interaction with the spouse at the outset of the marital relationship. These early patterns are believed to establish a lifetime policy. The principle is expressed through the proverb "Kill your cat on your wedding night"—i.e., if you intend to show your spouse how tough you are, do it at the outset of your relationship. Our story illustrates the importance of laying down these rules, but with an interesting humorous ending.

TWO FRIENDS MET. The first said to the second, "How are you So-and-so? We have not met for a long time. Those were the days. How are things going for you now?"

The second answered, "Well, by God, I got married, and my wife is the 'daughter of good people.' Just as one wishes a wife to be."

The first asked, "Have you beaten her yet or not?"

"No, by God, there is no reason to beat her. She does everything as I wish."

"She has to get at least one beating, just so that she may know who the master of the house is!"

"By God, yes! You are right."

A week passed, and they met again. The first asked the second, "Hey, what did you do? Did you beat her?"

"No! I just can't find a reason!"

"I will give you a reason. Buy fish, plenty of it, and take it to her and say, 'Cook it, because we will have a guest for dinner,' and leave the house. When you go home later, whatever she has cooked, say that you wanted it some other way!"

The man said, "Fine." He bought some catfish and went home. At the door, he shoved the fish at his wife and said, "Cook it, for we will have guests," and he flew outside.

The woman said to herself, "My girl, what are you going to do with all this fish? He didn't tell you how to fix it." She thought and thought and finally said, "I will fry some, bake some, and make some in a casserole [with onions and tomatoes]."

She cleaned the house and prepared everything. As dinner time approached, her infant son made a mess on the floor right next to the [knee-high] table where they sit [cross-legged on the floor] to eat. As she went to get something to clean it, she heard her husband and his friend knocking at the door. She ran to the door, and in order not to leave the mess like that, she covered it with a dish which happened to be in her hand.

They walked in and sat down [on the floor] at the table and said to her, "Bring the food, mother of So-and-so."

First she took out the fried fish. He said, "Fried! I want it baked!" Immediately she took out the baked fish. He shouted, "Not baked; I mean in a casserole!" Immediately she took out the casserole. He became frustrated and confused. He said, "I want—I want—"

She asked, "What?"

He replied [in bafflement], "I want shit!"

She immediately said [lifting the dish off the floor], "Here it is!"

Recorded in December 1969 from a 50-year-old middle-class woman in Cairo. She heard it from a woman neighbor, who comes from Sharquiyya Province, about fifteen years before.

Three important objects with stable symbolic significance are used—the watermelon, the knife, and the scissors. Both watermelon and scissors symbolize a female (see introductory note to tale no. 6), while the knife symbolizes the male. Thus the symbolic meaning of the story is more serious than a simple dispute over the object with which a watermelon is cut.

AN EGYPTIAN and a Turk were once talking together. The Egyptian said, "By God, yesterday I bought a watermelon. When I got the knife to cut it—"

The Turk shouted, "You cut the watermelon with a knife?"

The Egyptian replied, "Naturally!"

The Turk said, "No!"

The Egyptian said, "With what then?"

The Turk replied, "With scissors!"

"No, with a knife!"

"With scissors!"

"No, with a knife!"

They got hold of each other and started fighting. Hit! Takh! Takh! Takh!

A big crowd gathered and said to them, "Pray on behalf of the Prophet, brothers," and pulled them apart.

"What is the story?" asked a good man.

The Egyptian said, "This Turk says a watermelon is to be cut with scissors!"

The Turk replied, "Naturally, watermelons are cut with scissors!"

That good man said to him, "Brother, watermelons are too large for scissors; they are cut with knives."

The Turk replied, "With scissors, stupid!"

The people around them started laughing and said, "Brother, this is wrong. Watermelons are cut with knives."

The Turk said, "Never! With scissors!"

They (the people) went away and left them fighting.

They were fighting near a river. The Egyptian pushed the Turk, and the Turk pushed the Egyptian. The Turk's foot twisted (like this), and he fell in the stream. He could not swim. He began floundering about and going under the water shouting, "Scissors! Scissors!"

Water was getting into his mouth and his throat, and he still shouted [as he was drowning], "Scis—ba, ba, ba—sors, ba, ba, ba—! Scis—ba, ba, ba—sors!"

Finally, when he could not stay up any more, he stuck out his arm from underneath the water and went like this [moving his index and middle fingers vertically against each other, signifying cutting with scissors]. All this in order to show that he would not change his mind.

We always call a person who is very stubborn and never changes his mind "Scissors!"

The Trickster Cycle: Goha and Abu-Nawwas

Tricks played by animals and humans on others abound in Arabic lore. Not every act of trickery, however, qualifies its perpetrator as a "trickster." In contemporary Egyptian culture the animal trickster is virtually nonexistent. Two human tricksters appear: Goha and Abu-Nawwas. The Goha cycle of humorous jests and anecdotes is doubtless the most recurrent in the Arab culture area, with the possible exception of south Arabia. The name "Goha" appears among all religious, ethnic, and racial groups in the Arab culture area extending from Morocco to Iraq and from northern Syria to the middle of Sudan. Some scholars consider Goha's character to be a representative of the "spirit" of Arab folk culture and argue on behalf of his Arabic original identity. Younis states that Goha is "Ibi-al-Ghusn Goha al-Fazāri; in Arabic *goha* refers to [a person] . . . who walks hurriedly, or whose motions are not based on deliberation dictated by rationality" (pp. 3–5). Younis suggests that because of the "transitional" and "transformational" nature of Goha's character, it could have developed during the transitional period between the decline of the Omayyad caliphate and the establishment of the Abbasid era in the eighth century.

It has also been argued that Goha is the Arabic variant of the Turkish Mulla Nasruddin Hodscha, a courtier of the fourteenth century, Mongol Taymour Lank. However, the name "Goha," or "Joha," antedates the historical Turkish "Hodscha"; it appears in Arabic literature of the tenth century in Ibn al-Nadeem's bibliographic survey of Arabic and Moslem writing entitled *al-Fihrist,* written in Baghdad in the year 981. The word *goha* appears in later works also. Al-Maidani (d. 1124) cites the proverbial comparison "more foolish than Goha," which indicates that the name and the character it stands for were known prior to the eleventh century.

In many cases Abu-Nawwas duplicates Goha's character and deeds. Historically, al-Hasan Ibn Hani', nicknamed Abu-Nuwās (A.D. 762–814) was a distinguished poet in the court of the Abbasid calif Haroun al-Rasheed (d. A.D. 809). He is renowned for his poetry on love, sex, homosexuality, drinking, satire, and anti-Arab racism. It is popularly believed, as amply evidenced in oral literature, that Abu-Nuwās was al-Rasheed's joker; however, Ṣidqi states that al-Rasheed's joker was "Ibn-'abi Maryam al-Madani, who was known for his unusual utterances and deeds which were highly daring and made al-Rasheed laugh until breathless. This is exactly what is attributed to 'Abu-Nuwās.'... [But] these reports [about Abu-Nuwās] are fabricated, or at least they are assigned to someone other than their real doer" (p. 176).

Although Goha appears in oral tradition more frequently, Abu-Nawwas is found over a broader geographic area, particularly in south Arabia. Abu-Nawwas, unlike Goha, is also known among the Swahili of east Africa and various groups in Ethiopia. His name appears in Knappert (pp. 111–12) and Littmann's *Tales* (nos. 24, 26). It is also reported among the Somali in Courlander and Leslau (pp. 81–88).

A curious figure which appears among the Swahili as a substitute for Abu-Nawwas is "Mutanabbi"; Knappert (pp. 125–27) reports three trickster tales involving this character. Clearly the reference here is to the prominent Arab poet Abu-al-Ṭayyib

Aḥmad ibn-Ḥusayn (A.D. 915–65), nicknamed al-Mutanabbi, the prophecy claimer. Among Arabs, al-Mutanabbi is famous for his panegyric, lampoon, heroic, and the uncommon "self-praise" poetry; he is also well known for his selfishness and cowardice, two basic personality traits characteristic of the trickster. Al-Mutanabbi, however, unlike Abu-Nawwas, never appears as a trickster in Arab oral tradition. In the eastern section of Africa, particularly around the Horn area, both the indigenous animal tricksters and the Arab human tricksters appear (see notes to tale no. 51); this is also the case among the Berbers of north Africa.

Arguments about the origin of a specific name of a trickster may be legitimate in determining the time and place where that name developed. However, such arguments assume that the name of the trickster and the deeds he commits originated simultaneously. This is not so. A great many of the tricky acts performed by contemporary tricksters hark back to antiquity. The ancient Egyptian god Seth (as Te Velde points out, pp. 13–26, 109–52) was essentially a diety trickster. A number of the "Sethian animals" such as the ass, the hyena, and the jackal still play the role of the animal trickster with human and sometimes supernatural characteristics.

This pattern of distribution for the animal and human trickster in the Middle East and Africa suggests that, first, the trickster is an ancient indigenous character; second, a number of acts of trickery probably go back to antiquity; and third, the name of a human trickster simply supplants that of the animal trickster.

The contemporary Swahili case of Mutanabbi, where a new trickster character is in the making, and the case of Abu-Nawwas demonstrate that the substitution of a human name for that of an animal is determined according to the perceived qualities of that human. Similarly, the narrative cycle of the trickster expands through adding new stories with acts which are congruent with the trickster's character.

In Arabic lore the trickster is always a male; he plays both the tricky and the wise roles and appears over a wide spectrum of expressive forms, including proverbs. Both the trickster and his acts are perceived as real, at least symbolically.

Narrated in July 1969 by M. El-Fallah, a 36-year-old clerk. He heard the anecdote from his friends in the village when he "was still a boy of about 9 or 10 years of age."

This anecdote illustrates the conflict in a polygynous house from the viewpoint of a male child. In spite of its incestuous nature, the tale should not be viewed as oedipal, for both the step-mother and the stepson belong to the same age group; the stepmother is thus not a maternal figure. The symbolic associa-tion between putting on shoes and sexual intercourse appears in other folkloric contexts, especially pseudo-erotic riddles.

WHEN GOHA WAS YOUNG, he lived with his father and his mother. His mother was getting old and, his father wanted to marry a younger woman. People said to him, "Why do you have to do this? *'Um* Goha [Goha's mother] is a good woman."

His father answered, "I need a young wife to patch up my bones."

People said, "May God lead your path. May God satisfy you [i.e., please change your mind]!"

He said, "Never!"

His father married a young girl and brought her home to live with his old wife and Goha. Because she was the new wife, the old man became like a piece of dough in her hand. She drove Goha and his mother out of their minds and 'made them see the stars at mid-day.'

Finally, Goha said to himself, "By God, I must show this woman whose house this is!"

He waited until his father bought a new pair of slippers. And on a Friday, his father ordered him, "Goha, go get me my new *bulgha* [soft, slipper-like shoes], for I want to go to the mosque."

Goha ran inside to his stepmother and said to her, "My father ordered me to sleep with you."

The woman was startled and said, "What did you say? Your day is black!"

Goha put his head out of the door and shouted, "Hey father, the new or the old?"

The father replied in anger, "I told you a hundred times, the new, stupid!"

And the woman had to let him do what he said he would do.

· 59 · Goha and the Pair of Calf Legs

Narrated in July 1969 by S. el-Qirsh, a 36-year-old store hand from the town of Zagazig, Sharqiyyah Province.

Tricks and countertricks between Goha and his wife are very common occurrences. The initial deception here concerns the consumption of choice food. The fact that Goha cannot assert himself over his wife and resorts to a countertrick to establish the truth is uncharacteristic of the image of an average husband; it is a trickster's device.

ONE TIME Goha was in the market. He saw calf legs at a butcher shop. His mouth watered for them. He could not resist buying a pair of them. They cost him all he had in his pocket.

Goha took the pair of legs and flew home. He proudly gave them to his wife and said, "Woman, cook these as quickly as possible"; and he went out to buy some groceries, rice, and things to go with them.

When he was out, his wife took the lid off the pan and saw that the legs were done. She said to herself, "I'd better make sure."

She took one leg out and had a bite. She hadn't had meat since the last 'Aeed [Bairam: a religious feast day], and it tasted good. One bite after another; the leg was finished.

A short while later Goha returned. He sat down and shouted, "The pair of legs, woman!" and his wife brought a dish with one leg in it.

Goha asked in amazement, "Where is the other one?"

She answered, "What other one? You bought only one."

One word from him, and one word from her, and it became a big fight. Goha said to himself, "By God, I'll prove to her that it was a pair!"

He stuck his hand into his coat (like this, putting his hand on

his heart) and started moaning, "Oh, my heart, oh, my heart."
He pretended to be dead.

Quickly his wife called the undertaker, and they carried him
on a bier. The procession passed through the market on its way
to the cemetery. As it went by the butcher's shop, the butcher
asked a member of the procession, "Whose funeral is this?"

The man said, "It is Goha's funeral."

The butcher replied in sorrow, "'We belong to God and to
God we return!' He just bought a pair of calf legs from me this
morning."

On hearing this, Goha removed the cover from the bier and
stood up in one jump. "Tell my wife, that 'daughter of sixty
dogs,' that it was a pair!"

· 60 ·   *Goha on the Death Bed*

Narrated by S. el-Qirsh; see informant note to tale no. 59.

Cowardice is a salient personality trait of the trickster. In
dangerous situations men are expected to step forward and place
women as far away as possible from the danger; Goha is an
exception. Simpleminded Goha does not understand that "there
is no escape from death."

ONCE GOHA GOT VERY ILL and was about to die. He called his
wife and said to her, "Beloved wife, put on your best clothes and
perfume, and comb your hair—in short, do all you can to look as
beautiful as you can be!"

She answered sobbing, "Don't say things like that! How can I
do all these things with you dying! I will never think of these
things again after you [have passed away]!"

Goha said, "Do it for me, and come and sit at the head of my
bed."

The woman did all she could to fix her looks and sat down
next to him. She asked him, "Did you want to look at my beauty
before you die?"

Goha answered, "No. They say 'death chooses the best,' and I thought Azrael might see you and decide to take you instead of me."

· 61 · *The Quick Ass*

Recorded in October 1969 from Isma'Aeel (see informant note to tale no. 16). He heard this anecdote in Cairo.

The application of red pepper to the anus of an animal was reported to me as a practical joke by village students commuting by donkeyback to schools in nearby towns; the rider is usually thrown off. It is also a ruse used by some merchants in livestock markets to stir up a sluggish animal that they have for sale.

Goha is usually thought of in combination with his donkey; this association between the trickster and donkey harks back to the trickster god Seth and the ass, a Sethian animal, in ancient Egyptian beliefs.

GOHA ONCE HAD a very weak and sickly donkey. The donkey was so weak and scrawny that its bones were sticking out. It could hardly stand up. Goha wanted to sell the donkey, but no one would buy it. He said to himself, "I have to sell this donkey for ten pounds."

Of course nobody would buy this donkey even for fifty piasters [half a pound].

Goha went to the spice man and bought four piasters' worth of red pepper. Again he had an afterthought, and he bought another four piaster's worth of red pepper, "Just for emergencies."

On market day Goha took his donkey and went to the market. He began applying the red pepper to the rear of the animal little by little. All of a sudden, the dying donkey became almost like the most spirited stallion. Not even the best Arabian stallion could match its liveliness. It jumped up and down, bucked back and forth, reared up, and finally, when the pepper became too much, it broke the leash and ran away.

Of course Goha got awfully upset. People started chasing the animal, and he wanted to get his capital back. The animal was going so fast that no one could catch up with it. Finally Goha applied the rest of the red pepper to himself and took off after the donkey. He *ran* so fast that he couldn't stop himself! Finally he started yelling to the people, "Let the animal go! I'm the one who needs to be harnessed!"

· 62 ·   *Who Is the Laziest?*

Recorded in October 1969 from Isma'Aeel (see informant note to tale no. 16). He heard it a long time ago in his native village.

The trickster in the following narrative is Abu Nawwas. In numerous other variants the trickster is a *tanbal,* an obese, joker-like figure found in the courts or palaces of Turkish sultans. His role was to be comically lazy.

ONE TIME Haroun al-Rasheed had a pitcher of silver and gold. He ordered three of his courtiers to be brought before him. One of these three was Abu Nawwas. Haroun al-Rasheed said to them, "He who proves to be the laziest of you will have this pitcher."

"Now! Master So-and-so, tell your story."

He said, "One day as I was lying down beside a wall, it started falling down over my head. Little stones and sand started falling down, but I was too lazy to move."

Haroun al-Rasheed said to him, "Well."

"Now you tell your story, Tahir" (for example). [Tahir is the name of the narrator's son.]

Tahir said, "One day I was leaning against a tree. A huge serpent came and crept over me and made its way to the top of the tree. I was too lazy to move off his path."

He said, "Well."

"Now, Abu Nawwas, you tell your story."

Abu Nawwas did not want to tell any story. The calif said, "Fellow, tell your story."

Abu Nawwas did not want to tell any story. He did not even want to open his mouth. Haroun al-Rasheed shouted, "Don't you heed the order of the calif?"

Abu Nawwas answered, "To-o la-a-azy." The prize was his.

Jokes: An Urban Phenomenon

The following narratives represent the joke, *nùktàh,* as a genre known only in urban centers. Structurally, jokes emphasize brevity, dramatic presentation, and climactic action. The climax of a joke is represented by an abrupt, terse ending which is usually uttered in a different pace, tone, or emphasis. The content of jokes addresses every aspect of life; however, the majority fall into three main categories: political, erotic, and sterotypical of other groups. One joke, however, may belong to all three categories.

Within small groups and cliques where jokes are normally told, a "good joke" is relatively ephemeral. Since both the joke teller and his audience expect and emphasize novelty, the same joke may not be told repeatedly to the same listeners. In addition, a new joke circulates rapidly in a community. The teller of a well-known joke may be interrupted by his listener, who will cooly state, *"Adeemah!"* i.e., "It is old!" (see notes to tale no. 62). Thus a joke will tend to circulate for a short period of time, after which it loses its appeal and is relegated to a passive status where it is only referred to but not told in full. Jokes, however, are constantly adapted to new situations, personalities, and issues.

In the countryside and desert areas, as well as among the nonurbane folks of the city and towns, humorous narratives are limited to anecdotes, jests, and merry tales. These are generally speaking longer, more elaborate, more descriptive than dramatic, and, when compared with the urban joke, less climactic.

· 63 · *"Left or Right?"*

Narrated by a young male graduate student in May 1972. He heard it from his colleagues.

Shortly after Nasser's death in 1970, observers of the political scene noticed that although President Sadat continued to pay lip service to the "socialist camp," his actions were oriented toward rapprochement with the West. The following joke sums up this situation. It should be pointed out that the folk joke accurately gauged the political situation before officials and political commentators.

WHEN ANWAR EL-SADAT became president, he sat in Gamal 'Aabd-el-Naser's Mercedes, and said to the chauffeur, "Go."
"Where?"
"To wherever 'Aabd-el-Naser used to go."
The chauffeur drove, and people cheered. "El-Sadat is following 'Aabd-el-Naser's path!"
Soon the car came to a spot where the road branched out in wo directions. The chauffeur stopped and asked, "Left or right?"
"Which did 'Aabd-el-Naser take?"
"He always went left!"
"Hmmmmm; give a left-turn signal and turn right!"

· 64 · *The Coerced Confession*

Told by a graduate student in business in the winter of 1964. He heard it from colleagues in Egypt before leaving to study in the United States.

Bitter humor is expressed in the joke. It alludes to secret police tactics used to extract confessions from "enemies of the state."

A LITTLE ancient Egyptian statue was found, but no one could find out anything about it. They summoned experts from abroad, and still they couldn't find out a single thing about it.

The secret police heard about the statue, and they said, "Give it to us for twenty-four hours."

"Twenty-four hours! What can you do in twenty-four hours?"

"None of your business. Just give it to us."

They took it, and before the day was over, they came back with it and said, "This is King So-and-so, son of So-and-so; he ruled at such-and-such a time and place, and . . . , and . . . , and!" They told them everything.

"How did you find all that out? Did you locate his tomb?"

"No, sir! He confessed!"

· 65 · *Foreigner and Citizen*

Told in September 1968 by a young male government employee. The informant is a university graduate.

The courtesy and consideration which the Egyptian government is thought to accord European foreigners contrast sharply with the rough, inconsiderate treatment the average citizen receives, particularly in foreign travel matters. This issue can be of dramatic magnitude. The following joke was in circulation about two years before the death of Nasser in 1970.

GAMAL 'AABD-EL-NASER DIED, and his soul went to heaven. There the angels of paradise and the angels of hell disputed over him. When they weighed his good deeds against his bad deeds, they were exactly equal. They finally said, "Let him go to paradise." He entered paradise and found that everyone was happy; he couldn't live there. He thought, "I should visit hell and see how things are there." He took out a tourist visa and went to hell.

As soon as hell's angels saw his visa, they received him with all kinds of honor and respect and gave him a tour of all the torture chambers. Here were people burning in fire, and there others were being skewered; all were shrieking and crying in agony. He was very pleased with the tour. After the tour was over, he returned to paradise. This time he decided to transfer to hell, so he took out an immigrant visa to hell.

When he got there, hell's angels received him, but as soon as they saw his visa, they seized and chained him. As they were carrying him to hell, he said to them, "What is the matter! I was just here a few days ago, and you were wonderful to me!"

They replied, "Then you were a tourist; now you are a citizen!"

· 66 ·   *A Problem of Documentation*

Told by a male university student in 1964.

Bureaucratic procedures in Egyptian government offices are notoriously complex. The following joke expresses a native viewpoint; it illustrates how civil servants blindly follow formal procedures even concerning the most obvious facts.

A FOX ESCAPING from Egypt was running in the [western] desert. He met a camel going toward Egypt. The fox stopped and said to him [panting], "Uhh...uhhh...Don't go to Egypt! There they get hold of camels and work them to death!"

The camel [frowning in amazement] said, "But why are you running away? You are not a camel!"

The fox replied, "You know it and I know it. But I would have had a hell of a time [trying to produce the papers] proving it!"

· 67 ·   *The High Bridge*

Told in the summer of 1969 by a man about 30 years old to a group of his friends as they met in a coffeehouse. The narrator works as a clerk in a department store.

Hashish smoking has always been associated with wit and male sexual stamina. It is also believed that liquor causes dullness and phallic depression. The joke represents a fantasy about a super phallus.

A WOMAN HAD TWO LOVERS; one was a *hashshash* (a hashish smoker), and the other was a *khamorgi* (liquor drinker). One night both of them stopped by her place at the same time. What should she do? She said to them, "We will go to the Nile, and the two of you race. The one that wins spends the night with me!"

They went to the Nile and the two [men] jumped into the water. The liquor drinker swam fast, and quickly he was at the other bank. The woman took him home.

The following day the *hashshash* and the woman met. She said to him [reprimandingly], "How come? You have failed me! I suggested the race knowing that you would win. The liquor drinker, as you know, couldn't do a thing."

He replied, "What could I have done! My 'thing' was hard, and it stuck in the mud where I jumped!"

She said, "This is not an excuse. Why didn't you swim on your back?"

He replied, "What about the bridge!"

· 68 · *Instant Virginity*

Told by a college student in the winter of 1964.

A maiden's virginity is of paramount importance in Arab culture; bleeding after the ritual-like defloration procedure is the only acceptable proof of a girl's virginity. Although the defloration ceremony is not a part of wedding procedures among the middle class, a bride's bleeding as a sign of virginity is still closely watched for.

A GIRL HAD A BOY FRIEND. They used to meet and dally. One time things went too far, and he perforated her. She went to a surgeon and cried, "Save me, doctor! My virginity is gone!"

The doctor said to her, "Simple. There is an operation that would restore you. You will be as you were before."

She said, "Hurry with it!"

He performed the operation; of course, it was a minor one, and he sewed her back together again.

"How much?"

"Fifteen pounds."

"Fine," and she paid him and left.

Once more things went too far and she ran to the doctor.

"Save me doctor! . . . How much?"

"Fifteen pounds."

"Fine, here they are."

This happened a number of times. They meet, things go too far, she runs to the doctor. "Save me, save me, doctor!"

"Fifteen pounds."

The last time, the doctor said, "A hundred pounds."

"A hundred pounds! It has always been fifteen. Why a hundred?"

"This time I installed a zipper."

· 69 ·   *The Body Scrub*

Told in 1970 by a high school teacher. The narrator works in Cairo, but he is originally from southern Egypt.

The stereotyped image of a *si'Aidi* (southern Egyptian) is generally one which portrays him as stubborn, unyielding, aggressive, and stupid. This joke seems not to be restricted to describing southern Egyptians; it is also told about *fellahin,* delta farmers.

It is not unusual for an Egyptian to tell a joke which mocks his own social group. Thus a joke may represent one of the few institutionalized channels for self-criticism.

ONCE a *si'Aidi* [southerner] went to Cairo. They told him about the public bath. He said [in dialect], "What is that?"

They answered, "A place where you may get your body washed in hot water, rubbed, and scrubbed with a sponge."

He exclaimed, *"Wah,* oh, Fa-a-a-th-e-e-er!"

When he went there, he took his clothes off and got into the deep tub. After that, they got him, and wash, wash, wash; scrub, scrub, scrub for hours! He finally got tired and said, "That is enough."

They answered, "Patience; we are just about to reach your undershirt."

· 70 · *How the Cat Died*

Told by a university student in the summer of 1968. He heard it from friends.

This joke reveals an aspect of the stereotyped image of the Nubian. Although Nubians are considered honest and peaceful, they are also unfairly thought of as being stupid and lazy.

The Nubian accent in speaking Arabic, the use of male gender to refer to feminine words, and the slow pace with which the characters speak enhance the comic situation in the joke.

MORGAN WAS SITTING DOWN, and "Bakeet" passed by him carrying a cat. Morgan said [sluggishly], "Where are you going, Bakeet?"

Bakeet answered [sluggishly], "To the river to wash the cat."

Morgan said, "It is very cold. The cat will die."

Bakeet said, "No, it will not die."

A while later Bakeet returned without the cat. Morgan asked, "Where is the cat, Bakeet?"

Bakeet answered [sorrowfully], "It died."

Morgan said, "Didn't I tell you! It is very cold!"

Bakeet said, "It didn't die from the cold."

Morgan asked, "From what did it die?"

Bakeet replied [with considerable stress, and tight fists to show how it was done], "It died as I was wringing it dry!"

Notes to the Tales

The Aarne-Thompson Type Index and Egyptian Folktales

The notes to each of the tales identify their narrative contents according to the indexing systems for folktales and relate these contents to their cross-cultural matrix. Tale type numbers are assigned wherever applicable, according to Antti Aarne and Stith Thompson's *Types of the Folktale*. Salient motifs from the revised and enlarged edition of Stith Thompson's *Motif-Index of Folk-Literature* are also listed. As the present work shows, the overwhelming majority of Egyptian folk narratives comply with the major components of international tale types. The type index is, however, seriously limited with regard to the treatment of Arabic and Berber folktales and especially Egyptian tales.

Three major deficiencies limit the applicability of the type index to Middle Eastern materials. First, only a fragment of the published collections from the Middle East was included. The bibliography of the present book shows that Arabic and Berber collections available before 1961, 1928, and 1910 were abundant. Second, only a fraction of the tales which comply with the designated contents of the tale types in the works treated in the type index were recognized in the list of references to a tale type. For example, Spitta's *Contes* includes twelve tales of which ten are of indisputable typological character: these are nos. 1 (type 325), 4 (type 465), 5 (type 621), 6 (types 881 and 883A), 7 (types 706 and 872*), 8 (type 410), 9 (type 567), 10 (type 590), 11 (type 707), and 12 (type 314). None of these tale types was acknowledged in the index. Although type 883A may appear in Victor Chauvin's *Bibliographie des ouvrages arabes,* which the type index lists in this particular case, the index's coverage of Chauvin's *Bibliographie* is at best incomplete. The type index does not cite Chauvin's work in reference to types 155 (Chauvin 2, no. 109), 332 (Chauvin 6, no. 349), 707 (Chauvin 7, no. 375), or 1510 (Chauvin 8, no. 254), to name a few. Every one of the few Arabic and Berber references listed in the type index's bibliography received the same sketchy treatment given to Spitta's collection. Third, in its present format the type index does not recognize the emotional aspects of a tale, nor does it handle adequately the symbolic significance of actors and their actions. (For further information on specific issues, see notes to tales no. 1, 2, 8, 9, 11, 48, 50, and 51. See also the discussion on "The Trickster Cycle.") It was only by reading through the entire type index that I was able to identify certain of the type numbers sketchily rendered in that reference work.

Annotations.—The notes to the present work are meant to complement available type and motif indexes. In order to supply additional data, I located and read hundreds of relevant tale collections published in Arabic, English, French, and German. Wherever possible, I identified international tale type numbers and outlined the distribution of the tales, largely on the evidence derived from this survey of previously untreated collections.

This statement on the distribution of the tale and other related issues concentrates on two main spheres: Arab-Berber and sub-Saharan Africa, a division more political and geographic than cultural. The distribution of the tale in Egypt, as indicated by archival variants and sparse published materials, is given first. Since the Nile Valley region of the northern Sudan is considered an extension of the Nile Valley culture area in Egypt, variants from this region are cited next. The appearance of the tale in countries surrounding Egypt is presented as follows: north Africa (Morocco, Algeria, Tunisia, Libya), the Levant coast (Syria, Lebanon, Palestine), Mesopotamia (Iraq), and the Arabian peninsula and southern Arabia.

A note on the distribution of the tale in sub-Saharan Africa follows. As this work demonstrates, the sub-Saharan African tale is closely related to its counterpart in the north. Indeed it is difficult to distinguish between north and south with regard to certain areas which have served as melting pots for different social and cultural groups: Sudan, Somaliland, the Swahili coast of east Africa, south Arabia, Mauritania, Mali, and the entire southern strip of the Sahara.

Factors which affect the placement of a group or individual include race and color of skin, language, religion, and political and kinship-group affiliation, as well as geographic location. There is one geographical area in which Arab and African traditions intermingle: shaped like an arch, it extends from the tip of the African Horn and Dar es Salaam in the east across the continent to the northern borders of Mauritania and some diffuse point south of Dakar in the West. With regard to narratives and other traditions, many groups in this area manifest varying degrees of similarity to groups in the extreme north of the African continent.

Nevertheless, we find that some of the renditions most similar to tales told in Egypt come from the Hottentots, the Basotho, and other southern Bantu-speaking groups. Such similarities are identified in the notes to tales no. 4, 8, 37, 50, and 51. The nature of these parallels to contemporary as well as ancient traditions in Egypt awaits further research. Notes on the ancient counterparts of contemporary folk traditions are provided whenever possible.

Attempting to establish the relationship between contemporary narratives and their ancient Egyptian counterparts constitutes not a quest for origins but, rather, an effort to ascertain the stability of a tradition and its social, cultural, and emotional relevance. Had these ideas and values not been of continuous significance to their bearers, they would have survived only in the form of scrolls or rock paintings.

PART I
FANTASY TALES

· 1 · *The Trip to 'Wag-el-Wag'*

Our story combines serially a number of tale types; it revolves around a variation on type 303A, *Six Brothers Seek Seven Sisters as Wives.* Other tale types that play secondary roles are types 956, *Robbers' Heads Cut off One by One as They Enter House;* 302, *The Ogre's (Devil's) Heart in the Egg;* 300, *The Dragon Slayer,* pts. 2–5; and 550, *Search for the Golden Bird,* pt. 5. The narrative also incorporates numerous motifs; these include H1242, "Youngest brother alone successful on quest"; E761.4.4, "Life token: ring rusts"; D231, "Transformation: man to stone"; K2211, "Treacherous brother"; and H95, "Recognition by bracelet."

The present story is characterized by conflict among male siblings over marriage to the same female. Type 303A, which appears at the outset of events, determines the nature of sentiments expressed in the narrative. Unlike type 303, which expresses strong feelings of affection and altruism among brothers, type 303A in the Middle East manifests jealousy and conflict of interests. In this respect the Middle East texts differ radically from the contents of type 303A as outlined in the type index, and therefore it should be viewed as an independent tale type (303B is suggested). For further information on the theme of the "jealous brothers" in Middle Eastern folk literature, see Chauvin 6:1–9; Elisséeff, p. 125; and Laoust, *Contes,* p. 216, n. 1.

This complex story recurs in Egypt with a fair degree of stability; six archival variants have been collected recently from various regions, including Siwa Oasis. A rendition from Fayyoum Province is given in Morsi, no. 57. One variant from Sudan is given in Frobenius, vol. 4, no. 11, and an identical text appears in Kamil, p. 95.

The story has also been collected from north Africa. A recent Arab rendition from Algeria is included in Galley, no. 3, while a Berber variant appears in Lacoste, no. 1.

This composite story appears also in the eastern part of the Arab culture area. A variant from Palestine is given in Littman's *Modern Arabic Tales,* p. 225 (German translations in Littmann's *Arabische Märchen,* p. 350). Two renditions told by a Syrian Christian narrator appear in Prym and Socin, nos. 33 and 39.

In the Arabian peninsula, this story seems to be little known; only one rendition told by a Jewish female is abstracted in Noy's *Jefet*, p. 349. In published works from south Arabia type 303 dominates.

In sub-Saharan Africa individual tale types which appear in our narrative are recurrent. Type 302, for example, appears in western Africa; Klipple's index cites one Bambara variant. A recent Hausa rendition appears in Johnston, no. 28. For a discussion on the pattern of distribution for type 300, see notes to tale no. 34 in this collection. Only two variants of our tale appear in eastern Africa, however; both manifest the same theme of sibling rivalry and the composite organization of tale types: a variant from the Tanga, a northwestern Bantu group in the Congo, and a second from the Tanalas of Madagascar are cited in Klipple, type 301A. A story from the Digo of the east coastal Bantu, in which the conflict is between two friends, is cited as type 303 in Arewa, no. 3027.

Judging by Egyptian cases and a number of other Arab and Berber variants where the age and sex of informants are provided, our story seems to be narrated mainly by adult males. In most cases where the informant is a female, the punishment of the culprit brothers is either not included in the story or is extremely weak; see, e.g., the variants given by female narrators in Galley and Noy (*Jefet*).

In Egypt the tale is told mainly in areas where strong nomadic-Arab influence is present. Significantly, Frobenius's Sudanese variant is entitled "Albedewui," i.e., "The Arab Nomad." The pattern of distribution suggests that in its present format the tale was introduced into the Nile Valley area by immigrant nomadic groups subsequent to the Arab conquest in the seventh century A.D.

Similarly, all variants from sub-Saharan Africa come from areas which have had prolonged contacts with Arab or recently Islamized groups. Murdock, p. 271, 274, reports that the Tanga of the Congo are among "the latest to leave the original [Bantu] homeland and the most strongly influenced by recent historical developments there." Thus it may be concluded that, with the exception of the Tanalas' rendition, the narrative seems to be limited to Bantu groups influenced by Arab and Muslim culture. Likewise, the absence of our narrative in collections from west African communities adjacent to north African groups tends to support the claim of recent borrowing.

· 2 ·   *The Black Crow and the White Cheese*

The main section in this composite story belongs to types 590, *The Prince and the Arm Band;* and 300, *The Dragon Slayer,* pts. 2–4. The introductory event is based on motifs M302.2, "Man's fate written on his skull"; and H617, "Symbolic interpretation of dreams." Other detail motifs include S12.1.1, "Treacherous mother and paramour plan son's death"; E80.1, "Resuscitation by bathing"; and D2121.5, "Magic journey, man carried by spirit or devil."

The first part of our narrative is usually referred to as the story of "The Skull." It appears both independently and in combination with other tales, as in the case with our present text. A number of variants of "The Skull" story have been collected from Egypt, Sudan, and Iraq. For published examples, see Green, no. 12; El-Shamy, "An Annotated Collection," no. 12; Kamil, p. 35; and Stevens, no. 44.

Although the first portion of our narrative does not seem to appear in black Africa, the general theme of a skull which communicates with humans is found on a fairly wide scale; see Lindblom, pt. 2, no. 9, and his comprehensive comparative notes, p. 130.

Type 315, *The Faithless Sister,* occurs throughout the entire Arab culture area, as well as sub-Saharan Africa, as a variation on types 590 and 509A, *The Treacherous Wife;* it is not related to type 315A, *The Cannibal Sister,* as the type number might suggest.

Narratives that may be classified under types 315, 590, and 590A actually belong to the same tale type. In type 315 the sister plots against her brother, in type 590 the mother plots against her son, while in type 590A it is the wife who plots against her husband. The differences among these three branches of the same tale type are mainly differences of sentiment toward a female relative rather than of narrative content.

In Arab lore the brother-sister theme is decidedly dominant. The ratio of its occurrence, when compared with the son-mother theme, is roughly 2:1. The husband-wife theme appears infrequently.

Forty variants are available from Arab and Berber areas. In Egypt ten variants collected from various regions, including Nubia and Siwa Oasis, are available in archives. Two published renditions appear in Spitta, no. 10, and Dulac, no. 3.

In north Africa type 315-590 is recurrent, particularly among Berber groups. Examples are to be found in such older collections as Socin's "Arabischen Dialekt," no. 2; Frobenius, vol. 2, no. 2; Lacoste, no. 5; and Laoust, no. 20. Recent renditions are given in Amrouche, p. 117; and Scelles-Millie, *Contes sahariens,* p. 313. A rendition from north Africa appears in Noy's *Moroccan Jewish Folktales,* no. 17.

This tale is also well known in the eastern part of the Arab culture area. A variant from Palestine is given in Schmidt and Kahle, vol. 1, no. 42. A Lebanese rendition appears in al-Bustani, p. 219 (for a German translation and comparative notes on this text, see Samia Jahn, no. 11).

Type 315–590 appears frequently in Iraq, where a number of texts have been published. These include Weissbach, no. 8; Stevens, no. 8; and a recent text in *al-Turāth* 3, pts. 5–6: 180; another variant from the Kurds of Iraq is given ibid., pt. 10, p. 145.

The tale is well known in the entire Arabian peninsula, especially in the south. Al-Guhayman, 2:57, gives a recent rendition of the story from the central part of Arabia. Seven variants of our story were secured with meticulous care from various south Arabian communities and published in a monumental linguistic collection, along with many other aspects of lore, in a ten-volume work titled *Südarabische Expedition.* These include two variants in Alfred Jahn's *Südarabische,* vol. 3, nos. 7 and 9; two additional variants of particular importance to us in tracing the tale's movement between south Arabia and Africa are given from the jumping off point island of Socotra; these are in Müller's *Südarabische,* vol. 4, no. C, and vol. 8, no. 22. A fairly recent rendition from Yemenite Jewish traditions appears in Noy's *Jefet,* no. 15.

The identification of our story in African communities seems to present a problem. Although Klipple does not cite any occurrences of types 315 or 590 in sub-Saharan Africa, at least one African rendition of type 590 has been reported from the Bura of Nigeria in Helser, no. 43. This story deals with a boy and his grandmother, who falls in love with a leopard and plots against her grandson's life. In this respect the Bura rendition is similar to Noy's north African variant, which revolves around a boy and his mother, who plots with her second husband, a lion, to kill her son. Conversely, in his index, no. 3228, Arewa classifies a story from the Safwa of eastern Africa as type 590; although this story contains elements of the tale type and may have been derived from its variants, it displays a different narrative pattern and probably should not be viewed as a variant of type 590.

A number of recent collections from sub-Saharan Africa, however, indicate that type 315-590-590A is fairly recurrent. It appears among the Kambas of Kenya; Mbiti gives two renditions, nos. 26 and 33, which are very similar to Arabic traditions dealing with brother and sister (type 315); another related variant is reported under no. 8. Knappert, p. 140, also gives an additional east African Swahili variant involving brother and sister.

In western Africa, the story has been reported from Nigeria; in addition to the Bura rendition cited above, it occurs in a legendary context in the historical account of "Sanau and Korau," where the motifs of magic strength and the treacherous wife plotting against her husband (type 590A) appear. See S. J. Hogben and A. H. M. Kirk-Greene, *The Emirates of Northern Nigeria* (London, 1966), p. 158; and Gretchen

Dihoff, *Katsina* (New York, 1972), p. 44. Strong elements of our story also appear in a Limba tale from Sierra Leone given in Finnegan, no. 1.

The most important sub-Saharan African text is found among the Zande of southern Sudan; it appears in Evans-Pritchard, no. 32. In this story a sister plots against her twin brother and has him killed. She then plants the bones, which are gradually transformed into a man whom she marries. This story manifests characteristics not found in other variants and may well prove to be one of the oldest oral forms of this narrative account. It may also provide the missing link between the modern renditions of the part dealing with bringing back to life a dismembered person found in this tale type and its ancient Egyptian counterpart found in the myth of Isis and Osiris (see Budge, *The Gods,* 2:186–94; and Spence, pp. 68–80). The ancient Egyptian account, it should be pointed out, is found among various east African groups who tell it with astonishing fidelity to the corresponding portions of the ancient text. See, e.g., Lindblom, vol. 2, no. 16, "The Man Who Was Killed by His Brothers, but Came to Life Again," and no. 17, "The Brothers Sun and Moon and the Pretty Girl."

It is worth noting here that the religious account of Isis and Osiris cited above, particularly with reference to the themes of treachery, dismemberment, resuscitation, and loss of phallus, overlaps with the ancient Egyptian tale of "The Two Brothers," type 318, *The Faithless Wife.* See Pritchart, p. 25, no. 8; and Simpson, p. 92. Similarly, our present text (type 315-590-590A) overlaps with a current tale which is doubtlessly associated with the portion which represents type 318 in the ancient Egyptian tale of "The Two Brothers." Two extremely important variants of type 318 have so far been ignored; they appear in Müller's *Südarabische,* vol. 4, no. F, and vol. 6, no. 16. Additional Egyptian variants from Nubia, Siwa Oasis, and eastern Africa were recently collected. This tale may be summarized as follows:

Because of the treachery of the wife of the older brother, or the wife (or the father's wife, which appears only in the east African renditions), a young man has his phallus severed (in the Nubian variants, as is the case in the ancient text, the injury is self-inflicted). The hero regains his missing organ through the help of angels or other supernatural beings (compare the role of the seven Hathors in the ancient text). The culprit is punished.

Previous folkloristic studies on the tale of the two brothers and related tale types have ignored the modern oral texts. For example, Liungman's often quoted study (résumé in French entitled, "Le conte de Bata et Anubis et l'origine du conte merveilleux oriental-européen," p. 114) fails to include the readily available data from south Arabia.

Liungman's findings about the origin and the dissemination of the tale, as represented by his maps (pp. 11, 51) will have to be reconsidered.

· 3 · *The One Sesame Seed*

This *Märchen* is composed of two major tale types: 465, *The Man Persecuted Because of his Beautiful Wife*, pts. 2, 2a; and 1930, *Schlaraffenland*. It also incorporates the following motifs: H1053, "Task: coming neither on horse nor on foot (neither riding nor walking)"; H1054.1, "Task: coming neither naked nor clad (comes wrapped in a net or the like)"; F885, "Extraordinary field"; J1920, "Absurd searches for the lost"; H509.5, "Test: telling skillful lies"; and T585.2, "Child speaks at birth." For further information on the theme of the speaking infant, see Chauvin, 8:63.

This tale is popular in Egypt, particularly among females. It occurs with a fair degree of stability, especially in combining types 465 and 1930. However, pt. 1 of type 465, which accounts for the origin of the supernatural beautiful wife, is often missing, as in our present text. In variants where this episode is present, it is diverse and unstable.

Seven additional variants were collected form various Egyptian communities, including Nubia and the western oasis areas. See Spitta, no. 4.

Type 465 seems not to be widely spread in other Arab culture areas; two variants from Palestine were given in Spoer and Haddad, p. 167, and Schmidt and Kahle, vol. 1, no. 33 (a third variant was collected in Egypt in 1971). The Yemenite Jewish variants appear in Noy, *Jefet*, nos. 21, 22; their contents, however, differ considerably from that of our main text. (A variant which is very close to our own was reported from Afghanistan; it appears in Amina Shah, no. 10.

Type 465 has not been reported from north African Arab or Berber traditions, including Siwa Oasis in Egypt.

In sub-Saharan Africa, marriage to a water spirit is frequently reported; see Liyong, p. 60, and Jacottet, p. 108; yet type 465 does not appear. One Limba narrative, however, which is sufficiently similar to type 465 to suggest a direct relationship with Middle Eastern traditions, is given by Finnegan, no. 27; cf. also no. 5.

Type 1930 appears as an independent narrative throughout the entire Middle East. It usually revolves around the theme of a contest in lying. It also appears in numerous sub-Saharan African cultures. Klipple cites examples from the Nuba, Somali, and Hausa groups. An additional Shilluk text is provided in Westermann, no. 80. Lambrecht, nos. 3169, 3170, and 3815, also reports this tale type from central Africa.

Brunner-Traut, p. 262, argues that *Lügenmärchen* (lying tales) stem from the ancient Egyptian religious story of "Truth and Falsehood," which dates back to 1300–1200 B.C. (see also notes to tale no. 14 below).

· 4 · *The Magic Filly*

This narrative belongs to type 314, *The Youth Transformed to a Horse,* pts. 3, 5, and 6. It also includes the following basic motifs: B184.1, "Magic horse"; B521.1, "Animal warns against poison"; H1516, "Poisoned clothing test"; K1514.11, "Illness feigned to call physician paramour"; B335.2, "Life of helpful animal demanded as cure for feigned sickness"; T55.1, "Princess declares love for lowly hero"; R222, "Unknown knight: the three days tournament"; and H56, "Recognition by wound."

Preliminary evidence indicates that type 314 is not well known in Egypt. Its appearance is sporadic, and the contents are unstable. It is best known among Bedouin groups and, to a lesser extent, Nubians and Berber Siwans. Among peasants and townsfolk the narrative is virtually unknown except in areas where Bedouin influence is strong. Nine other variants are available from Egypt.

This tale type is widely spread throughout north Africa, where it appears among Arab as well as Berber groups in combination with other tale types, notably type 938B, *Better in Youth.* See, e.g., Galley, no. 2, and Dermenghem, p. 119. However, type 551, *The Sons on a Quest for a Wonderful Remedy for Their Father,* as a subsidiary event, seems to dominate the entire Arab-Berber culture area. A closely related rendition is cited from an Arabic-speaking group in Chad; see Abu 'Absi and Sinaud, no. 19. Type 314 has also been reported from Sudan (Cordofan Province), Palestine, Iraq, and Arabia as well as south Arabia; see, e.g., Campbell, *Market Place,* p. 125; al-Guhayman, 2:310; and Müller, *Südarabische,* vol. 7, no. 26.

Type 314 is also found in sub-Saharan Africa. Klipple's and Arewa's indexes cite the same two Swahili variants. More recent texts from the general east African area may be found in Knappert, p. 198, and Mbiti, no. 15. Closely related texts from cattle-raising Bantu groups in the southern section of Africa do appear but have not been included in present indexes. Savory, p. 76, gives a Tswana rendition, while Jaccottet, p. 76, includes another from Basotho. Both these southern African renditions as well as the Kamba story are merged with type 511A, *The Little Red Ox,* which is also widely recurrent in all parts of the Arab and Berber culture areas, especially in south Arabia.

The tale seems to be little known in west Africa; Klipple cites only one Hausa text, while Johnston's recent collection, with fairly wide coverage (86 narratives), does not include this tale type. In addition to the Arabic version from Chad mentioned earlier, another west African rendition from the Mogho, in the Upper Volta area, appears in Guirma, p. 57.

· 5 · *The Grateful Fish*

This narrative is composed of two major tale types. The first belongs to type 505, *Dead Man as Helper*. The "Grateful dead" motif is rare in Arab and Muslim cultures; a grateful animal, fish, or bird usually plays the role of the helper (a new tale type, 505A, is suggested for the animal-helper variation of type 505). The second and more important type is 681, *King in the Bath; Years of Experience in a Moment*. The tale also incorporates a number of motifs with key narrative functions. The presence of motif B375.1, "Fish returned to water: grateful," transforms the grateful dead theme into a grateful fish; motif D10, "Transformation to person of a different sex," also plays a cardinal role in defining the nature of the experience referred to in type 681. Other motifs include N844, "Dervish as helper"; K1314, "Seduction by invisibility"; and a variation on D2176.6, "Exorcising invisible man by flailing air with peach branch."

Five variants of this story are available in Egyptian archives; all were collected recently from various parts of Egypt, including Aswan Province. One rendition comes from the al-Khattara tribe, a group of black Arabs whose habitat extends into Sudan.

Type 681 appears in learned Arabic writings fo the tenth century A.D. Ibn-'Aaṣim, p. 169, accounts for the origin of the proverbial phrase "It is [like] Khurafa's talk!" which is also alleged to be a *ḥadeeth* (tradition) uttered by Prophet Muhammad. Ibn-'Aaṣim reports that Khurafa was a human captured by the jinn (motif F375, "Mortals as captives in fairyland"). Three other humans narrate fantastic personal experiences; thus they become partners with the jinn in owning Khurafa. Finally he is set free (cf. type 953, *The Old Robber Relates Three Adventures*). Type 681 is one of the stories narrated by Khurafa's rescuers. In Arabic the word *khurafa* means "myth."

The tale appears in north Africa. One Tunisian version is given in al-Màrzouqi, p. 34 (for German translation and comparative notes on this text, see Samia Jahn, no. 24). Type 681 also appears in the eastern section of the Arab culture area. A Lebanese rendition is included in Jamali, p. 99.

The element of the relativity of time is recurrent in religious literature; it appears as an Egyptian saint's legend in al-Nabhani, 1:625 and 2:23. Lane, p. 432, gives a résumé of a "tale" which he heard from a dervish in Cairo in the early 1800s. Lane's narrative has an etiological

function which explains the occurrence of a saint's festival on the eve of
mi'Arag (see foreword, pp. xxxvi–xxvii). A non-Arab variant associated
with Sufi mystics is given in Idries Shah, p. 35. Type 681 has also been
reported in a religious context from Yemenite Jewish traditions in
Noy's *Jefet,* no. 64.

One sub-Saharan African variant of type 681 has been reported from
west Africa; Terisse, no. 1, gives a story from Senegal entitled "Issa
Long-Legs in the Land of the Ancients," in which a young man under-
goes a series of supernatural time flight experiences; he finally ends up
old, dignified, and rich. The Islamic influence on this story is evidenced
in the name "Issa" (Arabic "'Aeesa," i.e., "Jesus"). However, its exact
source in Arabic or Islamic traditions is not readily identifiable.

· 6 · *The* Maghrabi's *Apprentice*

This *Märchen* belongs to type 325, *The Magician and His Pupil.* It
includes numerous basic motifs in the following order: T527, "Magic
impregnation by use of charm (amulet)"; S212, "Child sold to magician"; D1711.0.1, "Magician's apprentice"; C611, "Forbidden
chamber"; D612, "Protean sale: man sells youth in successive transfor-
mations"; C837, "Tabu: losing bridle in selling man transformed to a
horse; disenchantment follows"; and D671, "Transformation flight." A
number of other detail motifs are also used, including S162.2, "Ham-
stringing," and D1183, "Magic scissors (shears)."

Type 325 is well known in Egypt; it usually appears as an independent
tale. Only rarely are other minor tale types such as 921E, *Never Heard
Before,* and 926A, *The Clever Judge and the Demon in the Pot,* combined
with type 325 to provide detail episodes. A variant collected in Cairo
appears in Spitta, no. 1; another from Fayyoum Province in the western
desert is given in Morsi, no. 37.

Type 325 is particularly recurrent in north Africa among Berber
groups, where six variants have been collected and published; see
Laoust, *Contes,* no. 103; a more recent rendition appears in Loubignac,
no. 8; also another variant from the Libyan Jewish traditions is given in
Noy's *Folktales,* no. 55.

Present collections from the eastern part of the Arab culture area do
not include type 325; only one variant has been reported from either
southern Iraq or Oman, in south Arabia, in Campbells *Town and Tribe,*
p. 81.

In sub-Saharan Africa type 325 appears sporadically. Although exist-
ing type indexes by Klipple and Arewa do not cite this narrative, at
least one Swahili variant was published as early as 1901 in Bateman,
no. 9. Another more recent Swahili text appears in Knappert, p. 210.

A variant from the neighboring Kamba of Kenya appears in Mbiti, no. 46.

Only one variant from western Africa has been cited; see Guirma, p. 45.

In spite of the rare occurrence of type 325 in sub-Saharan Africa and its conspicuous absence in Nubia (see El-Shamy, "Beide," p. 58), a single variant of this tale type from southern Sudan may prove to be of extreme importance. Westermann, no. 89, gives a Shilluk variant of type 325 which is clearly not derived from either the modern Swahili or the Egyptian tradition. This variant uniquely includes the motif of a woman spearing the hero's adversary in the water during the transformation combat episode. This event appears only in the ancient Egyptian sacred account of "The Contendings of Horus and Seth," where Isis drives her magic harpoon into Seth during the transformation combat between the two gods; see Simpson, pp. 108, 118.

Type 325 appears in an ancient Egyptian account as one of the adventures involving Khamuas and his son Sa-Asar; it is found in two papyri written in Demotic, dating back to A.D. 46–47. In this "official" report a prodigious child is born to a prayer; he learns from his teachers quickly, then becomes involved in a contest in magical deeds with an Ethiopian master magician. The combat takes place in the presence of a pharaoh. The prodigious boy, however, vanishes at the end of the combat to be reborn; see Budge's *Egyptian Tales,* pp. 170–189, esp. pp. 171, 180–89. This ancient story also includes a number of other important motifs which recur in the modern lore of the area. These include wax statues come to life: motif D435.1.1, "Transformation: statue comes to life"; magic transportation—pharaoh magically transported to another land, beaten, and returned to his palace in six hours: motif D2122, "Journey with magic speed" (see tale no. 5); magic smoke which causes total darkness: motif D908, "Magic darkness"; the Nile magically caused not to flow; a drought results: motif D2143.2, "Drought produced by magic" (see notes to tale no. 34); Ethiopian magician and his mother returned to their country in an airship: motifs D1118, "Magic airship," and D2135, "Magic air journey." See also notes to tale no. 12, where other feats of Sa-Asar are cited.

The modern story is a combination of elements from two seemingly independent ancient religious accounts: the prodigious boy defeating a master magician, which dates back at least to the Greek period, and the "transformation combat" which harks back to the Early Middle Kingdom (Dynasties XII–XIX, beginning about 2200 and ending about 1200 B.C.). In its present format type 325 is evidently not a newcomer to the Egyptian-African scene.

· 7 · *The Royal Candlestick*

Our tale is composed of a number of distinct units. The first is a frame story containing the other three. The frame story is an elaboration on motif H343, "Suitor's test: bringing dumb princess to speak." This kind of narrative belongs to the cycle designated under types 571–74, *Making the Princess Laugh.* The frame incorporates three other units as the description of how the test is accomplished. The first two units are represented by two tale types: 653A, *The Rarest Thing in the World;* and 945, *Luck and Intelligence,* pt. 2, *The Wooden Doll.* The third unit of the contents of the frame story is actually an event, not a story per se, based on motif F699.1, "Marvelous dancers." Motif Z16, "Tales ending with a question," designates a structural quality and is present in all three stories.

A new type number, 572, is suggested to designate narratives based on the motif complex of bringing a dumb princess to speak. This theme is very well known and is fairly stable in Egyptian and other Arabic traditions. It also appears in older semiliterary works; see Bassett, *Mille et un contes,* vol. 2, p. 313.

Other motifs which appear in this narrative include F535, "Pygmy. Remarkably small man"; S110.3, "Princess builds tower of skulls of unsuccessful suitors"; D1155, "Magic Carpet"; D1163, "Magic Mirror"; and a variation on E106, "Resuscitation by magic apple," in our case magic water. Motif H621, "Skilful companions create woman: to whom does she belong?" plays a major role in the tale; the contents of this motif are identical with type 945, pt. 2.

This complex frame story is infrequently encountered in Egypt. Two additional composite texts are available; one is from Mansoura City in the Nile Delta; the other is from Fayyoum Province in the western desert; it appears in Morsi, no. 35.

Variants of our text also appear among north African Berbers; Frobenius, 3:98, gives a story in which an ape helps a fisherman make a princess speak by telling controversial stories. Also, a more recent rendition is provided in Amrouche, p. 65. One rendition of our story from the Arabian peninsula is given in al-Guhayman, 2:11.

Type 653A also appears independently on a fairly limited scale. Five variants of this narrative have been collected in Cairo; in a separate booklet for young readers, an Egyptian weekly magazine, *Sabah al-Khair* (no. 462), published a text of type 653A. Three of the Egyptian renditions were written down by high school students as an essay for an English language class. A Sudanese variant is given in Trimingham, p. 124.

Type 653A also seems to be not widely distributed in north Africa.

Besides the frame story text given in Amrouche's collection, two additional renditions are given in Legey, no. 49, and Holding, no. 3.

In spite of its appearance in semiliterary works such as *The Arabian Nights* and mystic Muslim literature (see Elisséeff, no. 163, p. 204; also Idries Shah, p. 108), type 653A seems to be rare in the oral traditions of the eastern part of the Arab culture area.

In sub-Saharan Africa this tale type is very popular, especially as a verbal puzzle; Bascom, no. 36, cites thirty-seven African variants of type 653A. It also appears as a regular nonriddling tale; see, e.g. Mbiti, no. 22 and Basden, p. 424.

Although type 945 proper is well known in Egypt, it normally occurs without *The Wooden Doll* episode. This event seems to be of even more restricted distribution in Egypt than type 653A; only one other rendition is found in Morsi, no. 35, as part of the frame story. Motif H631 (type 945, p. 2) has its widest circulation in north Africa, where seven variants have been reported from both Arab and Berber communities; see, e.g., Legey, no. 49; Dermenghem and El-Fasi, p. 178; Laoust, *Contes,* p. 70; and Basset, *Mille et un contes,* 2:313n.

The only rendition of type 945, pt. 2 that I know of from the eastern part of the Arab culture area is that given by al-Guhayman, cited above.

In sub-Saharan Africa, type 945, pt. 2, has a very limited distribution, especially when compared with type 653A. Klipple's, Arewa's, and Lambrecht's indexes do not include any listings under motif H621 or type 945, pt. 2. However, Thompson cites in the *Motif-Index* one African occurrence of motif H621, while Bascom, no. 125, lists two variants, of which one is east African Swahili, while the other is the north African Berber variant cited above. See also Finnegan, no. 45, where a closely related Limba narrative is given.

The dominance of the dilemma form of type 653A and, to a lesser extent, type 945, pt. 2 in Africa south of the Sahara and the rare occurrence of this verbal puzzle form in the northerly parts of Africa pose an interesting problem. As demonstrated by the Nubian text provided here, Arabic and Berber texts of northern groups address specific aspects of the communal value system; the answers are explicitly stated in accordance with these values. In view of the close geographic and historical contacts between the two portions of Africa, two arguments may be advanced: (1) the northern Africans borrowed dilemma tales from the south and provided stable answers for them, thus converting them into nondilemma tales; or (2) the sub-Saharan groups took nondilemma tales from the north and omitted the concluding episodes which rest on value systems different from their own, thus converting them into dilemma tales. A third argument, which is extremely unlikely, is that both traditions developed totally independently.

· 8 · Louliyya, Daughter of Morgan

Our story is composed of types 310, The Maiden in the Tower, and 313, The Girl as Helper in the Hero's Flight, pts. 3–5. Salient motifs include T548.1, "Child born in answer to prayer"; M301.2.1, "Enraged old woman prophesies for youth"; F571.2, "Sending to the older"; G123, "Giant ogress with breasts thrown over shoulder"; T671, "Adoption by suckling. Ogress who suckles hero claims him as her son"; D1313.12, "Magic cake indicates road"; F848.1, "Girl's long hair as ladder into tower"; G84, "Fee-fi-fo-fum"; D1611, "Magic objects answer for fugitive, left behind to impersonate fugitive and delay pursuit"; D672, "Obstacle flight"; D582, "Transformation by sticking magic pin into head"; D150, "Transformation: man to bird"; D765.1.2, "Disenchantment by removal of enchanting pin (thorn)."

This Märchen of "Louliyya bint Morgan" (Literally, "Pearl, daughter of Ruby") is well known in various parts of Egypt. Eight other variants were collected recently from the Nile Delta, middle southern Egypt, and the oasis area in the western desert. All were told by adult females and learned from females. (In one instance a man from an "Arab lineage" started telling me this story but could not go beyond the opening episode. He suggested that I lend him my recording equipment so that he could record the story for me from his wife.)

The tale is fairly stable and revolves around the emotional core of a daughter's hostility toward a parent. It always contains variations of themes designated under types 310 and 313. The names of both the hero and heroine seem to be restricted to this tale. Yousif (Joseph), however, appears in religious narratives associated with the biblical and Koranic character. The majority of variants from the northern parts of Africa and the Levant coast (Lebanon and Palestine) use the two names or derivatives therefrom as titles for the story. This title also appears elsewhere, but sporadically. One such case is a Somali tale cited below.

It should be pointed out at the outset that in the Arab-Berber culture area narrative events designated under types 310 and 312A, The Brother Rescues His Sister from the Tiger, are merely variations on the contents of type 313. The overwhelming majority of tales dealing with the main themes of our own texts may be classified as either type 313 plus 310 or 313 plus 312A; the presence or absence of a brother or brothers who rescue a sister (type 312A) being the main distinguishing factor. Occasionally the brother appears in the 313-310 combination, while more frequently, a parallel paternal cousin (who may also be called "brother" in actual life) is involved. In the context where a brother is involved, the main sentiment expressed is that of a woman's hostility toward her husband (or abductor).

Two stories (types 312A and 313) related to our text were reported from Sudan. 'Aabdullah al-Tayyib, no. 3, gives a variant from the town of Berber; the second appears in Hurreiz, no. 6.

In north Africa the tale seems to enjoy considerable popularity. It also shows remarkable similarities to our present text. In his *Contes,* no. 97, Laoust gives two variants of the tale and cites references to a number of Berber and Arabic renditions in countries extending from Libya to Morocco. Additional Berber texts may be found in Lacoste, no. 23, and in Amrouche, p. 21. A related story (type 312A) in the Hassaniya Arabic dialect of Mauritania is given in Norris, p. 122.

The story is also known in the eastern part of the Arab world; it appears on both the Levant coast and in the Mesopotamian Arab culture areas. Texts belonging to our present story appear in al-Bustani, p. 140 (for a German translation of this text, see Samia Jahn, no. 8). Another Lebanese rendition recorded in Iraq is given in Jamali, p. 107. A variant from Palestine appears in Schmidt and Kahle, vol. 1, no. 27; an archival rendition which was learned "either in Haifa or Nazareth" was narrated by a Palestinian Christian woman in Cairo in 1970. In Iraq type 310 seems not to be well known; one rendition of type 312A appears in *al-Turath* 3, pt. 10:67.

An Arabian rendition, closely related to the Iraqi story, is given in al-Guhayman, p. 195. (A story which is akin to the Iraqi and Arabian texts is reported from Afghanistan; see Amina Shah, no. 1).

Although type 310 and its companion events do not appear in major collections from the southern parts of the Arabian peninsula, a text which I secured from Qatar shows surprising similarity to our tale (types 310 and 313), including the title. This variant was narrated by a 38-year-old Somali woman who had learned the tale from her mother in their native Somalia.

Type 312A is found mainly on the outskirts of the Arab-Berber culture area, in regions which are largely dependent on pastoral nomadism, while type 310 is characteristically found in areas closer to the Mediterranean.

In sub-Saharan Africa, major components of our story appear in a number of communities. Like type 312A in Arab-Berber areas, they are also found mainly among pastoral groups. These African renditions lack the salient motif cluster of the tower, where the maiden was confined, and its companion motif of the girl's hair as ladder. Evidently because of their cognitive salience, these motifs were selected to serve as the identifying marks for type 310, *The Maiden in the Tower,* which as pointed out earlier is only an elaboration on a theme within type 313.

The nature of traditional sub-Saharan material culture and the physical qualities of most of its original inhabitants make the appearance in cultural expressions of a tall stone or brick tower and long, silky hair unlikely. Consequently the present type indexes do not report type 310 from any part of Africa. However, type 312, *The Giant-Killer and His Dogs* (actually type 312A, *The Brother Rescues His Sister from the Tiger*), and 313, *The Girl as Helper in the Hero's Flight,* are cited. Klipple reports a "Kaffir" and a Chaga text of type 312. She also cites the occurrence of type 313 in the same culture area among the "Khaffir" and Shangani groups of Rhodesia. A third rendition of type 313 from Madagascar is also reported.

Arewa lists only one variant of type 312 and cites the same Chaga source previously given by Klipple.

The occurrence of our tale, particularly in the format which comprises types 312A and 313, is, however, much more frequent than the indexes indicate. Stories from "Larousa", Shambala, and Ngonde groups, listed as nos. 3901, 3930, and 3991 of Arewa's own classification system, show major degrees of similarity to our tale.

Besides the Somali variant mentioned above, additional previously uncited stories which are related to our text appear in a number of older sources from the same general area in the eastern part of Africa. A Hottentot story (type 312A) given in Bleek, no. 27, shows remarkable similarity of action to our tale. A closely related Bushman story with solar etiological contents appears in Markowitz, no. 29.

Another related story (type 312A) is reported from the Xhosa group of the Nguni cluster, in Theal, p. 127. A similar narrative from the same area is given in Jacottet, p. 160. A rendition which ends with the cannibal father devouring his fugitive daughter while the hero lives the rest of his life in shame appears in Savory, no. 9.

When compared with their counterparts, especially type 310, in the Arab-Berber areas in northern Africa, most of these southern African tales seem relatively less complex (probably due to lack of accurate recording techniques). However, a recently published Xhosa text which was narrated by an adult female reveals the actual complexity of the sub-Saharan tale and its further ties with its counterparts in the northern parts of Africa; see Scheub.

In western Africa our tale seems to have limited circulation. In addition to the Arabic variant from Mauritania cited earlier, a variant from Sierra Leone which deals with a witch who prevents her daughter from finding a husband appears in Finnegan, no. 14. In many respects, especially the presence of a supernatural mother for the heroine, this Limba text resembles many adjacent Berber traditions. Cf. Amrouche and Laoust, p. 154.

In addition to the virtual identity of the basic plot of types 310, 312A, and 313, a number of detail elements which appear in sub-Saharan

African renditions enhance the possibility of a direct historical relationship between the northern and southern renditions. A magic pearl which helps the fugitives in their escape appears in the Larousa variant (see Arewa, no. 3901); "Pearl" is the name of the heroine in the majority of North African variants. Similarly, the hair of the heroine, a salient motif in north African texts, becomes instrumental in the fugitives' escape in Theal's "Xosa" variant. In Scheub's Xhosa rendition the heroine finds the bewitched hero inside the stomach of an eland and rescues him. In a number of north African variants, especially Berber, an identical event appears; the hero is swallowed by an eagle; the heroine slaughters a sheep or a calf; eagles perch to eat, but the one with the hero in its belly is too heavy to fly. It is captured and the hero rescued.

Our tale's pattern of distribution in Africa suggests that the type 313-312A combination is an older form of the narratives which linked components of types 310, 312, and 312A with type 313. The pattern also indicates that these narratives are of considerable antiquity in Africa, especially among pastoralists in the southeastern section. This argument is further enhanced when we consider the limited distribution of type 310 in Asia, especially in India and Turkey, where the tale is virtually unknown. Similarly, in Europe type 310 is known mainly in southern Mediterranean areas and has had only a limited history on the continent. See Thompson, *The Folktale,* p. 102. See also Massignon, no. 29, and her notes on p. 265; it is worth noting that Massignon's French rendition is combined with elements of type 402, *The Mouse (Cat, Frog, etc.) as Bride.* In this respect it is similar to a number of north African versions and also to al-Bustani's Lebanese rendition, where major elements of type 409A, *The Girl as a Goat (Jackdaw),* appear. Although the transformation of the heroine into a female dog appears in a number of other texts, including our own, it does not elicit other components of type 409A. It would therefore be safe to argue that the southern European variants of type 310 had their roots in Arab and Berber communities in north Africa or possibly in the Levant coast area.

· 9 · *The Promises of the Three Sisters*

This tale belongs to type 707, *The Three Golden Sons.* Its motifs include N201, "Wish for exalted husband realized"; H71.2, "Gold (silver) hairs as sign of royalty"; K2212, "Treacherous sisters"; D902, "Magic rain"; H1331.1.1, "Quest for Bird of Truth"; and B184.1, "Magic horse."

This tale is extremely popular in Egypt; it is usually referred to as "the story of the three sisters who said, 'If the king were to marry me I'd do such and such for him. . . .'" It is normally narrated by females. Of the fourteen variants available in Egyptian archives, only one was told by an adult male. Two printed texts appear in Spitta, no. 11, and Artin, no. 22. A Sudanese variant from the town of Sinnar was collected in Cairo from Muhammad 'Aali Sulaymān, 55, a teacher and tale collector; another variant appears in Khidr, 1:103. Al-Zayn, p. 99, also provides a variant of this tale; this Musabba'Aat story, however, is closer to the sub-Saharan African renditions of type 707, in which conflict is between two co-wives and the abandoned children are two brothers.

Numerous variants have also been culled from various north African Berber and Arab communities. In his *Contes,* Laoust gives a poor text of the tale (no. 106) which he collected from a male Berber narrator and cites several Berber and Arab renditions, p. 188. Similarly, Dermenghem, p. 49, gives a text of the tale and a bibliography for sixteen Berber and Arab variants which he compares with European and oriental counterparts, pp. 153–63.

Type 707 is also well known in the eastern part of the Arab culture area. It has been collected from Palestine, Syria, Lebanon, and Iraq; see, e.g., Schmidt and Kahle, vol. 1, no. 56; Østrup, p. 23; McCarthy and Raffouli, p. 532; and al-Soufi, p. 93.

Meanwhile, Stevens, no. 33, gives a variant of our tale (type 707, pts. 1 and 2, and type 894, *The Ghoulish Schoolmaster and the Stone of Pity,* pt. 4) which an "Armenian lady" in Baghdad narrated to her in English; on p. 299, Stevens also mentions an Arabic variant which she heard and cites further references in which the tale appears.

It is worth noting here that the central aspect in the Arab and Berber variants is the tale's emotional core of the affectionate bond between brother and sister (see El-Shamy, "The Traditional Structure"), this sentiment is lacking in the Armenian rendition. (For a European variant in which the tale acquires a definite oedipal trend, see O'Sullivan, no. 19. This Irish narrative combines strong elements of the tale of "Batu: The Egyptian 'Two Brothers'" which were probably derived from recent literary sources. The type index cites this tale as type 318, *The Faithless Wife;* O'Sullivan, however, classifies the tale as type 425, *The Search for the Lost Husband,* and only compares it with type 707. This Irish rendition has retained the themes of the hostility among sisters over the same man and the children's hostility toward the maternal aunt).

Surprisingly, however, type 707 has not been reported from any part of the Arabian peninsula, a gap that may be due to the fact that most collectors dealt with male informants only.

The tale has recently entered into the semiliterary traditions of *The Arabian Nights;* see Elisséeff, p. 163. Chauvin, vol. 7, no. 375, gives an abstract of the tale as it appears in Antoine Galland's edition of *The*

Arabian Nights; Galland's story is based on an oral rendition which he had heard, presumably in Damascus. Chauvin, incorrectly observed that "a [printed] text of the tale of the 'jealous sisters' has not been found yet" (p. 95). Two texts were already available; Spitta's text was published in 1883, while Artin's appeared in 1895.

Numerous variants of this tale type have been reported from sub-Saharan Africa. Klipple cites nine variants from the Venda, Larusa, Kamba, and Masai groups in east Africa. Also included in Klipple's index are one variant from the Suto of southern Africa and one from the Hausa of west Africa. All the African renditions show various degrees of similarity with their north African counterparts. The variant from the Suto given in Jacottet, p. 190, is of particular importance; it includes the theme of the emotional attachment between brother and sister which underlies all Arab and Berber renditions.

In *The Folktale*, p. 122, Thompson observes that this extremely widespread tale has had a brief literary history, going back only to Straparola's collection, which dates from the sixteenth century. Thompson also states that the distribution of the some 400 variants available then (1946) suggests European origins for the tale. This view should be reconsidered in light of the new evidence provided by Arab, Berber, and African variants of type 707.

PART II

REALISTIC AND PHILOSOPHICAL TALES

· 10 ·   *The Liver of the Wise and the Liver of the Foolish*

This realistic story, a novella, is composed of two distinct segments. The first, though involving human actors, is typologically affiliated with type 50, *The Sick Lion*. The second belongs to the category of tales designated as types 920–26, *Clever Acts and Words;* it is a part of the cycle dealing with riddling questions wisely expounded (types 921–21E). A new type number, 921F, *Wife Solves Riddles by Deception,* is suggested for this recurrent narrative.

The inaugural episode also incorporates such basic motifs as D1248, "Human liver as medicine," and a variation on motif K1673, "Sage's advice followed: he is killed so that sacrifice can be mixed with his blood." The second segment includes a number of motifs clustered around the general theme of motif H600, "Symbolic interpretations." These include H652, "Riddle: what is the softest?"; H645.1, "Riddle: what is the heaviest?" (here we may add a new motif, H645.2, "Riddle:

what is the lightest?"); H653, "Riddle: what is the fattest?" and H636.1, "Riddle: what is the richest? Autumn."

The belief that liver, which is viewed as blood, cures certain ailments is widespread in Middle Eastern narratives and folk remedial practices. See Laoust, *Contes,* p. 234, where liver or blood is reported to be a cure for serious illnesses, especially leprosy. This belief appears in the traditions of the area as early as the thirteenth century B.C. in the tale of "The Two Brothers" (see Maspéro, p. 17).

As an animal tale, type 50 appears in Arabic literary collections such as *Kaleelah wa dimnah,* the Arabic translation of *The Panchatantra;* see Chauvin, vol. 3, no. 56. Although many of the tales in such collections are well known among the literate, they hardly ever circulate in oral traditions. Sometimes, as in our present text, the basic plot of a literary animal tale appears in oral circulation, but with human actors. Evidently the literary and the oral texts exist independently of each other.

Three other variants of this composite narrative were collected in Nubia, southern Egypt, and the Nile Delta. Other variants from Arab countries appear in Scelles-Millie, *Contes arabes,* no. 16, Weissbach, no. 36, and Dickson, p. 315.

Our tale seems not to appear in sub-Saharan African cultures. This fact corresponds to the rare appearance of the story in south Arabian and north African Berber communities, two important contact areas. Type 50, however, appears frequently as an animal tale in numerous black African communities. See Klipple, and Arewa, no. 566, where examples from Nuba, Hottentot, Fulah, and Bambara groups are cited. Another recent variant from Senegal may be found in Terisse, no. 8.

· 11 · The Man Who Put His Mother over His Shoulder and Rode His Father

This realistic story, a novella, belongs to type 851, *The Princess Who Cannot Solve the Riddle.* The entire tale may be designated as motif H792, "Riddle of the unborn." According to the *Motif-Index,* the contents of this motif are virtually identical with the contents of type 851 except for the nature of the water involved in the riddle part, which is classified under motif H1073, "Task: filling glasses with water that has neither fallen from heaven nor sprung from the earth." The tale also incorporates a number of other basic motifs, including H551, "Princess offered to man who can out-riddle her," and H81.2, "Clandestine visit of princess to hero betrayed by token."

In Egypt this tale is widely reported but infrequently recorded. Several informants mentioned hearing the story but were not able to narrate it. The riddle part was always the stumbling block for them.

Four other variants and three fragments are available in archives; all of them come from the Nile Delta area. The four complete renditions are very similar, especially in the riddle part. The tale is conspicuously absent in major collections from the Middle Eastern culture area, including Eberhard and Boratav's Turkish index. Only one variant from Yeman is given in Noy's *Jefet,* no. 71, where type 851 appears as a component in a composite text. However, the riddles involved in the narrative are known in both oral and literary Arab traditions. For a bibliography on "enigmas" in Middle Eastern traditional literature, see Chauvin, 6:42.

In sub-Saharan Africa this tale appears infrequently. The type index cites two variants, one Swahili from east Africa and one west African from the Gold Coast (Ghana). In the Ghanaian rendition, a young man outriddles a king instead of a princess, and he is rewarded with the chieftainship rather than with a princess. Emphasizing this aspect of the tale, Klipple cited it under type 927, *Out-Riddling the Judge.* The type index includes type 927 within the broader category of *Clever Acts and Words;* types 920–29, whereas type 851 is included under *The Princess's Hand Is Won,* types 850–69.

A more recent variant appears in Mbiti, no. 65; this Kamba rendition, which is unquestionably related to our main text and other Egyptian renditions, indicates that the absence of this tale type from most Middle Eastern collections is due to insufficient and inadequate collecting rather than to its nonexistence in the area.

· 12 ·   *"It Serves Me Right!"*

Our narrative bears a strong resemblance to types 801, *Master Pfriem,* and 470, *Friends in Life and Death,* pt. 2, *The Journey.* It would be useful to assign a new type number to this Middle Eastern tale. There are two possibilities. First, the tale could be classified within the category designated in the type index under "Supernatural Tales," which is assigned the numbers from 460 to 485, as type 470C, *Man in a Utopian World Cannot Resist Interfering;* second, it could be classified under "The Man in Heaven" category, which is assigned the numbers from 800 to 809, as type 801A, *The Man in Earthly Heaven.*

The tale also incorporates the following basic motifs: C411.1, "Tabu: asking for reason of an unusual action"; and F171.0.1, "Enigmatic happenings in other world which are later explained." Variations on the following motifs also appear: F769.1, "Town where everything is sold at one price"; F171.6.2, "People in other world pour water into tub full of holes"; F171.6.4, "People in other world with horses both before and behind wagon"; and the general motif H600, "Symbolic interpretation."

A narrative with a similar theme and structure appears in the Koran (18:66-83); in this sacred Islamic account Prophet Moses asked a pious sage (often thought to be el-Khiḍr) to allow him to travel in his company so that he might learn some of his wisdom. The sage agreed on the condition that Moses did not ask any questions. Moses consented. The sage dug a hole in the bottom of a ship in which they were traveling, killed a young boy for no apparent reason, and rebuilt a tumbling wall in a village whose inhabitants had refused to be hospitable to them. As in our folk text, Moses protested each of the strange acts; each time the sage told him that their agreement has been broken, Moses pleaded for one more chance, and the sage agreed. After the third time the sage explained his acts, and the two of them had to part company.

Although this Koranic narrative is recited in every mosque every Friday, narrators never associate it with the folk text. Evidently each story belongs to a separate cognitive system (the correlation between the two narratives dawned upon me in 1978, seventeen years after collecting my first text of the folk story). Our oral narrative is not related to contemporary formal Islamic teachings; it is also unlikely that the folk story developed out of Islamic traditions in the recent past. The story seems to have its roots in ancient Egyptian religious literature. The earliest form of the story dates back to A.D. 46–47 and was written in Demotic. It carries the title of "The Story of Khamus and His Son Sa-Asar"; see Budge, *Egyptian Tales,* pt. 1, no. 11, esp. pp. 172–77; also Maspéro, p. 148, and Brunner-Traut, no. 34. It also appears in some editions of *The Arabian Nights;* see Elisséeff, p. 106, no. 3c.

The ancient Egyptian narrative is very close to the modern tale. It contains most of the motifs in our story, but in a different sequence. The boy prodigy Senosiris (actually Horus; see notes to tale no. 6) wishes his father, Satmi, the same fate of a poor dead man who is being buried without proper funerary rites, rather than the fate of a rich man with a lavish funeral; the father is dismayed. Senosiris takes his father to the Mountain of Memphis, and they enter a place composed of seven large halls representing Amentit, the other world. There, enigmatic occurrences are witnessed and explained by Senosiris. *(a)* The pivot of the door is fixed on the single right eye of a man who prays and utters great cries (a motif which appears in the variant given in *The Arabian Nights*), and another personage of distinction is near the place where Osiris is. The first is the rich man with the lavish funeral who was a sinner, and the second is the poor man whom no one lamented, a virtuous man (this is a common theme in current Muslim religious literature; see notes to tale no. 19). *(b)* "Persons who run and move about while asses eat behind them" are people whose women waste what they earn (see Maspéro, p. 149, no. 3, for Greek parallels). *(c)* Others who have their food, bread, and water hung above them and

who leap in order to pull it down while others dig holes at their feet to
prevent their reaching it are figures of people in this world who have
their food before them but the god digs out holes to prevent their
finding it. Satmi cannot reveal these things to any man in the world
(motif C420, "Tabu: uttering secrets"). Evidently the modern Egyptian
tale is a direct descendant of the ancient one. Both traditions reflect the
same fatalistic patterns, especially with reference to economic matters.

Nine variants of this story were collected from the Egyptian Nile
Valley area, including Nubia. A rendition given by an Egyptian woman
living in New York City is included in El-Shamy, "An Annotated Collection," no. 2. In other parts of the Arab culture area, the tale seems
not to be well known. One variant from Lebanon appears in al-Bustani,
p. 276; another Iraqi rendition is cited in *al-Turath* 3, pt. 10:159.

Strong elements of the story appear in Hadromount, south Arabia;
during his search for a wife, the young hero witnesses eight strange
occurrences. When he inquires about their meaning, he is told, "It is not
your concern." This theme, however, is abandoned for type 890, *A
Pound of Flesh*. See Hein and Müller, *Südarabische*, vol. 9, no. 43.

In its modern format this tale does not seem to be known in sub-
Saharan Africa. However, Knappert, p. 107, gives an etiological legend
from east Africa which bears a strong resemblance to the ancient Egyptian story. In this tale a man buries himself alive after a child is born to
him. In the other world he sees industrious and idle women; this contrast is explained to him later. The Swahili story is closer to the ancient
Egyptian text than to the modern Egyptian tradition.

A number of west African stories show marked similarities to the
introductory part to our present text. E.g., see Terisse, p. 72, and Fuja,
p. 125.

· 13 ·   *"I've Seen [It] with My Own Eyes; Nobody Told Me!"*

This tale belongs to the general theme of type 947, *The Man Followed by
Bad Luck*. It also includes the following basic motifs: N101, "Inexorable
fate," and N131, "Acts performed for changing luck." Other motifs
which appear in our story in slightly different renditions are X111.7,
"Misunderstood words lead to comic results"; K185.6, "Deceptive land
purchase: bounds fixed by throwing objects (axe, spear)"; and H1584.2,
"Land measured according to amount encompassed during certain
hours."

This rendition of type 947 seems to be limited to the Middle East.
Two other variants are available from Egypt: one of these appears in
Fayyoum Province and is given in Morsi, no. 39. The tale has also been
collected sporadically from other parts of the Arab culture area. One

variant from Morocco is given in Scelles-Millie, *Contes arabes,* no. 44, while another from Palestine is given in Schmidt and Kahle, vol. 1, no. 60. A rendition from the nomadic Shammar tribe of Iraq is given by Maligoud.

· 14 · *The Noble and the Vile*

This story belongs to type 613, *The Two Travelers (Truth and Falsehood).* It also includes the following basic motifs: M225, "Eyes exchanged for food"; N451.1, "Secrets of animals (demons) accidentally overheard from tree (bridge) hiding place"; and H346, "Princess given to man who can heal her." A variation on motif N471, "Foolish attempt of second man to overhear secrets (from animals, demons, etc.); he is punished," functions as a concluding episode.

Our present tale seems to have its roots in an ancient Egyptian religious account of a conflict between Truth and Fasehood. The written text dates back to the 19th Dynasty of the thirteenth century B.C. The translation of the ancient text appears in Gardiner, p. 2. It is also given with valuable comments in Lefèbvre, p. 159, and Brunner-Traut, no. 6. A more recent translation and notes are provided in Simpson, p. 127.

In the ancient account, Falsehood accuses his older brother, Truth, of having lost or damaged an extraordinarily huge knife or sword and asks the Ennead that Truth be blinded and forced to serve as the keeper of his gate. They agree (cf. motif K451.1, "Unjust umpire decides a religious dispute").

Still jealous of Truth's virtue, Falsehood orders two of his brother's servants to take him to the desert and throw him to lions. They spare his life, leave him at the foot of a hill, and report to Falsehood that his brother has been torn apart by a lion (motif K512, "Compassionate executioner"). Truth is discovered by some maids who report his beauty to their mistress. She sleeps with him and he begets a child; nonetheless, Truth still serves as her doorkeeper. The child grows and goes to school, where he is reproached for being fatherless. He inquires of his mother, and she points out his father (motif H1381.2.2.1, "Boy twitted with illegitimacy seeks unknown father"). The father tells him the story. To vindicate his father, the son leaves a fine steer with Falsehood's shepherds. Falsehood admires the calf, slaughters it, and eats it. The son demands his calf back and claims that it was of supernatural size or that it gave birth to sixty calves daily (motif X1237, "Lie: remarkable ox or steer"). The matter is taken to the gods, and they state that such a calf cannot exist. The youth then asks them, "How can there be a knife as large as you had stated before?" (motif J1163, "Pleading for accused by means of parable"). The son then reveals his identity. Falsehood contests the youth's claim and swears that Truth is dead and wagers to lose his eyes and to serve as Truth's doorkeeper if Truth is proved to be alive (motif N2.3.3, "Eyes wagered"). The youth produces Truth, his father, and the punishment is carried out. And thus the dispute between Truth and Falsehood is resolved.

This ancient Egyptian account seems to have developed into two independent narratives in modern Egyptian lore and to have generated a number of proverbial expressions and songs. The first part concerning the unjust decision and the blinding of Truth appears as a belief legend recurrent in rural areas. It combines motif K451.1 of the unjust umpire with motif N61, "Wager that falsehood is better than truth." Briefly stated, Truth and Falsehood are partners who own a farm jointly. Falsehood cheats Truth out of his share, then his land, then his house, and finally wants him to leave the village. They agree to ask the first man they meet to judge their case—the umpire states, "Truth should leave the village, and Falsehood should remain." This entire narrative is usually summed up in the proverbial form: "We said, 'Truth!' They replied, 'Get out of the village!'"

A number of narrators have pointed out that the contents of the tale and those of a frequently recurrent folk song are identical. The song may have originated as a reference to the incident cited in the ancient account. The song states, "Vile said to Noble, 'Come, we will make you a servant. You will eat and drink and be a servant among servants. . . .'"

The second part of the ancient narrative concerning the restoration of Truth's eyesight is doubtless associated with type 613. In his introduction to Erman's *Ancient Egyptians,* p. xv, Simpson states that this narrative "certainly reflects the avenging of Osiris by Horus." Similarly, Brunner-Traut, addressing herself to F. von der Leyen's inquiry into the nature of the "clever youth" who does not know his father, concludes that this youth is "no one but the boy Horus who strove for justice for his father Osiris" (p. 262). Thus the conflict between Falsehood and Truth is actually the conflict between Osiris and his younger brother Seth. Although the episode of the son is missing from all available variants, the general pattern and beliefs associated with the ancient Egyptian account still live in current oral traditions of Egypt.

Type 613 is very popular in Egypt, where nine variants were collected recently. One rendition from the Sudan is given in Hurreiz, no. 49. The story also appears in north Africa; one Berber variant is given in Lacoste, no. 2. Two additional variants from Morocco and Tunisia appear in Noy, *Moroccan Jewish Folktales,* no. 18; and *Folktales,* no. 22.

The story is also known in the eastern part of the Arab culture area. An early variant dating back to the fifteenth century deals with the conflict between a crown prince and his evil paternal uncle; it appears in a collection compiled by the Damascene historian Ibn 'Aarabshāh (d. 1450), p. 35; see Chauvin, vol. 2, no. 14, pt. 12. (A number of scholars judge Ibn 'Aarabshah's work to be a "free" translation of Indian or other foreign narrative sources. This view is erroneous; the author begins many of his chapters by stating, "We have been informed by . . . Abul-Mahāsin [which can be either a proper name or a praise name meaning "the virtuous"] Ḥassān." Ibn 'Aarabshāh may therefore be considered a collector who rendered folk narratives in his own intricate and often boring style). Iraqi variants have also been published; see Stevens, no. 46, and Noy, *Folktales,* no. 23; references to Kurdish and Persian variants are also cited by Kazim, p. 9.

Only a few variants have been reported from the Arabian peninsula. Müller gives a text from Socotra, off the tip of the African Horn in *Südarabische,* vol. 7, no. 15; also a closely related rendition from Yemen appears in Noy, *Jefet,* no. 11. It is interesting to observe that in the Jewish traditions from Morocco, Tunisia, and Yemen the theme of the conflict of two brothers, which appears in the ancient Egyptian account, dominates.

The story has also found its way into literary collections; it appears in *The Arabian Nights,* see Chauvin, vol. 5, no. 10, and Elisséeff, no. 153, p. 202. Idries Shah, p. 183, gives a variant of type 613 and attributes it to the teachings of dervishes of the middle of the seventh century A.D. However, Shah does not give his source for the date.

In sub-Saharan Africa the occurrence of type 613 seems to be limited mostly to areas adjacent to the northern parts of the continent. Klipple cites one variant from each of the following groups: the Swahili of east Africa, the Duala of the Congo, and the Bolanchi of western Sudan. In addition to the Arab-African variants from Sudan and Socotra cited above, a number of renditions have been collected from other northerly parts of Africa. Two variants from Ethiopia appear in Littmann, *Tales,* no. 15, and in Courlander and Leslau, p. 119. A Shilluk variant, but with a different ending in which the two travelers are reconciled, is given in Westermann, no. 92.

Strong elements from type 613 also appear in west African traditions reported from Nigeria and Senegal; see Tremearne, p. 238, and Diop, no. 3.

On the basis of R. Th. Christiansen's monographic study of type 613 and other investigations by K. Krohn and M. Gaster, Thompson states that "as a literary story the tale is not less than fifteen hundred years old. It is found in Chinese Buddhistic literature" (*The Folktale,* p. 80). Thompson also concludes that "its rather remote and oriental origin seems clear. . . ." Eberhard and Boratav, p. 306, quote the same literature attributing the origins of the tale to Indian and related Buddhist literature. In light of the new evidence from ancient Egyptian literature of 3,300 years ago, these conclusions must be reconsidered.

· 15 · *Sultan Hasan*

This story was told as a "true happening"; it belongs to type 938B, *Better in Youth.* The narrative incorporates a number of important motifs, including M340, "Unfavorable prophecies"; J214, "Choice: suffering in youth or old age"; L410, "Proud ruler (deity) humbled"; and M202, "Fulfilling of bargain or promise." The recurrent theme in Arab and Islamic literature of "seven lean years" appears in the story; a new motif, Z71.5.9, is suggested for this narrative element (cf. motif D791.1.1, "Disenchantment at end of seven years").

Our story seems to appear with moderate frequency in Egypt. Six additional archival variants are available. The story is normally told as a true historical legend and tends to cite a historical figure as the hero. Another variant from the city of Minya in Upper Egypt links the tale to Emir Ahmad Ibn Tūlūn (d. A.D. 883), whose name is also associated with a famous mosque in Cairo. It is interesting to note that the actual Ḥasan, son of Muhammad son of Qalawūn, surnamed al-Nāṣir, was the *seventh* son to succeed his father, Sultan Mohamad son of Qalawūn, to the sultanate of Egypt and that he did rule twice. His first reign (1347–51) began when he was only thirteen years old and ended when the general of his army overthrew and imprisoned him and installed his brother in his stead. His second rule (1354–60) began when the same general overthrew his brother and reinstated him in the sultanate. Ḥasan's end is unknown, however, and it is believed that he was murdered by his enemies. His father (d. 1340), who was responsible for halting the Mongol holocaust, had a similar experience. Beginning as a child of nine years of age, he ruled during three periods (1293–94, 1298–1308, 1309–40).

It was the father, however, who was first "exiled" to the Sham countries (Syria, Lebanon, and Palestine). He was later brought back, only to escape again to Damascus, where he received support from loyal emirs. The two Mamluk generals who were directly responsible for his flight became associated in the minds of the people with the bad economic conditions caused by the sharp decline in the water of the Nile. Finally, when the sultan returned to Cairo, he sought revenge over his mutinous generals.

The reign of Sultan Hasan came during harsh, turbulent times. It followed two major wars, the first with the Mongols and the second with the Bedouins of southern Egypt. Also in 1349, during his first nominal reign, Egypt and the rest of the world around her were struck with the plague. For the average Egyptian, times were harsh indeed. Native Egyptian historians of that period viewed both Sultan Hasan and his father very favorably.

The folk story and the actual historical events associated with the two historical figures show strong similarities: the need to abandon the throne; the formalistic number of seven years of hardships in el-Sham; the return to Egypt; and the recovery of the throne from an usurper. It is therefore likely that the folk narrative has some roots in that turbulent period of Egyptian history.

A limited number of variants of type 938B appear in north Africa. Two Algerian Arabic renditions are given in Galley, no. 2, and Hilton-Simpson, p. 85; two Berber variants appear in Dermenghem, p. 119, and Lacoste, no. 63, pt. 3.

The distribution of type 938B forms an intriguing pattern. It seems to be limited to the northern part of Africa, extending only from the Nile Delta to Morocco. Of the six available Egyptian variants, only one was recorded from Aswan City in the southern end of Egypt; its narrator stated that he had heard it from some workers, presumably from the north, while working on the construction of the Aswan High Dam. Moreover, this variant is the only case in which the story occurs as an ordinary tale; it is combined with type 726*, *The Dream Visit,* where the king regains his throne with the help of a magic coffee pot in which he can see all the treasures of the world. It would be safe to assume that this variant from Aswan is not typical of type 938B, as it occurs in Egypt, and that it is characterized by major individualistic changes.

In the north African variants the story is usually associated with Haroun al-Rasheed, the fifth Abbasid calif (A.D. 786–809). As is the case with our text, all north African variants are also associated with the proverbial saying "When it goes. . . ." Tale type 314, *The Youth Transformed to a Horse* (which is not recurrent in the Egyptian rural areas; see notes to tale no. 4) appears as the hero's adventures during the harsh years in all north African variants except Hilton-Simpson's.

Type 938B is closely related to type 938, *Placidas (Eustacius).* Four variants of type 938 were collected in Egypt as legends. Available data, though limited, suggests that type 938 is better known among Egyptian Copts than among Muslims. The data on the distribution of this type outside Egypt provided by Samia Jahn, p. 534, tends to corroborate this observation.

Type 938B has not been reported from sub-Saharan Africa. Meanwhile, type 938 appears rarely in an area adjacent to Egypt; one variant from the Kordofan region in Sudan and another from the Amharas of Ethiopia are cited by Klipple.

· 16 · *Which Muhammad?*

This story incorporates types 655, *The Wise Brothers;* 655A, *The Strayed Camel and the Clever Deductions;* and 920C, *Shooting at the Father's Corpse.* It also includes the following basic motifs: J1661.1.1, "Deduction: the one-eyed camel"; F647.5.1, "Marvelous sensitiveness: meat is dog's flesh; animal has been suckled by a dog"; J1661.1.3, "Deduction: bread made by a sick woman" (menstruating); J1661.1.2, "Deduction: the king is a bastard."

Five additional renditions of this composite narrative were collected recently from different parts of Egypt. The tale seems to be best known, however, in areas where nomadic influence is strong, especially in the northwestern Delta, middle Upper Egypt, and the eastern desert. One variant was recorded from Siwa Oasis.

The story is well known in north Africa, where a number of published variants appear in Arab and Berber collections from Morocco, Algeria, and Tunisia. These include Legey, no. 36; and Holding, no. 3; Laoust, in his *Contes,* gives a variant from Ntifa Berbers, no. 72, and cites reference to a number of other published variants.

A number of excellent recordings of this tale are available from the eastern part of the Arab culture area. A Lebanese text is given in Jiha, no. 9, and Iraqi variants appear in Meissner, no. 18, and Weissbach, no. 12. Other less accurate texts (from Iraq or Muscat and Oman) appear in Campbell's *Town and Tribe,* p. 171, and in *al-Turath* 1, pt. 7:84. Only one variant is available from southern Arabia; it appears in Noy, *Jefet,* no. 114.

Types 655 and 655A usually appear as episodes within the same story. This tradition seems to have played a more important role as an etiological historical account which explains the origin of various Arab tribes. For a detailed description of these oral historical events, see al-Ālūci, 3:264; see also al-Mas'Aūdi, 1:302. The story is also referred to in other Arabic forms of lore, especially old proverbs; see al-Maidani, vol. 1, no. 15, and Ibn-'Aasim, p. 189. Major events from our tale also appear in the epic-romance of 'Aantar; see Chauvin, 7:158. A historical account from the Humrān tribe of Sudan—whose name could mean "the reds"—cites events from our narrative to explain the origin of their name; see al-Tayyib, p. 3.

In sub-Saharan Africa the tale seems to be little known. It does not appear in major collections from east Africa, including Swahili traditions; this absence corresponds to the rarity of its occurrence in south Arabia.

Three variants of the tale appear in west African communities. Klipple cites a Malinke and a Hausa variant. A third and more recently recorded rendition from Senegal is given by a Wolof Muslim griot in Diop, no. 18. This Wolof story of wisdom is, however, limited to the episode of dividing the father's property symbolically among the three sons according to the father's enigmatic statement. All three renditions are closely related to North African variants and seem to have been derived from the north fairly recently.

PART III
TALES BASED ON RELIGIOUS THEMES

· 17 · *The Contract with Azrael*

The tale belongs to type 332, *Godfather Death,* and includes the following basic motifs: N101.3, "Man cannot die; snake will not bite him though it is provoked by him"; D1825.3.1, "Magic power of seeing death at head or foot of bed and thus forecasting progress of sickness"; and Z111, "Death personified." A variation on motif G303.3.1.12.2, "Devil as a beautiful young woman seduces man," is also found.

Belief in a supernatural being whose task is to take the lives of human beings at the command of a supreme deity harks back to the ancient Egyptian "savage-faced messenger." Osiris, the god of the underworld or the hereafter, could order this agent to "fetch the heart of any god or mortal who performed evil deeds"; see Ions, p. 75. Although the Koran speaks only of the "angel of death," the name and characteristics of this angel in Islamic teachings evidently stem from other secondary sources.

This story has not been frequently recorded in Egypt. Only two other variants have been collected from the Nile Delta area.

Type 332 was reported from north Africa in Noy, *Folktales,* no. 8. It also appears in the east; Hanauer, p. 171, reports the tale from Palestine, while Stevens, no. 28, gives an Iraqi story which belongs to type 1164D, *The Demon and the Man Join Forces,* with strong resemblance to type 332.

From the Arabian peninsula, Noy's *Jefet* includes a rendition of this story from the Jewish tradition of Yemen. It also appears in a number of literary works; see Chauvin, vol. 6, no. 349, where a number of north African literary and oral references are cited; cf. also Basset, *Mille et un contes,* 3:558.

In sub-Saharan Africa, although the narrative has not been reported in the indexes, three renditions may be cited. Helser gives a tale, no. 25, from the Bura of Nigeria which shows strong affinity to type 332. Similarly, Rattray, no. 61, gives a story about "How Abosom, the Lesser

Gods, Came into the Tribe," where the general pattern of this Ashanti narrative conforms to that of type 332. An additional Hausa variant is found in Johnston, no. 39; in this rendition Azrael, as in our own text, plays the major role; however, the contract that Azrael forms is with a little boy, and no trickery is involved. Both the Ashanti and the Hausa variants have etiological endings.

· 18 · When Azrael Laughed, Cried, and Felt Fear

Our story is composed of a series of events revolving around motif V233, "Angel of death." It also includes variations of the following motifs: J700, "Forethought in provision for life (general)" (a new motif, J701.1.1, "Forethought in provision for the future: punished," is suggested), and G303.9.8.10, "Satan weeps." Because of their recurrence in religious lore, the following new motifs are proposed: V249.3 "Angel weeps"; V249.4, "Angel laughs"; and V249.5, "Angel feels fear."

Three variants of this frequently recurrent religious story have been collected from the Nile Delta area. The tale is often used in religious sermons; an eleventh-century variant appears in al-Tha'Alabi, p. 172. In this rendition an afreet being arraigned before Prophet Solomon laughs (motif N456, "Enigmatic smile (laugh) reveals secret knowledge"); Prophet Solomon asks for an explanation. The afreet tells about a series of curious events which he has seen; one of these was a man who was having his shoes mended and demanding from the cobbler that the repair must last for four years, while he was predestined to die soon (see also tale no. 32).

One rendition of this narrative appears in Sierra Leone; Finnegan gives a Limba tale entitled "Kanu and the Star," no. 69, in which the Limba deity asks a star why it is laughing. The star cites people's foolishness for thinking that they can alter what Kanu Masala has made. It is likely that this account is related to Islamic teachings, recently introduced to the Limbas.

· 19 · The Man Who Didn't Perform His Prayers

This exemplum belongs to type 809*, Rich Man Allowed to Stay in Heaven; it also involves motifs E411, "Dead cannot rest because of sin," and Q212.2, "Grave-robbing punished."

A great number of Egyptian religious stories focus on eschatological beliefs. Our story illustrates the much disputed belief that a dead person receives his due reward or punishment from the moment he or she is buried. The other viewpoint is that the reward awaits the hereafter.

The belief in a rewarding or torturous life in the grave dates back to ancient Egyptian religious writings. A narrative account of grave life appears in the story of Senosiris and his father, Satmi, cited earlier (see notes to tale no. 12). A Moroccan story dealing with the same topic is given in Scelles-Millie, *Contes arabes,* no. 36. For an Arabic story illustrating compulsive stealing, see "Der Zwang zum Stehlen" in Schmidt and Kahle, vol. 1, no. 22.

· 20 · *The Beast That Took a Wife*

This religious narrative belongs to type 433A, *A Serpent Carries a Princess into Its Castle.* A number of motifs also appear in this story: S215.1, "Girl promises herself to animal suitor"; B640.1, "Marriage to beast by day and man by night"; C611, "Forbidden chamber"; and B41.2.1, "Angel horse."

The general theme of this narrative is the marriage between a human female and a supernatural being in the form of a serpent. This motif is particularly recurrent in the cycle of *Märchen* associated with type 425, *The Search for the Lost Husband,* which is very popular in the entire Arab culture area.

The *burāq* does not appear outside religious literature; however, the motif of the flying horse (B41.2) is well known throughout the various categories of folk narratives. For further data on the *burāq,* see Chauvin, 5:228.

Type 443A has been reported from the southern parts of Africa; Klipple cites references to three variants from Bantu-speaking groups. See also Lambrecht, no. 3130.

· 21 · *The Three Robbers and el-Khidr*

This moralistic story belongs to type 750D, *Three Brothers Each Granted a Wish by an Angel Visitor;* it is also associated with type 550A, *Only One Brother Grateful.* Major motifs in this narrative are variations on motifs D1470, "Magic object as provider"; D1300, "Magic object gives supernatural wisdom"; and D1001, "Magic spittle."

Four variants of this narrative are available in Egyptian archives. A number of literary sources also include this didactic account. In some cases it is cited as a *ḥadeeth,* attributed to Prophet Muhammad, to teach respect for the elderly and the weak; see, e.g., Shihatah and Taqiy-al-Deen, p. 15. It also appears in Basset, *Mille et un contes,* 3:302.

In sub-Saharan Africa two variants of this tale are cited from Sierra Leone. Finnegan gives two accounts of "Kanu Gives Chiefship," nos. 52 and 53, in which the Limba deity plays the role performed by el-Khidr in our story. Both variants have explicit etiological functions.

· 22 ·   *The Killer of Ninety-Nine*

This belief story belongs to type 756C, *The Greater Sinner*. It incorporates a number of basic motifs which include motif F971.1, "Dry rod
blossoms," and a variation on motif T466, "Necrophilism: sexual intercourse with dead human body." In our story the sexual act is only
attempted (a new motif, T466.1, is suggested). Another important element may be designated under a new motif number, T466.2, "Corpse
protects itself against sexual assault."

Our story belongs to a large cycle of belief legends involving unusual
acts which result in the redemption of the seemingly eternally damned.
This religious legend is widely distributed and is sometimes associated
with a specific enshrined minor saint named Abu-Nabboot ("the one
with the staff"). One informant who studied at al-Azhar University told
me, "I read it in one of the books," but he could not specify his printed
source. Five additional variants were collected mostly from the Nile
Delta area of Egypt. Only one Nubian rendition was found; the narrator
stated that he heard it in Cairo in 1922.

The motif of the blooming staff is well known in religious literature,
especially in connection with Prophet Moses' miraculous cane. Similarly, the event of the corpse protecting itself against assault appears in
semiliterary religious writings as a saint's miraculous manifestations; see
al-Nabhani, 2:379.

One Greek-Egyptian rendition of this legend has a political and historical setting. It was told to me by a 20-year-old female Greek student
from Cairo; she had heard the story from one of her schoolteachers.
The action in this historical legend takes place in Mistra, a small place
outside Sparta, where a Turk and a Greek disputed over Greece becoming independent of the Turkish Empire. The Turk said, "When my
cane blossoms," and drove it into the ground. The following year it
became a huge tree, and Greece won her independence.

The story is also known in north Africa; see Scelles-Millie, *Contes
arabes*, no. 35, and Chimenti, no. 42. One Berber variant is given in
Dermenghen, p. 95.

Type 756C has been occasionally encountered in the eastern part of
the Arab culture area. One variant from Palestine appears in Schmidt
and Kahle, vol. 1, no. 61. Similarly, only one variant has been reported
from the Arabian peninsula; see Noy, *Jefet*, no. 49.

Type 756C has not been reported from sub-Saharan Africa.

For a résumé of the studies on the distribution of this tale in Europe,
see Thompson, *The Folktale*, p. 132.

PART IV

ETIOLOGICAL BELIEF NARRATIVES

· 23 ·   *How el-Khidr Gained Immortality*

A number of motifs are found in this historical and belief legend: D1338.1.2, "Water of youth"; H1376.7, "Quest for immortality"; and H1321.3, "Quest for the water of youth." The theme of a human becoming a spirit through gaining eternal life may be viewed as a variation on motif F251.5, "Fairies as spirits who have been given immortality."

This belief legend appears frequently in oral tradition; however, it seems to be derived from literary religious sources, where it is an episode in the adventures of Alexander. Lane, p. 211n., refers to the narrative and attributes it to the "learned." The source of our present account is probably al-Tha'Alabi, p. 205. This portion of the Alexander legend cycle was also treated by individual Persian poets; see Ḥasanyn, esp. p. 116. A closely related story about the adventures of Bolouqiya appears in some of the editions of *The Arabian Nights;* see Elisséeff, p. 198, no. 123A; also Chauvin, vol. 7, no. 373, pt. 41. See also al-Tha'Alabi, pp. 195–200.

A Greek variant of our story in which Alexander's cook André and Alexander's daughter Cali become "demons" is summarized in Chauvin's *Bibliographie.* For additional information on Alexander the Dual-Horned, see Basset, *Mille et un contes,* 2:40n., vol. 3, no. 87.

A number of elements in our story may be traced back to ancient Egyptian beliefs. Some of the characteristics and functions of el-Khidr parallel those of the god Heh and goddess Buto. The name of the deity Heh means "eternity." He was portrayed as a man carrying the symbol of long life and happiness. Buto was also named "the green one" and "she who supplies cool water." Similarly, we may argue that the "dual-horned" motif, which has become one of the basic traits of Alexander in Islamic Eastern traditions, was derived from an actual historical event. Ions, p. 96, reports that when Alexander arrived in Egypt "he went through a ceremony at the oasis of Amon-Ra which gave him rebirth as the son of God and entitled him to wear the curved ram's horns of Amon." However, the majority of the episodes which constitute the Alexander legend cycle seem to hark back to ancient Babylonian traditions.

The general theme of this historical tale as well as numerous parts of the Alexander legend cycle are found in the Babylonian Gilgamesh epic, which dates back to 2000–1600 B.C. These themes include the hero's invincibility, his search for immortality, the discovery of precious stones in the dark part of the earth, the plant (or water) of immortality, the acquisition of the plant (or water) of immortality by an animal or person who was not originally interested in it, and the hero's inevitable death and the perpetual life of the creature who got the plant or water.

The strength of the contemporary tradition in areas which were the lands of ancient Babylon tends to support this viewpoint. Al-Tha'Alabi (d. A.D. 1035 or 1037), one of the main sources for the entire Alexander adventure cycle in Islamic literature, was born in the region of Khorasan in Persia.

In both Egyptian Coptic and Islamic traditions, Mar Girgis (Saint George) and el-Khidr are considered identical. In Palestine, Iraq, and Kuwait, "al-Khidr" has been reported to be an enshrined saint; no shrines for el-Khidr were reported to me in Egypt. Hanauer, p. 51, describes the multiple identity of el-Khidr and reports that he is an enshrined saint with many names, known among Christians as "Mar Jiryis" and among the Jews as "Elijah."

· 24 · *Why the Turks Were Called "Tùrk"*

This alleged historical account is based on the key motif F510.1, "Monstrous race." It also includes a theme related to that of motif A1611.6, "Origin of various Near Eastern peoples." A new motif, A11611.7, "Origin of Turks: a subdivision of Gog and Magog who escaped being walled in," is suggested.

This recurrent story represents a case of folk etymology. The Arabic root *taraka* means "to leave." The association of the Turks with Gog and Magog seems to date back at least to the tenth century. Al-Tha'Alabi, p. 36, cites Yafeth, one of Noah's sons, as the "father of the Turks and Gog and Magog." The attribution to Alexander the Great of building the wall around Gog and Magog is given in the Koran (21:92–98); also in al-Tha'Alabi, p. 204 (see also tale no. 23).

Al-Tha'Alabi's description of the geographic location of the wall suggests that it is the Great Wall of China. Similarly, his account of the physical characteristics of Gog and Magog and the destruction they had caused to frontier Muslim regions and towns adjacent to China indicates that he was referring to raids carried out by Mongol nomads. These violent events preceded and climaxed in the horrendous Mongol invasion which ravished the Abbasid califate in 1258. The Mongol holocaust continued; it reached the outskirts of Egypt and was stopped by the Egyptian Mamluk army (see notes to tale no. 15).

The legend of Alexander building the wall recurs in the works of the thirteenth- and fourteenth-century Persian poets (see Hasanyn). It also appears in medieval European Christian sources; Tubach, no. 147, cites the event under the title "Alexander Walls In Jews."

A subtype of the story appears in Greek traditions in Egypt. A 20-year-old student heard the following tale from her mother, who had heard it on Leros, a Greek island: "It is said that earth rests on a huge tree trunk and the *kalikanzaroi,* little malicious creatures which resemble the devil, try throughout the whole year to cut down this trunk with a big saw so that they may laugh at the sight of the falling earth. But on Christmas Eve they can't resist going up to the earth's surface to have fun as people do. During this time the trunk heals again, so when the *kalikanzaroi* go down again, they have to start anew. This happens every year, and they are never able to look at and enjoy the sight of the earth falling.

It is worth noting that I have not encountered this Greek rendition among native Egyptians, either Copts or Muslims. However, one variant of the Islamic legend which I collected from southern Egypt states that "the wall gets back to its original form at every Friday Prayer at the moment the Cave Sura [Koran 18] is read." Thus both the Greek and this southern Egyptian rendition have the saving of the world from destruction dependent on the regular performance of a sacred ritual.

· 25 · *Why the Copts Were Called "Blue Bone"*

This etiological legend may be classified under the general motif Z183, "Symbolic names." The main theme of the story is based on motif Z144, "Symbolic color: blue."

The story seems to be of limited distribution. Two other variants of this specific explanation for the name "Blue Bone" were reported; both accounts were told by educated men who came from the Asyout City area in southern Egypt. The most widely known explanation for the name is that the Copts were forced by the Romans to carry heavy crosses hung by iron chains around their necks; the chains bruised the bone at the nape of the neck blue. Both accounts of the name seem to be restricted to Coptic tradition. Muslims who use the expression, however, do not seem to have an explanation for its origin.

The theme of using a deceased person's bones to determine his social and cultural characteristics appears in another context. Hanauer, p. 141, reports that in Palestine a bone bleached by the sun signifies a nobleman who has been executed and whose skull has been left in the sun. Meanwhile Ameen, p. 30, states that "Egyptians often call blue [things] green because of the belief in the [good] nature of the green color and dislike for the blue." Blue symbolizing Christians appears in other contexts of verbal lore. In a story in *The Arabian Nights,* blue fish are the Christian segment of a transformed human population of a kingdom; see Elisséeff, p. 143, no. 2b. Another example appears in Green, p. 60, where a blue snake is the son of the sultan of Christian jinn.

· 26 · *Why There is a "Saint the Forty" in Every Town*

This religious legend incorporates a number of essential motifs: Z71.12, "Formulistic number: forty"; D1719.1.1, "Contest in magic between saint and druid"; and D2135.0.1, "Levitation."

Our narrative, which manifestly accounts for the origin of the "Saint the Forty" phenomenon, is well known throughout Egypt. However, another didactic story explains the same phenomenon but in a slightly different context; the etiological nature of the legend is only implicit. On his way to the mountain to converse with God, Prophet Moses stops in a village which has a tyrant mayor. A father of four sons asks him to ask God, "When will the tyrant ruler die?" In the hills Moses finds a hermit who has been in solitude for forty years. The hermit has been receiving food for himself alone from God; when Moses appears the hermit receives food for two, but he hides the additional rations. The hermit asks Moses to ask God whether he will enter Paradise. Lastly, deep in the hills Moses meets forty robbers. They are generous to him and offer him all the food they have (Motif H1291, "Questions asked on way to other world"). God's answers are (1) The ruler will still live for forty more years; however, the four sons exclaim (actually a curse), "No ability or power except with God's aid!" The ruler dies immediately, because each prayer "took away ten years of the tyrant's life" (D2061.2.4, "Death by curse"). (2) The hermit will not enter paradise because he hid the extra rations sent from heaven for the guest (Q292.1, "Inhospitality to saint (god) punished"). (3) The forty robbers will enter paradise because they were hospitable to the guest. Upon hearing the verdict, they decide to repent; they disperse and become saints (cf. 751D*, *Saint Peter Blesses Hospitable Thieves*). The theme "Moses converses with God" forms a large narrative cycle in Muslim traditions. This cycle parallels that associated with type 461, *Three Hairs from the Devil's Beard,* pts. 3, 4, which occurs in Europe as an "ordinary folktale."

Mitwalli, the narrator of the main text, also told one of the variants of type 751D*, as outlined above. Both narratives explain the "Saint the Forty" occurrence, but in a different context. The narrator saw no incongruity in this. Evidently each story belongs to a separate cognitive system.

Other rational accounts of the phenomenon have been offered. Ameen, p. 241, states, "With the Cairenes Sidi el-arb'Aeen [the Forty] is a celebrated sheik. They claim that he has forty tombs. However, the [word] 'forty saints' symbolizes multiplicity and not the [actual] number." Ameen offers a more empirical explanation; he states that the owners of seemingly abandoned places plagued by people urinating or defecating next to their property "would claim overnight that a Sidi el-arb'Aeen was buried nearby and build a small shrine."

Younis (personal communication, May 1971) stated that the "Saint the Forty" phenomenon is a survival from the ancient Egyptian myth of Isis and Osiris. After having been cut to pieces by his brother Seth, Osiris's corpse was thrown into the Nile. Isis gathered all parts except the phallic organ. She claimed to the priests of different regions of the country that this missing part was buried in their own region and that therefore fertility should follow. Thus shrines were erected at those spots (see notes to tale no. 2). This explanation has not survived in folk tradition.

For a description of similar conflicts between religious antagonists in ancient Egypt, see Simpson, p. 127.

· 27 ·   "Blow for Blow"

Our narrative expresses a theme which may be viewed as a patterned combination of two motifs, Q241.1, "Desire to commit adultery punished," and Q550, "Miraculous punishment." The basic theme in the story is the cause-and-effect relationship between two acts; this relationship is not per se "miraculous."

Although the philosophy of life which underlies our present text is attributed to Islamic teachings, its roots are found in ancient Egyptian religious views. In the early stages of development of their religious systems, Egyptians saw a direct relationship between the divine king and nature. The prosperity of the royal house meant the prosperity of the land and agriculture. This prosperity was achieved through magic and fetish rituals addressed to the gods who controlled nature. Under the influence of the Osirian cult, which developed at a later stage, a shift from the magical system to the ethical code took place. The main concern of the Egyptian was to follow the moral code of conduct in this life to gain eternal salvation in the hereafter. Osiris, the king-god, exemplified this approach. The earlier connection between the deeds of the divine king and the rest of the universe remained. Thus ethical deeds produced benevolent results, while immoral acts produced evil ones. See Budge, *From Fetish to God;* also Ions, p. 137.

Our present folk story is very well known; it is normally cited through the use of the first part of the proverb associated with it, "Blow for blow...." Ameen, p. 210, refers to this tale and states that it is found in *The Arabian Nights.*

Narratives which reflect the same theme of interconnectedness among the various aspects of the universe are found in literary works. Ibn-'Aarabshah gives an account in which nature itself changes when the king's conduct changes. In this supposedly true occurrence the king considers violating a young shepherdess, and consequently the animals' milk runs dry. When he gives up his mischievous thought, the milk flows back (see Chauvin, vol. 2, no. 148, pt. 4, p. 190). The same causal theme appears in another moralistic story with important political significance which is also coded in a proverbial utterance: "The justice of the ruler is [the effect] of the justice of the subjects. . . ." A Lebanese variant of this subtype appears in a booklet for children (al-Maqdisi, p. 8): a king watches a white bird dive into a fountain and come out black, thus indicating to the king that his subjects are unjust among themselves; the king also becomes unjust. Then the opposite happens.

A variant of our main text appears in the work of the Sufi philosopher al-Ghazzali (A.D. 1058–1111), p. 132. In this mystic context the tale involves a water carrier and a goldsmith who had rubbed the hand of one of his female customers. Evidently al-Ghazzali's account served as a guideline for some craftsmen. Al-Sharbatti cites the tale and states that it circulates orally among Iraqi goldsmiths as the code of ethics for their craft, which requires close contacts with female customers.

For a similar story in literary tradition see Chauvin, vol. 6:26, no. 198; Chauvin also cites a reference to a Swahili east African narrative which is thematically related to our text.

· 28 · *Why the Kite Always Attacks the Crow*

This narrative incorporates a peripheral belief, i.e., a superstition. It is based on a number of motifs which include B291.1.2, "Crow as messenger"; A1335.1.1, "Origin of death: wrong messenger goes to God"; B147.2.2.1, "Crow as bird of ill omen"; and A2494.13.2, "Enmity between kite and crow."

Although the crow (or raven) as unreliable messenger is known best through the biblical and Koranic event of the Deluge, its appearance in this role dates back to the Babylonian Gilgamesh epic of the second or possibly third millennium B.C. The description of the Deluge in this ancient work is surprisingly similar to or actually identical with the biblical events; see Heidel, pp. 80–89, esp. p. 85.

The crow as Noah's first messenger does not appear in the Koran, but it is assigned this role in later parareligious literature; see al-Tha'Alabi, p. 35. According to the Islamic account, Noah curses the crow when it fails to return with the news about dry land and blesses the dove for doing so. The distrustful and wild nature of the crow is believed to be due to Noah's curse, whereas the peaceful homing nature of the dove is attributed to Noah's blessing.

The crow plays the same role assigned to it in our narrative in another etiological story dealing with equality between the sexes in southern Egypt. 'Aadly Ibrahim, an Egyptian folklorist, reported in a personal communication the following narrative which he had heard from a 75-year old man in his own native village in southern Egypt: "Women sent the crow to Satan asking for equality with men. The crow has not returned since then. That is why whenever women hear a crow, they say, '[May God make it] good, crow.'"

The crow as untrustworthy messenger also appears among the Berbers of North Africa. Two variants are given in Laoust, *Contes,* no. 31; and Basset, *Contes,* no. 11. In these variants the crow exchanges God's parcels for Muslims and Europeans. It gives lice intended for Europeans to Muslims and gold intended for Muslims to Europeans. Laoust has observed that this theme is recurrent among the Berbers.

A related subtype from Morocco is given in Chementi, no. 18, where the queen bee, instead of asking God that men she stings should die, asks that she herself should die after stinging a man. Her wish is granted. In spite of its occurrence among Muslim groups, the theme of a bird or animal messenger to God is incongruent with basic Islamic beliefs. Its roots must be sought in either relatively recent African sources or ancient belief systems.

In sub-Saharan Africa this story appears repeatedly as a creation belief narrative; however, in these African accounts other types of animals are involved. Examples from the Hottentot and Zulu groups of southern Africa are given in Klipple, motif A1335.1. The narrative has also been reported from east Africa; Arewa, nos. 33 and 40, quotes references to Kamba and Nyamwazi variants. Also Beier, p. 56, cites west African examples from the Ibo of Nigeria and the Marge of the Central African Republic.

PART V

AXES, SAINTS, AND CULTURE HEROS

· 29 ·   *When the Arch-Saints Exchanged Jobs*

This belief narrative belongs to type 774D, *Peter Acts as God for a Day: Tires of Bargain;* it also refers to type 1910, *The Bear (Wolf) Harnessed.* The story includes the following motifs: A417, "Gods of the Quarters"; A840, "Support of earth" (cf. A841.2, "Four maidens as earth support"); and A1348, "Mankind escapes from trouble." We may add a new motif, A1348.2, "Arch-saints bear trouble instead of man."

In its present form this narrative is more of an explanatory statement to the collector than an actual narrative unit circulating orally within a community. Yet as mental facts, the contents of this account are highly stable. In most cases the "minor" deeds of arch-saints are only referred to rather than narrated as independent accounts. A number of the deeds that each of the arch-saints claimed for himself are incorporated in a powerful folk epic which is normally chanted by wandering religious bards (*maddaheen*). In this epic a maiden becomes a tyrant ruler and oppresses the fakirs. Only el-Sayyid is able to defeat her armies and convert her to his "path." She wants him to marry her, but he proves to her symbolically that it is impossible for her to withstand the weight of being his wife. See El-Shamy, "The Story of el-Sayyid." Ameen, p. 183, reports that the arch-saints are called *hawwasheen*, preventers. However, he does not cite any examples.

"El-Sayyid el-Badawi" is the nickname for Ahmad ibn Ibrahim (d. 1276); he studied and practiced mysticism under the followers of 'Aabd al-Qādir al-Jīlāni (d. 1166) and Ahmad al-Rifā'Ai (d. 1175). Today all three figures have Sufi brotherhood organizations named after them whose members follow their teachings.

· 30 · *An Arch-Saint's Attempt to Punish Sinners*

The most important motif in this religious account is a variation on motif A167.1, "Council of gods." Motifs J21.1, "Consider the end," and J21.2, "Do not act when angry," appear implicitly.

Presently available data suggest that the concept of the Diwān exists mainly in the Nile Valley area. A number of informants from the western coastal area told me that they have not heard of it.

The first part of this account is a poetic stanza which explains the composition of the Diwān. Normally a deed performed by a saint would not be told by a narrator; the listeners already know it.

· 31 · *"Imamu" 'Aali and 'Aantar*

The narrative includes the following motifs: E26, "Resuscitation by shouting at dead," and J911, "Wise man acknowledges his ignorance." Also found in the story is a theme related to motif K1093, "Goddess arouses heroes' jealousy and eternal fighting."

This narrative lies on the periphery of religious beliefs. The story as well as a number of similar reports establish relations of emotional congruence between two positively held yet contradictory cognitive systems: the paganism of 'Aantar (d. ca. A.D. 600) on one hand and Islamic ideology, which discourages admiration of pagan values and characters, on the other. In another account told by the same informant, 'Aantar's daughter 'Aenaitràh meets with Prophet Muhammad, fights on his side against pagans, and loses her thigh in a battle. The Prophet restores it for her and promises her God's mercy for her pagan father. Thus the two contradictory views are reconciled.

A number of modern literary works have been written about 'Aantar. These include a theatrical poetic piece performed in Paris in 1910, in which 'Aantar plays the role of the promoter of Arab nationalism and unity; see Ronart 1:44.

· 32 · *The Twelfth Month*

The most important motifs in this religious didactic legend are J710, "Forethought in provision for food"; C785, "Tabu: trying to save provisions for another day"; and Q221.6, "Lack of trust in God punished."

The theme of punishment for futuristic thinking and planning is recurrent in all Middle Eastern folk literature (see tale no. 18). I collected another variant of this legend in Nubia in 1969. For a story with parallel themes from Moroccan Jewish traditions, see Noy, *Folktales,* no. 8.

· 33 · *The Betrayal*

This religious legend is based on a variation on motif A530, "Culture hero establishes law and order." The actual motif in our account is "Culture hero maintains law and order among animals"; a new motif number, A530.1.1, is proposed for this theme.

One closely related rendition of this narrative was told to me in 1970 by the Egyptian folk art specialist Saber el-'Aadily. He heard it from his father in his village in the Nile Delta.

· 34 · *Mari Girgis and the Beast*

This religious legend contains two basic episodes found in type 300, *The Dragon Slayer,* pts. 2 and 3. A number of motifs also appear, including B11.7.1, "Dragon controls water supply"; B11.10, "Sacrifice of a human being to dragon"; and S263.3, "Person sacrificed to water spirit to secure water supply."

The motif of the hero who slays a monster, releases impounded waters, and thus wins a maiden who would have been the sacrifice is widely recurrent in the *Märchen*-novelle traditions of Egypt and the rest of the Middle East (see Chauvin, vol. 6, no. 274). However, in our present Coptic case, the narrative is presented as an actual historical event. This account, type 300, pts. 2 and 3, appears in historical and religious contexts in other parts of the Arab culture area. It has been reported to me to be a component in the epic-like account of Abu-Zaid the Hilalite current in the southern parts of Algeria and Tunisia. These poetic variants of our narrative which record the establishment of the residence of the Hilāli Arabs in Berber areas of north Africa (beginning in the year 1052) seem to be associated with the Hausa legend labeled "Abuyazid" (see below).

One rendition from Syria appears in Contineau, p. 112; it associates the adventure with "Prophet Sulayman" (i.e., King Solomon) who kills a *ḥayyi*, which has blocked the water stream, with his ring of prophecy"; from this time on he prohibits snakes from dwelling in streams. It should be noted that Contineau translated *ḥayyi*, which signifies viper and is invariably perceived as female, as "dragon," which is perceived as male. Obviously his substitution of one creature for the other, though understandable, is erroneous. Another variant from Palestine in Hanauer, p. 56, cites Saint George as the dragon slayer.

The cult of Mar Girgis, including his role as the dragon slayer, appears among the Copts of Ethiopia. Buxton, pp. 126, 142, reports the appearance of Saint "Giorghis" in early works of the Ethiopian Coptic church and states that "the equestrian saints so characteristic of Abyssinian painting were almost certainly of Coptic derivation." Buxton has also observed that "it was in Egypt too that characteristic colours became associated with the mounts of particular saints: St. George's horse is white; St. Mercurius's black; St. Theodore's red." The Abyssinian church has upheld this tradition since the fifteenth century.

The dragon slayer tradition is recurrent in sub-Saharan Africa and in a number of cases is associated with nationhood. A salient example is the "Legend of Daura," which accounts for the establishment of the seven Hausa states. This narrative is also referred to as the story of "Bayazida," or "Abuyazid" or "Bayajida"; see Johnston, no. 41; also nos. 28 and 32.

Several additional variants of the dragon slayer theme appear across the African continent without being of explicit historical nature. Recently published examples from the Luhya and Gisu groups may be found in Liyong, pp. 8, and 77. Both narratives are classified by the native writers, who are also the informants for the published data, as "legends." The tale also appears frequently among the Zande of southern Sudan as an adventure of Ture, the spider trickster; see Evans-Pritchard, nos. 1 and 2. It should be noted in this respect that the Zande accounts are of legendary nature; the Zande think of Ture as real because their fathers have told them so.

The earliest account of a sacred figure slaying a serpent or a similar monster threatening a particular group with destruction appears in ancient Egyptian religious beliefs. Apep or Apophis, a huge serpent which lived in the waters of the Nun, or the celestial Nile, was the chief enemy of Ra, the supreme deity. Apep daily attempted to obstruct the solar barque carrying Ra, the sun god, and his entourage across the heavens; it was the god Seth who succeeded in slaying Apep and thus delivering mankind. Similar accounts involving other Egyptian deities, including the popular Horus, recur.

Egyptologists agree that these ancient Egyptian sacred accounts are related to Christian legends expressing similar themes. Budge, *The Gods*, 1:489, states that these ancient encounters between gods and demons are "of course one of the sources of the pre-Christian legends of the overthrow of dragons by kings and heroes, e.g. Alexander the Great and Saint George."

Similarly, Buxton, p. 142, has independently observed that the Ethiopian painting of Saint George slaying a dragon resembles an ancient Egyptian relief of the god Horus slaying a crocodile.

The contemporary African accounts of dragon slaying seem to be of considerable antiquity, and they are probably related to ancient Egyptian traditions. (This viewpoint can be substantiated and is the subject of a current study by the present writer.) E.g., Ture, the Zande trickster, is associated with deeds and exhibits characteristics identical with those of the ancient Egyptian trickster god Seth.

In Europe the account of Saint George and the dragon slaying appears and is very close to the Middle Eastern versions; see Tubach, no. 2272. Historically, the European Saint George cult was transplanted by crusaders who had adopted the tradition during their stay in the Holy Land.

· 35 · *The Golden Signature*

The main themes in our story may be classified under motif V229, "Saints—miscellaneous"; these include "Saint's sudden appearance after hearing cry for help," "Saint in officer's uniform," and "Saint signs his name in gold." These narrative elements are recurrent in religious legendary tradition.

· 36 · *Letter to the "Justice of Legislation"*

A motif akin to A464, "God of justice," is the basic belief element in this memorate. However, it should be pointed out that the nature of the deceased legislator is one of sainthood; it belongs to motif V220, "Saints."

Commenting on "A Ghost Story," Edward F. Wente (see Simpson, p. 137) states that in ancient Egypt "the living could communicate with the dead by means of letters.... Egyptian's ghosts were not so much eerie

beings as personalities to whom the living reacted pragmatically."
Clearly this is still the view of modern Egyptians.

For a monographic study of the basic theme expressed in this account, see 'Auways.

· 37 ·   Sidi 'Aabdul-Rahman

This saint's legend belongs to types 780C, *The Tell-Tale Calf's Head,* and
960, *The Sun Brings All to Light.* It also incorporates a number of
important motifs, including E631, "Reincarnation in plant (tree) growing from grave," and Q551.3.3.1, "Punishment: melon in murderer's
hand turns to murdered man's head." Motif V222, "Miraculous manifestation acclaims saint," is implicitly expressed in the narrative; this
motif is universal in all accounts of how an average person attains sainthood.

A number of similar accounts of this "historic" event have been collected from the same area. One variant is given in Maṭar, p. 274. Similar
legends revolving around the theme expressed in types 780C and 960
have been reported from various parts of Egypt. A story from Upper
Egypt, collected in New York City, is given in El-Shamy, "Annotated
Collection," no. 8. In the Nile Valley area, however, this narrative
usually excludes motif E631 concerning the reincarnation in the form of
a plant; thus these accounts tend to be closer to type 960 than to 780C.
Wilmore, no. 42, reports a belief related to the theme of our story;
according to local tradition, the *reeḥ* (soul or ghost) of a person who has
been murdered by a sword or knife will dwell in the murder weapon
and shout out the name of the murderer. A number of other belief
legends include the motif of a "bleeding tree" as the means of discov-
ering a murder.

The story is also recurrent in north Africa. See, e.g., Laoust, *Contes,*
no. 55, Lacoste, no. 6, and Socin and Stumme, no. 11. In most of the
north African cases it is difficult to determine whether the story is
actually a belief narrative. Laoust, e.g., places his variant in the section
of "Contes merveilleux." However, a Jewish rendition from Morocco in
Noy, *Moroccan Jewish Folktales,* no. 21, is reported as a true occurrence.
In this account the grave of a murdered rabbi becomes a shrine where
tuberculosis is miraculously healed.

A number of Arabic writings dating back to the twelfth and thirteenth
centuries A.D. cite variants of our story as historical events. One rendition cites the court of Calif 'Aumar ibn 'Aabdul-'Aaziz (d. 720) as the
stage for the climactic event in the story. For a comprehensive survey of
literature related to this narrative, see Basset, *Mille et un contes,* vol. 2,
no. 109.

The story has been reported from various parts of sub-Saharan Africa, especially the southern and eastern portions. See, e.g., Jacottet, p. 56. Other east African sources are cited in Arewa, no. 900, where he quotes a Yao variant of type 780; another closely related story is given from the same group, but under no. 3046.

The tale is also known in west Africa; Klipple cites a Fulah variant (motif Q551.5). Two renditions from the Ibo group are given in Thomas, *Anthropological Report*, 3:58, 67. Cf. Lambrecht, no. 3070, where the theme is reported from central Africa.

Both Basotho and Ibo renditions deal with fratricide; this is also the case in the Kabylie Berber tradition given in Lacoste.

Laoust, p. 181, no. 1, has observed that the motif *(donnée)* of a tree growing from the corpse of a man, usually murdered, and revealing the crime is frequent in Indo-European "myths" and "contes populaires" but is lacking in Semitic traditions. This observation seems to be inaccurate. The motif is recurrent in Egyptian (and other African) narratives, particularly in types 720, *My Mother Slew Me; My Father Ate Me, The Juniper Tree,* and 511A, *The Little Red Ox.* Both traditions are extremely popular in Arab Semitic traditions.

· 38 ·   *The Grave That Wouldn't Dig*

This local belief legend contains a number of motifs, including D1654.9.1, "Corpse cannot be moved," and Q552.2.3, "Earth swallowings as punishment." A variation on motif Q551.2.4, "Corpse of murdered man sticks to murderer's back," is also expressed.

Reports about the immovable and the "flying" bier or coffin (motif D1641.13, "Coffin moves itself") are relatively frequent. Their occurrence is viewed as a testimony to the purity of the deceased and may serve as a rationale for considering the dead person a saint. A number of accounts of both types of phenomena have been recorded in Egypt. Al-Nabhani, 1:368, 416, cites a number of cases of "flying biers."

· 39 ·   *The Mountain That Moved*

The story is based on three basic motifs: K2298, "Treacherous counselor"; D1610.21.1, "Image of the Virgin Mary speaks"; and F1006.2, "Mountain moves to person." The hero's decision to die instead of standing the chance of being worshiped is related to the general motif J210, "Choice between evils"; it may also be considered a variation on motif J216.5, "Early death with fame preferred," but in our case it is "Death preferred to the fame of sainthood"; a new motif number, J216.5.1, is suggested for this theme.

Among Egyptian Copts there is strong belief in this religious legend. Another informant, a 24-year-old engineer from Asyout City, told me an identical account. Ameen, p. 74, reports his own personal knowledge of this Christian legend.

The same miraculous event appears in European medieval literature. Tubach, no. 3424, cites a legend in which a sultan asks Christians to move a mountain, and a poor smith performs the task.

PART VI

LOCAL BELIEF LEGENDS AND PERSONAL MEMORATES

· 40 · *The Thigh of the Duck*

This memorate contains the following motifs: F401.3, "Spirit in animal form"; Q572.2, "Magic sickness as punishment for uncharitableness, remitted"; and F473.6.4, "Spirit eats food."

Uncle 'Aabdu's account represents the modal pattern for supernatural sickness and healing as encountered in Egypt. In our narrative the jinn retaliate only mildly, with sickness; in worse cases they may retaliate with possession, where the spirit enters the body and refuses to leave. The treatment recommended, offering food, has no sacrificial nature.

The offering to the jinn is reported by al-Ālūci, 2:354, to be an old Arab practice called "the ransom of the ailing." In this old ritual small camel statues made of mud and loaded with rations were left out for the jinn; if the statues were found scattered, that signified that the jinn had accepted the "ransom" and the sick person was expected to be cured.

· 41 · *The Possessed Husband and His* Zar

The basic motifs in this report are related to motifs E728, "Evil spirit possesses person," and D2176, "Exorcising by magic." Cf. also motif E433, "Ghosts placated by sacrifices." These two motifs only approximate the nature of the action in our account. From a healer's viewpoint, or what is being called ethnoscience, the spirit need not be evil, nor is the process used in the treatment magic, nor does the process seek to exorcise or expel the spirit.

References to possession by the spirits and to exorcism exist in ancient Egyptian literature. A text entitled "The Legend of the Possessed Princess," which claims to date back to a period which corresponds to the thirteenth century B.C. but is dated only to the "4th or 3rd century

B.C." is reported in Pritchard, p. 29; see also Budge's introduction to "How the God Khonsu expelled a Devil from the Princess of Bekhten" in his *Egyptian Tales,* no. 9, p. 142. Clearly Budge's use of the word "devil" is an approximation influenced by Western views of possession; modern psychiatrists make the same error of equating local possessing spirits with the devil.

However, it is agreed that in its present format the *zar* cult in Egypt is of Ethiopian origin. It is assumed that it was introduced into Egypt at a fairly late date, probably during the eighteenth or the nineteenth century. Cf. the "Mari Girgis" cult.

· 42 · *The Only Murder in Girshah*

The basic motif found in this "true" local historical event is T591, "Barrenness or impotence induced by magic."

This belief appears among various groups throughout Egypt. It is the cause of a great many incidents of conflict. Two other identical accounts of this event were reported to me; one of these was told in 1961 in Brooklyn, by a 53-year-old Nubian immigrant originally from the village of Girshah.

The theme of magically induced impotence, motif T591, is known in sub-Saharan Africa. *Xala,* a 1973 novel by the Senegalese author Ousmane Sembene, is named after this motif. The literary work illustrates the importance of this belief among the educated elite of the Wolof and other groups in Senegal. A Hausa historical account of a case of supernaturally induced impotence is included in Johnston, no. 55.

· 43 · *The Changeling*

This account, which is based on a belief, includes the following motifs: F321.1.2.2, "Changeling is always hungry, demands food all the time"; F321.1.2.3, "Changeling is sickly"; and F321.1.4.6, "Changeling beaten and left outside; the mortal child is returned."

This extremely important belief and the drastic practices associated with it are virtually untouched by scholars. The only published reference, as far as I know, appears in Ameen, p. 324, where the author reports the belief and the practice of abandoning infants because they are "changelings." Ameen attributes this phenomenon to "mothers hating their children."

Motif F321.1, "Changeling," is widespread in northern Europe; it also appears in India. Interestingly enough, our belief narrative shows remarkable affinity with the English, Scottish, and Irish traditions.

· 44 · *El-Muzayyara*

This local legend dealing with the supernatural is based on two main motifs, F420.1.2, "Water-spirit as woman (water-nymph, water-nix)," and F420.1.4.10, "Water-spirit with extraordinary long hair." The salient characteristic of the "mermaid's iron breast" and "mermaid's fire-squirting breast" may be viewed as a variation on motif B81.9.2, "Mermaid has large breasts."

Local belief legends involving encounters with female supernatural beings are virtually infinite but have not been recorded. However, Willmore, p. 373, cites "il-Mezayara" as described by an informant from Cairo. It is presented as a female being which appears at midday during the summer (she is not associated with water); she has iron breasts and kills with pointed, needle-like nipples.

One of the earliest references to a female water nymph characterized by her long hair comes from the 18th Dynasty (1200 B.C.) in ancient Egypt. Maspéro, p. 265, gives an account of two shepherds encountering such a creature.

The motif of a human-like supernatural being which issues fire has also been reported in the Arabic writings of the ninth century. Al-Āluci, 2:354, quotes a story reported by al-Aṣma'Ai (ca. 830) in which two friends meet a little boy in the desert. They allow him to ride behind one of them on his camel. The two friends notice that fire is showing from inside the boy's mouth. He disappears when they show no fear.

For a parallel belief story from Iraq, see Stevens, no. 9, in which a female water spirit captures a man and licks his legs until they become "like wicks of candles," but he finally escapes.

· 45 · *The Stone in Bed*

The basic motif in this account is D2071, "Evil eye."

Belief in the evil power of an eye seems to have its roots in the ancient Egyptian account of the destructive eye of the god Atum. According to this religious belief, Atum sent his eye to look for two missing deities. The eye was not heard from for a long time. Atum thought it was lost forever and replaced it with a "brighter" eye. But the old eye returned, and upon learning that it had been replaced, it wreaked havoc on the country. The god Toth finally mollified the vengeance-seeking eye; see Ions, p. 27.

Narrative accounts of incidents involving "the eye" are myriad. Other recurrent motifs associated with this belief include D2071.0.1, "Evil eye covered with seven veils, person kills with evil eye," and D2071.2.1, "Person kills animal with a glance of evil eye." For further information on this belief, see Chauvin, 5:161, no. 48, and 8:143, no. 144, n. 1.

The belief in the evil eye is known in various parts of Africa; see, e.g., Liyong, p. 17.

· 46 ·   *The New Car*

The basic motif in this report is D2071, "Evil eye."

PART VII
ANIMAL AND FORMULA TALES

· 47 ·   *Son-of-Adam and the Crocodile*

This animal tale incorporates type 155, *The Ungrateful Serpent Returned to Captivity,* and an episode based on motif J1172.3.2, "Animals render unjust decisions against man since man has always been unjust to them."

The pattern of the geographic distribution of type 155 and its appearance among different ethnic groups in the Arab culture area represent a unique folkloric phenomenon. The tale was found only at the two extreme northern and southern ends of Egypt; it is virtually nonexistent in the collections from the eastern part of the Arab culture area, yet it has been frequently recorded in the western parts, that is, in north Africa, especially among Berber groups. At the outset of this statement it should be pointed out that in Egypt, type 155 is known through literary sources; the present writer read the story in an Arabic reader in primary school. As a school text, the story was clearly a translation of an Indian narrative; it dealt with a Brahman who set a tiger free from a cage. This literary and foreign text fails to appear in oral traditions in any significant measure. In spite of my deliberate efforts in questioning old classmates and others who must have read the textbook, most of those interviewed replied, "I remember vaguely that we had the story, but I don't recall how it went." I encountered only one presentation of the textbook story; it was given by an educated woman to her daughter, a college student. This rendition, which was derived from a printed source, deals with a little girl who sets a tiger free from a cage. The tree and the cow render unjust decisions, and finally a rabbit tricks the tiger into the cage. Both the tiger and the rabbit are totally alien to the oral traditions of this area.

Only two other oral variants from Egypt are known to exist; both are extremely similar to our main text. One was published in de

Rochemonteix, no. 6, almost a century ago. From the Nuba of the Sudan, two closely related variants were reported by Reinisch in 1879; in both texts a crocodile, a Bedouin and a fox are involved; see Klipple, p. 187.

Type 155 has been reported only three times from the eastern part of the Arab culture area. Dickson, p. 326, cites one variant which was told by a woman from the Kuwait area. In this rendition a man named Nesop, a snake which winds itself around him, and a fox as judge are involved; this rendition is clearly of African origin. A Yemenite variant similar to that cited by Dickson but fused with type 923B, *The Princess Who Was Responsible for Her Own Future*, is given in Noy, *Folktales,* no. 57. Meanwhile another Yemenite variant involving a jinni let out of a bottle, a man, and a fox as judge appears in Noy, *Jefet,* no. 6.

In the western part of the Middle Eastern area, the situation is different. Nine variants from north African communities appear in print, including Arab variants from Morocco in Legey, no. 64, and from Algeria in Lévy-Provençal, p. 142. In his *Contes,* p. 42, Laoust gives three Berber variants and cites a number of other Berber renditions. In the north African area, type 155 is unmistakably affiliated with the sub-Saharan traditions rather than with the Egyptian variants.

Type 155 is well known throughout sub-Saharan Africa; Klipple cites forty-nine variants; Arewa, no. 2751, adds a number of east African texts to Klipple's lists; while, Lambrecht, no. 2571C, reports the tale from central Africa.

Additional variants from areas adjacent to the Nile Valley include two renditions from Ethiopia which do not seem related to our own text; both, however, are affiliated with the dominant snake, man, and animal helper subtype. One appears among the Tigré, a Semitic group, and is given in Littmann's *Tales,* no. 4. The other is given in Courlander and Leslau, p. 51; this text, however, contains the unjust umpire motif (J1172.3.2) which appears in our main text and seems to be lacking in most other African renditions.

Recently published east African texts include Knappert, p. 130, and Mbiti, no. 25.

In western parts of Africa fresh texts are reported from the Hausa of Nigeria in Jablow, p. 78, and in Johnston, no. 23; also from the Yoruba of southern Nigeria in Idewu and Adu, p. 40, and in Fuja, no. 10; and from Senegal in Terisse, no. 12.3 and 24; Diop, no. 8. A variant from Sierra Leone appears in Finnegan, no. 79. One variant from the Banyanji of Cameroon was collected in Cairo in 1970 by the present writer.

In sub-Saharan African traditions, type 155 commonly appears as an independent "ordinary" tale. It sometimes has an etiological ending, as is the case in texts provided by Johnston, Finnegan, and Fuja. Less often the story appears as a dilemma tale. Although Bascom cites no examples of type 155, at least one Hausa rendition, in Jablow, is a verbal puzzle.

Brunner-Traut, p. 282, reports that the theme of animals rendering unjust decisions against man (motif J1172.3.2) is found in ancient Egyptian writings dating back to the fourteenth century B.C. This episode is found only sporadically in Africa. It appears, however, in variants which do not comply with the dominant man-snake combination, especially the two variants from the northwestern Egyptian Delta and the Ethiopian rendition given by Courlander and Leslau. Significantly, it does not appear in the neighboring Semitic Tigré rendition.

Type 155 is reported to have been introduced to Arab culture through one of the numerous translations of *Kaleelah wa dimnah,* i.e., *The Panchatantra;* see Chauvin, vol. 2, no. 109. The first translation of *Kaleelah* into Arabic is usually accredited to M. Ibn al-Muqaffa'A (d. ca. A.D. 760). A great many Arabic animal tales of folk extraction are mechanically attributed to *Kaleelah,* which came to be known as *the* collection of animal (moralistic) stories (see notes to tales no. 10 and 14, esp. p. 263).

Chauvin outlines the tale as dealing with a man, a snake, and a fox as judge; it also includes the unjust decision by a cow and a tree. His description is virtually identical with Turkish traditions described in Eberhard and Boratav, no. 48. This subtype, however, does not appear in the oral traditions of Egypt, north Africa, or the Arabian peninsula, where Turkish influence on narrative traditions is sometimes clearly visible.

Eberhard and Boratav, p. 58, conclude that "the entire *Märchen* has come from the Indian *Panchatantra,* through Persian literature." However, the new information advanced by Brunner-Traut and the present pattern of distribution of the tale may raise some doubts about this conclusion. The tale is virtually absent from the oral traditions of Arab countries where the translation of *The Panchatantra* has been known for more than a millennium (Iraq, Syria, Lebanon, and the northern parts of the Arabian peninsula). A number of considerations suggest that the Egyptian and Ethiopian texts are not derived from the literary variants. These include the closeness of the non-Semitic Ethiopian variants to those found in Nubia and northwestern Egypt; the wide distribution of the tale throughout the whole of Africa, most notably among Bushmanoid hunters of South Africa who once lived as far north as Singa in the middle of Sudan (see Murdock, p. 59); the virtual absence of the tale in major collections from the contact points between the Arabian peninsula and Africa; and the differences between our main text and literary traditions. However, more research is needed to determine whether type 155, like motif J1172.3.2, was known in ancient

Egypt. If this proves to be the case, then the modern Egyptian and some African renditions should be judged older than any literary presentation of this narrative.

· 48 ·   Son-of-Adam and the Lion

This animal tale is composed of three tale types: 157, *Learning to Fear Man;* 121, *Wolves Climb on Top of One Another to Tree;* and 152A*, *The Wife Scalds the Wolf.* The story also includes elements of type 75, *The Help of the Weak.*

This tale is well known throughout Egypt. Five archival variants are available; a rendition from Fayyoum Province is given in Morsi, no. 42. Although type 157 has not been recorded from Nubia, one of its basic themes, "the fire spitter," is used by Nubians to refer to themselves (see informant note to tale no. 10). It has also been reported from the Kordofan province in Sudan in Frobenius, 4:91; an extremely close variant (probably a translation of Frobenius's German text) appears in Kamil, p. 40.

This composite story is also well known in north Africa, where it appears in print in a number of basic collections. See Laoust, *Contes,* p. 41n., and Legey, no. 61B. Episodes based on types 121 and 152A* are reported from northern Morocco in Loubignac, p. 338.

Klipple reports one variant of type 157 from a Kanure-speaking group of the Bornu region who live west of Lake Chad. Aside from this case, Klipple, Arewa, and Lambrecht do not cite any of the main tale types which appear in our story, 157, 121, and 152A*. However, in addition to Frobenius's text from Sudan, type 157 appears among the Bondei of eastern Africa; see Arewa's no. 567. It has also been recently reported from western Africa, where examples may be found in Johnston, no. 3; see also no. 9 where strong elements of type 157 appear in combination with type 75; and in Finnegan, no. 71; see also nos. 36 and 94, where the concluding episodes converge with the themes of "learning to fear man."

In Egyptian traditions types 121 and 152A* appear only as episodes within type 157. It is not clear why Aarne and Thompson designate *Wolves Climb on Top of One Another to Tree* and *The Wife Scalds the Wolf* as two separate types, especially when we take into consideration the extremely limited distribution of the latter in Europe.

Thompson, *The Folktale,* p. 218, views type 157 as a literary fable stemming from the literary tradition of India and Greece. However, this narrative does not seem to be included in any Arabic literary work which might have been influenced by such Greek or Indian literature and could have served as the source for the tale in Arabic lore. It also

fails to appear in the eastern parts of the Arab culture area. Brunner-
Traut, p. 282, concludes that on the basis of references made in
"mythische Novellen" and themes appearing in wall paintings in ancient
Egypt, the contents of type 157 were a part of the Egyptian narrative
tradition as early as the fourteenth century B.C.

The pattern of distribution of the tale, in both time and space, tends
to support Brunner-Traut's hypothesis.

· 49 · *The Partnership between Wolf and Mouse*

This animal story with a touch of humor combines two tale types serially. The first is type 1030, *The Crop Division,* and the second is 1074,
Race Won by Deception: Relative Helpers.

A number of variants of type 1030 have been collected from different
parts of Egypt. One variant in which the partnership is between a *fellah*
and an afreet was told to me by a police officer to demonstrate that "a
peasant can trick even the afreet." Type 1030 has been infrequently
recorded from north Africa. It appears in Legey, no. 63, pt. 2; and in
Laoust, *Contes,* no. 12b (see also p. 13 for notes and references to other
Berber variants).

Only one variant of type 1030 has been cited in major collections
from Arab countries east of Egypt; it is given in al-Guhayman, 2:119.
Tubach, no. 1921, reports this tale type from European religious literature where Good and Evil share a wife, Evil taking the lower half and
Good the upper half. Tubach cites Chauvin, II, 43" as one of his references, but I could not find this tale in Chauvin's *Bibliographie.*

Type 1030 has not been reported from sub-Saharan Africa. One close
variant from Somalia is given in Shalabi, p. 23. In this rendition two
men, one of whom is the trickster Miyo, are partners. First they plant
onions, then wheat. The trickster loses simply by making the wrong
choice.

The theme of deceptive division is also found in other African collections. Fuja, p. 151, gives a Yoruba story with an etiological ending
which belongs to type 1030. In this Yoruba tale, cat and dog try to
divide a cow. Cat gives dog all parts against which the knife makes
noise, i.e., bone. That is why dogs eat bones. Later they argue over the
leftover meat. This ends their friendship, and that is why cats and dogs
now arch their backs when they meet. With the exception of the Somali
rendition, the crop division expressed in type 1030 seems not to appear
in sub-Saharan Africa.

On the basis of available data, type 1074, the second episode in our
tale, poses an interesting problem. Although all the participants in our
recording session (about six persons) agreed that they had heard that

portion of the tale before, type 1074 had not been reported anywhere before in Egypt, including Nubia. A rare appearance of type 1030 in combination with type 1074 in Persia has been recorded in Lorimer, p. 304, yet type 1074 is conspicuously absent from collections from Turkey, the Arabian peninsula, and, strangely enough, north Africa.

The absence of type 1074 from Nubia, Sudan, south Arabia, and the interior of north African countries, all of which are strong contact points between the African north and the African south, contrasts sharply with the recurrence of this tale type in all sections of sub-Saharan communities. Klipple lists thirty-eight variants from various groups, including the Nuer of Sudan. Lambrecht, no. 1157, also reports this tale type from central Africa. Interestingly enough, type 1074 seems also to be absent among the Hausa of northern Nigeria, as is the case among the Berbers of north Africa; both groups have had long and close historical contacts. Additional recently collected African texts are given in Mbiti, no. 32, and Finnegan, no. 89.

The recurrence of type 1074 in east African communities and (as pointed out by Thompson in *The Folktale,* p. 196) eastern Asia suggests that Madagascar was the contact area between the two traditions. The Egyptian rendition, unless future collections indicate the contrary, seems to be an individual case of transplantation.

· 50 ·   *The Sparrow*

This narrative balances precariously on the borderline between animal tale type 170A, *The Clever Animal and the Fortunate Exchange,* and the human actors tale type 1655, *The Profitable Exchange,* pts. 1 and 2a; in either case, the action of the main characters is based on the key motif Z47, "Series of trick exchanges." Other motifs in the narrative include K251, "Deceptive damage claim," and K2152, "Unresponsive corpse."

The type complex 170A-1655 seems to be concentrated in Nubia and southern Egypt. All four variants now available were collected in that area; these include a semiliterary renarration in Sha'Arawi, p. 53, and a re-presentation of a child's narrative in Ammar, p. 169. A Sudanese rendition is given in al-Zayn, p. 69.

A number of north African variants are available in print. Two renditions from Tunis appear in the same children's booklet series by Verji and Rouḥah. Variants from Libya are given in al-Qishat, p. 34, and in al-Mazoughi, p. 96.

From the eastern part of the Arab culture area, only one Iraqi variant appears in al-Ṣoufi, p. 106. The story seems to be well known in south Arabia, where it usually involves Abu-Nuwās, a human trickster. One variant from Socotra is given in Hein and Müller in *Südarabische,* vol.

9, no. 2; another variant from the hills of Dhafar in Oman is cited by Rhodokanakis in the same series, no. 11. A Yemenite variant which also involves Abu-Nuwās appears in Noy, *Jefet*, no. 115. The variant from Dhafar is combined with other acts of trickery, including type 15, *The Theft of Butter* (see notes to tale no. 51; type 136A*); it fuses the animal trickster (a fox) with the human trickster (Abu-Nuwās). This Socotri variant, like numerous other tale types found on the island, proves to be a model of a tradition in transition between sub-Saharan African and Arabic cultures.

Our tale appears frequently in sub-Saharan Africa; Klipple cites twelve variants of type 1655 appearing across the continent. Arewa cites a number of additional occurrences of type 1655 in the eastern section of sub-Saharan Africa under numbers 4266 and 4266A. Also narratives which Arewa classifies under nos. 4251 and 4269 may be viewed as variations on the basic themes of our tale. Available type indexes do not differentiate between type 170A, the animal tale variant of our narrative, and type 1655, which has the same narrative content as type 170A, but with human principal actors. The two tale types actually stand for the same type of action.

The dozen variants cited by Klipple do not represent the degree of frequency or the extent of the geographic spread of this tale type. Our story appears as far south as the Cape of Good Hope, where a Hottentot variant of the tale had been cited in Bleek, no. 42. Another Bantu rendition from the same general area is given in Theal, p. 89, where type 1655 appears in combination with elements from type 328, *The Boy Steals the Giant's Treasure*. A third overlooked rendition is given in Torrend, p. 169; this Tonga story combines types 1655 (actually 170A) and 55, *The Animals Build a Road (Dig Well)*. These three renditions from southern east Africa show remarkable similarities to the south Arabian tradition.

Type 1655-170A is found also in central and western portions of sub-Saharan Africa. Here we may add one rendition of the tale from the Niger branch of the Ibo to Klipple's index; it appears in Thomas's "Stories," p. 25.

Fresh African texts of this tale may be found in Evans-Pritchard, no. 40; Finnegan, no. 18; and Johnston, no. 27.

In *The Folktale*, p. 169, Thompson quotes Reidar Christiansen's conclusion that, with particular reference to the profitable exchange motif and the winning of a princess (pt. 2a), the tale is "perhaps a combination, made in Italy or somewhere in southern Europe, from those two motifs."

The data just presented from the Middle East tends not to support this assumption. Although winning a bride or a princess is recurrent in

Arab variants, the episode of the dead woman's corpse (motif K2152, pt. 2a of type 1655) is found only in Nubia. It appears in all three Nubian variants but is absent from adjacent culture areas. The Nubian renditions, it may be argued, were either transplanted by intruding groups (black Africans, Arabs, or Turks) or were indigenously developed. The first possibility of transplantation by black Africans or Arabs seems very unlikely, since neither group possesses this narrative component; while the introduction of this element by the Turks, who maintained garrisons in Nubia for a few centuries, seems more likely. However, since all fourteen Turkish renditions cited in Eberhard and Boratav lack this episode, we must conclude that the likelihood of a Turkish origin for this tale in Nubia is extremely remote. The logical conclusion is that the tale, including motif K2152, "Unresponsive corpse," is indigenous to the Nubian cultural setting. However, additional research is required before this possibility can be ascertained.

· 51 · *The Biyera Well*

This animal tale belongs to type 136A*, *Confession of Animals;* it is also affiliated with type 44, *The Oath on the Iron,* and to a lesser extent with type 15, *The Theft of Butter (Honey) by Playing Godfather.* Types 44 and 15 are both known in Egypt but are not recurrent. Unlike these two tale types, our story does not include deception in punishing the thief (type 44) or in blaming the theft on someone else (type 15). In type 136A*, justice is achieved supernaturally.

The main motifs in this tale are variations on J1117, "Animal as trickster" (a new motif, J1117.3, "Ass as trickster," is proposed), and H220, "Ordeals."

This children's story is one of the most popular animal tales in Egypt. It is virtually never told by an adult to another adult. One variant from the southern end of Egypt appears in an abridged form in Ammar, p. 168. A variant from Sudan (type number provided by the present writer in 1971) is given in Hurreiz, no. 3.

The story is also known in north Africa; one variant from Tunisia appears as a children's booklet by 'Aatiyyah. East of Egypt, type 136A* has been reported from Palestine in Stephan, p. 176. A number of variants appear in collections from Iraq; one is given in al-Ṣoufi, p. 118 (German translation in Samia Jahn, p. 9; Jahn also cites a reference to an Iraqi Jewish rendition). An abstract of a third Iraqi variant is given by Kaẓim, p. 9.

In its Arabic context the story is exclusively an animal tale. Human actors do not appear even in secondary roles. The animals involved are overwhelmingly domestic animals. Only the Palestinian variant cites a wild animal, the fox, as one of the actors. The trickster is invariably the donkey.

Although none of the type indexes cites type 136A* from sub-Saharan Africa, it does appear frequently. A number of close variants have been reported, particularly among Bantu-speaking groups in the eastern and southern parts. Jacottet, p. 180, gives a story in which the head wife of a chief eats his tortoise. All the wives are made to walk a tightrope stretched across a pool; only the head wife falls and dies. A close variant from the Bene-Mukuni is given in Torrend, p. 56. In this rendition a father accuses all the members of his family of having eaten a guinea fowl; they must walk a tightrope across a river. The guilty one cannot complete the crossing, thus indicating his guilt, and he is killed. This Bene-Mukuni variant includes a verse portion performed by a chorus, but with contents very similar to the verse in our text. A virtually identical variant from the Safwa, a branch of "Tanganyika [Tanzania] Bantu," is cited in Arewa, but under no. 3248.

The tale also appears among the Kambas of Kenya. It seems that at this geographical point the tale involves animal rather than human actors, and elements of type 15, *The Theft of Butter,* appear in combination with type 136A*. Lindblom, pt. 1, no. 17, gives a variant from the Machakos branch, in which a hyena and a hare are involved in a dispute over who ate the tail of a ram. Jumping over fire is proposed, but the guilty hare jumps successfully, while the innocent hyena burns his rear.

Another Kamba rendition, Mbiti, no. 59, combines types 136A* and 15 with other acts of trickery which are recurrent in both African and Arab traditions. A related Tigré variant is in Littmann, *Tales,* no. 13. It is worth reporting in this context that an extremely similar composite story in which type 136A* is eclipsed by type 15 and other acts of trickery has been reported from the Dhofar area in south Arabia in Rhodokanakis, *Südarabische,* vol. 8, no. 11. This south Arabian rendition demonstrates the ease with which an animal trickster metamorphoses in the mind of the narrator into a human one (see "The Trickster Cycle").

The tale has been reported from western Africa. One Hausa variant from Nigeria which also shows affinity with type 15 is given in Johnston, no. 19. Similarly, a story which combines elements from types 136A* and 44 is reported from the Niger branch of the Ibo tribe; see Thomas, "Stories," no. 5, pt. 2, p. 24.

Type 136A* seems to be confined to Africa and adjacent Arab areas; the type index reports it only from Lithuania. The main motif in the narrative, H220, "Ordeals," may be historically related to the ancient Egyptian belief in the Pool of Justice: in the hereafter, sinners will fail to cross this pool safely. See Maspéro, p. 50, n. 3. This ancient belief has its counterpart in the modern Islamic ṣirāṭ, a path bridging hell and leading to paradise. All humans, it is believed, must cross it before

reaching paradise; the sinners will fall off it into hell. For a description
of the *ṣirāṭ* in Hausa Muslim tradition, see Johnston, no. 44.

· 52 ·   *The Little, Little Woman*

This children's story is composed of two basic parts; the first is based on
motif J1442, "A cynic's retorts." The second is affiliated with type 210,
Cock, Hen, Duck, Pin, and Needle on a Journey, and with motif K1161,
"Animals hidden in various parts of a house attack owner with their
characteristic powers and kill him when he enters."

The tale is very popular in Egypt. Nine variants from the Nile Delta
area are available. One Palestinian variant was collected in Cairo in
1971.

The first part of our tale is similar to a tenth-century etiological story
cited by Ibn-'Aasim, p. 76. The story accounts for the origin of the
classical Arabic adage "It is at his own dwelling that an arbitrator is to be
met":

The rabbit found a date; the fox stole it. She [the rabbit] went to the
hedgehog to arbitrate.

She called, "*Aba-al-Ḥusàyn* [a hedgehog's nickname]!"
He answered, "You have called on a sage."
She said, "We have come to you to arbitrate, so come out."
"It is at his own dwelling that an arbitrator is to be met."
"I found a date."
"It is sweet, eat it."
"The fox stole it from me and ate it."
"He only sought his own welfare."
"I struck him."
"You got even."
"He struck me back."
"A free [person] seeking to assert his rights."
"Arbitrate between us."
"Advise the numbskull twice; if she refuses, then stop."
I.e., a rabbit is in no position to fight a fox.

This old Arab story (based on motif B274, "Animal as judge") may
have provided a pattern for the first part of our narrative. Neither the
story nor the proverb seems to have survived in contemporary Arabic
lore; on the absence of the rabbit in contemporary Arab oral traditions,
see notes to tale no. 47.

The second part of the tale, type 210, is also related to type 130, *The
Animals in the Night Quarters,* which has been reported from Cairo and
other Egyptian cities. In Egypt the two do not overlap. Thompson, *The
Folktale,* p. 223, cites Aarne's study which concludes that the original

Asiatic form of type 210 tells how an egg, a scorpion, a needle, a piece of dung, and another object, usually hard, go together on a journey. They hide in an old woman's house and attack and kill her. The modern Egyptian tale seems to be a combination of an indigenous, now extinct tradition and the international tale type. Some of the main actors in type 210 also appear in our tale, yet it has a completely different structural pattern and emotional trend.

· 53 · *Once There Were Three*

This narrative verbal puzzle belongs to type 2335, *Tales Filled with Contradictions.*

Formula tales are recurrent in Egypt and other Arab and African cultures. The most common example of this category of folk narratives is type 2030, *The Old Woman and Her Pig.*

A limited number of variants of our recurrent tale have been collected, presumably because they are not considered "stories." A Persian narrative which closely resembles our present text appears in Lorimer, p. 94.

PART VIII
HUMOROUS NARRATIVES AND JOKES

· 54 · *The Judge and the Baker*

This merry tale belongs to type 1534, *Series of Clever Unjust Decisions.*

Our story is well known in all parts of Egypt. Two English translations of oral texts appear in Sayce, pp. 177–180, and in Green, p. 39. Tawfīq al-Ḥakīm, Egypt's most prominent and honored novelist and playwright, gives a literary rendition in the form of a short drama which maintains all the characteristics of the oral tradition except for language and the extended dialogues. Al-Ḥakīm, a Cairene, states that he heard the story during his childhood and that it is "reminiscent of some [current] international events."

A Sudanese rendition is given in Hurreiz, no. 57. Type 1534 also appears in north Africa. A variant in the Arabic dialect of the city of Tetouan is given in 'Aabdul-'Aal, p. 385. A Berber story combining type 1534 as a sequel to type 567A, *The Magic Bird Heart and the Separated Brothers,* is given in Dermenghem, p. 81.

The story is also found in the eastern part of the Arab culture area; a Palestinian variant is given in Campbell, *Market Place,* p. 40. A rendition from southern Iraq appears in al-Ṣoufi, p. 145.

Two texts of type 1534 are available from the Arabian peninsula: al-Guhayman, 2:204 and Noy, *Jefet*, no. 128.

In sub-Saharan Africa, type 1534 seems to be little known. Klipple does not cite this tale type. Yet one rendition of the Bura of Nigeria appears in Helser, no. 18. Another recently published Swahili variant is reported from east Africa in Knappert, p. 208. Both African renditions are clearly derived from Arabic-Berber sources.

· 55 · *Stingy and Naggy*

This humorous tale belongs to type 1654 (formerly 1653* and 1654**), *The Robbers in the Death Chamber*. It also includes the following motifs: K1867, "Trickster shams death to get food," and K335.1.2.2, "Robbers frightened from goods by sham-dead man." The theme of "substituting excrement for stolen food" is recurrent in other narratives; it is similar to motif J1772.9.1, "Excrement thought to be berries." However, the theme belongs to the general motif K476, "Cheating by substitution of worthless articles." A new motif, K476.1.3, is proposed for "Substitution of excrement for stolen food."

Type 1654 is fairly well known in Egypt; five archival variants are available. Frequently it involves "The Thief from Egypt and the Thief from el-Sham," i.e., the Levant coast; cf. the Hausa variant cited below. A rendition from Cairo appears in Willmore, p. 335.

The story also appears among the Berbers of north Africa; Laoust, *Contes*, no. 69, gives a variant from the Ntifa tribe. Type 1654, however, seems to occur more frequently in the eastern part of the Arab culture area. Two variants from Palestine were cited in Schmidt and Kahle, vol. 1, no. 28, and Littmann, *Modern Arabic Tales*, p. 235. (German translation in Littmann, *Arabische Märchen*, p. 365).

From Syria a neo-Aramaic variant is given in Bergsträsser, no. 8. Two related texts are cited from Syria and from Iraq in Lewin, p. 70, and Meissner, p. 35. From south Arabia a Yemenite variant of the story appears in Noy, *Jefet*, no. 138.

Available indexes do not include any African variants of this type; a number of recent publications, however, reveal its presence in sub-Saharan Africa. These African stories have varying degrees of similarity to our text and to related Arabic and Berber renditions. Johnston, no. 82, gives a Hausa variant entitled "Dan-Kano and Dan-Katsina"; this rendition involves elements of type 1525N, *The Two Thieves Trick Each Other*, which is recurrent in the Middle East, particularly among the Berbers of north Africa and in south Arabia. A variant from Sierra Leone entitled "Sara Miser and Sara Scrounger" appears in Finnegan, no. 33; cf. also no. 82, where a number of individual motifs from type 1654 appear. Another variant from Senegal is given in Diop, p. 125.

It should be pointed out that all three west African variants appear among mainly Muslim peoples. They also show stronger affiliation with the Palestinian and Syrian variants of type 1654, where one friend tries to get a share of the other's food, than with our own rendition.

· 56 · *Reason to Beat Your Wife*

The climactic event in this humorous anecdote belongs under the general motif J2070, "Absurd wish." The overall theme of the story may be contrasted to type 901, *Taming of the Shrew*, which carries the local title of "Kill Your Cat on Your Wedding Night."

Two additional variants of this anecdote are available in Egyptian archives; both were told by females from rural areas.

· 57 · *"Scissors!"*

This humorous anecdote belongs to type 1365B, *Cutting with the Knife or the Scissors.*

The present semietiological story, which partly accounts for the origin of the expression "Scissors!" is recurrent in Egypt. It is usually referred to through the code word "scissors!" rather than narrated in full. Four other variants are available in Egyptian archives. The characters involved may vary; sometimes the stubborn man is a *ṣi'Aidi,* a southern Egyptian, but the watermelon-knife-scissors combination is highly stable.

· 58 · *"The New or the Old?"*

This humorous anecdote belongs to type 1563, *"Both?"* Motif K1354.1 bears the exact title of the tale type; the story also incorporates a variation on motif T412, "mother-son incest." In our present case it is stepmother-stepson incest; a new motif, T412.5, is proposed for this specific theme.

The narrative is recurrent in various parts of Egypt. It also appears in some editions of *The Arabian Nights;* see Chauvin, 6:180, no. 342.

Two variants from south Arabia appear in print. Rhodokanakis, vol. 8, no. 12, gives a story involving "Shbyra," (i.e., "Hand length," a human trickster similar to the Western character Tom Thumb); type 1563 appears as one event in a series of tricks. Also, a Yemenite rendition involving the less specific motif K1354, "Seduction by bearing false order from husband or father" is given in Noy, *Jefet,* no. 133. Although the theme of "Both?" in referring to two females appears only in a few Arab renditions, most of the variants include a dual act of sexual trick-ery, thus indicating their affinity with the renditions where "Both?" appears.

Thompson, *The Folktale,* p. 203, states that this tale type is frequently recounted as a part of the Anger bargain cycle (types 1000–1029). On the basis of available data, this does not seem to be the case in Egypt. Seven variants of type 1000, *Bargain Not to Become Angry,* are available in Egyptian archives; none of them involves type 1563. For a fuller discus-sion of this tale type, see El-Shamy, "Beide?"

· 59 · *Goha and the Pair of Calf Legs*

This anecdote is based on motif K1860, "Deception by feigned death (sleep)." The theme of motif J2511.1.1, "Husband to spite wife plays dead," is implicitly expressed.

The narrative is recurrent in oral tradition and appears in various parts of Egypt, including Nubia.

The themes of a trickster and his wife fighting over goods and of the trickster playing dead to deceive his wife are also common in sub-Saharan Africa. An Akan-Ashanti story in which Ananse the spider trickster hides the crop from his wife and pretends to be dead to avoid the subject appears in Rattray, no. 38.

· 60 · *Goha on the Death Bed*

This anecdote is based on a variation of motif T211.1, "Wife dies so that husband's death may be postponed." However, the theme expressed in this story belongs to the general motif J1540, "Retorts between hus-band and wife." A new motif, J1547, is proposed: "Husband wants wife to die so that he may escape death."

· 61 · *The Quick Ass*

This anecdote belongs to type 1682*, *Pitch on Tail of Ass;* it is also more accurately depicted in motif X11, "Red pepper for the slow ass: man tries it on himself." The type and motif indexes, however, do not cor-relate these two numbers.

Type 1682* is very widely distributed in Egypt and also known in other Arab countries. A variant from Iraq appears in al-Ṣoufi, p. 114.

· 62 · *Who is the Laziest?*

This humorous anecdote belongs to type 1950, *The Three Lazy Ones;* it also incorporates motif W111.1, "Contest in laziness."

The story is well known in Egypt. It is, however, not frequently told as a "joke" because, as one informant explained to me, "it is not novel!"; see "Jokes: An Urban Phenomenon."

Type 1950 is reported in Tubach, no. 3005, as a literary European exemplum. Thompson, *The Folktale,* p. 210, points out that such contests in laziness "appear in folktale collections from nearly all parts of Europe, though none seem to have thus far [1946] been reported outside that continent." Collectors of verbal lore in Egypt have shunned such materials and consider them "trivial."

· 64 ·   *The Coerced Confession*

Motif N482, "Secret learned by torture," is the basic theme in this joke.

In John Fowles's *Daniel Martin* (Boston, 1977), p, 469, the main character visits Cairo and attends a party where political jokes are told; a close variant of our present joke appears.

· 65 ·   *Foreigner and Citizen*

The basic theme in this joke is "Hell preferred to heaven." It appears in the *Motif-Index* in a different context and a more elaborate form as motif T251.1.2.1, "Husband chooses to go to hell rather than join shrewish wife in heaven." Our joke, however, belongs to a completely different sort of narrative.

· 66 ·   *A Problem of Documentation*

The basic theme of the joke belongs to the category included under motifs J1850–J1999, "Absurd disregard of facts"; the theme is also similar to motif J2532, "Bureaucrats debate as to who shall put out palace fire; meantime palace burns."

· 67 ·   *The High Bridge*

The basic theme of this joke is motif F547.3, "Extraordinary penis."

· 68 ·   *Instant Virginity*

The theme expressed in this joke is related to general motif T300, "Chastity and celibacy." However, the idea of "Restoration of damaged virginity" may be designated as a new motif; T319 is suggested.

· 69 ·   *The Body Scrub*

This joke belongs to type 1447*, *The Dirty Woman.* However, in Egyptian tradition it is invariably told about a dirty man.

· 70 ·   *How the Cat Died*

The joke is based on motif J1900, "Absurd disregard or ignorance of
animal's nature or habits."

Bibliography

See A Note on Transliteration, p. lviii.

'AABDUL-'AĀL, 'AABDUL-MUN'AIM S. *Lahgat shamāl al-Maghrib, Ṭùtwān wa ma ḥawlaha* [The dialect of northern Morocco, Tetouan, and its environs]. Cairo, 1968.

AARNE, ANTTI, and THOMPSON, STITH. *The Types of the Folktale: A Classification and Bibliography.* Helsinki, 1964.

'AAṬIYYAH, 'AABDUL-MAGEED. *Al-deek wa al-mā'Aiz wa al-kabsh wa al-ḥimār* [The cock, the goat, the ram, and the donkey]. Tunis, n.d.

ABU 'ABSI ['AABSI], SAMIR, and SINAUD, ANDRE. "Spoken Chad Arabic." Mimeographed. Part 3. International Language Center, Indiana University, November 1966.

AL-ĀLŪCI, MAḤMOUD SHOKRY. *Bulough al-arab fī ma'Arifat aḥwāl al-'Aarab* [The attainment of goal in knowing of the affairs of Arabs]. 3 vols. Cairo, [1964].

AMEEN, AḤMAD. *Qāmous al-'Aadāt wa al-taqāleed wa al-ta'Aābeer al-miṣriyyàh* [Dictionary of Egyptian customs, traditions, and expressions]. Cairo, 1953.

AMELINEAU, EMILE. *Contes et romans de l'Egypte chrétienne.* Paris, 1888.

AMMAR, HAMED. *Growing Up in an Egyptian Village: Silwa, Province of Aswan.* London, 1966.

AMROUCHE, MARGUERITE TAOS. *Le grain magique: contes, poèmes, et proverbes berbères de Kabylie.* Paris, 1966.

AREWA, ERASTUS OJO. "A Classification of Folktales of Northern East African Cattle Area by Types." Ph.D. dissertation, University of California at Berkeley, 1967.

ARTIN, YACOUB. *Contes populaires inédits de la vallée du Nil.* Paris, 1895.

'AUWAYS, SAYYID. *Min malāmiḥ al-mugtama'A al-miṣrī al-mu'Aāṣir: ẓāhirat 'irsāl al-rasā'il ilā ḍareeḥ al-imām al-*

Shāfi'Ai [From the traits of contemporary Egyptian society: the phenomenon of sending letters to the shrine of Imam al-Shafi'Ai]. Cairo 1965.

BASCOM, WILLIAM. *African Dilemma Tales*. The Hague, 1975.

BASDEN, GEORGE THOMAS. *Niger Ibos*. New York, 1938.

BASSET, RENE. *Contes populaires berbères*. Paris, 1887.

———. *Mille et un contes, récits, & legendes arabes*. 3 vols. Paris, 1924–26.

BATEMAN, GEORGE W. *Zanzibar Tales*. Chicago, 1969.

BEIER, ULLI. *The Origin of Life and Death: African Creation Myths*. London, 1966.

BERGSTRÄSSER, GOTTHELF. *Neuaramäische Märchen und andere Texte aus Ma'lūla*. Leipzig, 1915.

BLEEK, WILHELM H. *Reynard the Fox in South Africa: Hottentot Fables and Tales*. London, 1864.

BRUNNER-TRAUT, EMMA. *Altägyptische Märchen*. Düsseldorf, 1965.

BUDGE, ERNEST A. W. *Egyptian Tales and Romances: Pagan, Christian, and Muslim*. London, 1931.

———. *From Fetish to God in Ancient Egypt*. London, 1934.

———. *The Gods of the Egyptians, or Studies in Egyptian Mythology*. 2 vols. London, 1904.

AL-BUSTĀNI, KARAM. *Ḥikāyāt lubnaniyyāh* [Lebanese folktales]. Beirut, 1961.

BUXTON, DAVID. *The Abyssinians*. New York, 1970.

CAMPBELL, CHARLES G. *From Ṭown and Tribe*. London, 1952.

———. *Told in the Market Place*. London, 1954.

CHAUVIN, VICTOR. *Bibliographie des ouvrages arabes ou relatifs aux arabes*. 12 vols. Liège, 1892–1922.

CHIMENTI, ELISA. *Tales and Legends of Morocco*. Translated by AARON BENAMI. New York, 1965.

CONTINEAU, J. *Le dialecte arabe de Palmyre*. 2 vols. Beirut, 1934.

COURLANDER, HAROLD, and LESLAU, WOLF. *"The Fire on the Mountain" and Other Ethiopian Stories*. New York, 1959.

DERMINGHEM, EMILE. *Contes Kabyles*. Algiers, 1945.

DERMENGHEM, EMILE, and EL-FASI, M. *Contes Fasis*. Paris, 1925.

DICKSON, HAROLD R. P. *The Arabs of the Desert: A Glimpse into Badawin Life in Kuwait and Sau'di Arabia*. London, 1951.

DIOP, BIRAGO. *Tales of Amadou Koumba*. Translated by DOROTHY S. BLAIR. Oxford, 1966.

DORSON, RICHARD M., ed. *African Folklore*. New York, 1972.

———. *Folktales Told around the World*. Chicago, 1976.

DULAC, H. M. "Contes arabes, en dialecte de la haute-Egypt." *Journal asiatique* 5 (1885): 5–38.

EBERHARD, WOLFRAM, and BORATAV, PERTEV-NAILI. *Typen türkischer Volksmärchen*. Wiesbaden, 1953.

ELISSEEFF, NIKITA. *Thèmes et motifs de mille et une nuits: essai de classification*. Beirut, 1949.

ENNIS, MERLIN. *Umbundu: Folk Tales from Angola*. Boston, 1962.

ERMAN, ADOLF. *The Ancient Egyptians*. New York, 1966.

EVANS-PRITCHARD, E. E. *The Zande Trickster*. London, 1967.

FINNEGAN, RUTH. *Limba Stories and Story-Telling*. Oxford, 1967.

FROBENIUS, LEO. *Atlantis: Volksdichtung und Volksmärchen Afrikas*. 12 vols. Jena, 1921–28.

FUJA, ABAYOMI. *Fourteen Hundred Cowries*. Oxford, 1962.

Al-Funūn Al-Sha'Abiyyah [Folk arts]. Cairo, 1965, 1966–1971.

GALLEY, MICHELINE. *"Badr az-Zîn" et six contes algeriens*. Paris, 1971.

GARDINER, ALAN H. *Hieratic Papyri*. London, 1935.

AL-GHAZZALI, MUḤAMMAD IBN MUḤAMMAD. *Al-tibr al-masbūk fi naṣīḥàt al-mulūk* [The molded ore]. Cairo, 1967.

GREEN, ARTHUR OCTAVIUS. *Modern Arabic Stories, Ballads, Proverbs, and Idioms*. Cairo, 1909.

AL-GUHAYMĀN, 'AABDUL-KAREEN. *Min 'asaṭeerina al-sha'Abiyyah* [From our folk legends]. 3 vols. Beirut, 1967–69.

GUIRMA, FREDERIC. *Tales of the Mogho: African Stories from the Upper Volta*. New York, 1971.

AL-ḤAKĪM, TAWFĪQ. "[The Judge and the Baker]." *Al-ahram*, no. 30499 (June 12, 1970), pp. 6–7.

HANAUER, JAMES E. *Folk-Lore of the Holy Land: Moslem, Christian, and Jewish*. London, 1910.

HARRIES, LYNDON. *Swahili Poetry*. London, 1962.

ḤASANYN, 'AABDUL-NA'AEEM M. "Baḥth fi qiṣṣat al-Iskandar dhil-qarnàyn kamā ṣawwaraha al-adab al-fàrisi al-islàmi"

[Research into the story of Alexander the Dual-Horned as illustrated by Islamic Persian literature], *Annals of the Faculty of Arts,* Ain Shams University 12 (1969): 103–28.

HEIDEL, ALEXANDER. *The Gilgamesh Epic and Old Testament Parallels.* Chicago, 1970.

HEIN, WILHELM, and MÜLLER, DAVID H. *Südarabische Expedition.* Vol. 9, *Mehri- und Hàdrami-Texte.* Vienna, 1909.

HELSER, ALBERT D. *African Stories.* New York, 1930.

HILTON-SIMPSON, M. W. "Algerian Folktales [abstracts]." *Folk-Lore* 35 (1924): 83–86.

HOLDING, JAMES. *The King's Contes and Other North African Tales.* London, 1964.

HURREIZ, SAYYID H. "Ja'aliyyin Folktales: An Interplay of African, Arabian, and Islamic Elements." Ph.D. dissertation, Indiana University, 1972.

IBN-'AARABSHĀH, ABU MUḤAMMAD SHAHAB AL-DEEN. *Fākihàt al-khulafā' wa mufākahàt al-ẓurafā'* [The caliphs' delicacy]. Cairo, n.d.

IBN-'AĀṢIM, ABU-ṬĀLIB AL-MUFFAḌAL. *Al-Fākhir.* Cairo, 1960.

IBN AL-KALBI, ABU-AL-MUNDHIR HISHĀM. *Kitāb al'aṣnām* [The book of idols]. Cairo, 1960.

IBN-AL-NADEEM, MUḤAMMAD IBN-ISḤĀQ. *Al-Fihrist.* Cairo, 1960.

IDEWU, OLAWALE, and ADU, OMOTAYO. *Nigerian Folktales.* Edited by BARBARA K. and WARREN S. WALKER. New Brunswick, N.J., 1961.

IONS, VERONICA. *Egyptian Mythology.* Feltham, Middx., 1968.

JABLOW, ALTA. *Yes and No: An Anthology of West African Folklore.* London, 1961.

JACOTTET, EMILE. *The Treasury of Ba-Suto Lore.* London, 1908.

JAHN, ALFRED. *Südarabische Expedition.* Vol. 3, *Die Mehri-Sprache in Südarabien.* Vienna, 1902.

JAHN, SAMIA A. *Arabische Volksmärchen.* Berlin, 1970.

JAMALI, SARAH POWELL. *Folktales from the City of Golden Domes.* Beirut, 1965.

JIHA, MICHEL. *Der arabische Dialekt von Bišmizzin.* Beirut, 1964.

JOHNSTON, H. A. S. *Hausa Stories.* London, 1966.

JULLIEN, R. P. M. *L'Egypte–souvenirs bibliques et chrétiens.* Lille, 1879.

KĀMIL, MURĀD. *Qiṣaṣ soudāniyyàh* [Sudanese stories]. Cairo, 1963.

KĀZIM, SAʻAD AL-DEEN. "Al-ḥikāyah al-shaʻAbiyyàh al-ʻAirāqiyyàh" [The Iraqi folktale]. *Al-Turāth* 3, no. 10 (1971–72): 7–32.

KHIḌR, ʻAABBAS. *Ḥawādeet ʻAarabiyyàh* [Arab folktales]. 2 vols. Cairo, 1960–64.

KLIPPLE, MAY AUGUSTA. "African Folktales with Foreign Analogues." 2 vols. Ph.D. dissertation, Indiana University, 1938.

KNAPPERT, JAN. *Myths and Legends of the Swahili*. London, 1970.

LACOSTE, CAMILLE. *Légendes et contes merveilleux de la grande Kabylie, recueillis par Auguste Mouliéras*. 2 vols. Paris, 1965.

LAMBRECHT, WINIFRED. "A Tale Type Index for Central Africa." Ph.D. dissertation, University of California at Berkeley, 1967.

LANE, EDWARD WILLIAM. *An Account of the Manners and Customs of the Modern Egyptians*. London, 1902.

LAOUST, EMILE. *Contes berbères du Maroc*. Paris, 1949–50.

———. *Etude sur le dialecte berbère du Chenoua*. Paris, 1912.

LEFEBVRE, GUSTAVE. *Romans et contes égyptiens de l'époque pharaoniqe*. Paris, 1949.

LEGEY, FRANÇOISE. *Contes et légendes populaires du Maroc, recueillis à Marrakech*. Paris, 1926.

LÉVI-PROVENÇAL, E. *Textes arabes de l'Ourgla*. Paris, 1922.

LEWIN, BERNHARD. *Arabische Texte im Dialekt von Hama*. Beirut, 1966.

LINDBLOM, GERHARD. *Kamba Folklore*. Pt. 1, *Tales of Animals*. Uppsala, 1928.

———. *Kamba Folklore*. Pt. 2, *Tales of Supernatural Beings and Adventures*. Uppsala, 1935.

LITTMANN, ENNO. *Arabische Märchen aus mündlichen Überlieferung*. Leipzig, 1935. (German translation from the Arabic edition of *Modern Arabic Tales*.)

———. *Modern Arabic Tales*. Leiden, 1905.

———. *Tales, Customs, Names, and Dirges of the Tigré Tribes*. Leiden, 1910.

LIUNGMAN, WALDEMAR. *Sagan om Bata och Anubis och den orientalisk-eurpeiska undersagans urspring.* Djursholm, 1946.

LIYONG, TABAN LO. *Popular Cultures of East Africa.* Nairobi, 1972.

LORIMER, DAVID L. and LORIMER, EMILY D. *Persian Tales.* London, 1919.

LOUBIGNAC, VICTORIEN. *Textes arabes des Zaërs.* Paris, 1952.

AL-MAIDĀNI [AL-MAYDĀNI], ABUL-FADL AHMAD. *Magma'A al-amthāl* [The collection of proverbs]. 2 vols. Cairo, 1959.

MALIGOUD, COMMANDANT. "Contes bedouins." *Revue africaine* 64 (1924): 541–47.

AL-MAQDISI, WIDĀD. *Al-sàyyād wa al-'Aàfreet* [The fisherman and the afreet]. Beirut, n.d.

MARKOWITZ, ARTHUR. *With Uplifted Tongue: Stories, Myths, and Fables of the South African Bushmen Told in their Manner.* Johannesburg, n.d.

AL-MÀRZOUQI, MUHAMMAD. *Min turāthina al-fanniyy* [From our artistic legacy]. Tunis, 1964.

AL-MAS'AŪDI, ABUL-HASAN 'AALI. *Muroug al-dhahab wa ma'Aādin al-gawhar* [Prairies of gold]. Edited by MUHAMMAD MOHIYY-AL-DEEN 'AABDUL-HAMEED. 4 vols. Cairo, 1958.

MASPÉRO, GASTON. *Popular Stories of Ancient Egypt.* New York, 1967.

MASSIGNON, GENEVIEVE, ed. *Folktales of France.* Translated by JACQUELINE HYLAND. Chicago, 1968.

MATAR, 'AABDUL-'AAZEEZ. *Lahgàt al-badw fī iqleem sāḥil maryouṭ* [The dialect of Bedouins in the Maryout Coast province]. Cairo, 1967.

AL-MAZOUGHI, 'AUMAR. "'AAROUS AL-REEF . . ." [Bride of the countryside: some aspects of folk traditions in the Libyan Arab Republic). Mimeographed. Cairo, 1971.

MBITI, JOHN S. *Akamba Stories.* Oxford, 1966.

MCCARTHY, RICHARD, and RAFFOULI, FARAJ. *Spoken Arabic of Baghdad.* Vol. 2, pt. 1. Beirut, 1965.

MEISSNER, BRUNO. "Neuarabische Geschichten aus dem Iraq." *Beiträge zur Assyriologie und semitischen Sprachwissenschaft* 5 (1903–1906): 1–148.

MORSI, AḤMAD 'AALI. *Al-ma'thoorāt al-sha'Abiyyàh al-shāfahiyyàh: dirāsah maydāniyyàh fī muḥāfazàt al-fayyoum"* [Folk oral traditions: a field study in Fayyoum Governate]. Ph.D. dissertation, Cairo University, 1969.

MÜLLER, DAVID H. *Südarabische Expedition.* Vol. 4, *Die Mehri- und Soqutri-Sprache.* Pt. 1, *Texte.* Vienna, 1902.

———. *Südarabische Expedition.* Vol. 6, *Mehri- und Soqutri-Sprache.* Pt. 2, *Soqutri-Texte.* Vienna, 1905.

———. *Südarabische Expedition.* Vol. 7, *Mehri- und Soqutri-Sprache.* Pt. 3, *Shauri-Texte.* Vienna, 1907.

MURDOCK, GEORGE PETER. *Africa: Its Peoples and Their Culture History.* New York, 1959.

AL-NABHANI, YOUSIF IBN-ISMA'AEEL. *Gāmi'A karāmāt al-awliyā'* [(Inclusive) collection of saints (miraculous) manifestations]. 2 vols. Cairo, 1962.

NORRIS, H. *Shinqiṭi Folk Literature and Song.* London, 1968.

NOY, DOV, ed. *Folktales of Israel.* Translated by GENE BAHARAV. Chicago, 1963.

———. *Jefet Schwili Erzählt.* Berlin, 1963.

———. *Moroccan Jewish Folktales.* New York, 1966.

O'SULLIVAN, SEAN, ed. and trans. *Folktales of Ireland.* Chicago, 1966.

ØSTRUP, JOHANNES. *Contes de Damas recueillis et traduits.* Leiden, 1897.

PRITCHART, JAMES BENNETT, ed. *Ancient Near Eastern Texts Relating to the Old Testament.* Princeton, 1950.

PRYM, EUGENE, and SOCIN, ALBERT. *Der neu-aramaeische Dialekt des Tūr 'Abdīn: syrische Sagen und Märchen.* Vol. 2. Göttingen, 1881.

AL-QISHĀṬ, MUḤAMMAD S. *Al-adab al-sha'Abi fī Libya* [Folk literature in Libya]. Beirut, 1968.

RATTRAY, ROBERT SUTHERLAND. *Akan-Ashanti Folk-Tales.* London, 1930.

REINISCH, LEO. *Südarabische Expedition.* Vol. 1, *Somali-Sprache.* Vienna, 1900.

RHODOKANAKIS, NIKOLAUS. *Südarabische Expedition.* Vol. 8, *Vulgärarabische Dialekt im Ḍofâr (Zfâr).* Vienna, 1908.

DE ROCHEMONTEIX, JOSEPH MAXENCE. *Quelques contes nubiens.* Cairo, 1888.

RONART, STEPHAN and NANDY. *Concise Encyclopaedia of Arabic Civilization*. 2 vols. Amsterdam, 1966.

ROUḤAH, MAḤMOUD SHAYKH. *Fuwàylati* [My little bean]. Tunis, 1969.

Ṣabāḥ Al-Khair [Enclosure for young readers]. Weekly magazine, Cairo.

SALEḤ, AḤMAD RUSHDI. *Funūn al-'adab al-sha'Abi* [The genres of folk literature]. Cairo, 1956.

SAVORY, PHYLLIS. *Bechuana Fireside Tales*. Capetown, 1965.

SAYCE, ARCHIBALD HENRY. "Cairene and Upper Egyptian Folklore." *Folk-Lore* 31 (1920): 173–204.

SCELLES-MILLIE, JEANNE. *Contes arabes du Maghreb*. Paris, 1970.

———. *Contes sahariens du Souf*. Paris, 1963.

SCHEUB, HAROLD. "Sikuluma: A Xhosa Narrative." In *African Folklore*, ed. Richard M. Dorson, pp. 525–61. New York, 1972.

SCHMIDT, HANS, and KHALE, PAUL. *Volkserzählungen aus Palästina*. 2 vols. Göttingen, 1918, 1930.

SHA'ARĀWI, IBRAHĪM. *Rādyah: 'Aan alqaṣaṣ al-sha'Abi al-noubi* [Rādyah: after Nubian folk narratives]. Cairo, 1968.

SHAH, AMINA. *Folk Tales of Central Asia*. London, 1970.

SHAH, IDRIES. *Tales of the Dervishes: Teaching Stories of the Sufi Masters over the Past Thousand Years*. London, 1967.

SHALABI, ḤUSAYN AḤMAD. *Aqaṣees min al-ṣoomāl* [Short narratives from Somaliland]. Cairo, 1962.

EL-SHAMY, HASAN M. "An Annotated Collection of Egyptian Folktales Collected from an Egyptian Sailor in Brooklyn, New York." M.A. thesis, Indiana University, 1964.

———. "Beide? (AaTh 1563)." *Enzyklopädie des Märchen* 2, nos. 1–2 (1977): 55–63.

———. "The Story of el-Sayyid Ahmad el-Badawi with Fatma Bint-Birry." *Folklore Forum* 9 (1976): 140–64; 10 (1977): 1–13.

———. "The Traditional Structure of Sentiments in Maḥfouz's Trilogy: A Behaviorist Text Analysis." *Al-'Arabiyya: Journal of the American Association of Teachers of Arabic* 9, nos. 1–2 (1976): 53–74.

AL-SHARBATTI, HĀDI. "Asātidhàt fànn al-ṣan'Ash ladā al-ṭabaqāt al-shaʻAbiyyàh" (Master craftsmen among folk strata). *Al-Turāth* 1, no. 10 (1969–70): 63–68.

SHIḤATAH, AL-SAYYID, and TAQIY-AL-DEEN, AL-SAYYID. *Al-qaṣàṣ al-nabawi* [Prophet's stories]. Cairo, n.d.

ṢIDQI, ʻAABDUL-RAḤMĀN. *Abu-Nuwās, qiṣṣatu ḥayātihi fi giddihi wa hàzlih* [Abu-Nuwas: his life story in his solemnness and frolic]. Cairo, 1965.

SIMPSON, WILLIAM KELLY, ed. *The Literature of Ancient Egypt*. New Haven, 1972.

SOCIN, ALBERT. "Zum arabischen Dialekt von Marokko." *Abhandlungen der philologisch-historische klasse de königlische sächsischen Gesellschaft der Wissenschaften zu Leipsig* 14 (1893): 149–203.

SOCIN, ALBERT, and STUMME, HANS. "Der arabische Dialekt der Houwāra des Wād Sūs in Marokko." *Abhandlungen der philologisch-historische Klasse de Königlische sächsischen Gessellschaft der Wissenschaften zu Leipzig* 15 (1884): 1–144.

AL-ṢOUFI, AḤMAD. *Ḥikāyāt al-mouṣil al-shaʻAbiyyàh* [Folktales of Mosul]. Baghdad, 1962.

SPENCE, LEWIS. *Myths and Legends of Ancient Egypt*. New York, 1927.

SPITTA, WILHELM. *Contes arabes modernes*. Leiden, 1883.

SPOER, H. H., and HADDAD, E. NASRALLAH. *Manual of Spoken Palestinian Arabic*. Jerusalem, 1909.

STANNUS, HUGH S. "The Wayao of Nyasaland." *Harvard African Studies* 3 (1922): 299–340.

STEPHAN, STEPHAN H. "Palestinian Animal Stories and Fables." *Journal of the Palestine Oriental Society* 3 (1923): 167–90.

STEVENS, ETHEL S. *Folktales of Iraq*. London, 1931.

AL-ṬAYYIB, ʻAABDULLĀH. *Al-ahāji al-soudaniyyah* [Sudanese folktales]. Khartoum, 1955–61.

AL-ṬAYYIB, AL-ṬAYYIB MOHAMMAD. "Al-turāth al-shaʻAbi li-qabeelat al-ḥumrān" [Folk traditions of the Ḥumrān tribe]. Mimeographed. University of Khartoum, 1970.

TERISSE, ANDRE. *Contes et légendes du Sénégal*. Paris, 1963.

TE VELDE, HERMAN. *Seth, God of Confusion*. Leiden, 1967.

AL-THAʻALABI, AḤMAD IBN MUḤAMMAD. *Kitāb qiṣaṣ al-'anbiyā' al-musamma bi al'Aarā'is* [Prophets' stories]. Cairo, n.d.

THEAL, GEORGE MCCALL. *Kaffir Folk-Lore*. West Point, N.Y., 1970.

THOMAS, NORTHCOTE W. *Anthropological Report on the Ibo-speaking Peoples of Nigeria*. Pt. 3. New York, 1913.

―――. "Stories (Abstract) from Awka Neighbourhood." *Man* (1918), pp. 27–47, 56–87.

THOMPSON, STITH, *The Folktale*. New York, 1946.

―――. *Motif-Index of Folk-Literature*. 6 vols. Copenhagen and Bloomington, 1955–58.

TORREND, JAMES. *Specimens of Bantu Folklore from Northern Rhodesia*. London, 1921.

TREMEARNE, A. J. N. *Hausa Superstitions and Customs*. London, 1913.

TRIMINGHAM, J. SPENCER. *Sudan Colloquial Arabic*. London, 1939.

TUBACH, FREDERIC C. *"Index Exemplorum": A Handbook of Medieval Religious Tales*. Folklore Fellows Communications, no. 204. Helsinki, 1969.

Al-Turāth Al-Sha'Abiy [Folk legacy]. Baghdad, 1969– .

VERJI, MUḤAMMAD EL-RA'OUF. *Al-'Ausfour al-akhḍàr* [The green sparrow]. Tunis, 1969.

WEISSBACH, FRANZ HEINRICH. *Beiträge zur Kunde des Irak-arabischen*. Leipzig, 1930.

WESTERMANN, DEIDRICH. *The Shilluk People, Their Language and Folklore*. Philadelphia, 1912.

WILLMORE, J. SELDON. *The Spoken Arabic of Egypt*. London, 1901.

YOUNIS, 'AABDUL-ḤAMEED. "Goha: shakhṣiyyah 'Aālamiyyah" (Goha: a universal character). *Al-funun al-sha'Abiyyàh* 3 (1969): 3–5.

AL-ZAYN, ADAM. *Al-turāth al-sha'Abi li-qabeelat al-musàbba'Aāt"* [Folk traditions of the Musabba'Aāt tribe]. Mimeographed. University of Khartoum, 1970.

Index of Motifs

(Motif numbers are from Stith Thompson, *Motif-Index of Folk-Literature*, [6 vols.; Copenhagen and Bloomington, Ind., 1955–58]. Suggested new motifs are in brackets.)

A. MYTHOLOGICAL MOTIFS

B. ANIMALS

E. THE DEAD

F. MARVELS

H. TESTS

J. THE WISE AND THE FOOLISH

K. DECEPTIONS

Index of Tale Types

(Type numbers are from Antti Aarne and Stith Thompson, *The Types of the Folktale* [Helsinki, 1961]. Suggested new type numbers are in brackets.)

I. ANIMAL TALES (1–299)

II. ORDINARY FOLKTALES

A. Tales of Magic (300–749)

General Index